Olof Palme, Sweden, and the Vietnam War

Olof Palme, Sweden, and the Vietnam War

A Diplomatic History

Lubna Z. Qureshi

LEXINGTON BOOKS
Lanham • Boulder • New York • London

Rowman & Littlefield
Bloomsbury Publishing Inc, 1359 Broadway, New York, NY 10018, USA
Bloomsbury Publishing Plc, 50 Bedford Square, London, WC1B 3DP, UK
Bloomsbury Publishing Ireland, 29 Earlsfort Terrace, Dublin 2, D02 AY28, Ireland
www.bloomsbury.com

Published by Lexington Books
An imprint of The Rowman & Littlefield Publishing Group, Inc.
4501 Forbes Boulevard, Suite 200, Lanham, Maryland 20706
www.rowman.com
86-90 Paul Street, London EC2A 4NE

British Library Cataloguing in Publication Information available

Library of Congress Cataloging-in-Publication Data

Names: Qureshi, Lubna Z., 1974- author.
Title: Olof Palme, Sweden, and the Vietnam War : a diplomatic history / Lubna Z. Qureshi.
Description: Lanham : Lexington Books, 2023. | Includes bibliographical references and
    index. | Summary: "Over the years, the 1986 assassination of Swedish Prime Minister
    Olof Palme has attracted considerable international attention. Yet, far more interesting
    than Palme's death is his opposition to the Vietnam War. Neutral Sweden had the
    independence to challenge the Nixon Administration that members of NATO did
    not have"– Provided by publisher.
Identifiers: LCCN 2023004321 (print) | LCCN 2023004322 (ebook) | ISBN
    9781793638441 (cloth) | ISBN 9781793638458 (ebook)
Subjects: LCSH: Vietnam War, 1961-1975–Sweden. | Vietnam
    War, 1961-1975–Diplomatic history. | Palme, Olof, 1927-1986. | United States–
    Foreign relations–Sweden. | Sweden–Foreign relations–United States. |
    Sweden–Foreign relations–Vietnam (Democratic Republic) | Vietnam (Democratic
    Republic)–Foreign relations–Sweden.
Classification: LCC DS559.62.S8 Q747 2023 (print) | LCC DS559.62.S8 (ebook) |
    DDC 959.704/33485–dc23/eng/20230214
LC record available at https://lccn.loc.gov/2023004321
LC ebook record available at https://lccn.loc.gov/2023004322

♾™ The paper used in this publication meets the minimum requirements of American
National Standard for Information Sciences—Permanence of Paper for Printed
Library Materials, ANSI/NISO Z39.48-1992.

Contents

Preface: Prime Minister Olof Palme, Sweden, and the Vietnam
    War: A Diplomatic History Preface   vii
    By Lubna Z. Qureshi

Chapter 1 : The Early Evolution of Olof Palme and Swedish
    Vietnam Policy   1

Chapter 2 : The Accession of Olof Palme   23

Chapter 3 : The Christmas Bombing and Consequent Diplomatic
    Freeze   89

Chapter 4 : Sweden and the American Prisoners of War in North
    Vietnam   123

Chapter 5 : Reconciliation with Washington   209

Chapter 6 : The Postwar Reconstruction of Vietnam and
    Swedish-American Relations   227

Afterword   247

Bibliography   251

Index   263

About the Author   273

Preface

Prime Minister Olof Palme, Sweden, and the Vietnam War: A Diplomatic History Preface

By Lubna Z. Qureshi

My interest in the statecraft of Swedish Prime Minister Olof Palme goes back to February 28, 1986. While I was watching television with my parents, a news bulletin announced the assassination of the prime minister. I was only twelve years old, a typical American child, and I had never even heard of Palme, but my father's reaction has remained with me ever since. "A very good man," he said, with a disturbed expression on his face.

As I grew older and more aware of the wider world, I developed a fascination with contemporary history and international affairs. Even though I focused on US foreign policy in graduate school, Palme lurked somewhere in my mental background. One of my professors mentioned Sweden's provision of iron ore to Nazi Germany and then brought up Palme's vocal opposition to the Vietnam War more than two decades afterward, suggesting that the late prime minister's moral outrage had been hypocritical. "I abhor the self-righteous," my professor said. I was not sure that my professor's charge of hypocrisy was fair. Palme had been a teenager during the Second World War and, as such, bore no responsibility for Swedish foreign policy of the period.

Once I completed my graduate studies, I encountered historical scholarship that dismissed Palme's opposition to the Vietnam War as little more than political grandstanding.[1] Allegedly, it was an attempt to strengthen the leftist appeal of his own Social Democratic party at the expense of the Left Party

Communists.[2] Such scholarship scoffed at the notion that a country as small as Sweden could have had an impact on the course of events in Southeast Asia or substantially challenge the United States. I sensed something was wrong with this argument. If Sweden was so irrelevant to international affairs, why even bother writing about the country? It did not make sense to me. So, I decided to examine the evidence for myself.

Based on the research I have done, I can conclude that Palme's position on the Vietnam War was, essentially and substantially, a moral one, indicating a significant shift in Swedish foreign policy. Political scientist Ann-Marie Ekengren has influenced my argument in this regard. Unlike many theorists of international relations, she sets aside structuralism in favor of individual personality and political psychology. Rather than following the path of his predecessors, Palme, guided by his ideology, cleared his own. According to Ekengren, Palme's ideology had four essential principles:

1. "Relations between states should be regulated according to international law."
2. "The inhabitants of poorer states should have the same economic, social, and political rights, which in the West hanged together with the causal idea that underdevelopment in this respect could contribute to instability in different regions, and the entire world over time."
3. "All people have the right to self-determination."
4. "Sweden should preserve its sovereignty at any price."[3]

The application of this ideology had a considerable impact on both Vietnam and the United States. Palme's relations with President Richard M. Nixon may have been antagonistic, but he enjoyed positive and productive interactions with many sectors of American society and even with some US government officials.

NOTES

1. Carl-Gustaf Scott, "A Good Offense is the Best Defense": Swedish Social Democracy, Europe, and the Vietnam War," PhD dissertation, University of Wisconsin-Madison, 2005. Scott has now published a monograph, *Swedish Social Democracy and the Vietnam War* (Huddinge, Sweden: Södertörn University, 2017).

2. From 1967 until 1990, Sweden's extreme left-wing party represented in the Swedish Parliament was known as *Vänsterpartiet Kommunisterna* (the Left Party Communists). Today, it is called *Vänsterpartiet* (the Left Party).

3. Ann-Marie Ekengren, *Olof Palme och Utrikespolitiken* (Umeå, Sweden: Boréa, 2005) 46 – 47.

Chapter 1

The Early Evolution of Olof Palme and Swedish Vietnam Policy

Olof Palme's Early Life

Olof Palme was born January 30, 1927, to a wealthy family in Stockholm. His father, Gunnar, was the chief operating officer of Thule, the insurance company that was run by the Palme family. Eventually, Gunnar would succeed his father as chief executive officer. His mother, Elisabeth von Knieriem, came from a German-speaking aristocratic family in Latvia. During World War I, Elisabeth had moved to Stockholm as a refugee from her homeland, then under the domination of tsarist Russia. Both parents held the politically conservative views typical of the upper class.[1]

Gunnar died when Olof was only seven years old, so the little boy fell under the strong influence of his mother. Elisabeth actively participated in women's groups and charitable organizations. Olof often accompanied Elisabeth when she paid calls on poor families.[2] In spite of his mother's political conservatism, her charitable work exposed him to people far outside his own social milieu.

Nevertheless, Elisabeth dispatched her ten-year-old son to Sigtuna humanistiska läroverk, an exclusive boarding school in Sweden.[3]

Such a rarefied environment would not have enlightened Palme politically. His undergraduate experience in the United States changed everything. At Kenyon College in Gambier, Ohio, Palme studied political science and economics. He came under the influence of his economics professor, Paul M. Titus, a progressive who taught the ideas of both Adam Smith and Karl Marx to his students. For his thesis, which Titus supervised, Palme even interviewed Walter Reuther, the president of the United Auto Workers, in Detroit. Following graduation in 1948, Palme remained in the United States, relying on busses and his own thumb for his tour of thirty-four states. He met widespread poverty and racism on his sojourn. If not a socialist at this point in his life, he had learned to think critically.[4] As much as he loved American society and culture, he concluded that American-style capitalism did not have all the answers.

Returning to Sweden, Palme enrolled in law school at Stockholm University, then Stockholm University College. He got his first taste of politics through his participation in the International Union of Students (IUS). As a student politician, Palme traveled throughout Eastern Europe. He had always been an anti-Communist, but his distaste for the Soviet occupation of the region was now first-hand.[5] Resenting the Communist influence on the IUS, he joined the student representatives of other Western countries to create a breakaway organization, the International Student Conference (ISC). The ISC received funding from the US government, mainly the Central Intelligence Agency (CIA). It is unclear if Palme was aware of the CIA's role.[6] Disturbingly, Palme did know what he was doing when he spoke with US embassy officials. He named three Swedish radicals who had attended the 1950 Congress of the IUS in Prague, Czechoslovakia, which he had also attended.[7]

When Palme completed his law degree in 1951, he was already a second lieutenant in the cavalry unit of the Swedish army. Apart from the standard military exercises, Palme also became an intelligence analyst for the defense staff in Stockholm that year. He already had thoughts about a distant land. Regarding the French phase of the Vietnam War, Palme concluded:

> Despite the military successes, the French have not yet succeeded in winning the native population behind their policy. Certainly, they have built a coalition government with great difficulty, but influential interest groups still stand outside, and cooperation between the government and the French authorities are far from friction-free. Nor has the promised popular representation come to pass. Even if the military situation were to develop favorably, significant diplomatic flexibility is required from the French side to convince the Vietnamese of the advantages of continued collaboration within the French Union.[8]

At this stage in his political development, however, Palme had the mentality of a cold warrior. Just as his journeys to the United States and Eastern Europe had shaped him, his 1953 trip to Asia would push him further leftward. On behalf of the ISC, Palme attended a student seminar in India, even though he had completed his education. Beyond the former jewel in the crown of the declining British Empire, Palme traveled to Sri Lanka, Burma, Thailand, Indonesia, Singapore, and British Malaya (now Malaysia). Ironically, Vietnam was not on his itinerary. His engagement with the students of Asia convinced him of the evils of European colonialism, and of the legitimacy of Communist participation in nationalist struggles.[9] Violent repression of indigenous Communist movements would only backfire. As Palme observed after his departure from Malaya, "It is a remarkable paradox that the British government spends millions of pounds to kill some Communists in the jungle resulting in the careful propulsion of an unknown number to the university in Malaya."[10]

The visitor from a small, neutral nation could empathize with countries under the domination of great powers. He regarded Communism in Eastern Europe as a malign force, for it was the product of Soviet aggression, but he respected anticolonial movements that used Communism as a tool of national liberation. It would a mistake, he believed, to apply European standards to developing countries.[11]

The year of his Asian tour, Palme made further professional progress. The defense staff, his employer at the time, now appointed him as an intelligence analyst for its military/political department. A concurrent part-time job proved more fateful. He took up a post as private secretary to Social Democratic Prime Minister Tage Erlander, who would become the most important man in his life. In 1954, Palme became the prime minister's right-hand man on a full-time basis.[12]

PALME AND EARLY SWEDISH POLICY ON VIETNAM

To be sure, the Vietnam policy of Palme's predecessor and mentor, Erlander, was rather equivocal. Sweden recognized South Vietnam in 1958, and in 1960, established a diplomatic presence in Saigon.[13] "But . . . we had no ambassador there because the ambassador in Bangkok [Thailand], he covered Saigon in Vietnam as well," explained Kai Falkman, a foreign ministry official at the time.[14] Ambassador Tord Hagen, who had believed in Saigon's potential and then grew disillusioned, resigned from his Bangkok post. Jean-Christophe Öberg, as the newly appointed secretary, would manage the embassy in the six months before Hagen's replacement arrived. The departing ambassador encouraged Öberg to take advantage of his position by traveling through the region.[15]

Hagen's successor, Ambassador Åke Sjölin, regarded the American position more sympathetically. "Oh, yes," Falkman recalled, "he said because the Vietnamese people could never win that war against America, the strongest power on earth."[16]

Öberg's youth had given him a broad perspective. He had been born in Rouen, France, to a Swedish father and a French mother. Later, in 1946, when his father was working at the Swedish embassy in Paris, the young Öberg accompanied him to a military parade. It was at this parade that Öberg caught his first glimpse of Ho Chi Minh, who was paying tribute to the Tomb of the Unknown Soldier located under the Arc de Triomphe.[17]

Several years later in Sweden, Öberg prepared to take his final examinations required for high school graduation. With so much already on his adolescent mind, he still followed the progress of the siege at Dien Bien Phu in Vietnam: "I could not understand why the French insisted on remaining in Indochina. Why could not the French agree to granting the Vietnamese people their longed-for independence? Why could not France, the France of 1789, show greater understanding for the Vietnamese people's longing for freedom?"[18]

By 1964, the fully grown Öberg was a diplomat, paying a call on US ambassador Henry Cabot Lodge. Öberg, cognizant of the precarious state of the Saigon regime, suggested negotiations with the insurgent forces in the South. Lodge exploded:

> Negotiate what? There is nothing to negotiate about. It is enough to get the situation under military control to make it possible for the government to establish enduring superiority outside Saigon, too. If one could only reach that goal, it would create no difficulties to convince the population that it had everything to gain by submitting to the government's administration. With that, the guerrillas will die a natural death.[19]

The audience with the American ambassador left Öberg feeling dispirited, his friend Falkman remembered, "And I think that was the time when he started to wishing to support Vietnam."[20]

His service to the antiwar cause would come soon enough. Shortly after his return to Stockholm in 1965, Öberg encountered Palme, already a veteran of several government posts. "I have read your reports on Vietnam," Palme told Öberg.[21]

Öberg would have considerable influence with the Palme government.

The spring of 1965 saw the beginning of antiwar demonstrations on Sweden. Sharing the views of the demonstrators, Palme questioned its morality. The US intervention had generated some controversy among Swedish youth but had not yet become a burning issue. Prime Minister Erlander, who had assumed power at the dawn of the Cold War, studiously avoided controversy in international affairs, emphasizing that Swedish "neutrality policy was based on not strongly committing ourselves to one side in the political rivalry between East and West."[22]

In a May 1965 speech, Foreign Minister Torsten Nilsson told his Gothenburg audience that he did not blame one side for the continuing war, only calling on all sides to embark on serious negotiations. Nilsson refrained from determining the ultimate goal of Vietnamese nationalism and suggested that the influence of unidentified foreign powers prevented the identification of that goal.[23]

Palme, now minister without portfolio, took the argument several steps further. Unlike Erlander, or Nilsson, Palme did not believe that military neutrality precluded forthright moral commitments. Despite his different approach to world politics, he sought the counsel of the prime minister and the foreign minister while composing the draft of his speech.[24]

Promoted to acting foreign minister for the summer, Palme revealed a sophisticated appreciation of Southeast Asian realities in his speech before the Brotherhood Movement's Congress in Gävle.[25] Well before the Vietnam War would inflame in Europe, Palme correctly perceived that the Vietnamese military campaign against the Americans was part of a larger third world movement for national liberation. The junior minister described the Vietnamese as "people who have lived for centuries under foreign domination and oppression."[26] The nationalist impulse may have gone out of fashion in Sweden and other parts of the first world, "but in Asia and Africa, nationalism was an explosive force of unprecedented strength."[27] Industrialized nations could not halt this revolutionary trend. "We must learn to live with it and perhaps also for it," Palme advised.[28] Moreover, the socialist principles of his own political party compelled its members to give these movements their moral support. "I do not know if the peasants in the villages of Vietnam—for it is about Vietnam that I have mostly spoken—have some utopias, a few dreams about the future," but Palme could imagine that villagers dreamed of "a future in peace without starvation, and when their personal dignity is respected."[29] Indeed, Palme argued, the Vietnamese people only sought the same things for which the Swedish labor movement had struggled in the past. The young cabinet minister probably said the things that Erlander lacked the boldness to say. Although the prime minister had supported Palme's rhetorical initiative, he publicly distanced himself from his protégé's moral stand: "We have no reason now to try to analyze and assess what could have been correct or incorrect in the U.S.A.'s Vietnam policy so far."[30]

Soon afterward, Leonard S. Unger, the assistant secretary of state for Far Eastern Affairs in Washington, summoned Jean-Jacques von Dardel, counselor at the Swedish embassy. Unger proceeded to scold von Dardel, accusing Palme of violating Swedish neutrality and distorting the truth of the war. Von Dardel did not aggressively challenge Unger, only responding that "Palme's speech did not only pertain to Vietnam but was also a more principled statement concerning the striving for freedom around the world."[31]

Palme had an opportunity to elaborate on his views on the war when Bertil Ohlin, the leader of the Liberal Party, attacked him. Ohlin accused him of siding with the Soviet Union and China, along with the Communist-dominated National Liberation Front in South Vietnam. The popular National Liberation

Front (NLF), which had been founded in 1960, operated under the guidance of North Vietnam. In response, Palme explained that he did not necessarily support the Vietcong, as the NLF was pejoratively labeled. Only the support of the Vietnamese people themselves for the NLF had any relevance. Palme wondered if Ohlin really cared about the aims of the Vietnamese people, rhetorically inquiring, "Is Mr. Ohlin also an opponent to free elections that, according to the Geneva Accords' provisions, should be held in Vietnam?"[32] Moreover, Palme sharply and perceptively responded to Ohlin's charge about Red China: "Mr. Ohlin seems absolutely certain that the Vietcong is directed from North Vietnam and that North Vietnam is directed from Peking. How does Mr. Ohlin know that?"[33] The liberal leader was historically ignorant, Palme implied. From the very beginning, the NLF had struggled for Vietnam's right of self-determination, free from foreign interference, including that of the Chinese.[34]

It was this sophisticated moral and geopolitical awareness that gave Palme's antiwar criticism such substance. The American public, in comparison, was poorly informed about the Vietnam War. They assumed that Communist North Vietnam were committing aggression against the people of South Vietnam. Key Washington figures, such as Secretary of Defense Robert S. McNamara, would continue to propagate this myth after they left office.[35] Of course, the actual evidence contradicts this myth. Palme himself had referred to the Geneva Accords of 1954, which stipulated the holding of elections in two years that would reunify North and South Vietnam. These elections were never held because President Dwight D. Eisenhower, and his secretary of state, John Foster Dulles, knew that North Vietnamese leader Ho Chi Minh would have won.[36] McNamara, who authorized the classified study of the Vietnam War now known as the Pentagon Papers, was surely aware of this denial of democracy.[37] Furthermore, McNamara and his superior, President Lyndon B. Johnson, had ready access to dissident opinions as the American investment in Vietnam escalated in 1965. James Thomson, who served as the National Security Council's China specialist, maintained that Vietnamese Communism was not an expression of Chinese aggression. More significantly, Undersecretary of State George Ball also insisted that the Soviet Union and China had little stake in the North Vietnamese struggle. Even more hawkish figures such as John McNaughton, the assistant secretary of defense for international security affairs, and William Bundy, the assistant secretary of state for East Asian and Pacific Affairs, challenged the relevance of the Cold War to Vietnam.[38] When Democratic senator George McGovern of South Dakota, a trained historian who held a doctorate from Northwestern University, suggested that Ho Chi Minh could act as a bulwark against an aggressive China, Johnson retorted: "Goddamn it, George, don't give me another history lesson. I don't have time to be sitting around this desk reading history books."[39]

By this time, the aging Ho Chi Minh was a mere figurehead in Hanoi. Le Duan, the general secretary of the Communist Party, now directed the Vietnamese war effort from the north, and pursued a far more aggressive strategy than Ho Chi Minh himself preferred. Le Duan had opposed the Geneva Accords, as well as Ho Chi Minh's passive acceptance of them. Ho Chi Minh feared antagonizing the Soviets, who, along with the Chinese, had favored the Geneva Accords and opposed renewed conflict in Vietnam.

Ho Chi Minh may have lost most of his power, but that does not mean that McGovern was wrong about Hanoi's intentions. Johnson and McNamara still could not accept the inconvenient realities of Southeast Asia because it would have required too much integrity to come to terms with them. The Johnson administration did not design Operation Rolling Thunder, the bombing campaign against North Vietnam, as a guarantee for the political integrity of South Vietnam, but as a hindrance. As William Bundy, the assistant secretary of state for Far Eastern affairs, put it, Operation Rolling Thunder would prevent "a government of key groups starting to negotiate covertly with the Liberation Front or Hanoi, perhaps not asking in the first instance that we get out, with that necessarily following at a fairly early state."[40]

True, Erlander and his senior advisors worked for peace in Vietnam, but they operated quietly and behind the scenes, avoiding controversy as much as possible. As part of his efforts to broker a peace, Erlander visited Washington in the fall of 1965. Johnson, who was seriously displeased with Palme's address, had conveniently traveled to his home state of Texas. Nevertheless, Vice President Hubert Humphrey extended warm hospitality to Erlander. Humphrey hosted a lunch for the prime minister on Thursday, November 4. That weekend, the vice president and his wife entertained the prime minister and Mrs. Erlander at the famed Greenbriar resort in West Virginia.[41]

That year, the Swedish ambassador to Algeria met with the local NLF representative in Algiers. After that first contact, Swedish diplomats continued to meet with the NLF in Peking, Hanoi, Moscow, Warsaw, Washington, Bucharest, Helsinki, and even Hanoi. Öberg, who was now department secretary of the Swedish Foreign Ministry, frequently visited the NLF in Warsaw.

In October of 1966, Foreign Minister Torsten Nilsson met with Vice President Humphrey and Secretary of State Dean Rusk in Washington. Nilsson informed Humphrey that the Swedish ambassador to Peking was in communication with his North Vietnamese counterpart in the Chinese capital. This was a significant piece of intelligence because the Swedes did not yet have an embassy in Hanoi. Then, the Swedish foreign minister offered information that was even more important. According to the minutes taken by the Americans: "The Swedish ambassador in Peking is now going to visit

Hanoi to see what he can learn there. He learned very little from talking to the Chinese in Peking. The Swedish Government believes it worthwhile to test the atmosphere in Hanoi."[42]

The vice president dismissed this news, saying "that there is no real lack of contact with Hanoi as Canadians and the South Vietnamese have many contacts. Other countries have contacts and share their information with us."[43] If Americans had been truly sincere in their wish for peace, on the other hand, they would have sought to exploit every possible contact.

After Swedish diplomats held discussions with North Vietnamese contacts in Warsaw as well as in Hanoi, Nilsson met with Rusk for lunch in Washington in November. The Swede made no more headway with Rusk than he had with Humphrey. This was highly unfortunate because Rusk carried far greater weight with Johnson than the vice president did.

In Hanoi, Foreign Minister Nguyen Duy Trinh himself had received the Swedish ambassador to Peking. Rather than continued war, the North Vietnamese foreign minister desired a peaceful settlement with conditions that the United States would eventually accept in 1973, seven years later. According to Nilsson, Hanoi wanted a coalition government in South Vietnam that included the NLF.

Rusk had other ideas, as the Americans recorded: "The Secretary said we could not impose a coalition government on the South; we could not turn our men around and start them shooting in the other direction to impose a coalition government."[44]

For Rusk, negotiations would only have value if the Americans could gain through diplomacy what they were not winning on the battlefield: "We are prepared, he said, to accept the Communist world's interest in North Viet-Nam if they are prepared to accept our interest in the South. Until Hanoi abandoned its objective of seizing South Viet-Nam, there could be no peace. It was a simple as that."[45]

The Swedes, of course, had their own perspective on the luncheon with Rusk. "For my part," Nilsson later said, "when I told Dean Rusk that I was certain that it would become a long-term war, he was naturally very skeptical. And I was just as certain then as now that one cannot bomb one's way to a military settlement in Vietnam."[46]

The Swedes continued their mediation efforts, codenamed Operation Aspen by the Americans, from November 1966 to February 1968. Öberg, the future Swedish ambassador to North Vietnam, had attended the luncheon with Rusk in his capacity as secretary of the foreign ministry. Years later, Öberg provided Prime Minister Palme with a blunt assessment of Rusk, who had

tried to make a great impression on Torsten Nilsson through recounting his adventures in Burma during the war [World War II]. Rusk then added that the

Burmese, Thai, Koreans, or Vietnamese were all the same, equally impossible to understand, equally stubborn, equally unreasonable in negotiations. I had a feeling at the time that Rusk had simply never placed himself in Vietnamese shoes.[47]

An unassertive man, Rusk simply reflected the ethnocentric perspective of President Johnson, who was determined to prosecute the war to final victory. Öberg perceptively realized that Rusk "only looked at the USA's prestige and global interests in Indochina."[48] Neither Rusk nor Johnson could see anything else. In 1964, the special assistant to Undersecretary of State Ball complained to his superior about National Security Council memoranda: "Nowhere in these papers is there a consideration of your proposal for negotiations within the near future and without increased military action (although with the threat of such action)."[49]

They also rebuffed the peace-making efforts of Polish diplomat Janusz Lewandowski, as historian James Hershberg recounts in his ground-breaking research. Lewandowski's diplomatic efforts, codenamed Operation Marigold, had persuaded Hanoi officials to agree to meet with their Washington counterparts, who rejected the arrangement at the last minute in late 1966.[50]

Until its March 1968 exposure by the Swedish media, Operation Aspen compelled the Swedish government to maintain a relatively low profile, but there was one American official who encouraged Stockholm to speak up. As chairman of the US Senate Foreign Relations Committee, Senator J. William Fulbright of Arkansas carried considerable influence. In 1964, the worldly Democrat had sponsored the Gulf of Tonkin Resolution authorizing the use of force in Vietnam. With the honorable exceptions of Senators Ernest Gruening of Alaska and Wayne Morse of Oregon, Fulbright and other liberal members of Congress had been led to believe that the resolution would not lead to a wider war. The Johnson administration deceived them, claiming that North Vietnam had made two unprovoked attacks on US naval vessels in the Gulf of Tonkin. The legislators had assumed that the resolution merely legitimized an American response to these supposed assaults, only one of which had actually happened, and at US provocation.[51]

Fulbright made considerable efforts to atone for his past mistake. In early 1966, the senator from Arkansas held wildly publicized hearings on the Vietnam War. Secretary of State Dean Rusk and General Maxwell D. Taylor, the former US ambassador to Saigon, expressed conventional views about the conflict in Southeast Asia. By contrast, Lieutenant General James M. Gavin and the diplomat George F. Kennan both came out of a productive retirement to criticize the war.[52]

Fulbright will always be remembered for his opposition to the Vietnam War, but his competing legacy is the Fulbright Program for international educational exchange. In December of 1966, the senator traveled to Sweden to deliver an address before the Swedish Institute. Ostensibly, he only intended to address the needs of the Fulbright Program, which was sponsored by the US government, and to suggest that Stockholm increase its subsidy. Sweden had participated in the Fulbright Program since 1952 and had signed a cost-sharing agreement with the United States in 1963, the third country to do so after its founding.

In his address, 'Education for a New Kind of International Relations,' Fulbright uncannily and presciently called for the kind of world leader that Palme would eventually become. The senator, a former Rhodes Scholar, believed that international education broadened the mind, sensitizing the student to different cultures and societies. "In a world," Fulbright said, "we must seek through education to develop empathy, that rare and wonderful ability to perceive the world as others see it."[53]

Obviously, Fulbright was speaking of statesmen only in a general sense, but Palme himself had developed that empathy at Kenyon College and through his extensive travels abroad. Empathetic leaders could strive for a world where the international language was cooperation, not domination. When Fulbright spoke of these leaders, he also included leaders of the non-imperial nations such as Sweden, which he specifically mentioned: "Small countries can contribute to the building of a world community by overcoming their sense of impotence; big countries can contribute to the same end by overcoming their arrogance."[54]

The smaller countries could make their influence felt in multinational institutions, and Fulbright did not overlook the past contributions of Dag Hammarskjöld, the late secretary general of the United Nations and distinguished Swedish diplomat.

Beyond active participation in the UN and the World Bank, rhetoric could be an additional tool of effective international activism. Fulbright advised:

> By speaking out, by pressing unsolicited advice on the big countries—in much the same way that members of legislative bodies sometime provide unsolicited advice to their executives. Disinterested, knowledgeable and experienced as they often are, the leaders and scholars of small countries can exercise a moral authority which is convertible into greater political influence than they may realize.[55]

Just as Fulbright, as a member of US Senate, had offered Johnson constructive, but undesired, criticism, Sweden could do the same as a member of the world community. Although the senator did not explicitly criticize the Vietnam War in his speech, it is implausible that his was not a subtle call for Swedish criticism of America's intervention.

Indeed, the senator anticipated the oratorical role of the future Prime Minister Palme, perhaps even inspired it to some extent. The Swedish Institute address left Palme, the minister of transport and communications, with a positive impression, for he did write the forward to the Swedish translation of the Fulbright hearings transcript: "Fulbright's speech constituted an effective reply to those who anxiously seek to hush the Vietnam debate in our country and who seek to brand every critical statement on the American policy as 'one-sidedness' and 'anti-Americanism.'"[56]

Ever mindful of Operation Aspen, the Swedish government had not yet taken a public stand against the war, but that caution did not prevent Stockholm from provoking the Johnson White House. In 1967, the International War Crimes Tribunal sorely tried Swedish-American relations. The Tribunal, which was organized by the British philosopher Bertrand Russell, would take place both in Roskilde, Denmark, and Stockholm. Intended to illuminate atrocities in Vietnam, the proceedings promised to embarrass the United States. Consequently, they would also prove embarrassing for Sweden. Erlander wrote to Russell to dissuade him from holding the hearings, but the prime minister appealed to the philosopher in vain. The foreign minister blocked the Stockholms Arbetarekommun, the local branch of Social Democratic Party of which he was chairman, from making a financial contribution to the Tribunal.

When Erlander traveled to Bonn, West Germany, for the funeral of the former Chancellor Konrad Adenauer, he spoke with the American president. The prime minister explained that his government had tried to prevent the Tribunal, but this did not impress the angry president. Johnson's national security advisor, Walt Rostow, confronted Erlander with the view that neutral Sweden was an inappropriate site for such proceedings, while the prime minister justified them on the grounds of free speech. Moreover, Erlander pointed out, the Swedish government was not even the sponsor of the tribunal.[57]

While Erlander wanted to maintain good relations with the United States, his discretion did not prevent his government from quickly granting visas to the North Vietnamese participants in the tribunal. Sweden and North Vietnam did not yet have official diplomatic relations, but the North Vietnamese ambassador to Peking informed his Swedish counterpart, Lennart Petri, that Stockholm's assistance was "worth more than shiploads of weapons."[58]

As the war went on the Swedish people felt increasingly hostile toward the US government. At a 1966 May Day demonstration in Stockholm, a US flag was burned. In January of 1967, a student broke windows at the US embassy.[59]

The continued indifference of the Johnson White House to Operation Aspen made the Swedish government more willing to openly criticize the United States. The Swedish government officially turned against the Vietnam

War on November 4, 1967. Nilsson advocated the pull-out of foreign troops from Vietnam, and the inclusion of the NLF as a negotiating partner. Sweden would no longer have an ambassador to Saigon.[60] Still, Stockholm's comments would remain comparatively restrained until Palme took office.

The civil unrest continued. Torchlit processions challenged American imperialism. The Swedish police had to guard the American embassy, whose diplomats now dodged snowballs, raw eggs, and rotten tomatoes. "The positive attitude to the U.S. was gone," observed Ingvar Carlsson, a Social Democratic member of the Riksdag, or the Swedish Parliament. The future successor to Palme continued: "We were disappointed that a country, which we liked so much, could make such a great mistake and risk such great values."[61]

The Erlander administration feared that C. H. Hermansson of the Left Party Communists would draw antiwar voters away from the Social Democrats. The Left Party Communists, for their part, faced competition from the more radical Communist Party of Sweden, an ally of United NLF Groups, a group of young antiwar activists of a pronounced Maoist orientation. As a counterweight to this antiwar organization, the Social Democrats founded the Swedish Committee for Vietnam.[62]

Amid the protests, the Swedish Committee for Vietnam and the United NLF Groups jointly organized the torchlit procession that would take place in Stockholm on February 21, 1968. Palme, who was now education minister, would deliver the keynote address. During this planning, the foreign minister got wind that the North Vietnamese ambassador to Moscow would simultaneously visit the Swedish capital. The American ambassador to Stockholm, William Heath, did not yet know this. Nevertheless, Heath was still angry and confrontational when he met with Nilsson for lunch. Erlander was in Oslo, attending a meeting of the Nordic Council. The American ambassador argued that the Swedes were not looking at the war objectively.[63] Heath's accusation of partiality must have influenced the foreign minister. Shortly after the luncheon with the American ambassador, Nilsson publicly referred to "the mindless killing from all sides" in Vietnam, and the necessity of ending "every type of military involvement from abroad," which, of course, also alluded to the support that China and the Soviet Union provided to North Vietnam.[64]

The Swedish Committee for Vietnam had invited the North Vietnamese to Moscow, Nguyen Tho Chan, to the protest. The foreign minister received Chan at the Foreign Ministry. Count Wilhelm Wachtmeister, a Foreign Ministry official who had met Chan's plane at Stockholm-Arlanda Airport, also paid a call on the North Vietnamese diplomat at the Grand Hotel. The ambassador sought Wachtmeister's guidance on extending an invitation to Palme to the protest. "My answer was that it was the organizers' business to decide who they wanted to invite," Wachtmeister recalled. "I had no reason to give any advice in that respect. I informed Palme immediately about the meeting. He accepted the invitation to speak at the gathering."[65]

The indifference of the Johnson White House to Operation Aspen made the Swedish government more willing to openly criticize the United States.[66]

On the evening of February 21, the North Vietnamese diplomat showed up at Humlegården, a park in Stockholm. Palme showed no surprise as he welcomed Chan to the procession. The education minister walked side by side with the ambassador, both bearing torches aloft as they led a procession of five to six thousand people.[67]

The procession made its way to Sergels Torg, or Sergel's Square, where Palme delivered his speech. Some protesters bore signs that read: "Military Aid to NLF."[68] There was a common perception among the crowd that the United States was committing genocide in Vietnam. More radical attendees chanted "U.S.A. – murderer" and "Tage and Geijer—Lyndon's lackeys."[69] This last expression, which rhymes in Swedish, referred to the belief of the United NLF Groups that Tage Erlander and Lennart Geijer, a minister without portfolio, were appeasing the Johnson administration.[70] The Swedish Communist Party's youth organization did not spare Palme. They passed out flyers: "Palme turns which way the wind blows."[71]

Palme now had the opportunity to appeal to these Swedish leftists. The recent lowering of the voting age to twenty in Sweden made a more radical position on the Vietnam War politically advantageous for him and his party.[72] Jan Eliasson, who would soon take up an appointment as first secretary at the Washington embassy, admired Palme for his progressive principles, but could also see the electoral strategy that accompanied them: "He was also a politician, and of course, by this line he took, which was credible in my view, he also reached new people, a new generation. He brought the world into Sweden in a way which had never been the case before."[73]

Nevertheless, had Palme not truly cared about the Vietnamese people, it is unlikely that he would have taken such pains to understand their struggle, as he continued to do once he become education minister, and Vietnam gradually attracted more and more international attention. He would fulfil his ministerial role, in the broadest sense, by educating the Swedish public and the world at large about Vietnam.

Eliasson never overlooked the political calculus of the Social Democratic Party, yet he never overlooked Palme's essential character, either. Eliasson would also serve as a foreign policy advisor at the prime minister's office in Palme's second term. Over time, the two men would become close personal friends. Therefore, Eliasson knew Palme well in life, and after the prime minister's death, would deeply reflect on his character:

He never would have been credible if it hadn't been his personal convictions and values. He was very firm on those values. He was a proponent of the rights of small countries, and also realized the importance of respect for international law for smaller countries. He used the expression: "The first line of defense is a well-functioning international system, a well-functioning United Nations."[74]

In his 1968 address at Sergels Torg, Palme voiced those convictions. He deepened and refined his analysis of the war as a conflict between nationalism and imperialism. The education minister directly attributed the origins of the war to US maintenance of the old French empire, which had disintegrated in Southeast Asia in the face of Japanese aggression during the World War II. The Vietnamese, after driving out the Japanese, had established the Democratic Republic of Vietnam. "But the colonial power decided to violently recover and claim its dominion," Palme said. "And the United States decided to place itself on the French side."[75] He also noted that Washington had defrayed 70 to 80 percent of France's military expenses as the war progressed.[76] After the French defeat in 1954, the minister continued, the United States destroyed the prospect of free elections in their rejection of the Geneva Accords. The Americans established the artificial state of South Vietnam instead. The South Vietnamese government, which was based in Saigon, oppressed the people who had unluckily fallen under its control. Palme defended the Vietminh, the NLF forerunner that had fought the French, for its challenge to the propertied classes. "The Vietminh had distributed land to the peasants," Palme observed. "But it is reported that the old landowners and moneylenders followed," with the support of the South Vietnamese government, to reclaim what they regarded as their property.[77]

By the time of his speech in 1968, Palme was also far more critical of the United States. He did not wait until the Nixon presidency to condemn the aerial destruction of Vietnam. President Johnson's Operation Rolling Thunder sufficed. Palme pointed out that "in these three years, more bombs have fallen over North Vietnam than over Nazi Germany during the Second World War. We know what this has meant in material devastation, in suffering for individual people."[78] This suffering was completely unjustified. The claim that the Communist Chinese empire required a countering American response lacked any supporting evidence. "This argument was already brought forward in 1945 as grounds for the support of the French colonial power," the minister slyly stated. "The difference is only that the present regime then did not yet exist" until Chairman Mao's triumph in 1949.[79] In Palme's view, US foreign policy was a self-destructive model of capitalist imperialism. "My opinion is: no wise capitalist can be so unreasonably foolish," Palme said. "But no one can be so unreasonably foolish without economic interests also existing in the picture."[80]

Palme's reference to economic interests were not far off the mark. Eisenhower, the more forthright of the Cold War presidents, had acknowledged these interests at a press conference on April 7, 1954. Communist domination of Indochina, Eisenhower said, would take "away, in its economic aspects, that region that Japan must have as a trading area or Japan, in turn, will have only one place in the world to go—that is, toward the Communist areas in order to live."[81]

In other words, the United States had to prevent Japan from becoming a trading partner of Red China. Eisenhower, who also had the region's natural resources on his mind, pointed out that "two of the items from this particular area that the world uses are tin and tungsten. They are very important. There are others, of course, the rubber plantations and so on."[82]

Clearly, Palme's speech made an impression at home. Gösta Bohman, a Moderate member of the Riksdag, charged Palme in a radio debate of making a "simplistic and one-sided attack on the USA," of criticizing the American war effort in an "insulting" manner.[83] Addressing Palme directly again in a parliamentary debate: "If one, Mr. Minister Palme, really had been out to influence the course of events and one had tried to convey a real, honest, and convincing appeal that could have had an effect, one would not have chosen the approach and words that Mr. Palme chose in his address. It shows that he was out for something else.[84]

Putting Palme's supposed insincerity aside, the antisocialist Bohman proceeded to make a comment that was particularly telling: "At the same time, one chooses means of expression and methods of delivery that stand in clear opposition to the fundamental rules for the conduct of Swedish politicians and statesmen that earlier we had agreed should pertain to our appearances in such a context as this."[85]

Cynical scholars have claimed that Palme's wartime commentary had no impact, but if that were the case, would Bohman have criticized the education minister for failing to conform to the standards of Swedish statecraft? This nonconformity suggests that Palme brought something new to Sweden's international role.

Concurrently, Palme realized that his new approach to international affairs could potentially threaten Swedish-American relations. Soon after the march, Palme made the incredible claim that he had been "surprised" to find himself marching with the North Vietnamese ambassador.[86] "I saw the statement of some political giant who claimed that when I came to the demonstration and discovered the North Vietnamese I should have immediately taken a taxi and ridden home," Palme said afterward in the Riksdag, "but for me this was a moral issue. In this situation, should I have turned my back on the North Vietnamese, turned on the demonstration, turned my back on this struggle for peace and justice they aimed for? That I could not do."[87]

Palme may have fibbed to fend off controversy, but he refused to retract his public support for Vietnamese self-determination.

The impact of Palme's speech was evident in the American reaction. "You kick us in the teeth and go to bed with our enemy," Ambassador Heath said to Wachtmeister's face.[88]

Heath then paid a call on Erlander to complain about Palme's march with Chan. While an American diplomat had been struck with eggs and rotten tomatoes, Heath complained, the North Vietnamese ambassador had been treated as a "hero."[89] He went on to accuse the Swedish government of exploiting the Vietnam issue for its own domestic political advantage.

This conversation grew heated. The prime minister denied that Palme's participation had any connection with the upcoming elections, but did acknowledge that the ambassador "had a point" about Chan. Erlander added that the demonstration had been planned before the North Vietnamese ambassador's arrival.[90]

Erlander was as angry as Heath. After the American ambassador had taken his departure, the prime minister said, "I was close to throwing out the bastard, but in any case, he is the ambassador of the United States."[91]

In March of 1968, the Johnson administration summoned Heath home for discussions, and when the ambassador's official posting ended the following January, he would not be replaced for more than a year.[92] Publicly, Palme denied knowing why the ambassador had returned to the United States: "Doesn't the ambassador travel home occasionally?"[93]

Right-wing elements in Sweden continued to attack Palme's speech, including Yngve Holmberg, the leader of the Conservative Party. Holmberg publicly advised Palme to step down. Sven Wedén, the head of the Liberal People's party, advocated an official apology to the United States.[94]

The young education minister reached out to progressive members of the US Senate. "Thank you for sending me a copy of your February 21st speech concerning the war in Vietnam," Senator Robert F. Kennedy of New York responded. "I appreciate your thoughtfulness in doing so."[95]

A copy of the speech also reached the office of Senator Eugene J. McCarthy of Minnesota. "It has been said that I am violently anti-American," Palme wrote to McCarthy. "This is simply not true. I was partly educated in the United States/B.A., Kenyon College, 1948. I know and love your country and people."[96]

Like Robert Kennedy, McCarthy dismissed Palme in a polite manner.[97] As McCarthy and Kennedy both vied for the 1968 Democratic presidential nomination, they would not take the political risk of engaging a foreign critic of the war. The senator who treated Palme with the most serious consideration was, appropriately enough, the chairman of the Senate Foreign Relations Committee.

In the 1968 letter accompanying his enclosed speech, Palme reminded J. William Fulbright of their previous meetings in Stockholm and Geneva. Explaining the circumstances of the speech, Palme sought Fulbright's empathy and understanding:

> It was read beforehand by the Prime Minister and the Foreign Minister, and thus represented the views of the Swedish government. Shortly afterwards the American Ambassador in Sweden was called back to Washington for consultations. This has caused great uproar in this small country. The conservative party thus demanded that I resign immediately. I think you can easily visualize what questions of principle in the relations of a great power to a small country have been involved in the vivid public discussion.[98]

The Arkansas senator, deeply concerned about the damage done to American relations with Western Europe by the Vietnam War, fully appreciated the impact of Palme's rhetoric on the Johnson administration. Fulbright expressed that appreciation on the floor of the United States Senate: "The United States called its Ambassador home 'for consultation'—a diplomatic way of saying to the Swedish Government that the United States is unhappy."[99] According to the senator, it was too easy to attack Palme without bothering to understand the Swede's position. "I wonder how many Americans have read what the Swedish Minister of Education actually said," he commented. "Was he anti-American, or was he trying to help us?"[100] The senator proceeded to insert the entire English translation of Palme's speech into the Congressional Record.[101]

Within the United States, the domestic antiwar movement had enough of an impact to convince Johnson to abandon his reelection campaign in 1968. The Republican nominee, Richard M. Nixon, was so determined to win the race that he deliberately undermined the Johnson administration's negotiations with the North Vietnamese. A successful peace agreement would have benefited the Democratic candidate, Vice President Humphrey. Receiving intelligence about an imminent settlement from Professor Henry Kissinger of Harvard University, the Republican candidate did not waste time. Using Bui Diem, the South Vietnamese ambassador to Washington, and right-wing lobbyist Anna Chennault as go-betweens, Nixon informed South Vietnamese president Nguyen Van Thieu that a Republican victory would give Saigon a better deal. As a result, Thieu rejected the agreement, sabotaging it.[102] Historian Thomas A. Schwartz doubts that the Johnson administration could have reached a peace agreement at the last minute, and is also skeptical that Kissinger's conduct affected the 1968 election, but even he describes it as "self-serving and egregious."[103]

NOTES

1. Kjell Östberg, *I takt med tiden: Olof Palme 1927–1969* (Stockholm: Leopard Förlag, 2012), 33–37.

2. Ibid., 40–44.

3. Ibid., 47.

4. Henrik Berggren, *Underbara dagar framför oss: en biografi över Olof Palme* (Stockholm: Norstedts, 2010), 119, 123–124, 129–133; Östberg, *I takt med tiden*, 61–63.

5. Berggren, *Underbara dagar framför oss*, 156–160; Östberg, *I takt med tiden*, 74–79.

6. Berggren, *Underbara dagar framför oss*, 176; Östberg, *I takt med tiden*, 79–81.

7. Östberg, *I takt med tiden*, 88; Stellan Andersson, *"Biografiska notiser 1950"*: olofpalme.org.

8. Östberg, *I takt med tiden*, 170. Electronic mail correspondence with Archivist Emeritus Stellan Andersson of ARAB, November 12, 2020.

9. Östberg, *I takt med tiden*, 104–6. Berggren, *Underbara dagar framför oss*, 216.

10. Östberg, *I takt med tiden*, 106.

11. Berggren, *Underbara dagar framför oss*, 216, 279. Östberg, *I takt med tiden*, 128. Stellan Andersson electronic mail, November 12, 2020.

12. Ibid.

13. Gunnar Åselius, *Vietnamkriget och de svenska diplomaterna* (Dialogus: Stockholm, 2019), 137–38, 140.

14. Kai Falkman, Interview in Stockholm, Sweden, July 6, 2016. Åselius, *Vietnamkriget och de svenska diplomaterna*, 151.

15. Åselius, *Vietnamkriget och de svenska* diplomaterna, 137–38. Jean-Christophe Öberg, *Varför Vietnam?* (Stockholm: Rabén & Sjögren, 1985), 9, 17.

16. Falkman interview.

17. Kaj Falkman, *Ekot från Vietnam: En diplomats minnen från kriget och återbesök fyrtio år senare* (Stockholm: Carlssons, 2014), 92.

18. Ibid., 92–93. Åselius, *Vietnamkriget och de svenska diplomaterna*, 181.

19. Ibid., 94.

20. Falkman interview.

21. Björn Elmbrandt, *Palme* (Stockholm: Atlas Vintage, 2011), 54–55.

22. Staffan Thorsell, *Sverige i Vita Huset* (Stockholm: Bonnier Fakta, 2004), 100; Östberg, *I takt med tiden*, 266–67; Berggren, *Underbara dagar framför oss*, 342.

23. *"Anförande av utrikesministern i Göteborg den 1 maj,"* *Utrikesfrågor: Offentliga Dokument M.M. Rörande Viktigare Svenska Utrikespolitiska Frågor 1965* (Stockholm: Norstedts Tryckeri, 1966), 40.

24. Thorsell, *Sverige i Vita Huset*, 102.

25. Berggren, *Underbara dagar framför oss,* 352; Thorsell, *Sverige i Vita Huset*, 99.

26. *"Statsrådet Palmes anförande vid Broderskapsrörelsens kongress i Gävle den 30 juli 1965,"* *Volym* 676/2/4/0: 005, *Tal, Olof Palmes arkiv* (OPA), *Arbetarrörelsens arkiv och bibliotek* (ARAB), Flemingsberg, Sweden; Thomas Alan Schwartz, *Lyndon*

Johnson and Europe: In the Shadow of Europe (Cambridge, MA: Harvard University Press, 2003), 84.

27. Ibid.

28. Ibid.

29. Ibid.

30. Thorsell, *Sverige i Vita Huset*, 103.

31. Ibid., 104.

32. *"Bakgrunden till herr Ohlins och mitt mellanhavande är denna,"* August 24, 1965, *Volym* 676/2/4/0: 006, *Tal,* OPA, ARAB; Pierre Asselin, *Vietnam's American War: A History* (Cambridge, UK: Cambridge University Press, 2018), xxii, 96; Lien-Hang T. Nguyen, *Hanoi's War: An International History of the War for Peace in Vietnam* (Chapel Hill: The University of North Carolina Press, 2012), 49; John Prados, *Vietnam: The History of an Unwinnable War, 1945–1975* (Lawrence: University Press of Kansas, 2009, 71.

33. Ibid.

34. Ibid.

35. See Robert S. McNamara with Brian VanDeMark, *In Retrospect: The Tragedy and Lessons of Vietnam* (New York: Vintage, 1996).

36. Marilyn B. Young, *The Vietnam Wars: 1945–1990* (New York: Harper Perennial, 1991), 47; "Origins of the Insurgency in South Vietnam, 1954–1960," Vol. 1, Chapter 5, *The Pentagon Papers: Gravel Edition*, https://www.mtholyoke.edu/acad/intrel/pentagon/pent11.htm.

37. Young, *The Vietnam Wars*, 259–60.

38. Fredrik Logevall, *Choosing War: The Lost Chance for Peace and the Escalation of War in Vietnam* (Berkeley: University of California Press, 1999), 291–92; Young, *The Vietnam Wars*, 127–29.

39. Thomas J. Knock, "'Come Home, America': The Story of George McGovern," *Vietnam and the American Political Tradition: The Politics of Dissent*, ed. Randall B. Woods (New York: Cambridge University Press, 2003), 105–6.

40. Nancy Hershberger, *Traveling to Vietnam: American Peace Activists and the War* (Syracuse, NY: Syracuse University Press, 1998), 14; Asselin, *Vietnam's American War*, 10, 88–89, 95, 109; Nguyen, *Hanoi's War*, 42, 49, 51, 147; Christopher Goscha, *Vietnam: A New History* (New York: Basic Books, 2016), 270, 308.

41. Thorsell, *Sverige i Vita Huset*, 106–7.

42. Meeting between Hubert Humphrey and Torsten Nilsson, "Memorandum of Conversation," Office of the Vice President, Washington, October 17, 1966; *UD HP-Dossierer, Vietnamkriget, Mål: C, USA's politik,* 1966–1971, HP38:9, *Riksarkivet,* Arninge, Sweden (RA); Ulf Bjereld, *Kritiker eller medlare: Sveriges utrikespolitiska roller 1945–1990* (Stockholm: Nerenius & Santérus Förlag, 1992), 112–13.

43. Ibid.

44. "Memorandum of Conversation," Document 303, *Foreign Relations of the United States, 1964–1968, Volume IV, 1966*. U.S. Department of State, Office of the Historian, http://history.state.gov/historicaldocuments/frus1964-68v04/d303.

45. Ibid.

46. Transcript of Torsten Nilsson on Swedish Television's (*SVT*) *Aktuellt*, June 29, 1972. *UD HP-Dossierer, Vietnamkriget, Mål: F, Fredsträvanden*, 1971–1972, HP 38:20, RA.

47. Personal letter from Jean-Christophe Öberg in Hanoi to William Wachtmeister, *"Vietnam-problemet på 60-talet,"* August 6, 1972. *UD HP-Dossierer, Vietnamkriget, Mål: F, Fredstävanden*, 1971–1972, HP 38:20, RA.

48. Ibid.

49. "A Bureaucratic Insider Laments the Momentum Against Negotiation, November 1964," in *Major Problems in American Foreign Relations, Volume II: Since 1914*, Sixth Edition, eds. Dennis Merill and Thomas G. Paterson (Boston and New York: Houghton Mifflin Company, 2005), 422–23.

50. See James Hershberg, *Marigold: The Lost Chance for Peace in Vietnam* (Stanford, CA: Stanford University Press, 2012).

51. William C. Berman, *William Fulbright and the Vietnam* War (Kent, OH: Kent State University Press, 1988), 23–25; David F. Schmitz, "Congress Must Draw the Line: Senator Frank Church and Opposition to the Vietnam War and the Imperial Presidency," *Vietnam and the American Political Tradition: The Politics of Dissent*, ed. Randall B. Woods (New York: Cambridge University Press, 2003), 126–27; LeRoy Ashby and Rod Gramer, *Fighting the Odds: The Life of Senator Frank Church* (Pullman: Washington State University Press, 1994), 184; *The Vietnam Hearings, with an introduction by J. William Fulbright* (New York: Vintage Books, 1966), 44–47, 275; Bjereld, *Kritiker eller medlare?*, 120; Prados, *Vietnam*, 99. Young, *The Vietnam Wars*, 117–21.

52. See *The Vietnam Hearings, with an introduction by J. William Fulbright*.

53. "Education for a New Kind of International Relations," J. William Fulbright of Arkansas, Speech before the Council Meeting of the Swedish Institute, December 5, 1966. J. William Fulbright Papers (MS F956 144-B). Series 72, Box 27, Folder 21. Special Collections, University of Arkansas Libraries, Fayetteville, Arkansas. (JWF)";*Fran kritik mot Nordstaterna,"* *Dagens Nyheter*, December 5, 1966. Electronic mail from Eric Jönsson, Executive Director, Fulbright Commission in Sweden, October 15, 2019.

54. Ibid.

55. Ibid.

56. *Kommunikationsminister Olof Palmes förord. Senats förhören om Vietnam*, translated by Sture Biurström (Stockholm: Beckmans, 1967), 7.

57. Thorsell, *Sverige i Vita Huset*, 110–11; Ulf Bjereld, Alf W. Johansson, and Karl Molin, *Sveriges Säkerhet och Världens Fred: Svensk utrikespolitik under kalla kriget* (Stockholm: Santérus Förlag, 2008), 224";*Erlander vill ej ha ny Stockholmssession,"* *Dagens Nyheter*, May 9, 1967.

58. Thorsell, *Sverige i Vita Huset*, 113–14.

59. Berggren, *Underbara dagar framför oss*, 370. Scott, *Swedish Social Democracy and the Vietnam War*, 58.

60. Marder, "Pentagon Data Show Both Sides Stalled on Key Issue."; Bjereld, *Kritiker eller medlare?* 128; Östberg, *I takt med tiden*, 285.

61. Thorsell, *Sverige i Vita Huset*, 120.

62. Ibid., 121. Scott, *Swedish Social Democracy and the Vietnam* War, 33 and 56; Wilhelm Agrell, *Fred och fruktan: Sveriges säkerhetspolitiska historia 1918–2000* (Lund: Historiska Media, 2000), 174–75.

63. Thorsell, *Sverige i Vita Huset*, 123–24; Bjereld, *Kritiker eller medlare?* 102.

64. Thorsell, *Sverige i Vita Huset*, 125; Rolf Ekéus, Interview in Stockholm, Sweden, January 19, 2016.

65. Wilhelm Wachtmeister, *Som Jag Såg Det: Händelser och människor på världsscenen* (Stockholm: Norstedts, 1996)," 193; Gösta Julin, *"Ambassadören i Vietnammarsch: Sverige 'Informeras,'" Dagens Nyheter*, February 21, 1968.

66. Bjereld, *Kritiker eller medlare?* 128.

67. Ibid., 126; Berggren, *Underbara dagar framför* oss, 385";*Palme i attack mot USA:s krig: Ett Hot Mot Demokratin," Dagens Nyheter,* February 22, 1968.

68. Thorsell, *Sverige i Vita Huset*, 127.

69. *"Tage och Geijer—Lyndons lakejer"; Thorsell, Sverige i Vita Huset*, 127.

70. Ibid.

71. Berggren, *Underbara dagar framför oss*, 388.

72. Ibid., 385; Scott, *Swedish Social Democracy and the Vietnam War*, 32.

73. Jan Eliasson, Interview in Stockholm, Sweden, June 7, 2017.

74. Ibid.; Jan Eliasson, *Ord och Handling: Ett liv i diplomatins tjänst* (Stockholm: Albert Bonniers Förlag, 2022), 92–93.

75. *"Statsrådet Palmes anförande vid Vietnam-demonstrationen 21.2.1968," Volym* 2/4/0: 012, *Tal,* OPA, ARAB.

76. Ibid.

77. Ibid.; Asselin, *Vietnam's American War*, xxiv; Prados, *Vietnam*, 58, 68; Goscha, *Vietnam*, 301.

78. Ibid.

79. Ibid.

80. Ibid.

81. Document 716, "Editorial Note," *Foreign Relations of the United States, 1952–1954, Indochina, Volume XIII, Part I*: https://history.state.gov/historicaldocuments/frus1952-54v13p1/d716. Taken from *Public Papers of the Presidents of the United States, Dwight D. Eisenhower, 1954*, 381–90.

82. Ibid.

83. *"Maktbalans modell (h)," Arbetet*, February 25, 1968, *Volym* 2/4/0: 012, *Tal,* OLA, ARAB.

84. *"Utrikes- och handelspolitik debatt, Torsdagen den 21 mars 1968," Riksdagen, Volym* 2/4/0: 012, *Tal,* OLA, ARAB.

85. Ibid.

86. Thorsell, *Sverige i Vita Huset*, 128.

87. Ibid., 129.

88. Wachtmeister, *Som Jag Såg Det*, 193.

89. Thorsell, *Sverige i Vita Huset*, 135.

90. Ibid.; Wachtmeister, *Som Jag Såg Det*, 194.

91. Ibid., 136.

92. Alvin Schuster, "Swedish Chilliness Toward U.S. is Limited to Vietnam," *New York Times*, January 8, 1973; Thorsell, *Sverige i Vita Huset*, 148.

93. Thorsell, *Sverige i Vita Huset*, 137.

94. Bjereld, *Kritiker eller medlare?* 103.

95. Letter from Robert K. Kennedy to Olof Palme, April 2, 1968; letter from Olof Palme to Robert Kennedy, March 15, 1968. OLA, *Brevsamling, Volym* 3.2/48, ARAB, Courtesy of Joakim Palme.

96. Letter from Olof Palme to Eugene McCarthy, March 15, 1968. OLA, *Brevsamling, Volym* 3.2/48, ARAB, Courtesy of Joakim Palme.

97. Letter from Eugene J. McCarthy to Olof Palme, May 1 1968. OLA, *Brevsamling, Volym* 3.2/48, ARAB, Courtesy of Joakim Palme.

98. Courtesy of David Prentice. Letter from Olof Palme to J. William Fulbright, March 14, 1968. Folder N-Q, Box 55:2, Subseries 18 Vietnam Correspondence, Series 48 Foreign Relations Committee, JWF.

99. J. William Fulbright "Speech of Swedish Minister of Education at Vietnam Demonstration," March 22, 1968, *Congressional Record—Senate*, *Volym* 2/4/0: 012, *Tal, OPA,* ARAB.

100. Ibid.

101. Ibid.

102. John A. Farrell, *Richard Nixon: The Life* (New York: Doubleday, 2017), 342–43, 350.

103. Thomas A. Schwartz, *Henry Kissinger and American Power: A Political Biography* (New York: Hill and Wang, 2020), 58–59.

Chapter 2

The Accession of Olof Palme

History remembers January 1969 as the month that Richard M. Nixon became president of the United States, but it was also the month that Sweden became the first Western country to recognize the Democratic Republic of Vietnam.[1] This recognition took place nine months before Palme became prime minister, and nine days before Nixon took the presidential oath. Denmark and Norway, the two other Scandinavian countries, did so in 1971, along with Switzerland.[2] Yet both Copenhagen and Oslo had to wait two more years, after the signing of the Paris Peace Accords, for most of their NATO partners to join them. Those NATO partners were Canada, Belgium, the Netherlands, Italy, France, and the United Kingdom. Australia, a non-NATO member, fought with the United States, but also recognized Hanoi in 1973.[3] The United States, the final holdout, would not establish formal diplomatic relations with Vietnam until 1995.[4]

At least one historian sees an inconsistent application of principle in the Swedish recognition of North Vietnam and the Swedish nonrecognition of East Germany.[5] Yet it is important to remember that the Democratic Republic of Vietnam was an independent state fighting for national reunification. The German Democratic Republic, by contrast, was controlled by the Soviet Union.

Despite his campaign promise of "peace with honor," Nixon came to power with the intention of expanding the war in Southeast Asia, and ultimately winning it. This expansion involved extensive bombing campaigns over Laos and Cambodia, as well as ground incursions into those countries. The Johnson administration had also authorized bombing raids against Cambodia and Laos, but these were tactical rather than strategic, and did not involve B-52s.[6] Although the Nixon administration's bombing campaign, which did use B-52s, was concealed from Congress and the American public, both the president and his national security advisor, Henry Kissinger, would later point to the presence of the Ho Chi Minh Trail in Laos and Cambodia as a justification. The North Vietnamese used the Ho Chi Minh Trail to transport troops and supplies into the Central Highlands of South Vietnam.[7] Accompanying the air raids was the policy of Vietnamization, that, depending on the progress of the war, would gradually replace American ground troops with South Vietnamese forces.[8] Nixon and Kissinger opposed the abrupt withdrawal of all the American ground troops. Ultimately, the president hoped to preserve South Vietnam in the same manner as an American client state had been preserved on the Korean peninsula.[9] If geopolitical concerns assumed first place in the Nixonian consciousness, domestic politics, at least, took a very close second. In defiance of war fatigue and mounting protests among the general American population, Nixon's conservative base demanded victory in Vietnam.[10] Kissinger, as much as he liked to portray himself as a cosmopolitan statesman far removed from provincial matters, was also deeply concerned about the domestic impact of the war.[11]

Nixon laid out his motives before the National Security Council:

> We talk hard in private, but with an obvious peaceful public stance, seeking to gain time . . . giving the South Vietnamese a chance to strengthen the regime . . . while punishing the Viet Cong. Within three or four months bring home a few troops unilaterally . . . as a ploy for more time domestically, while we continue to press at the negotiation table for a military settlement.[12]

The Nixon administration was not happy to deal with the activist position of the Palme government. Nilsson, who remained at his post as foreign minister, had made a startling announcement at the 1969 Congress of the Social Democratic Party, the same gathering that had replaced Erlander with Palme as party leader. With his young colleagues Rolf Ekéus, Ulf Svensson, and Ethel Ringborg, Foreign Ministry Secretary Jean-Christophe Öberg had "outlined a policy, a radical policy of giving aid to Vietnam," in the words of Ekéus.[13] Lennart Klackenberg of the Finance Department was also a contributor.[14] When Nilsson accepted their advice, they drafted a speech for him.

The foreign minister did not make a proposal. Without consulting Palme beforehand, Nilson announced a new government policy, which was a clear case of insubordination. "We can contribute humanitarian aid to the victims of various conflicts," Nilsson said in his address before the party congress. "Such assistance can be made while a conflict is still going on. Up to now, we have offered and contributed more than 20 million in aid to Vietnam."[15] So far, so good.

Then, the foreign minister continued:

> The Vietnamese people's suffering has made a deep and indelible impression on us all. I am convinced that the government has strong public opinion behind it, when it now plans assistance and credits worth over 200 million

to North Vietnam to be disbursed over three years. . . . When the fighting in South Vietnam reaches its end, we also hope we could make more extensive efforts there.[16]

In 1969, 200 million kronor roughly equalled $40 million.[17]

Ekéus recalled of this surprise: "Torsten Nilsson saw this as a great gift to the new prime minister. Torsten Nilsson had strongly supported the government. So, he also thought that Palme would be happy."[18]

When Palme delivered the concluding speech of the Congress, he expressed no strong emotion. The new party leader acknowledged that the Social Democrats now favored providing 200 million Swedish kronor "in loans and assistance to North Vietnam for the humanitarian aid and reconstruction."[19]

Through the Red Cross, the Swedish government funnelled 450,000 kronor in humanitarian aid to North Vietnam between 1965 and 1968. At the same time, 150,000 kronor went to the NLF.[20] Nevertheless, Prime Minister Tage Erlander, and initially Finance Minister Gunnar Sträng, had had some reservations about a Swedish aid program for the Third World in general. While sympathetic to the scheme, Erlander feared it would never win widespread popular support. The elder statesman was more also inclined to dispense aid to further Sweden's strategic and economic aims.

In 1967, Palme himself had argued that the primary responsibility of the government was to ensure the economic well-being of the Swedish people. In contrast to his mentor, however, Palme envisioned aid as an expression of international solidarity: "I believe that a program for aid to developing countries must be far more strictly connected to a general principal focus, where our values in foreign policy must come into the picture, the attitude to social revolutions in the poor countries."[21]

In other words, Palme favored a cautious and calibrated approach to foreign aid, unlike the foreign minister and the finance minister, who now just wanted to charge ahead. Nilsson and Sträng, who both had working-class roots, jointly patronized Palme. In 1970, Ekéus remembered, they "presented to the prime minister the draft [of a] new development aid budget jointly prepared by them, containing radical financial increases including Vietnam support reflecting Nilsson's speech at the Party Congress" the year before.[22]

"These two old gentlemen were looking at a young kid because he had had no real career in the party," Ekéus observed. "He was a right-wing bourgeois, rich family, intellectual, picked by the very intellectual prime minister, Erlander . . . he picked that little boy as his replacement."[23]

Although Nilsson and Sträng condescended to the youthful Palme, the two elder statesmen had also fallen under the influence of the younger officials at the Foreign Ministry. "We had the fantastic ambition to go to one percent, first in the world, lots of money, which was a good part of the success of us young kids who had been pressing for that," Ekéus recalled of their desire to contribute 1 percent of Sweden's gross national product to foreign assistance.[24]

Essentially, Nilsson and Sträng were trying to dictate an entire new foreign aid program to Palme. "These two guys come to him and tell him what should be in the assistance budget," Ekéus said. "Including Vietnam. Including South Africa. If I had been Olof Palme, so young, I would say the same thing: 'I'm the prime minister. So, I would also like to be part of the decision-making.' But it never happened with Erlander. He never dared to with these important guys."[25]

Nevertheless, Palme's youth alone did not account for the manipulations of the foreign minister and the finance minister. Erlander had always approved the budgets presented by Nilsson and Sträng, but his successor proved tougher than expected. "If you are to be prime minister," Ekéus pointed out, "you must have an ego."[26] The Swedish leader would eventually find a replacement for Nilsson. In spite of these tensions, Palme would come around to favor an ambitious aid program for North Vietnam, but only under his firm leadership. "Yes," Ekéus agreed, "over time, yes . . . it was only that it was without asking him."[27]

The foreign minister said that the Swedish government would provide the North Vietnamese with 220 million kronor in aid over a three-year period starting on July 1, 1970. Two-thirds of this assistance would consist of credits, and the remaining one-third in actual aid. Among Nilsson's ambitious plans were the construction of a children's hospital in Hanoi, and the provision of synthetic fertilizer worth 10 million kronor. Even though fertilizer could be used to produce explosives, the new prime minister defended the idea to prevent starvation in Vietnam.[28]

This argument did not persuade Nixon. The national security advisor was instructed: "The President wants you to 'direct State to cut anything we can with Sweden.'"[29]

The Export-Import Bank, an agency of the US government, telephoned a Swedish diplomat, threatening to cut off loans to his country if it provided aid to an American enemy. Moreover, US Secretary of Commerce Maurice Stans personally warned the Swedish ambassador that if Sweden provided any aid outside of the Red Cross channel, no more financial assistance to Sweden would come from the Export-Import Bank. The Exim Bank would not support countries that, in turn, offered loans and credits to other countries engaged in war with America. This threat would hurt Scandinavian Airlines System (SAS), a carrier jointly owned by Sweden, Norway, and Denmark. SAS had just arranged to purchase new aircraft from Boeing.[30] "The threat of reprisals through the Export-Import Bank was given expression that could not be misunderstood," recalled Yngve Möller, a Swedish delegate to the United Nations.[31]

Stockholm also felt pressure from the US. business sector. Stora Kopparberg, a Swedish paper company, had received a seven-year order from an American company worth an annual 25 million kronor. Then, a telegram arrived: "When Sweden appropriates money to a country with which the United States finds itself at war, there is no reason to fulfill the contract."[32]

Another American concern put off an order for two turbines from ASEA, a Swedish electrical company. ASEA also received a common complaint from other American customers: "Sweden is sending money to North Vietnam so they can shoot down our boys."[33]

Foreign Minister Nilsson was forced to give his assurances that Sweden would only offer humanitarian aid to North Vietnam. As early as the spring of 1970, the Riksdag decided to set aside 225 million kronor for postwar reconstruction aid.[34] Vietnam would not receive any Swedish fertilizer, after all.

Publicly, at least, the Americans carried on with the peace negotiations begun by the Johnson administration. Kissinger, however, circumvented the official talks in Paris to meet secretly with North Vietnamese diplomat Le Duc Tho. These secret discussions, which also took place in the French capital, proved just as fruitless because the Americans sought peace solely on their own terms. Palme himself suspected that secret talks of some sort were going on, as he indicated privately to British Prime Minister Harold Wilson. Nixon would not publicly acknowledge these clandestine discussions until January 1972.[35]

On the first day of June of 1970, the North Vietnamese chargé d'affaires in Stockholm paid a call on the prime minister. Nguyen Dinh Thanh expressed grave concern over the continuation of the American war in Vietnam, and its extension into Laos and Cambodia. Thanh said to Palme:

> In November 1969, Nixon had declared . . . that there existed two possibilities of solving the Vietnam problem. The first was the so-called Vietnamization of the war, the second was through negotiations. The Americans had openly showed that they no longer gave priority to negotiations. The deadlock in Paris was a telling example of this. Nor had a chief negotiator been appointed by President Nixon. Vietnamization scarcely constituted a peace policy. It only aimed to prolong the war.[36]

Palme inquired if the North Vietnamese regarded a peaceful resolution to the conflict in Southeast Asia as feasible. "Thanh answered that a total unconditional and prompt withdrawal of the American troops in Vietnam, Laos, and Cambodia would solve all the problems," the minutes recorded.[37]

Curious about the potential for a coalition government in South Vietnam, the prime minister sought the opinion of the North Vietnamese diplomat: "Thanh replied that a coalition government in Saigon would be the quickest way to a politically reach a solution in Vietnam. All political differences of opinion could be represented in such a government."[38]

During the conversation, which was conducted entirely in French, Thanh did not forget to thank Palme for his support. The chargé d'affaires extended his thanks to the Swedish people as well. He also asked the prime minister for the Swedish government's views on the situation in Indochina. According to the minutes:

> The prime minister answered that on the Swedish side, one followed develop-
> ments with intense interest. The great question mark, however, was whether
> the Americans intended to keep their word and withdraw their troops from
> Cambodia before July 1st of this year. The situation concerning the intentions of
> the South Vietnamese troops was yet unclear, added the prime minister. On the
> Swedish side, one naturally regretted that the war had been widened to become
> a new Indochina war. The Swedish government thought—now as before—that
> only a political solution could bring the war to an end.[39]

It turned out that the American troops would withdraw from Cambodia by July 1, but the North Vietnamese diplomat was more concerned about the long term. Thanh made an interesting request. The Swedish Red Cross had agreed to supply the North Vietnamese with a medical laboratory, as well as cloth and milk. Due to a complete paper shortage in North Vietnam, nine million schoolchildren had neither textbooks nor exercise books. Since the Swedish Red Cross did not classify paper supplies as humanitarian aid, Thanh appealed to Palme. The prime minister stated he was unfamiliar with the issue, but that he would look into it. As we shall see later, Palme did far more than just that.

Perhaps most significantly, Thanh urged Palme to establish an embassy in Hanoi. The prime minister explained that the creation of an embassy would be a gradual process, partly because of budgetary considerations: "He added that despite the lack of a Swedish embassy in Hanoi, one could say to a certain degree our relationship <u>was</u> more intense than if an embassy did exist. My long stay in Hanoi during the winter was telling enough proof of this."[40] Indeed, the recorder of the minutes was Jean-Christophe Öberg, who had spent time in Hanoi, and would soon return in his new capacity as Swedish chargé d'affaires, and subsequently, ambassador.

Referring to Palme's plan to visit the United States in a few days, Thanh encouraged the prime minister to "use his influence to persuade the American government to withdraw its troops from Indochina and embark on a new political course."[41]

AMBASSADOR HOLLAND

Thanh may have overestimated Palme's influence, for the Swedish prime minister would not have an easy time in the United States. Since US-Swedish relations were increasingly tense, Palme would have had good reason to feel apprehensive. More than a year into his presidency, Nixon had finally appointed a new ambassador to Stockholm, Jerome Holland. Sweden had not had an American ambassador for fifteen months.[42] Holland arrived at Arlanda on April 8, 1970, accompanied by his wife, one daughter, and one son.[43] Protesters had assembled at the airport, bearing signs that read: "US Imperialism—The Greatest Enemy of All People" and "Fight US Imperialism" and "USA Must Leave Vietnam Immediately and Unconditionally."[44]

At least one sign bore an inappropriately racial reference: "Vietnamese Women and Children Die—Uncle Tom Comes to Sweden."[45]

A young Swedish protester shouted a greeting at the new ambassador: "Go home, Murderer! You're not welcome in Sweden!"[46]

When the African American diplomat rode in a glass coach to the Royal Palace to present his credentials to King Gustaf VI Adolf on April 14, a few antiwar protesters attacked the state carriage with fruit and eggs, while shouting, "Nigger, nigger." The disturbance obliged the new ambassador to exit the palace through the back door. Holland was understandably incensed: "You can say what you want about the Vietnam War. That is free speech and I believe in free speech. But when I am called a nigger that is a personal insult, and I resent it deeply."[47]

Granted, the notorious racial slur was not acceptable among Social Democratic circles. The extreme left also shunned the word. In all likelihood, the users of the "n-word" were unstable people who belonged to the margins of Swedish society.[48]

Similar volleys of eggs and tomatoes enhanced the flavor of other public appearances made by the new ambassador. A particularly dramatic incident took place in the town of Glanshammar. A young man named Björn Falkenäs was selling the *Vietnambulletinen*, a newspaper for the radical United NLF Groups, and collecting money for their cause: "When bombs fell over Vietnam, the American pilots said, 'Let's drop some eggs.' . . . We came out to Glanshammar, before they had arrived. So, the car turns up and we throw our eggs. The police rush out and then a great scuffle results."[49]

When asked nearly fifty years later if he regretted throwing the eggs, Falkenäs said: "No, never have. Honestly speaking, it was so long ago, but

I do not believe that I thought of him as anything other than a representative for the U.S. government that did this in Vietnam. I hope my egg hit its target, but I don't know."[50]

The eggs did not reach their intended target, but the State Department threatened to recall Holland.[51] Palme himself attributed the usage of the racial slur to a "lunatic fringe." He also said that the man who had used the slur on April 14 was a US citizen and former member of the Black Panthers.[52] In truth, some Black deserters referred to Holland as *mums-mums*, a Swedish pastry with chocolate coating an interior of egg-white foam.[53]

The US ambassador was not reassured. In a dispatch to the State Department, Holland referred to the episode in Glanshammar, calling it the "latest in long series of egregious incidents here which, while deplored by government, are inevitable result of government's criticism of U.S. policies in Southeast Asia and elsewhere and the anti-American atmosphere which has been built up."[54]

The American ambassador regarded Palme's position on the war as "one-sided."[55]

After the prime minister asked the Foreign Ministry to conduct a thorough investigation, which included statements from witnesses and data from the National Police Board, he suddenly claimed that "there has been found no evidence of an abuse of a racial character."[56]

Confused about the conclusion of this official investigation, I wrote to Joseph Holland. "I'm a bit surprised by your inquiry, that there is still specu-lation about whether the N-word was hurled at my father," Joseph wrote back. "It was not only hurled on April 14, 1970 . . . there were other incidents as well when I witnessed racial slurs against my father."[57]

Palme was disturbed enough about the matter to ask the American ambas-sador to see him in person. Holland recognized the prime minister as a sincere advocate of racial equality. At the same time, he also recognized the prime minister as a politician:

> Palme then came around to what appears to have been principal purpose of meeting by saying that election campaign is warming up and that he may have to say something about racism charges. He said that he proposed to say that gov-ernment investigation has not substantiated charges of racism directed against Ambassador Holland. We would add that ambassador is positive that he has heard epithet "nigger" shouted at him. . . . We would add, however that ambas-sador's overall impression is that he has had warm reception from overwhelm-ing majority of people.[58]

The U.S. ambassador was noncommittal.[59]

VISIT TO AMERICA

Of course, the Nixon administration was downright hostile. When the prime minister traveled to Gambier, Ohio, to accept in honorary doctorate from his undergraduate alma mater, Kenyon College, the president snubbed him by failing to extend an invitation to the White House. Publicly, the Palme administration denied asking to meet Nixon. On the day before Palme's departure for the United States, a Swedish reporter had asked the prime minister, "Has any attempt been made from the Swedish side to bring about an official invitation?" Palme had replied, "Absolutely not."[60]

The prime minister's visit to the United States was ostensibly a private one. Yet telegraphic exchanges between the Foreign Ministry in Stockholm and the Washington embassy indicate that Sweden viewed a meeting with the president as desirable. The US State Department could only promise a visit with Secretary of State William Rogers. Stockholm instructed Swedish Ambassador Hubert de Besche, "We are anxious that your statement . . . that Rogers would be a natural interlocutor for the prime minister not be understood by the Americans that Palme would not be interested in a meeting with the president."[61]

The State Department remained unreceptive, noting that Erlander had not met with Johnson during his own visit to the United States in 1965. "I refuted this by pointing out that Johnson was forced to leave Washington at the time of Erlander's visit but that [Vice President Hubert] Humphrey invited Erlander to a major lunch," de Besche reported. "I made no such demand of the White House, but a courtesy visit seemed important and appropriate."[62]

In fact, Kissinger had already performed his function as national security advisor, advising the president on the prime minister, "If he does come to Washington, he could not be seen by high U.S. officials, and so if he chooses to come, it would be best if his stay were long enough only to accomplish his purpose (e.g., address the Press Club)."[63]

Nixon scribbled his decision directly upon the memorandum: "Just completely ignore his visit—our Ambassador shall not comment—State shall not comment—background or otherwise—This is an order I expect to be followed without deviation."[64]

What did not help Palme's case was his official reaction to the US invasion of Cambodia. Two days after the invasion, which took place on May 1, the prime minister said that the offensive "went under the name Operation Complete Victory. Thus evidently referring to an victory for violence and military power, but in today's war there is no longer any victor. One can only lose the peace."[65]

Pressing his case, the Swedish ambassador even met with a protocol official at the State Department.[66] The National Security Council's Helmut Sonnenfeldt, aware of the Swedish contact with Protocol, had an interesting idea for Kissinger. Even as he referred to "the obnoxious official Swedish attitude toward our actions in Cambodia," Sonnenfeldt suggested that

> there may be some value in your talking to Palme; while he almost certainly is beyond persuasion, it may be desirable to have the record show that he was given an authoritative explanation of US policies and exposition of one view of Swedish conduct. Moreover, since he may be around for a long time, it may be wise not to administer a personal snub. Distasteful as it may be, the Swedes just might be useful to us some day, and personal animus should probably not be permitted to get in the way. I suppose there is also some value in taking the measure of the man and seeing what makes him tick.[67]

At the end of the memorandum, Sonnenfeldt left several options for Kissinger's response. The most significant option was, "I will see Palme privately."[68] Kissinger's handwritten answer was "No."[69]

Undeterred by White House coldness, the Swedish Foreign Ministry scheduled Palme's lunchtime appearance at the National Press Club in the US capital, which could be "possibly preceded by a visit with Nixon in the morning."[70] Through his intentional and deliberate snub, Nixon missed an opportunity to work out his differences with the prime minister. The only other head of a foreign government to receive such a slight in the history of the White House was Fidel Castro, during the Eisenhower presidency.[71]

The White House snub did not extend to the State Department. William Watts of the National Security Council informed the national security advisor that "Secretary Rogers (and maybe [Undersecretary of State] Elliott Richardson) were extremely upset on this directive, and has had it withdrawn."[72]

Secretary of State William Rogers explained to the president that shunning Palme would help the prime minister rather than hurt him: "We had considered indicating to Palme that this is not a good time for a visit but rejected the idea. He would undoubtedly make public that he had asked him not to come, and the public relations consequences would be adverse both here and abroad, well beyond the range of Swedish-American relations."[73]

It was significant that on the same day that Palme met with Rogers, Nixon received the prime minister of Morocco. Sweden certainly carried more geopolitical weight in the world than Morocco did. Yet it was Ahmad Laraki who enjoyed a private visit to the White House.[74]

Palme, nonetheless, appreciated his appointment with Rogers at his seventh-floor office of the State Department on June 4.[75] When they were photographed at the start of their private meeting, Rogers complained in jest that photographers always aimed from below in order to highlight his double chin. Such jocularity presaged a courteous discussion, but the secretary of state still had his differences with the prime minister.[76]

The three-hour long conversation included lunch. According to the State Department minutes, "Palme was verbally adroit in defending Sweden's position but appeared sincerely concerned to explain Sweden had not deviated from its traditional neutrality and to assure the secretary he intended to avoid any direct attacks on US and its policies while visiting here."[77]

Minister Per-Bertil Kollberg of the Swedish embassy witnessed the conversation. Afterward, Kollberg gave the scoop to Colonel Carl-Gustaf Ståhl, the embassy's military attaché. "Concerning Cambodia, Rogers conveyed the Americans' irritation that the Swedish government had compared the American action there to the Soviet invasion of Czechoslovakia," Ståhl reported to his military superiors in Stockholm. "Palme answered that he, as head of government of a small country, watched the actions of the superpowers against other small countries with trepidation."[78]

Rogers and Undersecretary Richardson, another participant in the discussion, defended the US intervention in Cambodia. They argued that Washington had briefed Phnom Penh beforehand, and that Prime Minister Lon Nol had privately expressed his desire for the intervention. Unconvinced by such reasoning, Palme maintained that a military intervention in a foreign country required an explicit and direct request from that country's government. The prime minister made a valid point. It is doubtful that Lon Nol's wishes coincided with the wishes of the Cambodian people. With the approval of the White House, Lon Nol had toppled Prince Norodom Sihanouk in a March 1970 coup.[79]

The State Department minutes largely coincided with the Swedish version of Palme's comments: "After Paris Talks opened, bombing halt began, and US troop withdrawal continuing, Swedish criticism was withheld. With Cambodian action Sweden 'had' to resume criticism because this action represented widening of war and intervention in a small country without permission of its government."[80]

As the State Department recorded, the subject of neutrality emerged during the argument over Cambodia. The secretary of state "noted some countries appear to take particular delight in criticizing us from a position of non-alignment and without responsibility for problems which require urgent solution."[81]

Defending Swedish nonalignment with as much vigor to Rogers in private as he would in his speeches before the American public, Palme observed that "Sweden's brand of well-armed and therefore credible neutrality was of great value to European security and a major contribution of the existing 'balance' in Northern Europe."[82]

As far as Cambodia was concerned, the prime minister also feared that the American invasion would damage Swedish efforts on behalf of the American prisoners of war (POW) in North Vietnam. On behalf of his government, Rogers thanked Palme for his POW work. Carrying on this conciliatory tone, the secretary of state suggested that Ambassador Holland could avoid travel and public appearances in Sweden, thereby also avoiding more unpleasant encounters with demonstrators. Palme, who liked Holland, declined, although he had previously expressed worry that continued travel would subject the ambassador to additional attacks.[83]

The tone again turned less pleasant when "Rogers, in relatively sharp terms, warned Palme against criticizing the American government while he was on American soil."[84] The prime minister denied making "such statements in his speeches that contained direct criticism of U.S. policy, but to the extent that questions were put to him on controversial subjects, he must essentially speak the same as he has done in Sweden."[85]

Even if Palme toned down his rhetoric, he would not completely censor himself. All the same, the well-mannered Rogers said that he would have liked to invite the prime minister and Mrs. Palme to dine at his home.[86] Palme never visited Rogers's home, but Treasury Secretary David M. Kennedy and Interior Secretary Walter J. Hickel did attend the dinner held at the Swedish embassy in the prime minister's honor. The rest of Nixon's cabinet, including Rogers, declined the same invitation.[87]

The good will between the secretary of state and the prime minister had little bearing on US foreign policy, however. Given the low status of Rogers within the Nixon administration, Palme's visit to the State Department meant that the prime minister had been dispatched to the doghouse. Nixon and Kissinger had effectively bypassed the nominal chief diplomat in their secretive and undemocratic management of US foreign policy.[88] Undeterred by the snub, Palme did not refrain from speaking his mind. His June 6, 1970, speech at Kenyon College only offered general coverage of international affairs, but did address issues relevant to the conflict in Indochina. In a probable allusion to his own extremely vocal position on the Vietnam War, Palme maintained the right of less powerful countries to express themselves in the face of US and Soviet domination:

> As things are today, a widening scope of tasks has become the exclusive pre-rogative of the superpowers. The superpowers are in a position to destroy themselves, but in so doing they will destroy the others. But the small nations cannot escape being affected by their actions. This is why the small nations would like to have a word in the councils.[89]

Even though Vietnam was hardly a tool of the Communist superpower, the fear existed that Nixon's military engagement could escalate into a Cold War conflict with Moscow. "I doubt whether peasants in Asia, of South America of Africa would relish being wiped out in the name of a global strategic doctrine," Palme warned, without a doubt thinking mainly of Southeast Asia.[90]

In their implementation of détente, Nixon and Kissinger sought to maintain a balance of power between the United States and the Soviet Union. Of course, they intended to keep Southeast Asia within the American sphere, and the prime minister hinted at this: "The balance of power in the world of today may be regarded as a guarantee of peace, however fragile. There is, however, the risk that the status quo is being maintained in the social and economic spheres, too. The social emancipation in the poor countries may be regarded as a threat to strategic interests."[91]

Protected by local sheriffs and the police while at Kenyon College, Palme encountered members of the International Longshoreman's Association (ILA). The ILA belonged to the same prowar sector of the organized working class as the so-called "hard hat" construction workers. In May, the hard hats had physically attacked antiwar demonstrators in New York. Fortunately, the ILA did not physically attack Palme. Still, they were an intimidating group of approximately one hundred men who wore steel helmets bearing "We Love America" stickers. The president of Toledo's Local 1379 explained their motives for the protest: "First, his country's treatment of our ambassador. Second, the fact that Sweden is in cahoots with North Vietnam and supporting North Vietnam. Third, the fact that they harbor our deserters."[92]

A Black longshoreman held a sign that referred to Ambassador Holland's experiences in Sweden: "ILA says Go Back to Sweden. Biggot [*sic*] Palme." A White longshoreman bore an identical sign. Another sign read, "Palme, take your Volvos and go home." Protesters tried to interrupt his speech with jeers and yelling, "Go home!" Palme scored points with the audience, who numbered between five hundred and one thousand, when he stated that academic freedom "also includes the right to be heard."[93]

Margareta Sjöström, a Swedish exchange student at a local high school, attended the speech: "The strongest memory is that the Palmes were so calm and seemed unaffected by the entire situation."[94]

In Washington and New York, Palme also benefited from protection by the FBI and the local police, courtesy of the State Department.[95] He probably needed it the most in New York, for hostile longshoremen held a protest outside his hotel. Like the longshoremen in Ohio, they objected to Swedish aid to North Vietnam, and to Swedish protection of draft resisters.[96]

Apart from his honorary doctorate, his visit to the United States did have some consolations. Senator Fulbright, in his capacity as chairman of the Senate Foreign Relations Committee, gave Palme the opportunity to share his views with that body.[97] The June 4 meeting was a production of one of the Swedish embassy's first secretaries, Jan Eliasson. "I was glad we mobilized so many high-flyers at that meeting," Eliasson recalled. "I had prepared that pretty much through these truly wonderful senators' aides and congressional aides."[98] As first secretary, his access to the senators themselves was minimal, his friendships with their aides proved beneficial.[99]

The meeting went well because it was largely one of the minds. Palme had spoken out against the war, as had the senator from Arkansas. "And Fulbright was, of course, very much critical himself with the Vietnam War, but he was also a gentleman," Eliasson recalled. "He was never . . . a firebrand, criticizing his country. He was a very, very, dignified opponent of the war, but basically he understood Palme's position."[100]

The prime minister also related well to Senator Ralph Yarborough of Texas, who was not even a member of the Foreign Relations Committee. Nevertheless, the liberal Democrat was kindly disposed toward Palme's views, and attended the meeting. Hitting it off on a personal level, the two men discussed the history of Swedish immigration to Texas, and Palme's own youthful visit there in 1948. The senator would follow up by sending the prime minister articles about distinguished Swedish immigrants to the Lone Star State.[101]

The Republican senators, for their part, gave the prime minister a very civil hearing. Whatever they may have felt about the war themselves, they were willing to listen to his critical views. Republican courtesy came as an immense relief to Eliasson. "And I was worried that we would get a beating from some of the Republicans," he said. "I don't recall it happening . . . Palme was very happy with it."[102]

An important component of the prime minister's discussion with the Foreign Relations Committee was the matter of American prisoners of war held in North Vietnam, which I shall address in chapter 2.

Throughout his tour of the United States, Palme adhered to his principles, maintaining a measured tone in his rhetoric, more measured, perhaps, than his rhetoric from 1968. As the State Department had predicted, "Palme may mute his criticism of the US during his visit here . . . but we doubt that he will drop it altogether."[103]

The State Department dismissed Palme's rhetoric as political food for Swedish domestic consumption, but his main aim was to explain Sweden's position to the American people, rather than to attack their country. Palme answered the charge that his antiwar stand violated Swedish neutrality. "It must be possible to rely on our sincerity when we declare that our policy of no alliances in peacetime is a demonstration of our firm resolve to maintain our neutrality in war," Palme assured the National Press Club on June 5 before four hundred members of the Fourth Estate. "People should be able to feel confident that neither Swedish territory nor Swedish resources will be used for aggression."[104]

Nevertheless, Swedish would remain active in international affairs:

> Our neutrality does not condemn us to silence. Participation is to hold views and take stands . . . the opinions of a small, neutral country like Sweden can never be reasonably conceived as an expression of ambitions of power politics or as hostility toward other nations. When we express opinions on different questions they are based on our own independent judgment. This is fully compatible with a foreign policy based on strict neutrality as far as the national security is concerned.[105]

Sweden had been officially neutral since 1834, simply meaning that it wished to stay out of any war. Over time, Stockholm had come to interpret the concept of neutrality as freedom from any military alliances.[106] Palme himself gave Swedish neutrality a morally responsive cast.[107]

Appearing on the June 7 broadcast of *Meet the Press*, a news program on NBC, the prime minister stressed his admiration for the United States. Palme acknowledged the painful conflict that he and his countrymen felt in challenging the Americans because "the Swedish people is [*sic*] in many ways the most pro-American, or Americanized people in Europe."[108] Therefore, the criticism "did not come conveniently or easy to it, but it was very honest and sincere when it was brought forward."[109]

So, the prime minister's tactful criticism continued. "You say that the people of Vietnam should have had the opportunity for self-determination," an interviewer noted on *Today*, another NBC program. "Do you think they would have that opportunity if the North Vietnamese and the Vietcong took over?"[110] Palme cautiously began: "It's very difficult to say. We can't speak of democracy in the same way as we do in our countries."[111] Of course, it would have been very easy, and logical, to say that a Hanoi victory would give the Vietnamese people the best opportunity for self-determination. The rank and file of the National Liberation Front was committed to the war effort, and to final victory. Even though that victory did not ultimately come about through electoral means, the war effort was a popular movement in both North and South Vietnam, and Palme knew this. The obvious answer, therefore, would have been a simple yes. The prime minister, however, did go on to explicitly state, "Only that I think the NLF, to a large extent, has represented the national aspirations of the Vietnamese people."[112]

Without a doubt, the North Vietnamese government of Le Duan was authoritarian.[113] If the *Today* interviewer cared so much about Vietnamese self-determination, however, he should have brought up the canceled elections that had been promised by the Geneva Accords. Surveying the history of the world, violent revolutions have brought about the most dramatic political change. This was certainly the case in China, Russia, and France. While the Continental Congress may have directed the American Revolution, the legis-lative body was hardly the product of universal manhood suffrage.

As cautious as the prime minister's language may have sometimes been, he still had the courage to carry on with his activism, even at considerable risk to Swedish trade. The United States and Sweden had a significant eco-nomic relationship. In fact, Swedish exports to the United States grew by 21 percent in the first quarter of 1970, while American imports jumped by 51 percent. To be sure, Washington never punished Sweden with trade sanc-tions. Still, the actions of the longshoremen represented a potential threat. They sat on their hands in Newark, New Jersey, refusing to remove Volvos from ships that had come from Sweden.[114] Palme regarded it as his duty to promote Swedish business, but apart from meeting the Business Council on International Understanding, he devoted relatively little attention to economic affairs during his official visit as prime minister. Primarily, his speeches and media appearances covered the great issues of war and peace. He did not spend his time touring Volvo dealerships.[115] What is more, the humanitar-ian concern expressed in internal documents within the Swedish Foreign Ministry matched the concern expressed in Swedish rhetoric. In addition to maintaining Swedish-American relations, Palme simply wanted to speak out against the war. Pressure from radical students in Sweden did not compel him to do so, as his 1970 election strategy focused on issues affecting Swedish workers.[116]

SWEDEN AND THE ARMS TRADE

Nevertheless, there was one aspect of Swedish trade that provoked charges of hypocrisy: the arms industry. Responding to a report in *The Washington Post* that American commando raids in Indochina had employed Swedish submachine guns, the Swedish government investigated the matter. The state munitions inspector informed the Foreign Ministry that the State Department and the Central Intelligence Agency had purchased Swedish submachine guns that were untraceable. He suspected that the submachine guns could have been sold indirectly to Washington through Samuel Cummings, a lead-ing American trader in small arms. Conversely, the Swedish weapons could have been acquired from a factory in Cairo, Egypt. The munitions inspector knew one thing: "In 1952, we sold . . . 50,000 submachine guns of Finnish manufacture from surplus stock to Western Arms Corporation, and 5,000 new submachine guns to Interarmco."[117] Interarmco was Samuel Cummings's company. Apparently, no direct sales from Sweden to the US government were made, but the munitions inspector did not think that mattered: "An interested buyer should not have any difficulty finding Swedish small arms on the international market."[118] At any rate, the sales took place long before the prime ministership of Olof Palme.

The North Vietnamese were particularly concerned about a story from United Press International that two American gunships, the AC-119 and the AC-130, employed radar detectors and 44-mm guns from Bofors, the Swedish arms manufacturer. Marc Giron of the Foreign Ministry assured the North Vietnamese ambassador that Bofors had not sold any war materiel, including guns, to the United States within the last decade. "Therefore, it seemed extraordinarily unlikely that the information from UPI had any foundation in reality," Giron said.[119] He went on to explain that export control laws in Sweden did not regulate the sale of radar detectors, which were not considered to be war materiel. Giron did not know if Bofors had sold radar detectors to the United States, and "we therefore could not exclude the possibility that these, or parts of them, could be of Swedish origin."[120]

The Swedish government had tightly regulated the export of war material since 1918. Giron wrote about a more comprehensive law passed that very year: 1971. The new law, although conditional, prohibited the export of Swedish arms to countries fighting wars either internally or externally.[121]

In any case, it seems Swedish laws prevented the American usage of the most lethal of Swedish arms in Vietnam. Falkman was far more confident that Swedish arms had not been employed in the conflict in Indochina, elaborating: "We had the export controls . . . countries that are at war should not get Swedish war materiel . . . no sort of hardware."[122] Of course, this meant that Sweden never delivered weapons to the North Vietnamese, either.[123]

Eliasson, who was also a naval officer, was not so sure. "I can't guarantee that Swedish weapons cannot have been used," he said.[124]

Ekéus recalled that during the war, "we didn't sell weapons to U.S., but we sold technology and we bought technology."[125] Nonaligned Sweden maintained its position through a strong defense, but paradoxically, this strong defense required technological exchange with the United States and Great Britain. Swedish sales of military technology abroad also financed Swedish defense. The arms industry in Sweden could not have sustained itself by domestic sales alone. According to Ekéus: "I mean if you produce your artillery, if you produce a hundred pieces, and instead of producing a thousand pieces, and you sell nine hundred off, then the per capita will be much less expensive."[126]

That did not mean that the Swedish military-industrial complex sought to engage solely with the Anglo-American Alliance. Ekéus remembered that "we tried to work with Norway, but they bought American planes instead."[127] He repeated his point: "Once you get longer production lines . . . we could afford fifty or something, but if we can sell two hundred more, so it's part of financing the Swedish defense system."[128]

Following the end of the Cold War, Eliasson came to believe geopolitics no longer offered the same justification for this vast military-industrial complex:

> All of my generation have served in the military, and we needed the best mate-
> riel. We were fearing that anything could happen. At the time, the line was that
> if we are neutral (we used the word neutrality) we are not part of any alliance.
> We need to be self-sufficient also in materiel. In today's world, it has become a
> less sufficient, less powerful argument.[129]

Nevertheless, the worldwide reach of the Swedish arms industry was disturbing. Ekéus himself conceded: "I have great respect for friends who work in the peace movement there, which are very critical about our policy."[130]

Eliasson took his own criticism to the next level: "I must admit that to me, this is one of the weak spots for us, that we have such an extensive arms industry, and also arms export. All through the years, I have had difficulty defending and explaining this, I must admit."[131]

Looking back, Eliasson was particularly disturbed by the exportation of arms to Singapore, an Asian city-state with a highly repressive government. The exports came from Swedish companies such as Bofors and Saab. "Singapore received a lot of goods," Eliasson remembered. "They don't know what Singapore then did with the export. We didn't react strongly enough against Singapore. My God, why should Singapore have all this?"[132]

Eliasson, recently retired from a long and extensive career in diplomacy, could only conclude, "The fact is that I think we should stand up with . . . the reputation we have to speak out on moral grounds, which I think should be our line. In that case you have to do it with credibility. You can't just be critical."[133]

Even at the height of the conflict in Southeast Asia, Eliasson also pointed out the Swedish government never imposed a general arms embargo against the United States. "And the contacts between defense officials in Sweden and the U.S. continued," he said. "And Palme didn't mind that. He thought it was good that we had that continued dialogue."[134]

It is important to also note that Palme's antiwar activism went against the best interests of the Swedish arms industry. Eliasson did note that Swedish arms manufacturers were not entirely pleased with Palme.[135] When asked about the industry's reaction to the prime minister's rhetoric, particularly his controversial address in December 1972, Ekéus replied, "I think they were very angry. They were not proud about that."[136]

Falkman had the same view about those involved in the Swedish arms industry. "They belonged to the conservative sector of the country, of course, and they were rather critical throughout because Palme was such a passionate politician," he said. "We don't have passionate politicians, and then he was an exception to the rules. People were a bit frightened of him."[137]

MILITARY COLLABORATION WITH
THE UNITED STATES

Stockholm's official opposition to the Vietnam War, and sympathy for the North Vietnamese, had a deleterious impact on the Swedish-American military collaboration. For example, in September of 1967, the Erlander administration had decided to order Redeye air defense missiles from the United States.[138] The Redeyes were scheduled for delivery in stages from April to September of 1969.[139] As the Johnson administration drew to a close, it deliberately put the delivery on hold.[140] Officially, the US Army blocked sales to all foreign countries. Unofficially, the Swedish military attaché would receive another message:

> On a classified basis, however, he will be informed that the situation in Southeast Asia has made the sale of REDEYE militarily unacceptable, and that except for a relatively small shipment of REDEYE missiles to Australia for training purposes within country, no deliveries are to be made to any other foreign country for the duration of hostilities in Southeast Asia. This approach will then afford the Swedes the option of either cancelling (at no expense to Sweden) or permitting their order to be stored until such time as delivery can be made.[141]

The succeeding Nixon administration waited one year to reverse this decision. In January of 1970, the White House authorized the deliveries, which began that summer, on the condition that the Americans could inspect the deployment of these missiles. There was some US apprehension that the Redeyes, once delivered to Sweden, could eventually end up in North Vietnamese hands. One such inspection took place in 1972. "Now when I fight with the Americans, for God's sake make sure we have good cooperation with the Americans on defense in all cases," Palme admonished General Stig Synnergren, the supreme commander of the Swedish Armed Forces.[142]

So, the military cooperation between the two countries continued, but not without American snubs. High-level US officers ceased their official visits to Sweden, and only their lower-level Swedish counterparts were welcome in the United States. The US chairman of the Joint Chiefs of Staff, Admiral Thomas Moorer, canceled a 1972 visit to Sweden in response to the statements made by prominent politicians at a May Day demonstration. This cancellation came upon the recommendation of Ambassador Holland. From 1969 to 1973, Sweden did not host any US naval ships.[143]

While the Swedes did have some dealings with the US military, and did lean westward ideologically, one should not underestimate the determination of the Palme government to maintain its independence and neutrality. Otherwise, the comments of Herman Kahn, the American geostrategist and systems theorist, would not have come as such a surprise. In a published interview, Kahn said: "It is as if—to take an extreme example—the Russians or East Germans started bombing Sweden. We've no treaty with Sweden, but we wouldn't stand idly by and watch it. Sweden is in what I call our 'zone of responsibility,' while Eastern Europe and perhaps Finland and Yugoslavia are not."[144]

The geostrategist justified US presence in Vietnam as a "stabilizing force" in Asia and believed that the United States could potentially perform the same function in Sweden. Kahn's argument deeply disturbed Wachtmeister at the Swedish Foreign Ministry:

"This reasoning is worrying, among other things, against the background of the pronounced parallel with Southeast Asia. The American government's actions in Indochina in the last ten months shows that the integrity of neutral states is set aside when the U.S.A. finds that its interest (or 'the world's interest') demands it."[145]

Wachtmeister resented the assumption that Sweden would automatically welcome American intervention: "Kahn's reasoning not only shows a lack of confidence in Sweden's own ability to preserve its own neutrality but also a lack of familiarity with the meaning of the Swedish policy of neutrality."[146]

Regardless of official Swedish policy, Washington viewed Sweden as a strategic asset. Back in 1952, Stockholm and Washington had reached an agreement that would permit the Swedes to purchase American military equipment and arms. Ten years later, the two countries signed a clandestine and self-explanatory Memorandum of Understanding Concerning Technical Information.[147] "Swedish neutrality is of value to the United States so long as its application continues to result a strong and stable nation which provides a buffer to Soviet expansionism in the Baltic area,' the U.S. State Department concluded in 1962.[148]

That year, Stockholm and Washington also secretly agreed to exchange military technology.[149]

During the Cold War, Sweden did not fully realize its importance to Washington. Decades later, veteran Swedish diplomat Rolf Ekéus led an investigation of Stockholm's national security policy during the Cold War.[150] Thanks to his collaboration with Swedish researcher Jerker Widén years later, Ekéus uncovered a surprising recommendation that the State Department had made in back in 1962:

In the event of Soviet aggression against Sweden alone we should undertake to come to the assistance of Sweden as part of a NATO or UN response to the aggression. Planning and preparation for this contingency must be conducted on a unilateral U.S. basis, since some NATO powers may be sensitive to a preferential assistance guarantee to a neutral non-member, and the Swedish Government has scrupulously avoided any identification with NATO.[151]

President John F. Kennedy proceeded to approve the State Department's proposal.[152]

"I'm sure that the Brits knew it," Ekéus said, "but not NATO . . . Sweden didn't know about that document."[153] In the course of his investigation, Ekéus "talked, of course, with both Kissinger and Brzezinski."[154] Another source was Helmut Sonnenfeldt of the NSC. Additionally, Sven Hirdman, the former state secretary of the Swedish Ministry of Defence, provided information he had received from an advisor to Reagan-era Secretary of Defense Caspar Weinberger. By means of this distinguished network, the Swedish diplomat verified the continuation if this secret policy until the early 1980s.[155]

Further substantiating Ekéus's conclusions was one document from September of 1975, which bore the signature of Secretary Henry Kissinger and was addressed to the US ambassador to Stockholm, Robert Strausz-Hupé.[156] Despite the tensions created by Palme's opposition to the recently ended Vietnam War, the secretary of state gave the "instruction to Strausz-Hupé that it was strategically vital that the Soviet Union was prevented from militarily exploiting Swedish territory."[157]

Tellingly, Kissinger only referred to US intervention in the event of a conventional Soviet attack on Sweden. As a nonmember of NATO, the Swedes would have been out of luck had the Soviets resorted to nuclear weapons.[158] Neutrality would still delimit American help.

At the same time, Sweden did consciously and deliberately engage in military collaboration with the United States. Many critics of US foreign policy must be sorely disappointed by this fact, including me. Despite this collaboration, Stockholm avoided collaboration with NATO. Since NATO was a US-dominated organization, what difference did it make for Sweden to just cooperate with America alone? As an explanation, Ekéus referred to the Nordic Balance. Neutral Sweden effectively functioned as a buffer zone in Northern Europe.[159]

Three decades after the dissolution of the Soviet Union, Kissinger also endorsed the concept of a buffer zone in Northern Europe, but in Ukraine. On the North Atlantic Treaty, he had favored the signatures of Poland and other former Soviet satellites but opposed the same for former Soviet republics such as Ukraine and Georgia. "I thought NATO overextended itself,"

Kissinger concluded about Western military overtures to those former Soviet republics.[160]

Reflecting on the crisis in Ukraine in 2014, the former secretary of state wrote: "Far too often the Ukrainian issue is posed as a showdown: whether Ukraine joins the East or the West. But if Ukraine is to survive and thrive, it must not be either side's outpost against the other—it should function as a bridge between them."[161]

Therefore, the former secretary of state advised Ukraine from seeking official membership in NATO: "Internationally, they should pursue a posture comparable to that of Finland. The nation leaves no doubt about its fierce independence and cooperates with the West in most fields but carefully avoids institutional hostility toward Russia."[162]

While Ekéus was critical of Kissinger, he also believed that the retired American diplomat's argument was relevant to the Nordic region as well:

> We should not build a sharp line between NATO and Russia up there, which would totally change the security structure in Europe. And that was, of course, American policy during that time, and our policy also. We should not increase the tension. That meant also that Sweden couldn't be a base, shouldn't be a base, for attacks on the Soviet Union, now Russia. . . . So I think that is a policy which is a contribution to stability and peace in Northern Europe. . . . It would be real, serious undermining of European security if we, maybe with the Finns, start to build up a major front, a new front towards Russia.[163]

During the Cold War, official Swedish neutrality not only provided Northern Europe with a secure buffer zone, but it allowed Stockholm greater independence of action in other international matters. Neutral Sweden was not a polite fiction, but something that truly existed.[164] Regardless of Sweden's friendship with the United States, the Scandinavian country did not feel obligated to consult with the members of the North Atlantic Alliance before acting. From time to time, the Swedes could even challenge the Western superpower itself, as they did over the war in Vietnam.

Since the Russian invasion of Ukraine in 2022, Kissinger has reluctantly shifted in favor of Ukrainian membership in NATO.[165] Regrettably, fear of Russian aggression has now driven Sweden to apply for NATO membership.[166] Neutral Sweden could have played a mediating, humanitarian role in the present conflict in Eastern Europe.

CONTINUED DIPLOMACY

Indeed, the war went on. When Dr. Daniel Ellsberg of the RAND Corporation leaked the classified Pentagon Papers in June of 1971, Palme expressed his approval in a public statement:

> Openness is the strength of democracy. It must not be betrayed. The documents which are now published concerning U.S. Vietnam policy during the Sixties and which show a clear contradiction between the news that the political and military leadership reported to the people and the preparations for aggression which were secretly carried on are from a democratic point of view something of a catastrophe.[167]

> Palme went on: "I have for several years said that the war in Vietnam, far from being a defense for democracy, is a threat to the ideals of democracy over the world. . . . The Vietnamese people must themselves be in a position to decide their own fate."[168]

Rogers may have had a pleasant meeting with Palme the year before, but now he conveyed his annoyance through his underling. Martin J. Hillenbrand, the assistant secretary of state for European and Eurasian affairs, summoned the Swedish ambassador to inform him of "the displeasure of my government," and that Palme's statement "had not made people here happier."[169] Hillenbrand assured de Besche that the secretary of state "had approved of this action. He is displeased."[170] Presumably, Nixon and Kissinger were also displeased.

Prior to the unauthorized release of the Pentagon Papers, it was already apparent that the Nixon administration would never concur with Palme. The North Vietnamese chargé d'affaires visited Palme again at the end of 1970. Speaking for his superiors in Hanoi, Nguyen Dinh Thanh expressed grave fear that the Americans would escalate the war even further. To prevent "adventurous American acts of war directed against the DRV [Democratic Republic of Vietnam]," the chargé d'affaires asked the Swedish prime minister to speak out.[171] The prime minister acknowledged that he found the belligerent tone from the US government "very worrying and difficult to understand."[172] Furthermore, Palme said that he had described US reconnaissance flights over North Vietnam as "indefensible" to the American media. When he asked the chargé d'affaires if Hanoi expected "resumed bombing against North Vietnam, Thanh answered with an unequivocal yes."[173]

Nevertheless, the Swedish government was careful to reject more radical proposals to end the war. Professor Gunnar Myrdal was a prominent economist at Stockholm University. Not only was he the founding chairman of the

Swedish Committee for Vietnam, Myrdal chaired the Stockholm International Peace Research Institute, which was partly funded by the Swedish government. When an American wrote to Myrdal to suggest that Sweden host hearings on American violations of international law in Indochina, the economist forwarded the letter to Hans Blix, the Foreign Ministry's resident expert on international jurisprudence.

Blix bluntly evaluated the proposal, calling it "high-flying and unrealistic."[174] He suggested that Myrdal respond to the proposal in the following way: "It has been a long-standing Swedish line, applied to a variety of matters, to favour inquiries, assessments and judgments by organs of the international community rather than by actions by individual states, which can always be suspected of partiality."[175]

In addition, Blix noted that his government had worked through the United Nations to promote the implementation of international law in response to armed conflicts. "The government has also sought to establish, in general terms at the U.N., that any use of teargas and herbicides in war is illegal," Blix pointed out. "This approach was a general one, but it had special reference to Viet Nam."[176]

Certainly, the wartime activism of Palme and his colleagues was sincere. It was not the product of a self-interested political agenda. When the prime minister returned to the United States for the twenty-fifth anniversary of the founding of the United Nations in the fall of 1970, he still faced hostile questions. On *Issues and Answers*, a program on ABC, an interviewer asked the following question: "Sir, it's been said that your government could not function without support of the small communist minority in Parliament. Does this fact, in any way, influence your government's attitude toward this whole situation, toward the governments in Hanoi and so forth?"[177] Palme gave an effective and convincing response. "Absolutely not, no," Palme answered. "On the question of Vietnam, there's been almost complete unanimity in the Swedish Parliament, say ninety-five percent of the members behind the policy of the government on that question."[178] As an elected official, Palme was only expressing the will of the majority of his people. He was not just playing a political game with the extreme left wing. The interviewer persisted: "They can't hold the whip hand in your government then?" Again, Palme denied this: "They can only have an influence if they join with the Conservatives, and that does not often happen."[179]

As part of the UN commemoration, Palme received an invitation to a formal dinner at the White House. "Of course, he would never have considered declining the invitation, so he went there," Eliasson explained many years later.[180]

Palme flew with the other world leaders to Washington on a State Department plane.[181] The dinner on October 24 was a dull affair. President and Mrs. Nixon greeted the guests briskly and efficiently. Nixon felt uncomfortable about meeting Palme, but the prime minister tried to break the ice. Referring to the president's recent visit to Gary, Indiana, Palme asked if the boxer Tony Zale hailed from that town. Nixon, a dedicated sports fan, perked up slightly.[182]

Palme returned to Europe immediately after the dinner, courtesy of British Prime Minister Edward Heath's Royal Air Force plane. The Swedish prime minister would never go back to the White House, and rarely discussed the dinner afterward.[183] Eliasson did try to broach the subject. "I have a feeling of discomfort generally, not irritation," Eliasson later recalled of Palme's evasive response. "He just sort of waved it off. It happened. I don't think it was his only impression. He wasn't discriminated in any way, or insulted by anyone. It wasn't his favorite conversational theme. Let's put it that way."[184]

The prime minister had wanted to meet with the president, but that meeting must have felt like a snub.

As Nixon embarked on his policy of détente with China and the Soviet Union, he carried on his war in Southeast Asia, dismaying most of the world. The president's opening to China impressed Palme. "The change in the American policy which is now signalled is justly greeted all over the world as a statesmanlike act," the prime minister conceded in an address in the spring of 1972. "It implied an acceptance of realities in the world of to-day and a step towards peace."[185] At the same time, Palme used Nixon's initiative to expose the inherent contradiction of the president's other foreign policy initiative, Vietnamization: "The basic idea behind the American involvement in Vietnam was to prevent what was considered to be a communist expansion which threatened the democracy of the Western world and its strategic interests. It has now been scuttled by . . . the new China policy."[186]

Since the new China policy indicated that Nixon did not anticipate world conquest by an international communist conspiracy, the pursuit of military victory was pointless. No good could come from the continued support of the repressive regime in Saigon, Palme believed. Only negotiations could resolve the conflict.[187] Acceptance of realities in Vietnam, as well as in China, would bring peace to Asia. Palme's British counterpart, Wilson, had not shared these views two years before. When Palme sought Wilson's opinion on the policy of Vietnamization, his response revealed a remarkable tolerance for American adventurism in Vietnam:

> The Prime Minister [Wilson] said that the policy had been exceptionally fully considered and worked out and he thought President Nixon would stand by it. He could see no circumstances which could change this, particularly as the policy, in contrast to that of President Johnson, enjoyed wide public support. But

if there was a major recrudescence of military activity or massive infiltration of North Vietnamese troops, the President might have to think again.[188]

Whatever reservations Wilson may have felt about the war, British economics had held him back since the tenure of LBJ. The British prime minister was reticent "because we can't kick our creditors in the balls."[189]

ON THE GROUND IN HANOI

The Swedes probably had a better grasp of the situation in Vietnam than the British did because they now enjoyed full diplomatic relations with North Vietnam. The British prime minister suspected the North Vietnamese sought independence from Moscow and Peking. Wilson also sensed that the Soviets themselves did not believe they had substantial influence in Hanoi.[190] By contrast, Öberg definitely knew that a truly unified Communist bloc did not exist because he was on the ground in Hanoi.

Öberg, with his considerable experience in Southeast Asian affairs, had come to Hanoi in July of 1970 to head the new Swedish embassy. A veteran of the Swedish foreign service in Indonesia, Thailand, and Singapore, Öberg had acquired a sensitivity to the issues of poverty and injustice in the developing world.[191] He had also been a key operative in Operation Aspen. "He was very important . . . going between the United States and Vietnam," said Rolf Ekéus, a close friend who replaced Öberg as department secretary at the Foreign Ministry.[192]

Operation Aspen had required Sweden to maintain some semblance of objectivity, but the formal mediation effort had come to an end. "We wanted to give aid to Vietnam," Ekéus noted, "and we wanted to have a presence in Vietnam, to understand what's going on."[193] If anyone could appreciate what was going on in North Vietnam, it was Jean-Christophe Öberg. He understood "the history of Vietnam, the Vietnam people. Their role was against China . . . always keeping China out."[194] Their role was not to spread Communism beyond their own borders, contrary to American popular belief.

Although Sweden was the first Western country to establish an embassy in Hanoi, Falkman said later it was slow in coming "because there was a strong opposition in the conservative parties here to recognize Vietnam."[195] He remembered that "the socialist government wanted to do it . . . but perhaps also they were scared because the Swedish business community said if we recognize North Vietnam then that would be very bad for our business."[196] As the United States was a major export market for Swedish companies, they disliked Palme's antiwar activism as a rule.[197]

In Sweden's wider business community, Palme had few fans. One exception among Swedish corporate executives was Pehr Gyllenhammar, the chief executive officer of Volvo. Sharp political differences would emerge between Gyllenhammar and Palme in later years, but the CEO commented: "I had a positive memory of Olof Palme at the time of the Vietnam War and do not know—nor was I interested in—what the business community thought at the time. I found that war atrocious and thought Palme was right."[198]

Stockholm had stopped receiving the South Vietnamese ambassador to Bonn in 1967.[199] There was no interest in reestablishing diplomatic relations with Saigon, for South Vietnam was an artificial entity, an unintended product of the 1954 Geneva Agreement. Once Stockholm had formalized its relationship with Hanoi in January of 1969, there was no point in maintaining a connection with Saigon.[200] "Vietnam was Vietnam," Ekéus explained.[201]

Arne Björnberg, the Swedish ambassador to Beijing, would officially handle relations with North Vietnam as well as Cambodia. Öberg, as chargé d'affaires in Hanoi, would run the embassy beginning in July of 1970. In spite of his experience, Öberg was reluctant to assume the post. "First, he didn't want to," Ekéus recalled. "He was so young, like me. He was the same age. So, he was put to chargé d'affaires."[202] Although Öberg was not yet ambassador, he had the responsibility of one. "It was a full embassy," Ekéus noted.[203]

Öberg's promotion to ambassadorial rank would soon come in 1972, but not without some controversy. Falkman, first secretary of the Foreign Ministry, moonlighted as chargé d'affaires at the Hanoi embassy while Öberg went on vacation in the summer of 1971. Falkman recalled that "there was a lot of opposition in the newspapers and also in the Foreign Ministry because they thought he was too young, and secondly, we shouldn't have an ambassador in Hanoi as the only Western country."[204]

Yet, like Ekéus, Falkman appreciated Öberg's strengths as a diplomat. Falkman pointed out that Öberg "had an advantage of being born in France to a French mother. So, he spoke perfect French, and you know we all spoke French in Hanoi, and the elite, the upper class I would say, in the party, and at the Ministry, they spoke French."[205]

Another advantage was that the leadership in Hanoi was warmly disposed to Öberg. He charmed them with his utter lack of pretension, even riding his bicycle to the Foreign Ministry.[206] Mai Van Bo, the chief of the North Vietnamese Foreign Ministry's Political Division, enthused to Falkman: "We in Hanoi have adopted Jean-Christophe Öberg."[207] Mai Van Bo's positive impression of Swedes in general was likely due to his positive impression of Öberg:

You Swedes have an ability to understand Vietnam that is exceptional for a Western country. I daresay you understand Vietnam better than even the French, even though they have been here a long time. It is a remarkable experience for us Vietnamese. It is not so easy to understand the reasons for this, but I believe it depends on your prolonged period of peace, your lack of colonial ambitions, your profound democratic development, your sympathy for the weakest members of society, and your feeling of solidarity with other small nations.[208]

By 1971, the chargé d'affaires had already proved worthy of an ambassadorial rank. He had cultivated an invaluable network of contacts in Hanoi, where Soviet personnel stationed there indicated a Russo-Vietnamese split rather than the long-studied Sino-Soviet version. North Vietnam took advantage of the Sino-Soviet split. The Soviets were so fearful of a closer relationship between Hanoi and Beijing that they contributed surface-to-air missiles accompanied by technical support, planes, and petroleum products. Nevertheless, the Soviet Union antagonized the North Vietnamese in October of 1971 by extending an invitation to Nixon to Moscow.

Officials at the Soviet embassy insisted to Öberg that Hanoi had not shared its plans with Moscow for the 1972 Easter Offensive. In truth, North Vietnam had informed the Soviets in advance, but they had been seriously displeased. The Soviets feared that the Easter Offensive would not meet with success. Moreover, the Soviets seemed more concerned about their connection to the United States than their friendship with North Vietnam. To the Swedish diplomat, it seemed that the Soviets were merely going through the ideological motions: "So much is however certain that Moscow's actions in Hanoi these days, despite all public statements on 'brotherly militant solidarity,' have little impressed the Vietnamese who still know how dependent they also will continue to be on deliveries of Soviet supplies."[209]

The Soviets were unhappy with Hanoi's aggressive prosecution of the 1972 Spring Offensive, and its aggressively outspoken objections to the US blockade of North Vietnam's ports. Öberg knew this because of his own contact with his diplomatic counterpart: "The Soviet ambassador, who has consistently toned down the developing crisis during the past weeks, is now requesting non-Communist embassies, the Swedish among them, to use their influence with Hanoi to explain to North Vietnam that they have more to win through negotiations than through further escalation of the fighting in South Vietnam."[210]

In response to the Spring Offensive, which began on March 30, Nixon on May 8 launched Operation Linebacker, even though heavy bombing had commenced some time before. Operation Linebacker was named for a playing position in American football, the president's favorite spectator sport, and involved large-scale aerial bombardment of North Vietnam, accompanied by the mining of Haiphong's harbors. Not that Operation Linebacker profoundly disturbed the Soviets, who still insisted on holding the Moscow summit with the American president. Moscow even refused to help the North Vietnamese remove the mines from their harbors.[211]

Even before his own stint as chargé d'affaires, Falkman had detected the tensions between Hanoi and its Communist patrons during his first visit there. He could see right away that the North Vietnamese did not like the Chinese very much. Almost immediately upon his arrival, an official from Hanoi's Foreign Ministry escorted Falkman to a historical museum. As the two men viewed old maps of Vietnam, the North Vietnamese official focused on his country's northern border, which had been violated over millennia by "northern feudal lords."[212] Falkman was quick to note that the official would only refer to the Chinese as "northern feudal lords," and nothing else. The Swedish diplomat also realized that this feeling of distrust was mutual:

> I listened to the Chinese ambassador, the Soviet ambassador, and they said, "We understand that you have very good relations with Vietnam, much better than we have. And we don't understand why they misjudge, how their illusions, etc., etc." They got weapons from these countries, of course, but they didn't get any, so to say, political support because the Soviet Union and China . . . had official relations with the United States. And they didn't want to disturb these relations by supporting the Vietnamese policies too much.[213]

The United States would not have official diplomatic relations with China until 1979, but the rapprochement had indeed begun during the Nixon administration. This very rapprochement only aggravated North Vietnamese distrust of Beijing, which began pressuring Hanoi to reach a settlement with Washington. Beijing did try to appease the Vietnamese by furnishing them with tanks.

The Soviets, for their part, envied Sweden's trustful relationship with North Vietnam. At the Soviet embassy, Minister Podolski made a surprising request of Falkman: "You Swedish diplomats have better knowledge of Vietnam than anyone else. That is a well-known fact. We would be very grateful if you would share some of your knowledge with us now and then."[214] Falkman tactfully and diplomatically declined, claiming that Soviet knowledge of Vietnam far surpassed what Sweden would have to share.[215]

The Vietnamese were fighting a national war of liberation. They did not intend to serve the aims of either Moscow or Beijing. Nguyen Co Thach, North Vietnam's deputy foreign minister, put this sentiment into words for Falkman: "Sweden is a country that we Vietnamese admire, for it is independent in both thought and deed."[216]

Ideological ties between Vietnam and other Communist countries seemed to be weak. In his dealings with North Vietnamese officials, Falkman never heard them use Marxist-Leninist terminology. "To Ho Chi Minh, revolution is less a matter of textual criticism than an organizational problem," Falkman reported to Stockholm. "First of all, the Vietnamese are empirical pragmatists, realists, organizers."[217]

True, aid from the Soviets and Chinese continued throughout the war. For the combined years of 1967, 1970, and 1971, Moscow provided Hanoi with an approximate total of $675 million in military aid. This military aid consisted of "such items as surface-to-air missiles, tanks, heavy artillery, and oil."[218] In these same years, Soviet economic aid added up to more than $500 million. US intelligence classified economic aid from Moscow as "military-economic" because it helped sustain North Vietnam's military capability both directly and indirectly. The Chinese, for their part, contributed a total of $305 million in military aid for the years 1967, 1970, and 1971 altogether. At the same time, China furnished North Vietnam with $240 million in economic help. Financial support from the Soviet Union remained relatively steady during this period, and from China, it increased. These numbers may seem substantial and impressive, but they also indicate a remarkable decline in military aid just before the Spring Offensive in 1972. From an estimated peak of $505 million in 1967, Soviet defense assistance had decreased to $100 million in 1971. As for China, military aid sank from $145 million in 1967 to $75 million in 1971.

Moreover, aid from Soviet-dominated Eastern Europe to Hanoi was insignificant in comparison to American expenditures for the preservation of the South Vietnamese regime. For the years 1967, 1970, and 1971, a combined sum of $480 million reached North Vietnam. By contrast, the United States provided South Vietnam with $9 billion in 1972 alone.[219] While noting that components for certain precision instruments came to North Vietnam from East Germany, Öberg described military aid from that country as "symbolic."[220]

By 1974, the US Defense Intelligence Agency would determine the United States had invested in the war twenty-nine times as much as the Soviet Union and China had combined. Over an eight-year period, Washington spent $107.10 billion, compared to $2.57 billion from Moscow, and $1.08 billion from Beijing. The expenditures for the entire US war effort, not just that eight-year period, added up to $200 billion.[221]

The North Vietnamese found dealing with their own allies frustrating, but probably not as frustrating as dealing with their adversaries at the official peace talks. Just as unsatisfactory were Le Duc Tho's secret discussions with Kissinger, the Americans still sought peace solely on their own terms.

Aerial destruction in Hanoi accompanied the secret talks in Paris. Even though the Soviets, in that age of détente, gave greater importance to their relationship with the United States than with North Vietnam, they still offered their assistance as the American bombs fell in 1971. Visiting Öberg in the

North Vietnamese capital, the political counsel of the Soviet embassy said as much. As Öberg reported: "The counsel told me that a sophisticated missile system had already been delivered and that the last days' shootdowns could be placed in direct connection with this."[222]

The North Vietnamese, for their part, continued to express their frustrations freely and frankly to the Swedes. On 24 July 1972, Foreign Minister Nguyen Duy Trinh met with Öberg, who had been promoted to full ambassador the previous month. "The foreign minister began by referring to the morning's violent bomb attack against Hanoi as proof that very little had changed in the American negotiating position," Öberg reported back to Stockholm. By this point, however, Trinh was a little more optimistic: "The foreign minister reckoned that a change in tone had come about on the American side."[223]

Trinh said that at Le Duc Tho's recent meeting with Kissinger, "one could notice less arrogance in the Americans' use of language."[224]Trinh concluded his conversation with a warm expression of thanks to the ambassador for his government's critical statements about the American intervention in Vietnam, which was "particularly important because they came from the side of a neutral state."[225]

Despite Trinh's newly emergent optimism about the secret talks, the Swedish ambassador could see the devastation for himself. This destruction was a subject of special concern not only for Öberg, but the prime minister, who took care in reading his ambassador's reports. Öberg was skeptical about the perfect accuracy of the official statements of the North Vietnamese, so he also provided Palme with firsthand accounts.[226] When asked if the prime minister had found Öberg's reports valuable, Ekéus replied: "Always . . . and the contacts were at the highest level."[227]

ÖBERG AND THE DIKES

The dams and dikes of the Red River Delta were a prominent subject. From April to the first twenty-seven days of July 1972, for example, the delta was the quarry of 173 air raids. American planes dropped a grand total of 1,243 bombs. Out of these 173 air raids, 149 resulted in a direct hit on eleven dams, and seven locks were blown to pieces.[228] The ambassador toured the Red River dams as the North Vietnamese frantically yet efficiently worked to repair these installations. There remained the incalculable threat to the surrounding civilian areas. "The North Vietnamese engineers, who are responsible for the repair work, still expressed their anxiety for what the bombings could have caused in invisible damage," Öberg reported to Stockholm.[229] This invisible damage came in the form of cracks.

Back home, Öberg made his concerns public before the Swedish Social Democratic Youth League:

> Practically all industry in North Vietnam has been destroyed. But the greater danger just now is the bombing of the dams and locks. If there are further attacks, there may be an enormous catastrophe, with villages submerged, and famine. The intention seems to be to weaken North Vietnam economically for a long period to come and to transform it into a second or third class nation in Southeast Asia. It is a typical policy of annihilation. The bigger the defeats of the U.S. and Saigon troops in the South, the more bombing in the North. Now, the dams and dikes are the greatest worry for the Vietnamese. The Red River has already started to rise; it reaches its highest level in July and August. If the river rises as high as last year, there may be an enormous catastrophe.[230]

Attending the speech was his friend and diplomatic colleague, Rolf Ekéus: "And I remember in Swedish he said: '*Det får helt enkelt inte ske.* . . . "Simply, it cannot be allowed."[231]

Öberg did not intend to only reach a Swedish audience, however. Öberg shared his concerns that July with an American visitor, John A. Sullivan of the American Friends Service Committee, a Quaker organization. "Oberg . . . said up to 3 weeks ago he believed the dike damage was not intentional, but accidental, now he suspects it may be intentional," Sullivan reported back to AFSC headquarters in Philadelphia. "He said that he had talked to State Department men who spoke of a plan to reduce North Vietnam to chaos so that it would be in no position to dominate the South."[232]

Combined with the blockade of Hanoi's ports, the bombing of the dikes could undermine the North Vietnamese economy. The Swedish ambassador feared that the US strategy would result in food shortages. Öberg's worry extended beyond Southeast Asia, indicating anxiety that "bitter anti-Americanism developing among young Europeans who are opposed to the war and whom their foreign offices and governments are ignoring."[233]

The Swedish ambassador told Sullivan that he was convinced that "American policy was doing damage to Western civilization and concepts of freedom and liberty."[234] Öberg won the admiration of another peace activist, Professor Richard Falk of Princeton University. The legal scholar had nothing but praise for the Swedish ambassador, who "was very informed about the Nixon initiative to start bombing the dikes in North Vietnam, which would have caused as many as two million casualties, and his exposure of that initiative to the media had a big effect on discouraging the U.S. from pursuing that kind of tactic."[235]

The reaction in the halls of Congress bears Falk out. Impressed with Öberg's audacity, Democratic senator John Tunney of California said that the

Swedish envoy "took a step virtually unprecedented for Western diplomats, who traditionally speak out only on issues of direct concern to their countries." Senator Tunney approvingly inserted some of Öberg's public remarks into the Congressional Record.[236]

Both Nixon and his secretary of defense, Melvin Laird, denied that the dikes were targets for bombing. At a press conference, Laird claimed: "Now, there are occasions, of course, when a dam or a dike could possibly be hit when an anti-aircraft installation is placed on a dam or dike or when there is a roadway or a bridgework that is also tied in with a dam or dike formation."[237]

Given that the National Security Council and the Joint Chiefs of Staff had discussed the idea of bombing the dikes as early as 1969, it is likely that the direct hits were intentional.[238] As late as April 1972, the presidential taping system captured Nixon's words: "I still think we ought to take out the dikes now."[239]

Laird's Pentagon took a disturbingly strong interest in Ambassador Öberg's opinions of its offensive operations in Vietnam. When the military attaché of the Swedish embassy, S. Geijer, visited the Pentagon in the late summer of 1972, he had an unpleasant surprise. The Swedish attaché met with three officers to arrange the visit of Sten Wåhlin, the general director of Sweden's Defence Materiel Administration, and Wåhlin's associates, as "self-invited guests."[240] The American officers did not expect anything to stand in the way of the planned visit, but then one of them ominously noted, "However, Sweden has an ambassador in Hanoi who sends reports."[241]

Later that evening, the Swedish attaché encountered the same man at a party. The aggressive officer resumed the subject of Öberg. "I replied that there naturally can be reports from entirely different perspectives that many times will diverge or be contradictory," the Swedish attaché reported.[242]"Yes," the officer repeated. "We read his reports."[243]

Some of Öberg's reports were coded, but Ekéus doubted that the Americans had broken the Swedish code:

> It is extremely difficult to believe that because, yes, they would have broken it, but not between Hanoi and Stockholm, but after it entered into Stockholm. The reason is that the code system we had, it was so old-fashioned, so it was practically impossible in any form to solve it. And the reason is that it was saved in the one time for each article. So, what we had was a very simple. . . . I think it was only letters . . . related to . . . an "A" means "C" or something else like that. But it was on hard paper, so it was not fed into a computer of any sort. . . . So one was in Stockholm, and the other was at the embassy.[244]

Ekéus went on to explain that the code was changed "every day. Every message had changed code."[245]

So, if the Americans did not break the code, how did they gain access to Öberg's reports? "Unfortunately," Ekéus concluded, "there were leaks, probably innocent, well-intentioned people maybe, who did it."[246]

Perhaps some leaks had come from the uncoded copies of Öberg's reports that Stockholm had forwarded to other Swedish embassies, including the one in Washington.

Falkman concurred with Ekéus's doubts that the Americans had broken the Swedish codes:

> I don't think they were so interested in decoding our messages because Öberg's reports were almost always written, typed-out, and sent by courier, you know, diplomatic dispatch. We flew every fortnight, so we took the plane to Vietniane [Laos]. We went to Bangkok [Thailand], and there we left it, the reports, in a secret bag to the embassy. And they sent it to Stockholm. . . . We sent very small messages on important things because we had to decode.[247]

Falkman, for his part, said that he had used a coding machine, "and I had to decode everything with fingertips. The coding system was complicated . . . you had to sort of code the different words coded in different ways."[248]

Like his colleagues Ekéus and Falkman, Eliasson doubted that Washington had cracked the Swedish code. "We have a vigorous system," he said. "I never heard that our coded messages spread out. . . . I have no sense that they could break our code. I have no sense that they really broke our code."[249]

Unlike his colleagues Ekéus and Falkman, however, Eliasson also doubted that there had been leaks. In spite of his doubts, Eliasson acknowledged that some Swedish officials did not appreciate the outspoken activism of the prime minister and his ambassador to Hanoi: "There was a conservative school of thought in the Foreign Ministry that thought that Palme had gone too far."[250] Eliasson simply could not conceive of diplomatic tattletales because "there is also tremendous discipline and loyalty in the corps. Leaks are considered morally unacceptable."[251]

Eliasson suspected that the Americans had obtained information about Öberg through other means. "I think they simply had a very close process of finding out what happened in the Swedish embassy," Eliasson speculated, "they may have sources or simply followed what he said and what he was doing."[252]

It did not shock Eliasson that Öberg had attracted American attention: "He was an enormously charismatic, colorful personality. He was not the classic image of the diplomat. He was enormously verbal, very persuasive. And he was a person who was really, by the White House and from the State Department, considered an evil genius."[253]

When Öberg himself learned of the Swedish attaché's encounters with the American officer, the diplomat refused to be intimidated. He thought the surveillance had done no harm, for the most part: "It may even be useful reading for the capable American officers to get to read something other than falsified bomb reports á la Levelle or doctored depictions of the bombing of civilian targets in DRV [North Vietnam]."[254] Lieutenant General John D. Lavelle of the US Air Force had been recently accused of directing bombing runs over North Vietnam, on his own initiative, and then distorting the information in the subsequent reports.[255] The Swedish ambassador would not live to see the 2010 posthumous exoneration of Lavelle, who had followed Nixon's orders.[256]

Öberg was only concerned that the Americans could also read his coded reports:

Through my Vietnamese friends, I often get access to quite unique information. They are easy to identify as sources to the degree that they are not even named in my reporting. What the Vietnamese occasionally say to me about their Soviet friends are also something that I would not wish to come to Washington's—and thus certainly also Moscow's—knowledge.[257]

By now, the Soviets enjoyed warmer relations with Washington than with Hanoi.

The Pentagon may have resented Öberg's statements, public or otherwise, but he had good reason to suspect that the dams were a deliberate target. As much as his claims may have angered the US Defense Department, examples from history give substance to them. The Korean War was one such example. According to an official US Air Force study, General Mark Clark had decided in 1953 to target irrigation dams as a means of pushing the North Koreans into making concessions in negotiations. A 1972 memorandum from the Swedish Foreign Ministry highlighted a telling passage from the Air Force study:

FEAF [Far East Air Force] intelligence officers reasoned that food was war materiel and they thought it was just a legitimate to destroy a growing crop as to seek the destroy rice once it was harvested. Target researchers soon determined how air attacks could destroy the rich rice crops of the Haeju provinces. Rice production in this area depended upon impounded irrigation water from some 20 large reservoirs. By destroying the impounding dams, air attacks could release floods which would destroy a year's rice planting.[258]

The FEAF Target Committee had reservations about such a scheme. Indeed, both General Clark, who was commander of the United Nations Command in Korea, as well as his subordinate, Air Force General Otto P. Weyland, believed it would be premature to ruin the North Korean rice crop.[259]

Nevertheless, the study reported "General Weyland was willing to approve irrigation-dam attacks where resultant floodwaters would interdict the enemy's line of communications."[260] The bombing of the Toksan Dam, one of three that were hit, released also floodwaters that "scoured five square miles of prime rice crops."[261] The Fifth Air Force noted that the "damage done by the deluge far exceeded the hopes of everyone."[262] This agricultural damage did not cause General Clark to regret the bombing, and he wrote to the joint chiefs of staff that the "breaching of the Toksan dam has been as effective as the weeks of rail interdiction."[263]

Since the Americans had deliberately targeted dams in the Korean War, it was logical for Stockholm to conclude that they repeated the tactic in the successive conflict. The dikes and dams of North Vietnam were already a target during the Johnson administration, as indicated in the Pentagon Papers. A classified report, which was produced by the Central Intelligence Agency and the Defense Intelligence Agency in 1966, indicated that the bombings were quite deliberate: "Of 91 known locks and dams in North Vietnam, only 8 targeted as significant to inland waterways, flood control, or irrigation. Only one hit . . . heavily damaged."[264] Indeed, the Johnson administration knew what it was doing. The Central Intelligence Agency reported to the White House: "Bombing the levee system which keeps the Red River under control, if timed correctly, could cause large crop losses and force North Vietnam to import large amounts of rice. Depending on the success of the interdiction efforts, such imports might overload the transport system."[265]

The bombing of dikes was a serious war crime. The Nuremberg Tribunal placed a noose around the neck of Arthur Seyss-Inquart, the former Reichskommissar of the occupied Dutch territories, in 1946. Among other evil deeds, Seyss-Inquart had released the dikes in Holland two years before, destroying five hundred thousand acres of agricultural land.[266]

OPERATION LINEBACKER

In addition to dikes and dams of North Vietnam, the strategic air war also targeted its cities. From early April to August 7, 1972, only five out of twenty-three provinces in North Vietnam escaped the US air campaign. Numerous cities suffered through bombing raids as often as ten times during this period, with Hanoi itself forced to test its own endurance on eighteen different days.[267]

Amid this aerial offensive, Öberg took refuge in the small air raid shelter that was located in the embassy garden. True to his own character, however, the Swedish ambassador worried less about his own safety and more about the health of Vietnamese society. The bombing campaign spared the central part of Hanoi but hit the industrial sector. North Vietnam's impressive economic development had now come to a halt. "The aim seems to be to weaken North Vietnam economically for the long-term, and make the country a second- or third-rate country in Southeast Asia," Öberg concluded.[268]

Far more serious were the assaults against schools, hospitals, and residential areas with antipersonnel bombs. The bombing of power stations also filled the Swedish ambassador with grave concern: "Because all industry is knocked out, not so much energy is needed. The worst is for the surgeons who stand and operate. The power supply has become so erratic."[269]

The hospitals were directly assaulted from the air, despite their visible Red Cross markings. Between April and July of 1972, twenty-one hospitals and nine other medical facilities had been hit in North Vietnam. The largest hospital in North Vietnam was the Bach Mai Hospital, which had 1,200 beds. Its location in central Hanoi should have provided some protection. The new hospital's major benefactor was the Swedish Red Cross.[270]

"For example, I have visited a damaged hospital, where the operating theater was gutted and the hospital pharmacy destroyed," Öberg reported to Stockholm. "Otherwise, the hospitals have been evacuated and moved underground. There are only emergency hospitals remaining in Hanoi."[271]

Often like the hospitals, the schools and residential areas of Hanoi could not escape the bombardment.[272] The North Vietnamese government turned to the Swedes for help. Mai Van Bo summoned the Swedish ambassador to Hanoi's Foreign Ministry to make an urgent request:

> He spoke of the thousands of civilians killed every week and expressed the hope that the Swedish government would find it possible, in an official form, to condemn the continued bombing against the North, as well as South Vietnam, and exert pressure on Washington to try to bring about a change in the Americans' unacceptable conditions for a political solution to the war.[273]

North Vietnamese Prime Minister Pham Van Dong offered his own assessment of Swedish foreign policy's true worth. Providing Öberg with a letter for the Swedish prime minister, Dong "expressed his thanks for Olof Palme's support for Vietnam's cause and the Swedish government's leading role in moulding public opinion in Western Europe."[274] Contrary to the official American conception of the North Vietnamese as a mere puppet of the Soviet Union and China, they sought friends west of the Iron Curtain

ECOCIDE

Meanwhile, the US military supplemented the conventional bombardment of Vietnam with herbicides. This novel form of chemical warfare was intended to deprive the indigenous forces of nutritional local crops, and vegetative cover for their operations. An additional aim of this herbicidal campaign was to pressure the local civilian population to move to sectors more firmly held by U.S. forces.[275] Between 1962 and 1971, the US military had subjected roughly 5,767,520 acres of South Vietnamese land to herbicidal treatment in South Vietnam.[276] This chemical warfare applied approximately one hundred million pounds of herbicides to approximately one-seventh of South Vietnam, the land that the United States was ironically claiming to defend against the north.[277]

Stockholm was very mindful of the dangers war presented to the environment.

Sverker Åström, the permanent representative to the United Nations for Sweden, began arrangements for the first international environmental conference four years before it even took place. Åstrom, backed by the Foreign Ministry in Stockholm, was a key figure in the emergence of environmental diplomacy. The permanent representative relied on the advice of Hans Palmstierna, a prominent chemist and consultant at the Swedish Environmental Protection Agency, who was profoundly concerned about the impact of human development on the natural world.[278]

From June 5–16, 1972, Sweden hosted the United Nations Conference on the Human Environment. The Stockholm conference was an international collaboration, but the Swedish government played the important role of host. Attending the conference were two American scientists, the wildlife biologist Dr. Egbert W. Pfeiffer and the forest ecologist Dr. Arthur H. Westing. Sponsored by the Scientists' Institute for Public Information (SIPI), both men had traveled together extensively in Cambodia and South Vietnam, where they had seen the destructive environmental impact of herbicides for themselves. They had also visited Indochina separately. They had now come to Stockholm to serve as delegates for SIPI at the conference.[279] Awaiting the conference, Drs. Pfeiffer and Westing delivered public lectures on behalf of Miljöcentrum (Environmental Center). According to Dr. Westing, "Several of my most graphic photos of environmental destruction in Viet Nam had been blown up to billboard size and were on public display in the heart of Stockholm."[280]

Fortunately for the scientific duo, their public presentations made a strong impression on Dr. Johan "John" Takman, a physician and Communist member of the Riksdag. Takman had long concerned about the effects of chemical warfare. At the 1967 Russell Tribunal, Takman had attracted considerable attention by presenting a nine-year-old napalm victim, Do Van Ngoc, as a witness to the panel. Coincidentally, the physician was also a personal friend of Palme. Thanks to that friendship, Westing and Pfeiffer soon found themselves face-to-face with the prime minister of Sweden. They gave Palme an hour-long lecture, accompanied by photographs. "He appeared to be very moved and asked many questions," Dr. Westing recalled.[281] The science lesson had political consequences. "As a result of the extensive briefing we were thus able to give on the anti-environmental US strategy in Indochina and its devastating outcome," Dr. Westing noted. Palme made an addition to the draft of his own inaugural address for the conference.[282]

In his speech to the plenary meeting on June 6, the prime minister addressed environmental concerns in a general sense, but he also made specific reference to ecological warfare:

> The immense destruction brought about by indiscriminate bombing, by large-scale use of bulldozers and herbicides is an outrage sometimes described as ecocide, which requires urgent international attention. It is shocking that only preliminary discussions of this matter have been possible so far in the United Nations and at the conferences of the International Red Cross, where it has been taken up by my country and others. We fear that the active use of these methods is coupled by a passive resistance to discuss them. We know that work for disarmament and peace must be viewed in a long perspective. It is of paramount importance, however, that ecological warfare cease immediately.[283]

The head of the US delegation was Russell Train, the chairman of the US Council on Environmental Quality. Right after Palme's speech, Train addressed the conference. According to the Swedish newspaper *Aftonbladet*, Train "made clear that he agreed with several of Palme's points. Not one word of criticism was heard from the chief of the American delegation."[284]

Predictably, Palme's plenary speech angered another member of the Nixon administration. John Ehrlichman, the White House Domestic Affairs advisor, had traveled to Stockholm as part of the US delegation. Palme later recounted the flare-up:

> Ehlichman sat in the hall. Scarcely had the speech been delivered before a sharp condemnation was issued from Washington, as the American delegation was forced to follow-up since Ehrlichman traveled home the same day. Privately, they were ashamed and despairing and related that this action happed on the express order of Ehrlichman to chastise Sweden. It just gave . . . an insight on what kind of people one had to deal with.[285]

No matter his feelings, Train also held a press conference. Before the media, he criticized Palme for politicizing the conference. Speaking on behalf of his government, Train objected that Sweden, as the host country, could take such a stand.[286] Train claimed that he had not expressed himself so forcefully beforehand because he had lacked the time to frame a considered response.[287]

On June 6, 1972, the very day of the speech, the Washington embassy held a reception in celebration of Sweden's National Day. "And then there was an urgent phone call from Stockholm coming in . . . the ambassador couldn't take it," Eliasson remembered. "Leifland couldn't take it."[288] That left Eliasson: "So, I went up and took the phone, and then they said: "Well, it seems like hell is breaking loose here because Palme is criticizing the use of herbicides in warfare."[289]

Ehrlichman "was very mad . . . and angry about" Palme's recent address against herbicidal warfare. "He probably called his own embassy in Stockholm," Eliasson explained, "or called his friends in Washington: 'You know what?' And raised hell."[290]

The domestic affairs advisor was a proxy for Nixon. "And then Stockholm realized that since Ehrlichman was so close to the president, they realized that we better be prepared."[291] The first secretary reported the alarming conversation to Ambassador de Besche. As minister of the embassy, Leifland felt the need to warn his subordinate: "Eliasson, get ready!"[292]

De Besche had to get ready as well. Three days later, he received a scolding at the US State Department from Undersecretary of State John Irwin. Sweden proceeded to reciprocate this diplomatic scolding. The foreign minister summoned the outgoing ambassador Jerome Holland, making it clear that the Swedes stood by their position on ecocide, and resented the official American overreaction to it. Moreover, Stockholm would work to ban ecocide as a military practice.[293]

In his memoir, Ehrlichman would mention his presence for part of the conference yet omit any reference to Palme's speech."[294]

Despite Ehrlichman's temper tantrum, Palme's environmental address did win some American admirers. "Your reference to the problem of military ecocide made during your opening speech to the U.N. Conference was an inspiration to all of us who have been trying for years to bring this subject to the public conscience," Dr. Pfeiffer wrote to the prime minister later. "Needless to say, the response of my country's government was the source of utmost embarrassment [*sic*] and disappointment to me."[295]

Naturally, the North Vietnamese government thanked Palme for his address on the subject at the environmental conference.[296] In spite of Washington's hostility, and with the support of Hanoi, Stockholm carried on with its campaign. The warnings of Pfeiffer and Westing had deeply impressed Palme, and the Swedish government noted articles that were published on herbicides. Although long employed in the United States for weed control and forest management, the chemicals that poisoned Vietnam were ten times more powerful.[297] It was the potent impact of herbicides on Vietnam that attracted the attention of the *Congressional Quarterly Weekly* Report, whose article, in turn, attracted the attention of the Swedish embassy. After receiving the article, the Foreign Ministry in Stockholm forwarded it directly to Palme.[298]

An observation from Dr. Westing, who had just met with the prime minister, introduced the piece:

> A number of statements have been made, half jokingly, that we should bomb Vietnam back to the stone age. The horrible thing about this is that Vietnam was darned close to the stone age when we started in over there. We've knocked their social fabric for a loop because the vast majority of the people are tied very closely to the land and we are destroying the natural resource base of a people who depend on the land on a day to day basis.[299]

The authoritative, well-sourced article detailed disturbing information. For example, herbicides had a destructive impact on mountain rice, a key component of the diet of the Montagnards, the indigenous peoples of Vietnam's Central Highlands. According to the article: "Although scientists found no sign of poisoning among the Montagnards, they did note cases of starvation and malnutrition, plus migrations away from the sprayed regions to the refugee camps."[300]

Scientists of the day may not have completely understood the health effects of the most notorious herbicide, Agent Orange, but the article was remarkably prescient. The *Congressional Quarterly* also cited Dr. Pfeiffer, who had detected the presence of dioxin in Agent Orange. Dr. Pfeiffer predicted that dioxin could produce birth defects.[301]

Moreover, Dr. Pfeiffer was also worried about the environmental destruction wrought by conventional bombs, 80 percent of which fell on South Vietnam. The article noted that the bombing "left hundreds of thousands of craters throughout Indochina, some as large as 40 feet across and 15 feet deep."[302] Hardwood lumber was an important economic resource in Vietnam. Not only would the pitted hardwood forests be lost to cultivation, Pfeiffer concluded, "they may provide additional breeding areas for insect vectors of disease."[303] Indeed, cases of malaria had risen in 1969 and 1970.[304]

Soon after the Stockholm conference, Palme spoke about environmental warfare more specifically to a congress of the Social Democratic Youth League. "The greatest destroyer of the environment is war," Palme said. "So, it has always been."[305] In the prime minister's speech, the passage about conventional bombing strongly indicated that he had closely read the Congressional Quarterly article: "The land is filled with the bomb craters. They are full of water—and a breeding ground for malaria-bearing mosquitoes. Soil, vegetation, crops are destroyed, depriving also future generations of the possibility of life and cultivation."[306]

Modern chemistry had rendered the environmental destruction infinitely worse. Phosphorus bombs, herbicides, and napalm had resulted in humanitarian atrocities. The effect of phosphorus was horrifying. "The burning phosphorus, which is said to be very poisonous, cannot be removed from the body but must be cut away," Palme informed his audience.[307] As for napalm, the prime minister did not need to go into detail: "Many of you saw on TV what napalm means for one child."[308]

The prime minister was referring to Phan Thi Kim Phuc, a nine-year-old South Vietnamese girl who had been severely burned in a recent napalm attack. A photograph of the naked child, fleeing in terror, is now a classic image of the war. Military technology made civilians more vulnerable in war than ever before in history. Whether state-of-the-art-planes dropped cluster bombs, toxic chemicals, or more traditional explosives, the result was in many ways the same. "The war has become automated and anonymous for the attacker—but not for the affected. Technology frees individuals from experiencing their deeds. . . . Massive bombing over large areas erases the boundary between military and civilian."[309]

Palme continued to ruminate over the ecocide in South Vietnam. His ruminations were fed by Palmstierna, the environmental scientist. Palmstierna employed a term favored by the prime minister himself: "What is ecocide? It is something even worse than genocide because the intention is not only to kill the people but also the world they live in, a war against all life."[310]

US defoliation policy, officially known as Operation Ranch Hand, affected civilians as well as active insurgents. "The USA's official reason for this ecocide is that they want to deprive NLF forces of their hiding places (the forest)," Palmstierna explained to Palme. "By destroying the rice cultivation and the harvests, they want to deprive them of access to food."[311]

Naturally, the NLF shared the same food source as the general population, but Palmstierna did not believe that South Vietnamese civilians were just collateral damage. He thought the objective of Operation Ranch Hand was to starve the civilians as well.[312]

The Swedish government remained deeply concerned about the use of herbicidal agents in Vietnam, and its embassy in Washington approached the US government for more information. At the State Department's Office of the Legal Adviser, the resident Vietnam expert "categorically stated no herbicides were used any longer by the Americans in either Vietnam, Laos, or Cambodia. He did, however, add that the South Vietnamese were possibly still spreading herbicides 'by hand' around military bases."[313]

Still, Stockholm would not drop the matter, continuing to press Washington. A White House official informed Leifland at the embassy that the South Vietnamese army had "recently" employed a form of herbicide: "The agent had not been spread on the opposing side of the controlled areas, however, but only had been used—often in combination with 'bulldozing'—around South Vietnamese military units' bases to defend against infiltration from the opposing side and to facilitate fire from the bases."[314]

The Swedes probably doubted these assurances, and they probably would have been right to do so, but what is truly significant is the extent of their concern about the issue. The controversy over chemical warfare could potentially invite yet another charge of Swedish hypocrisy. During this period, the Swedish corporation Boliden AB sold approximately six thousand tons of arsenic per year to the United States. Arsenic had civilian purposes such as in domestic agriculture as well as in the production of wood preservatives and insecticides; it was also the active ingredient in one military herbicide, Agent Blue, scientifically known as cacodylic acid. This contrasted with the more notorious Agent Orange, whose main component was dioxin. The US military released Agent Blue on Vietnam from 1962 to 1971. Four hundred thousand hectares in South Vietnam alone were sprayed. For part of this period, Laos and Cambodia also received applications of Agent Blue. Two days after Palme's public stand on ecocide, the Swedish newspaper *Aftonbladet* reported that Boliden had recently supplied one thousand tons of arsenic to the Ansul Company, the Agent Blue manufacturer based in Marinette, Wisconsin.[315] By the time of Palme's ecocide speech, it should be noted, Agent Blue was no longer used in Vietnam.

Johnson Controls, which has been the parent company of Ansul since 2016, wrote to me that no records from the period had been retained.[316] Boliden had the same response.[317] Domestically, Ansul could have purchased arsenic from the Anaconda Company in Montana, or American Smelting and Refining Company in Washington State. International alternatives to Swedish arsenic could have been found in Mexico and France, among other countries.[318]

Vietnam's mangrove forests sustained considerable damage from Agent Blue, but the primary target were the rice crops, the staple of the Vietnamese diet. By targeting the supply of rice, the US military hoped to starve the NLF and North Vietnamese forces. Other grains and cereals were affected too. To this day, drinking water drawn from the Red River remains contaminated with arsenic. The chemical is also a toxic presence in the water and soil of the Mekong Delta. Arsenic, which does not degrade, has deleterious effects on the neurological and immune systems. It is also linked to several cancers. Although Vietnam's own industrial development has contributed to this pollution, the US military first created it during the war.[319]

Yet if this particularly toxic form of international commerce had taken place, the available evidence suggests that the Swedish government had at least neither favored nor promoted it. Three months after the environmental conference, the cabinet in Stockholm ordered the Washington embassy to investigate the matter: "To what extent does the U.S.A. use this or possibly another arsenic compound for herbicidal warfare?. . . . Which company in the U.S.A. manufactures arsenic compounds for use in Vietnam? Do any of these companies use arsenic from Sweden?"[320]

Many years later, Stockholm's request did not ring a bell for Eliasson. "I can't recall any information or action on that," he said.[321] Had the US military used Swedish arsenic for herbicidal purposes in Vietnam, "it would have completely undermined our position."[322] Eliasson, for his part, doubted this had been the case.[323]

Whether the manufacture of Agent Blue included Swedish arsenic or not, the Foreign Ministry should have investigated the matter before Palme delivered his environmental speech.

At the United Nations in 1969, Sweden had sponsored a resolution that would have applied the 1925 Geneva Protocol against chemical and biological weapons to military herbicides. Eleven other countries supported Sweden, even the mutually hostile India and Pakistan.[324]

Shortly before Palme publicly addressed the issue of ecocide three years later, the Riksdag had already made an international ban against ecocide its official policy. Gunnar Helén, leader of the Liberal Party and the Communist Dr. John Takman deserved the credit for this legislative success, but they probably had Palme's crucial backing.[325]

If Boliden had contributed to the production of Agent Blue, the Swedish government was certainly not acting in the corporation's best interests.

In addition to herbicidal agents, Stockholm sought to internationally criminalize any application of military technology that failed to discriminate between civilian areas and combatant targets, or that destroyed the natural environment. This included cluster bombs, incendiary bombs such as napalm, and phosphorus munitions. Above all, Stockholm wanted to stop the kind of aerial assaults that turned civilians into victims, such as saturation bombing and the deliberate destruction of dams.[326]

A WHITE HOUSE CHAT

The September following the environmental conference, three Croatians hijacked a SAS plane en route from Gothenburg to Stockholm, forcing it to land in Malmö. The three hijackers called for Croatian independence and insisted that seven Croatian prisoners in Swedish custody be released. Three of these prisoners were the assassins of Vladimir Rolovic, the Yugoslav ambassador to Stockholm, who was shot in 1971. The others had taken hostages at the Yugoslav consulate in Gothenburg.[327]

Palme would have found no sympathy in the Oval Office for his predicament. In conversation with Nixon and George H. W. Bush, the US ambassador to the United Nations, Secretary of State Rogers mentioned, "The Swedish airline was hijacked by Croats. So, it doesn't involve the Middle East."[328]

Sweden owned SAS in partnership with Norway and Denmark. Not that would have mattered to the president, who jokingly inquired, "Was the prime minister on board?"[329]

Ambassador Bush, the future president, snickered.

Nixon continued: "[No?] That's too bad."[330]

Bush laughed again. Kissinger kept silent, making no objection to this tasteless bit of humor.[331]

OPERATION LINEBACKER CONTINUED

As Nixon and his policymakers waged war on Vietnam, the Swedish prime minister was a profound irritation to them. Palme's ambassador to Hanoi, who was equally irritating, served as a key eyewitness to the bombing of the North. Starting on Friday, October 6, 1972, the United States attacked the North Vietnamese capital with a particular ferocity that did not end until Monday, October 9. Öberg survived a relatively close call on that first day. "During Friday's raids an American missile was fired, which is said to be the type known as the 'Shrike,' toward the city center and claimed twenty-six dead and injured," Öberg reported. "The missile fell less than 300 meters from the embassy and hit a residential block."[332] The Shrike was an air-to-ground missile that targeted radar signals, flying at a maximum velocity of MACH 1.7, meaning 1.7 times the speed of sound.[333]

Shortly before noon on October 12, the French diplomatic mission in Hanoi did not prove as fortunate as the Swedish embassy. Even though the French mission was in a diplomatic area, far from any industrial targets or North Vietnamese government buildings, its residence was all but destroyed in yet another US bombing raid over the North Vietnamese capital. Pierre Susini, the delegate-general, was trapped in the rubble. The Swedish ambassador immediately visited the affected site, even trying to dig Susini out with a shovel. A Vietnamese soldier stopped the helmetless Öberg, warning him that the bombing could resume. Regardless of his lack of personal protection, he stated,

> I remained on the spot until Pierre Susini was dug out and carried away by ambulance. He still was conscious. The day before, he had borrowed a record from me, Mozart's "Piano Concerto No. 23 in A major." The theme of Elvira Madigan [a 1967 film by Swedish director Bo Widerberg]. The album cover lay scorched among the ruins. It was unreal, like a dream.[334]

Determined to help in some way, Öberg informed Stockholm via radio of the catastrophe: "The French radio connection was broken off. We were suddenly the only link with Western Europe."[335] Krister Wickman had replaced Foreign Minister Nilsson in June of 1971. Quickly getting word, Wickman addressed the atrocity before the UN General Assembly in New York that very day.[336]

As soon as he could, Öberg made available the Swedish embassy's own radio system to other members of the French delegation. They reached the French embassy in Stockholm.[337] Courtesy of the Swedish embassy in Hanoi, Susini's deputy could communicate with his superiors in Paris.[338]

The Swedish ambassador closely monitored the condition of the comatose Susini, who bore third-degree burns on more than half his body, among other injuries. Against the recommendation of his Vietnamese doctors, who insisted that Susini was in no condition to travel, the delegate-general was flown back to France several days later for additional medical care.[339] Sadly, Susini would die on October 19 at a Lyon hospital.[340]

Initially, Laird and Rogers attempted to blame North Vietnamese antiaircraft missiles for the bombing of French delegation's residence. Öberg had been very intimate friends with Susini, frequently meeting to play tennis together.[341] He had also known Susini's romantic partner, Aleya, who had been killed instantly.[342] Wiring Stockholm as Susini lay dying, the Swedish ambassador bitterly scoffed at Laird's explanation:

> One could maybe begin by asking Defense Secretary Laird how come the Vietnamese civil defense immediately after the direct hit found three additional, undetonated American bombs in the delegation's immediate vicinity right after the direct hit. One can further ask the American defense secretary how he is explaining that an additional building in the delegation's neighborhood was totally destroyed by two American bombs, of which one could be identified.[343]

Shortly afterward, a French investigative commission determined that the bombs did, in fact, come from the United States.[344] It was only then that the Americans owned up to their mistake.[345] The Swedish ambassador's humanitarianism was duly acknowledged. French Foreign Minister Maurice Schumann personally thanked the Swedish government for Öberg's aid after the bombing.[346]

Indeed, the Swedish ambassador's own diplomatic approach fit his prime minister's unique brand of Swedish foreign policy. Like Palme, Öberg felt free to make moral judgments. Forthrightness was far more important than tact for Sweden's chief diplomat in Hanoi. He politely but vigorously expressed his views to Wickman. "I beg your indulgence, Mr. Minister, if in this dispatch I choose to set aside the rules for conventional diplomatic reporting," Öberg began in his account of a visit to the North Vietnamese cities of Thai Binh, Nam Dinh, and Phu Ly in October of 1972. All three cities had been the target of American planes. "It would be too simple, to state with detachment that war is war, that even entire cities in South Vietnam have also been obliterated."[347]

What the ambassador saw in North Vietnam alone was enough to appall him. Thai Binh lost an entire hospital complex, which had also housed facilities for medical students and a pharmaceutical factory, a devastating blow for a city in a developing country. Not only did Nam Dinh lose a hospital complex, its entire city center was gone, taking with it a cultural center, library, sports center, and the local textile industry. As for Phu Ly, "I saw a totally obliterated city."[348] In attributing blame for the war, and the resulting atrocities that he had just seen, Öberg offered his observations in a refreshing but decidedly undiplomatic manner:

> The American war machine—the military-industrial complex, Wall Street or what one prefers to call it—are collectively responsible for what is happening out here, even if the highest military commanders who have sanctioned the bombings, that is to say the president himself, can be said to bear symbolic responsibility for every civilian casualty in Vietnam.[349]

Although Öberg had enjoyed a warm relationship with Foreign Minister Wickman, not everyone at the Foreign Ministry favored Öberg's unconventionality and firm political convictions. When Öberg had resigned his position as department secretary and relocated to Hanoi, the ministry carefully replaced him with Falkman. The previous foreign minister, Nilsson, had been a Social Democratic stalwart, and Öberg was a party member too. "We others didn't belong to a political party," Falkman went on. "And they wanted to have a neutral, shall we say, diplomat as a counterbalance to Jean-Christophe and so therefore I got that post."[350]

Over time, the apolitical Falkman grew very close with Öberg. "And I agreed with his policy, to support North Vietnam, and was very much opposed to American bombing," Falkman said.[351]

DIPLOMACY WITH THE PROVISIONAL REVOLUTIONARY GOVERNMENT

The friendship between Sweden and Vietnam was strong enough for Öberg, at Palme's prompting, to invite the legendary Madame Binh to speak at the 1972 Social Democratic Party Congress.[352] Madame Nguyen Thi Binh was the foreign minister for Vietnam's Provisional Revolutionary Government (PRG), which had replaced the NLF in the South in June 1969.[353] She addressed the congress: "To all Vietnam's loyal friends—men and women, boys and girls, inhabitants of Stockholm (this beautiful city), of all ages and from all social classes, who have worked incessantly for peace and our people's just cause— we want to say: A great thank you."[354]

Calling Nixon "history's greatest terrorist," Madame Binh also regarded him as a hypocrite: The American government speaks much about peace and tries to promote the view that a peaceful solution is within reach, but at the same time, Mr. Nixon sends in his air and naval forces to bomb the two zones of northern and southern Vietnam to the point of extermination, bombings that indiscriminately affect women, children, and the elderly.[355]

As sympathetic as the Swedish listeners would be to Madame Binh, they did not necessarily do her bidding. They rejected her request to recognize the PRG, which represented the insurgent movement in South Vietnam. Meeting with Madame Binh during her visit to Stockholm, the foreign minister offered an explanation. According to the minutes of the conversation, "The Swedish government applied strict principles in matters of recognition and attached decisive importance with regard to the governments with real control of the country's territory—Swedish recognition was therefore never an expression of sympathy or antipathy."[356]

Since the Vietminh had not yet gained complete control of South Vietnam, premature Swedish recognition of the PRG could cause problems. Years later, Ekéus confirmed what Wickman had told Madame Binh. "They were not in full control of the country," Ekéus said, "elementary international law demanded you control a place."[357]

Indeed, the PRG had a questionable position in international law.[358]

Yet Wickman's objection to Madame Binh's request extended beyond the concerns of international law. "There was yet another reason for Sweden not to recognize the PRG now," Wickman went on, "namely that someone in McGovern's closest circles learned that such recognition could be counterproductive in turning American public opinion against the war and for a coalition government as a means of a political solution."[359]

Senator George McGovern of South Dakota was the Democratic presidential candidate in 1972. He had come to deeply regret his vote for the 1964 Gulf of Tonkin Resolution. Speaking on the floor of the US Senate in 1970, McGovern had said that "every senator in this chamber is partly responsible for sending 50,000 Americans to an early grave. This chamber reeks of blood."[360]

As determined as he now was to terminate the "cruelest, most barbaric, and the most stupid war in our national history," the decorated World War II veteran also had no intention of leaving the American POWs behind, contradicting the implications of the Nixon administration that McGovern's plan would entail the abandonment of them. The failed McGovern-Hatfield

Amendment, which he had cosponsored, would have arranged for the release of these prisoners.[361]

When McGovern had accepted the Democratic nomination in the summer of 1972, he declared: "Within ninety days of my inauguration, every American soldier and every American prisoner will be out of the jungle, and out of their cells, and back home in America where they belong."[362]

Running on an antiwar platform, McGovern also realized that an American withdrawal had to avoid any appearance of humiliation. He promised an exit from South Vietnam that would leave the Saigon regime intact within a coalition government. If the American people rejected his platform, the alternative would be the reelection of Richard Nixon, whose goal was to preserve American domination of South Vietnam.[363]

Apart from that, the PRG was never an independent government. "Because then North Vietnam was called the Democratic Republic of Vietnam, and that also covered the liberation zones," Falkman pointed out. "So, the Communist side had only one government, and that was in Hanoi. . . . They said it's one party; it's our country."[364] Therefore, Sweden did not recognize the PRG because it would have created complications. Stockholm would only do so when the issue had become irrelevant, on the day Saigon fell, April 30, 1975.[365]

NOTES

1. To be exact, January 11, 1969. *Säkerhetspolitiska utredningen, Fred och säkerhet: Svensk säkerhetspolitik 1969–1989, Del* 1, SOU 2002:108 (Stockholm: *Statens Offentliga Utredningar,* 2002), 251, 273–74. Courtesy of Kaj Falkman and Pierre Schori. "The Legacy of Olof Palme and Sweden," Address by the Swedish Prime Minister's Special Representative, Pierre Schori, at the Ho Chi Minh Political Academy, Hanoi, June 2, 2016.

2. *Säkerhetspolitiska utredningen, Fred och säkerhet: Svensk säkerhetspolitik 1969–1989, Del* 1, 262.

3. Konrad G. Bühler, *State Succession and Membership in International Organizations: Legal Theories* versus *Political Pragmatism* (The Hague: Kluwer Law International, 2001), 76, n316–17.

4. Alison Mitchell, "Opening to Vietnam: The Overview; U.S. Grants Vietnam Full Ties; Time for Healing, Clinton Says," *New York Times*, July 12, 1995, 1. "Assistant Secretary Stilwell Remarks for 25th Anniversary of Diplomatic Relations," U.S. Embassy and Consulate of Hanoi, December 27, 2019:
https://vn.usembassy.gov/assistant-secretary-stilwell-remarks-for-25th-anniversary-of-diplomatic-relations/.

5. Scott, *Swedish Social Democracy and the Vietnam War*, 179–80.

6. Ben Kiernan and Taylor Owen, "Iraq, Another Vietnam? Consider Cambodia," in *The United States, Southeast Asia, and Historical Memory*, eds. Mark Pavlick with Caroline Luft (Chicago: Haymarket Books, 2019), 81; Pierre Asselin, *A Bitter Peace: Washington, Hanoi, and the Making of the Paris Agreement* (Chapel Hill: University of North Carolina Press, 2002), 13; Prados, *Vietnam*, 288.

7. Farrell, *Richard Nixon*, 321; Ellen D. Goldlust, "The Ho Chi Minh Trail," *Encyclopedia of the Vietnam War*, ed. Stanley I. Kutler (New York: Simon & Schuster Macmillan, 1996), 233.

8. See Young, *The Vietnam Wars*; Seymour Hersh, *The Price of Power: Kissinger in the Nixon White House*, New York: Summit Books, 1983; Jeffrey Kimball, *Nixon's Vietnam Wars*, Lawrence: University Press of Kansas, 1998.

9. Schwartz, *Henry Kissinger and American Power*, 69–70.

10. Ibid., 74–77.

11. Ibid., 70, 72.

12. Farrell, *Richard Nixon*, 360.

13. Ekéus interview. Åselius, *Vietnamkriget och de svenska diplomaterna*, 261.

14. Åselius, *Vietnamkriget och de svenska diplmaterna*, 261.

15. Address of Torsten Nilsson, September 30, 1969. *Protokoll, Del I, Sveriges Socialdemokratiska Arbetarepartis 24:e Kongress 28 september-4 oktober 1969* (Stockholm: Tiden-Barnängen, 1970), 247–48. ARAB.

16. Ibid.

17. Memorandum from Theodore E. Eliot Jr. to Henry A. Kissinger, October 6, 1969. Nixon Presidential Materials Staff, NSC Files, Country Files—Europe, Box 707, Richard Nixon Presidential Library, Yorba Linda, CA (RN).

18. Ekéus interview.

19. Address of Olof Palme, October 4, 1969. *Protokoll, Del II, Sveriges Socialdemokratiska Arbetarepartis 24:e Kongress 28 september-4 oktober 1969*, 742. ARAB.

20. Åselius, *Vietnamkriget och de svenska diplomaterna*, 279.

21. Ekengren, *Olof Palme och utrikespolitiken*, 162–65, 217.

22. Rolf Ekéus, email, July 28, 2017.

23. Ekéus interview. Berggren, *Underbara dagar framför oss*, 438.

24. Ekéus interview.

25. Ibid.

26. Ibid. Ekéus email.

27. Ibid.

28. Östberg, *I takt med tiden*, 295; Thorsell, *Sverige i Vita Huset*, 145.

29. Memorandum from Ken Cole to Henry A. Kissinger, October 3, 1969. Nixon Presidential Materials Staff, NSC Files, Country Files—Europe, Box 707, RN.

30. Thorsell, *Sverige i Vita Huset*, 146; Bjereld, Johansson, and Molin, *Sveriges Säkerhet och Världens Fred*, 239.

31. Thorsell, *Sverige i Vita Huset*, 148.

32. *"Bättre besked hade hindrat missförstånd,"* *Dagens Nyheter*, October 10, 1969.

33. Sven Åhman, *"Även Åsea får kritik i Amerika,"* *Dagens Nyheter*, October 10, 1969.

34. Bjereld, Johansson, and Molin, *Sveriges Säkerhet och Världens Fred*, 239.

35. Courtesy of David Prentice. Transcript of Harold Wilson's conversation with Olof Palme, April 7,1970. PREM 13/3552, Public Records Office, Kew, England; Asselin, *A Bitter Peace*, 32; Prados, *Vietnam*, 447.

36. Memorandum by Jean-Christophe Öberg, June 1, 1970. *UD HP-Dossierer, Vietnamkriget, Mål: A, 1970–1971,* HP38:1, RA.

37. Ibid.

38. Ibid.

39. Ibid.

40. Memorandum by Jean-Christophe Öberg, June 1, 1970. James P. Sterba, "Last U.S. Troops Leave Cambodia," *New York Times,* July 1, 1970.

41. Ibid.

42. "Swedish Leader on a Tightrope," *U.S. News and World Report*, June 15, 1970.

43. Excerpt from *From Harlem With Love: An Ivy Leaguer's Inner City Odyssey.* New York: Lantern Books, 2012. Courtesy of Joseph Holland.

44. Jonas Frohlin and Eva Tillberg, *Året var 1970* (Stockholm: Sveriges Television, 2019). Courtesy of Jonas Frohlin.

45. Reuters, "Demonstrators Greet U.S. Envoy in Sweden," *New York Times*, April 10, 1970.

46. Frohlin and Tillberg, *Året var 1970.*

47. Don Cook, "Black Envoy Changes U.S. Image in Sweden," *Washington Post*, March 12, 1970, originally published in *The Los Angeles Times*; Thorsell, *Sverige i Vita Huset*, 165.

48. Telephone interview with Håkan Blomqvist, Professor Emeritus, Institute of Contemporary History, Södertörn University, December 17, 2022.

49. Frohlin and Tillberg, *Året var 1970.*

50. Ibid.

51. Robert C. Toth, "U.S. May Recall Envoy to Sweden Over Insults," *Los Angeles Times*, May 28, 1970; Bjereld, Johansson, and Molin, *Sveriges Säkerhet och Världens Fred,* 236.

52. "Swedish Leader on a Tightrope," June 15, 1970. Frohlin and Tillberg, *Året var 1970.*

53. Blomqvist interview.

54. Telegram from Jerome Holland in Stockholm to the Secretary of State, "Approach to Palme Re Trip to U.S.," May 25, 1970. Nixon Presidential Materials Staff, NSC Files, VIP Visits, Box 938, RN.

55. Ibid.

56. Letter from Olof Palme to Jerome Holland, August 11, 1970. OLA, *Brevsamling, Volym* 3.2/52, ARAB, Courtesy of Joakim Palme.

57. Electronic mail correspondence with Joseph Holland, December 20, 2019.

58. Telegram from Joseph Holland in Stockholm to the Secretary of State, "Conversation with Prime Minister Palme on Subject of Racism," August 26, 1970. Nixon Presidential Materials Staff, NSC Files, Country Files—Europe, Box 707, RN.

59. Ibid.

60. Thorsell, *Sverige i Vita* Huset, 156; Thore Davidson,*"Har Nixon nobbat Palme? Nej—Palme har aldrig bett att få träffa Nixon,"* Aftonbladet, March 30, 1970. "Swedish Leader on a Tightrope," June 15, 1970.

61. *"Statsministerns besök I USA: Chiffertelegram,"* January 21, 1970 from *Utrikesrådet Wachtmeister* to the Swedish Embassy in Washington, *UD HP-Dossierer. Politiska avdelningens ärenden, Politik allmänt, Mål G, USA, Statsminister Palmes besök år* 1970, 1967–1974, HP1: 59, RA.

62. Telegram from Hubert de Besche in Washington to Swedish Foreign Ministry, January 29, 1970. *Politiska avdelningens ärenden, Politik allmänt, Mål G, A, Statsminister Palmes besök år* 1970, 1967–1974, HP1: 59, RA.

63. Memorandum from Henry A. Kissinger to the President, "Swedish Prime Minister Announces a Private Visit to the U.S.," January 6, 1970. Nixon Presidential Materials Staff, NSC Files, VIP Visits, Box 938, RN.

64. Ibid. Luke A. Nichter, email, May 10, 2022.

65. Fohlin and Tillberg, *Året var 1970.*

66. Memorandum from William R. Codus, May 11, 1970. Nixon Presidential Materials Staff, NSC Files, VIP Visits, Box 938, RN.

67. Memorandum from Helmut Sonnenfeldt to Henry A. Kissinger, "White House Involvement in Palme Visit," May 26,1970.

68. Ibid.

69. Ibid.

70. *"Statsministerns besök I USA: Chiffertelegram,"* January 30, 1970, from *Utrikesrådet Wachtmeister* to the Swedish Embassy in Washington, *UD HP-Dossierer. Politiska avdelningens ärenden, Politik allmänt, Mål G, USA, Statsminister Palmes besök år* 1970, 1967–1974, HP1: 59, RA.

71. Robert M. Smith, "Swedish Leader, in U.S., Avows Amity," *New York Times*, June 5, 1970. Carl-Gustaf Ståhl to Stig Synnergren, *Rapport med synpunkter i anslutning till statsministern Palmes besök I USA 4/6–11/6 1970,"* August 4, 1970. *Försvarsstaben, Section 2, Serie F2:1, Utgående och inkomma skrivelser, 1970, Arméattachés Hemliga Skr., Volym nr. 1, Krigsarkivet,* Stockholm, Sweden.

72. Memorandum from William Watts to Henry A. Kissinger, "Visit by Swedish Prime Minister Palme," February 10, 1970. Nixon Presidential Materials Staff, NSC Files, VIP Visits, Box 938. RN.

73. Memorandum from William Rogers to Richard Nixon, "Subject: Swedish Prime Minister Palme's visit," May 21, 1970 in Memorandum from Henry A. Kissinger to the President, "The Visit of Swedish Prime Minister Palme" and Telegram from American Embassy in Stockholm to the Secretary of State, "Schedule for Palme's U.S. Visit," May 12, 1970. Nixon Presidential Materials Staff, NSC Files, VIP Visits, Box 938, RN.

74. Carl-Gustaf Ståhl to Stig Synnergren, *"Rapport med synpunkter i anslutning till statsministern Palmes besök I USA 4/6–11/6 1970,"* August 4, 1970. "Visits By Foreign Leaders of Morocco," Office of the Historian, U.S. Department of State: https://history.state.gov/departmenthistory/visits/morocco.

75. "Transcript of question-answer period, National Press Club, June 5, 1970, Swedish Information Service," *Talserien, Volym* 2.40: 021, OPA, ARAB. Copy of Letter

from Olof Palme of Sweden to William P. Rogers, July 14, 1970. *HP UD-Dossierer, Vietnamkriget, Mål:K, Krigsfångefrågan,* June-December 1970, HP38:32, RA.

76. Thorsell, *Sverige i Vita Huset,* 160.

77. Memorandum from Secretary of State to American embassy in Stockholm, "Prime Minister Palme's Meeting with Secretary," June 9, 1970. Nixon Presidential Materials Staff, NSC Files, Country Files—Europe, Box 707, RN.

78. Carl-Gustaf Ståhl to Stig Synnergren, *"Rapport med synpunkter i anslutning till statsministern Palmes besök I USA 4/6–11/6 1970,"* August 4, 1970.

79. Ibid.; Seymour Hersh, *The Price of Power,* 175–76.

80. "Prime Minister Palme's Meeting with Secretary," June 9, 1970.

81. Ibid.

82. Ibid.

83. Carl-Gustaf Ståhl to Stig Synnergren, *"Rapport med synpunkter i anslutning till statsministern Palmes besök I USA 4/6–11/6 1970,"* August 4, 1970. "Conversation with Prime Minister Palme on Subject of Racism."

84. Ibid.

85. Ibid.

86. Thorsell, *Sverige i Vita Huset,* 160.

87. *"Rapport med synpunkter i anslutning till statsministern Palmes besök I USA 4/6–11/6 1970."*

88. Roger Morris, *Uncertain Greatness: Henry Kissinger and American Foreign Policy* (New York: Harper & Row, Publishers, 1977), 90–93. See also Hersh, *The Price of Power* and Walter Isaacson, *Kissinger: A Biography* (New York: Simon & Schuster, 2005).

89. "Address by Olof Palme at Kenyon College, Ohio, June 6, 1970," *Talserien, Volym* 2.4.0: 021, OPA, ARAB.

90. Ibid.

91. Ibid.

92. United Press International, "Workers Picket Palme Speech," *St. Paul Pioneer Press,* June 7, 1970; Jefferson Cowie, "The 'Hard Hat Riot' Was a Preview of Today's Political Divisions," *New York Times,* May 11, 2020.

93. Fohlin and Tillberg, *Året var 1970.* Associated Press, "The Prime Minister Who Refused to Be Silenced," *San Francisco Chronicle,* June 7, 1970. United Press International, "Workers Picket Palme Speech."

94. Ibid.

95. *"Palme får egen livvakt vid hotellsviten i USA,"* Expressen, June 2, 1970.

96/ "Dockers in Newark Refuse to Unload Swedish Cars," *New York Times,* June 14, 1970.

97. Courtesy of David Prentice. Speech of J. William Fulbright, December 4, 1970. Letter from Olof Palme to J. W. Fulbright of Arkansas, July 3, 1970. Folder 1970, Box 17:4, Subseries 3 Committee Administration, Series 48 Senate Foreign Relations Committee, JWF. Speech of J. William Fulbright of Arkansas, December 4, 1970, *The Congressional Record.*

98. Eliasson Stockholm interview. "Schedule for Palme's U.S. Visit."

99. Ibid.

100. Ibid.

101. Letter from Ralph W. Yarborough to Olof Palme, July 14, 1970. OPA, *Brevsamling, Volym* 3.2/54, courtesy of Joakim Palme. Letter from Olof Palme to the Alumni Secretary of Kenyon College, February 12, 1969. OPA, *Brevsamling, Volym* 3.2/48, ARAB, courtesy of Joakim Palme. *Committees in the U.S. Congress 1947–1992. Volume 1: Committee Jurisdictions and Member Rosters*, p. 151. Courtesy of the U.S. Senate Historical Office.

102. Eliasson Stockholm interview.

103. "Sweden: Palme Faces Serious Domestic Problems on Eve of Visit to US," Intelligence Note: Bureau of Intelligence and Research, June 2, 1970. Nixon Presidential Materials Staff, NSC Files, VIP Visits, Box 938, RN.

104. "Address by the Swedish Prime Minister, Mr. Olof Palme, to the National Press Club, Friday, June 5, 1970," *Talserien, Volym* 2.40: 021, OPA, ARAB. Östberg, *I take med tiden*, 301. "Sweden: Palme Faces Serious Domestic Problems on Eve of Visit to US."

105. Ibid.

106. Ove Bring, *Neutralitetens uppgång och fall—Eller Den Gemensamma Säkerhetens Historia* (Stockholm: Atlantis, 2008), 13–15, 106.

107. Andrew Cottey, "European Neutrality in Historical Perspective," in *The European Neutrals and NATO: Non-alignment, Partnership, Membership?* ed. Andrew Cottey (London: Palgrave Macmillan 2018), 26–27.

108. "*Meet the Press*: Television Interview," National Broadcasting Company, June 7, 1970, Swedish Information Service, *Talserien, Volym* 2.4.0: 021, OPA, ARAB.

109. Ibid.

110. "*The Today Show*: Television Interview," NBC, June 9, 1970, Swedish Information Service, *Talserien, Volym* 2.4.0: 021, OPA, ARAB.

111. Ibid.

112. Ibid.; Asselin, *Vietnam's American War*, 125. Nguyen, *Hanoi's War*, 309.

113. Nguyen, *Hanoi's War*, 262–63, 309–10.

114. "Dockers in Newark Refuse to Unload Swedish Cars." "Meet the Press," *Talserien, Volym* 2.40: 021, OPA, ARAB.

115. "*Chiffertelegram*" from Hubert de Besche in Washington to the Swedish Foreign Ministry, March 7, 1970, *UD HP-Dossierer. Politiska avdelningens ärenden, Politik allmänt, Mål: G, Statsminister Palmes besök år 1970*, 1967–1974, HP1: 59, RA. Östberg, *I takt med tiden*, 301.

116. Östberg, *I takt med* tiden, 302.

117. *Promemoria, "Svenska vapen,"* Swedish Foreign Ministry, December 9, 1970. *UD HP-Dossierer, Vietnamkriget, Mål:C, USA's politik*, 1966–1971, HP38:9, RA.

118. Ibid.

119. Memorandum from Marc Giron, December 15, 1971. *UD HP-Dossierer, Vietnamkriget, Mål:H, Hanoi's politik*, 1971–1972, HP38:27, RA.

120. Ibid.

121. Birgit Karlsson, *Svensk försvarsindustri 1945–1992* (Karlskrona: Printfabriken 2015), 65.

122. Falkman interview

123. Ibid.
124. Eliasson Stockholm interview.
125. Ekéus interview.
126. Ibid.
127. Ibid.
128. Ibid.
129. Eliasson Stockholm interview.
130. Ekéus interview.
131. Eliasson Stockholm interview.
132. Ibid.
133. Ibid.
134. Ibid.
135. Ibid.
136. Ekéus interview.
137. Falkman interview.
138. *Säkerhetspolitiska utredningen, Fred och säkerhet: Svensk säkerhetspolitik 1969–1989, Del* 1, 310.
139. *Säkerhetspolitiska utredningen, Fred och säkerhet: Svensk säkerhetspolitik 1969–1989, Del* 1, 316.
140. Ibid., 314–17.
141. Letter from Dean Rusk to Clark Clifford, October 18, 1968. *Säkerhetspolitiska utredningen, Fred och säkerhet: Svensk säkerhetspolitik 1969–1989, Bilagedel* SOU 2002:108 (Stockholm: *Statents Offentliga Utredningar,* 2002), 67.
142. Agrell, *Fred och fruktan,* 178–79. *Säkerhetspolitiska utredningen, Fred och säkerhet: Svensk säkerhetspolitik 1969–1989, Del* 1, 311, 325–26.
143. *Säkerhetspolitiska utredningen, Fred och säkerhet: Svensk säkerhetspolitik 1969–1989, Del* 1, 275–76, 282.
144. "Why U.S. Must Stay in Asia: Interview with Herman Kahn, Foreign-Affairs Expert," *U.S. News and World Report,* February 8, 1971.
145. Wilhelm Wachtmeister to Hubert de Besche, *Sverige ligger inom USA's ansvarszon,"* March 3, 1971. *UD HP-Dossierer, Vietnamkriget, Mål:C, USA's politik,* January-March 1971, HP38:10, RA.
146. Ibid.
147. *Säkerhetspolitiska utredningen, Fred och säkerhet: Svensk säkerhetspolitik 1969–1989, Del* 1, 293.
148. "Guidelines for Policy and Operations: Sweden," U.S. Department of State, June 1962. *Säkerhetspolitiska utredningen, Bilagdel,* 43; Agrell, *Fred och* fruktan, 201.
149. Bjereld, Johansson, and Molin, *Sveriges Säkerhet och Världens Fred,* 271.
150. Bengt Albons, *'USA hemlig vän i kalla kriget,'* Dagens Nyheter, 21 December 2002, p. A14. Rolf Ekéus, *"Mytbildning om Neutralitetetspolitiken,"* 26.
151. "Guidelines for Policy and Operations: Sweden," 60.
152. Bromley Smith, 'Notice to Holders of NSC 6006/1,' May 2, 1962. *Säkerhetspolitiska utredningen, Fred och säkerhet: Svensk säkerhetspolitik 1969–1989, Bilagedel,* 65.

153. Ekéus interview. Bjereld, Johansson, and Molin, *Sveriges säkerhet och världens fred*, 34–35, 311.

154. Ibid.

155. *Säkerhetspolitiska utredningen, Fred och säkerhet: Svensk säkerhetspolitik 1969–1989, Del* 1, 223–224. Rolf Ekéus, *"Mytbildning on Neutralitetspolitiken," Internationella Studier* (Spring 2005), 32.

156. Ekéus, *"Kissinger och Svensk Säkerhetspolitik under Det Kalla Kriget"* in *En diplomatins hantverkare: vänbok till Jan Eliasson* (Stockholm: Bokförlaget Atlantis, 2010), 277.

157. Ibid., 278.

158. Ibid., 279–80.

159. Ekéus interview.

160. Jonas Åhlund of FLX, Interview with Henry Kissinger by Jan Eliasson, *Toppmötet 2, Avsnitt 4,* (Stockholm: Sveriges Television, 2017).

161. Henry A. Kissinger, "Henry Kissinger: To settle the Ukraine crisis, start at the end," *Washington Post*, March 5, 2014.

162. Ibid.

163. Ekéus interview.

164. Bjereld Johansson, and Molin, *Sveriges Säkerhet och Världens Fred,* 164.

165. Laura Secor, "Henry Kissinger is Worried About 'Disequilibrium,'" *Wall Street Journal*, August 12, 2022.

166. "Sweden's road to NATO," Government Offices of Sweden, 5 October 2022: https://www.government.se/government-policy/sweden-and-nato/swedens-road-to -nato/.

167. Unofficial Translation of Prime Minister's Statement on Vietnam, Hubert de Besche to Cabinet Stockholm, June 16, 1971. Excerpt of Olof Palme's Address before the Food Workers' Union Congress, Telegram from Press Office, Swedish Foreign Ministry, June 16, 1971. *Utrikesdepartementet, HP-Dossierer, Vietnamkriget, 1970–1972, Svenska ställningstaganden,* HP38:57, RA.

168. Washington embassy's unofficial translation; Ibid.

169. Coded Telegram 137 from Ambassador Hubert de Besche, June 17, 1971. *Utrikesdepartementet*, UD HP-Dossierer, *Vietnamkriget, 1970–1972, Svenska ställningstaganden*, HP38:57, RA.

170. Ibid.

171. Wachtmeister, Ekéus from Öberg, *"Situationen Vietnam-Indokina,"* December 16, 1970. *UD HP-Dossierer, Vietnamkriget, Mål: H, Hanoi's politik, 1970–1971,* HP38:26, RA.

172. Ibid.

173. Ibid.

174. Letter from Hans Blix to Gunnar Myrdal, February 1, 1971. Letter from Sam Bass Warner, Jr. to Gunnar Myrdal, January 19, 1971. *UD HP-Dossierer, Vietnamkriget, Mål:A,* 1970–1971, RA.

175. Letter from Hans Blix.

176. Ibid.

177. "Olof Palme interview, ABC's *Issues and Answers*, New York, October 25, 1970," audio recording #XA-ARAB07–02913, OPA, ARAB. Olof Palme interview transcript, ABC's *Issues and Answers*, New York, October 25, 1970. *UD HP-Dossierer, Politiska avdelningens ärenden: Regeringsledamöternas resor, Politik allmänt, Mål: G, USA, Statsminister Palmes besök år* 1970, 1967–1974, *HP* 1:59, RA.

178. Ibid.

179. Ibid.

180. Eliasson Stockholm interview.

181. Thorsell, *Sverige i Vita Huset*, 168–69.

182. Kurt Mälarstedt, *"Frostens År,"* Dagens Nyheter, June 5, 1988.

183. Letter from Olof Palme to Edward Heath, October 27, 1970. OPA, *Brevsamling, Volym* 3.2/52, ARAB, Courtesy of Joakim Palme. Thorsell, *Sverige i Vita* Huset, 170–71.

184. Eliasson Stockholm interview.

185. "Extract from Prime Minister Olof Palme's speech at the Uppsala Society for Foreign Affairs on April 15, 1972. *Utrikesdepartementet, HP-Dossierer, Svenska ställningstaganden, Vietnamkriget,* HP 38:57, RA. *Pressbyrån, Utrikesdepartementet, "Utdrag ur statsminister Olof Palmes anförande infor Utrikespolitiska föreningen i Uppsala den 13 april 1972. Utrikesdepartementet, HP-Dossierer, Svenska ställningstaganden, Vietnamkriget,* HP 38:57, RA.

186. Ibid.

187. Ibid.

188. Courtesy of David Prentice. Transcript of Harold Wilson's conversation with Olof Palme, April 7, 1970. PREM 13/3552, Public Records Office, Kew, England.

189. Schwartz, *Lyndon Johnson and Europe*, 232.

190. Ibid.

191. Ekeus interview; Falkman, *Ekot från Vietnam*, 93; United Press International "Sweden Plans to Establish Permanent Hanoi Mission," *New York Times*, June 30, 1970.

192. Ekéus interview.

193. Ibid.

194. Ibid.

195. Falkman interview.

196. Ibid.

197. Scott, *Swedish Social Democracy and the Vietnam War*, 23.

198. Pehr Gyllenhammar, electronic mail, October 5, 2020.

199. Åselius, *Vietnamkriget och de svenska diplomaterna*, 238.

200. Falkman interview.

201. Ekéus interview.

202. Ekéus interview. Åselius, *Vietnamkriget och de svenska diplomaterna*, 308. Memorandum from John H. Holdridge to Henry A. Kissinger, "Oberg Named Swedish Charge In Hanoi," July 6, 1970. Nixon Presidential Materials Staff, NSC Files, Country Files—Europe, Box 707, RN. United Press International, "Sweden Plans to Establish Permanent Hanoi Mission," *New York Times*.

203. Ekéus interview.

204. Falkman interview. Åselius, *Vietnamkriget och de svenska diplomaterna*, 187.

205. Ibid.

206. Falkman, *Ekot från Vietnam*, 133.

207. Ibid., 130.

208. Ibid, 130–31.

209. Jean-Christophe Öberg to the Swedish Foreign Ministry, April 20, 1972. *UD HP-Dossierer, Vietnamkriget, Mål:A, 1971–1972*, HP 38:2, RA; Asselin, *Vietnam's American War*, 140, 187; Nguyen, *Hanoi's War*, 206–07, 224. Prados, *Vietnam*, 449.

210. Telegram from Jean-Christophe Öberg to the Swedish Foreign Ministry, May 10, 1972. *UD HP-Dossierer, Vietnamkriget, Mål:H, Hanoi's politik*, March-July 1972, HP 38:28, RA.

211. Asselin, *Vietnam's American War*, 193; Nguyen, *Hanoi's War*, 244, 250, 256; Prados, *Vietnam*, 471.

212. Falkman, *Ekot från Vietnam*, 18.

213. Falkman interview.

214. Falkman, *Ekot från Vietnam*, 131; Asselin, *Vietnam's American War*, 186, 189; Nguyen, *Hanoi's War*, 207, 242; Prados, *Vietnam*, 449.

215. Falkman, *Ekot från Vietnam*, 131.

216. Ibid., 132.

217. Ibid., 133.

218. Associated Press, "Soviet Arms Aid to Hanoi is Down," *New York Times*, April 13, 1972.

219. Ibid.

220. Coded Telegram from Jean-Christophe Öberg to the Swedish Foreign Ministry, December 9, 1971. *UD HP-Dossierer, Vietnamkriget, Mål:H, Hanoi's politik, 1971–1972*, HP38:27, RA.

221. Press Release from Les Aspin, June 3, 1974. *UD HP-Dossierer, Vietnamkriget, Mål:C, USA's politik, 1974-*, HP38:17, RA; Asselin, *Vietnam's American War*, 6.

222. Coded Telegram from Jean-Christophe Öberg to the Swedish Foreign Ministry, December 29, 1971. *UD HP-Dossierer, Vietnamkriget, Mål:H, Hanoi's politik, 1971–1972*, HP38:27, RA.

223. Ibid. *"Vår man i Hanoi m m,"* *Dagens Nyheter*, June 9, 1972.

224. Ibid.

225. Ibid.

226. Jean-Christophe Öberg to Cabinet Stockholm, *"Bombningar mot Röda Flodens fördämningar,"* May 29, 1972. *UD HP-Dossierer, Vietnamkriget, Mål: H,* March-July 1972, HP 38:28, RA.

227 Ekéus interview.

228. Telegram 400 from Ambassador Jean-Christophe Öberg to Cabinet Stockholm, *"Re Amerikanska Bombningar Flodfördämningssystemet DRV,"* July 31, 1972. *UD HP-Dossierer, Vietnamkriget, Mål: H. Hanoi's politik, juli-december 1972,* HP38:29, RA.

229. Jean-Christophe Öberg to the Swedish Foreign Ministry, *"Bombningar mot Röda Flodens fördämningar,"* May 29, 1972; Asselin, *A Bitter Peace*, 60.

230. Ambassador Jean-Christophe Öberg, *Aftonbladet*, June 28, 1972. This quote was used in "Eyewitness Reports by Westerners of Bombing of Dikes in North Vietnam by U.S. Military," *A Documentation of U.S. Bombing of Dikes and Dams in the Democratic Republic of Vietnam: Compiled by Project Air War and Indochina Summer/American Friends Service Committee*. *UD HP-Dossierer, Vietnamkriget, Mål: C, USA's politik,* August-December 1972, 1972–1973, HP 38:15, RA.

231. Ekéus interview.

232. "Report on Mission to Hanoi from John A. Sullivan," 10.

233. Ibid.

234. Ibid.

235. Richard Falk, Telephone interview, January 8, 2018.

236. The bolding of the Öberg quotation is my own. John Tunney, "Senate Resolution 342—Submission of a Resolution in Support of Policy of the President Not to Strike Dikes in Vietnam," August 4, 1972, Congressional Record—Senate, sent by Curt Lidgard to the Swedish Foreign Ministry, *UD HP-Dossierer, Vietnamkriget, Mål: C, USA's politik,* August-December 1972, 1972–1973, HP 38:15, RA.

237. Dale Van Atta, *With Honor: Melvin Laird in War, Peace, and Politics* (Madison: The University of Wisconsin Press, 2008), 410. Telegram 196 from the Swedish Embassy in Washington to Cabinet Stockholm, June 19, 1972. Telegram 959 from the Swedish Embassy in Washington to Cabinet Stockholm, June 30, 1972. *UD HP-Dossierer, Mål: C, USAs politik,* April-June 1972, HP 38:14. "News Conference by Secretary of Defense Melvin R. Laird at Pentagon," July 17, 1972. *UD-HP Dossierer, Mål: C, USA's politik,* HP 38:14, April-July 1972, *Vietnamkriget,* RA. Asselin, *A Bitter Peace*, 60.

238. Prados, *Vietnam*, 307–08, 419; Morris, *Uncertain Greatness,* 164–65.

239. Prados, *Vietnam*, 484.

240. *"Samtal med officer i Pentagon angående svenska ambassadörens i Hanoi rapporter,"* Copy of Memorandum by *Försvars- och arméattaché* S. Geijer, Office of the Armed Forces Attachés, Royal Swedish Embassy, Washington, D.C., August 10, 1972. *UD HP-Dossierer, Vietnamkriget, Mål: H, Hanoi's politik, juli-december 1972,* RA.

241 Ibid.

242 Ibid.

243. Ibid.

244. Ekéus interview.

245. Ibid.

246. Ibid.

247. Falkman interview.

248. Ibid.

249. Eliasson Stockholm interview. Eliasson telephone interview.

250. Eliasson Stockholm interview.

251. Ibid.

252. Ibid.

253. Ibid.

254. Jean-Christophe Öberg to Wilhelm Wachtmeister, September 28, 1972. *UD HP-Dossierer, Vietnamkriget, Mål: H, Hanoi's politik, juli-december 1972,* HP38:29, RA.

255. Seymour M. Hersh, "Aide Says Lavelle Ordered Bombings," *New York Times,* September 20, 1972.

256. Editorial, "Correction: The Lavelle Case," *New York Times,* August 7, 2010. Prados, *Vietnam,* 461–63.

257. Ibid.

258. Robert Frank Futrell, Brigadier General Lawson S. Moseley USAF, and Albert F. Simpson, *The United States Air Force in Korea 1950–1953* (New York: Duell, Sloan and Pearce, 1961), 626. The cited passage was highlighted in E. Rosenblad, *"Flygbombning av bevattningsanläggningar,"* July 1972. *UD HP-Dossierer, Mål: C, USA's politik, april-juli 1972,* HP 38:14, *Vietnamkriget,* RA.

259. Ibid.

260. Ibid.

261. Ibid and D. Gareth Porter, "Nixon's Next Options: Bombing the Dikes," *The New Republic* (June 3, 1972), 20. Porter wrote that the bombing of the Toksan dam flooded twenty-seven miles of agricultural land.

262. Ibid.

263. Ibid., 626–27.

264. *The Pentagon Papers* (Boston: Beacon Press), 56, referred by John Tunney in "Senate Resolution 342—Submission of a Resolution in Support of Policy of the President Not to Strike Dikes in Vietnam," August 4, 1972.

265. Porter, "Nixon's Next Option: Bombing the Dikes," 20.

266. Ibid.

267. "Statement by the Ministry of Foreign Affairs of the Democratic Republic of Viet Nam on the U.S. imperialists' deliberate attacks against dyke and water conservancy systems and densely-populated area in North Vietnam," August 8, 1972, as forwarded by the Swedish Embassy in Hanoi to the Swedish Foreign Ministry, August 16, 1972. *UD HP-Dossierer, Vietnamkriget, Mål: H. Hanois politik, juli-december 1972,* HP 38:29, RA.

268. Gunnar Fredriksson, *"En Diplomat Måste Också Reagera som en Människa,"* *Aftonbladet,* June 28, 1972.

269. Ibid.

270. "Declaration of the DRVN Ministry of Public Health on the deliberate attacks ordered by the Nixon administration against hospitals and other sanitary institutions in North Viet Nam," July 7, 1972, forwarded by Jean-Christophe Öberg in Hanoi to the Swedish Foreign Ministry, *"Bombningar av hälsovårdsetablissemang i DRV,"* July 21, 1972. *UD HP-Dossierer, Vietnamkriget, Mål: H. Hanoi's politik, juli-december 1972,* HP:38:29, RA. "Report on Mission to Hanoi from John A. Sullivan," American Friends Service Committee, August 16, 1972, 7. Courtesy of Don Davis, American Friends Service Committee.

271. Ibid.

272. Ibid.

273. Telegram 253 from Jean-Christophe Öberg to the Swedish Foreign Ministry, August 9, 1972. *UD HP-Dossierer, Vietnamkriget, Mål: H. Hanois politik, juli-december 1972,* HP38:29, RA.

274. Telegram 269 from Jean-Christophe Öberg to the Swedish Foreign Ministry, August 18, 1972. *UD-HP Dossierer, Vietnamkriget, Mål: H. Hanois politik, juli-december 1972,* HP38:29, RA.

275. Arthur H. Westing, *Ecological Consequences of the Second Indochina War* (Stockholm: Almqvist & Wiksell, 1976), 9.

276. "Vietnam: Impact of War on its Environment," *Congressional Quarterly Weekly Report,* June 29, 1972, 1880. The article was attached to a memorandum, *"Miljökrigföringen i Vietnam,"* Curt Lidgard to the Foreign Ministry in Stockholm, July 31, 1972. *UD-HP Dossierer, Vietnamkriget, Mål:C, USA's politik, augusti-december 1972, 1972–1973,* HP38:15, RA.

277. Ibid., 1879.

278. Eric Paglia, "The Swedish initiative and the 1972 Conference: the decisive role of science diplomacy in the emergence of global environmental governance," *Humanities & Social Sciences Communications* 8:2 (2021), 2–3, 5'; Bjereld, Johansson, and Molin, *Sveriges Säkerhet och Världens Fred,* 260; Sverker Åström, *Ögonblick: Från ett halvsekel i UD-tjänst* (Stockholm, 2003), 197–02, 214.

279. Arthur H. Westing, "Egbert W. Pfeiffer (1915–2004): A Remembrance and Appreciation," *Environmental Awareness* 27:2, 67–70; Arthur H. Westing, "A Meeting with Prime Minister Olof Palme (Stockholm, 1972)," *Incidents, Gripes & Reflections* (2017), 4647, unpublished memoirs, courtesy of Arthur H. Westing.

280. Westing, "A Meeting with Olof Palme."

281. Westing, "A Meeting with Olof Palme." *"Yngsta tribunalvittnet: 'När jag vaktade boskapen kom tre plan över fältet'" Dagens Nyheter,* May 7, 1967. *"Krigets offer klädde av sig på tribunalen," Aftonbladet,* May 6, 1967. See *Napalm,* ed. John Takman. Stockholm: Raben & Sjögren, 1968.

282. Westing, "Egbert W. Pfeiffer."

283. "Statement by Prime Minister Olof Palme in the Plenary Meeting," Swedish Delegation to the UN Conference on the Human Environment, June 6, 1972, ARAB: http://www.olofpalme.org/wp-content/dokument/720606a_fn_miljo.pdf. Palme Stockholm Conference 1972: https://www.youtube.com/watch?v=0dGIsMEQYgI.

284. Lars Svedgård, *"Palme Tar Kallt på Nya USA-Attacken," Aftonbladet,* June 8, 1972.

285. Letter from Olof Palme to Ted U. Hallberg, January 27, 1975. OPA, *Brevsamling, Volym 3.2/126,* ARAB, Courtesy of Joakim Palme.

286. *"USA till motattack: Skarp protest mot Palmes tal," Dagens Nyheter,* June 8, 1972.

287. Lars Svedgård, *"Palme Tar Kallt på Nya USA-Attacken."*

288. Eliasson Stockholm interview.

289. Ibid.

290. Eliasson Telephone interview.

291. Ibid.

292. Eliasson Stockholm interview.

293. *"Svenskt besked till USA':Vi vill stoppa miljömord,"* Dagens Nyheter, June 15, 1972. Lars Bjelf, *"'Irriterat Läge' Sverige-USA,"* Aftonbladet, June 14, 1972.

294. John Ehrlichman, *Witness to Power: The Nixon Years* (New York: Simon and Schuster, 1982), 317–19.

295. Letter from Dr. E. W. Pfeiffer to Olof Palme, July 10, 1972, OPA, *Volym* 3.2/82, Brevsamling, ARAB, courtesy of Joakim Palme.

296. Jean-Christophe Öberg in Hanoi to Cabinet Stockholm, June 12, 1972, as reported by the Swedish Foreign Ministry, June 14, 1972. *UD HP-Dossierer, Vietnamkriget, Mål: H, mars-juli 1972,* HP 38:28, RA.

297. Ibid., 1878–79.

298. Record of distribution for "Vietnam: Impact of War on its Environment," *Congressional Quarterly Weekly Report*, June 29, 1972, 1880. The article was attached to a memorandum, *"Miljökrigföringen i Vietnam,"* Curt Lidgard to the Swedish Foreign Ministry, July 31, 1972. The record was on the last page of the memorandum.

299. Vietnam: Impact of War on its Environment," *Congressional Quarterly Weekly Report*, 1878.

300. Ibid., 1879.

301. Ibid., 1878.

302. Ibid..

303. Ibid., 1880.

304. Ibid..

305. *"Statsminister Palmes tal infor SSU-kongressen (utdrag),"* Telegram 938 from Cabinet Stockholm to the Swedish Embassy in Washington, June 27, 1972. *Utrikesdepartementet, HP-Dossierer, Vietnamkriget,* HP38:57, *Svenska ställningstaganden,* RA.

306. Ibid.

307. Ibid.

308. Ibid.

309. Ibid.

310. *"Miljömord i Vietnam,"* Hans Palmstierna, August 30, 1972, OPA, *Volym* 3.2/82, *Brevsamling,* ARAB, Courtesy of Joakim Palme.

311. Ibid.

312. Ibid.

313. Telegram 202 from Hubert de Besche to the Swedish Foreign Ministry, October 25, 1972. *UD HP-Docsierer, Vietnamkriget, Mål: C. USA's politik, augusti-december 1972,* 1972–1973, HP38:15. RA.

314. Telegram 172 from Hubert de Besche to the Swedish Foreign Ministry, September 22, 1972. *UD HP-Dossierer, Vietnamkriget, Mål: C. USA's politik, augusti-december 1972,* 1972–1973, HP38:15, RA.

315. *"Mitt under Miljökonferensen i Stockholm: USA-fartyg 14 000 ton gift till Vietnam—Sverige,"* Aftonbladet, June 8, 1972. Telegram from Cabinet Stockholm to the Swedish Embassy in Washington, *"växtbekämpningsmedel,"* September 19, 1972. *UD HP-Dossierer, Vietnamkriget, Mål: C. USA's politik,* august-december 1972, 1972–1973, HP38:15, RA. *"Stoppa arsenik-exporten till USA,"* Proletären, No. 30 (1972); Erik Nordell, *"'Kolonialkriget hemma': Bilden av Amerika inom den svenska*

marxist-leninistiskaa vänstern 1963–1977." Master's Thesis in History, Uppsala University (August 2012), 53–54; Kenneth Olson and Larry Cihacek, "The Fate of Agent Blue, the Arsenic Based Herbicide, Used in South Vietnam during the Vietnam War, *Open Journal of Soil Science* 10 (2020) 518, 523, 533; Vladimir Bencko and Florence Yan Li Foong, "The history of arsenical pesticides and health risks related to Agent Blue," *Annals of Agricultural and Environmental Medicine* 24:2 (2017), 313; Jeanne Mager Stellman, Steven D. Stellman, Richard Christian, Tracy Weber, and Carrie Tomasallo, "The extent and patterns of usage of Agent Orange and other herbicides in Vietnam," *Nature* 422 (2003), 681, 684.

316. Tim Maciolek, Vice President of Litigation, Johnson Controls, email, May 11, 2021.

317. Text Message from Klas Nilsson, Director of Group Communications, Boliden, June 1, 2022.

318. Don H. Baker Jr. and Gertrude N. Greenspoon, "Arsenic," in Bureau of Mines, *Minerals yearbook: Metals and minerals (except fuels) 1961* (Washington, DC: U.S. Government Printing Office, 1962), 275–77; F. L. Wideman and Gertrude N. Greenspoon, "Arsenic," in Bureau of Mines, *Minerals yearbook: Metals and minerals (except fuels) 1962* (Washington, DC: U.S. Government Printing Office, 1963), 253, 255; Arnold M. Lansche, "Arsenic," Bureau of Mines, *Minerals yearbook: Metals and minerals (except fuels) 1963* (Washington, DC: U.S. Government Printing Office, 1964), 245, 247.

319. Vladimir Bencko and Florence Yan Li Foong, "The history of arsenical pesticides and health risks related to Agent Blue," 313–315; Kenneth R. Olson and Larry Cihacek, "The Fate of Agent Blue, the Arsenic Based Herbicide, Used in South Vietnam during the Vietnam War," 518–19, 521, 529, 544–45

320. Telegram from Cabinet Stockholm, *"växtbekämpningsmedel."*

321. Eliasson Stockholm interview.

322. Ibid.

323. Ibid.

324. "Campaign Pressed in U.N," *New York Times*, November 25, 1969.

325. *"Svenskt besked till USA':Vi vill stoppa miljömord.'"*

326. *"Utdrag ur 'Världen i Fokus,' TV 1 i den 1 juni 1972, Intervju med Krister Wickman,"* Pressbyrån. Utrikesdepartementet, HP-Dossierer, Vietnamkriget, 1970–1972, HP38:57, Svenska ställningstaganden, RA.

327. "Hijackers Hold Plane in Sweden, Forcing the Release of Croations," *New York Times*, September 16, 1972; Reuters, "Yugoslav Envoy to Sweden Dies of Wounds by Croats," *New York Times*, April 15, 1971.

328. Richard M. Nixon, William P. Rogers, Henry A. Kissinger, and George H.W. Bush. Oval Office Conversation 783–004, September 19, 1972, The Nixon Tapes, RN: https://www.nixonlibrary.gov/white-house-tapes/783; Luke A. Nichter, Chapman University, email, June 26, 2022; John Powers, National Archives and Records Administration, email, June 24, 2022.

329. Ibid.

330. Ibid.

331. Ibid.

332. Telegram 502 from Jean-Christophe Öberg to Cabinet Stockholm, "*Amerikanska Bombningar mot DRV för Pol och Press,*" October 9, 1972. *UD HP-Dossierer, Vietnamkriget, Mål:H. Hanois politik, juli-december 1972,* HP38:29. RA.

333. Courtesy of Dr. Timothy Castle. Translated excerpt of Lieutenant General Phan Thu, *An Unequal Contest* (Ho Chi Minh City, Vietnam: Tre Publishing House, 2014), 114, 121.

334. Falkman, *Ekot från Vietnam,* 148; Anthony Lewis, "Abroad at Home," *New York Times,* October 14, 1972.

335. Falkman, *Ekot från Vietnam,* 148.

336. Ibid.; Åselius, *Vietnamkriget och de svenska diplomaterna,* 476.

337. Falkman, *Ekot från Vietnam,* 148.

338. Ibid., 147; Telegram 50 from Jean-Christophe Öberg in Hanoi to Cabinet Stockholm, October 11, 1972. *UP HP-Dossierer, Vietnamkriget, Mål: H. Hanois politik, juli-december 1972,* HP38:29, RA.

339. "A Career Diplomat," *New York Times,* October 21, 1972; Telegram 513 from Jean-Christophe Öberg in Hanoi to Cabinet Stockholm, October 11, 1972; Telegram 516 from Öberg to Cabinet Stockholm, October 12, 1972. Telegram 527 from Öberg in Hanoi to Cabinet Stockholm, October 17, 1972. UD HP-Dossierer, Vietnamkriget, Mål: H. Hanois politik, *juli-december 1972,* HP38: 29, RA.

340. "A Career Diplomat," October 21, 1972; *Falkman, Ekot från Vietnam,* 148.

341. Falkman, *Ekot från Vietnam,* 149";*Intervju med utrikesminister Krister Wickman i NBC:s televisionsprogram* 'Today Show,' New York, *den 12 oktober 1972. UD HP-Dossierer, Vietnamkriget,* 1970–1972, HP38:57, RA.

342. Ibid., 147.

343. "*Amerikanska Bombningar Hanoi Onsday 11 Okt.,*" October 12, 1972. *HD UP-Dossierer, Vietnamkriget, Mål: H. Hanois politik, juli-december 1972,* HP: 38:29, RA.

344. Telegram 530 from Jean-Christophe Öberg to Cabinet Stockholm, October 17, 1972. *UD-HP Dossierer, Vietnamkriget, Mål: H. Hanois politik, juli-december 1972,* HP 38:29, RA.

345. Falkman, *Ekot från Vietnam,* 149.

346. Telegram 447 from Hamilton to Cabinet Stockholm, October 13, 1972. *UD-HP Dossierer, Vietnamkriget, Mål: H. Hanois politik, juli-december 1972,* HP 38:29, RA.

347. Report from Jean-Christophe Öberg to Krister Wickman, "*Thai Binh, Nam Dinh, Phu Ly,*" October 5, 1972. *UD HP-Dossierer, Vietnamkriget, Mål: H. Hanois politik, juli-december 1972,* HP 38:29, RA.

348. Ibid.

349. Ibid.

350. Falkman interview.

351. Ibid.

352. Falkman, *Ekot från Vietnam,* 178. Address of Madame Binh, Provisional Revolutionary Government of Vietnam, October 3, 1972. *Protokoll, Del I, Sveriges Socialdemokratiska Arbetarepartis 25:e Kongress 1 oktober-7 oktober 1972,* 444–446. ARAB.

353. Bühler, *State Succession and Membership in International Organizations*, 71; Asselin, *Vietnam's American War*, 175; Nguyen, *Hanoi's War*, 140.

354. In the transcript, her speech was translated into Swedish. Address of Madame Binh, 444.

355. Ibid.

356. Peter Landelius, *"Mme Binh besöker utrikesministern,"* October 2, 1972. *UD HP-Dossierer, Vietnamkriget, Mål:G, FNL's politik,* 1970–1974, HP38:25, RA.

357. Ekéus interview.

358. Bühler, *State Succession and Membership in International Organizations*, 78

359. *"Mme Binh besöker utrikesministern,"* Swedish Foreign Ministry, October 2, 1972.

360. Thomas J. Knock, "The Story of George McGovern," 104, 116.

361. Ibid., 116; Robert D. Schulzinger, "Nixon, Congress, and the Vietnam War. 1969–1974," *Vietnam and the American Political Tradition: The Politics of Dissent*, ed. Randall B. Woods (New York: Cambridge University Press, 2003), 295; John W. Finney, "Senate, 55 to 42, Defeats McGovern-Hatfield Plan," *New York Times*, June 17, 1971; Allen, *Until the Last Man Comes Home*, 50.

362. Acceptance Speech of George McGovern, 1972 Democratic National Convention: https://www.youtube.com/watch?v=orx63ix1y-o.

363. *"Mme Binh besöker utrikesministern,"* Swedish Foreign Ministry, October 2, 1972.

364. Falkman interview.

365. Bühler, *State Succession and Membership in International* Organizations, 79, n334.

Chapter 3

The Christmas Bombing and Consequent Diplomatic Freeze

Thwarted Negotiations

Diplomatic contact between Sweden and the Democratic Republic of Vietnam continued. In October of 1972, North Vietnamese ambassador Nguyen Huu Ngo saw Wickman in Stockholm. The ambassador reported on the frustrating negotiations that his country was conducting with the United States. North Vietnam insisted on several key points in these talks:

> Respect for the fundamental rights of the Vietnamese people. The end to all American involvement in Vietnam. The United States shall recognize the reality that two governments, two armies, and two different "action areas" exist in South Vietnam. The United States shall recognize the Vietnamese people's right to self-determination and leave the Vietnamese people this right. The United States shall provide the requested contribution for the reconstruction of Vietnam.[1]

Remarkably, the Americans would eventually agree to all these demands, but they dragged their feet, thereby prolonging the war. They prevented a rapid agreement by stalling on fine points. For instance, the United States agreed to permit a general election in South Vietnam and also agreed not to impose a pro-American regime there. "The foreign minister said he found an inconsistency in that the Americans, on one hand, said that they would accept not setting up a pro-American government in Saigon, and on the other, intended to continue military aid to Saigon," ran the minutes of the meeting.[2]

In addition, the Americans had agreed on a prisoner exchange that would coincide with the withdrawal of troops. Ngo complained that this did not include the release of political prisoners who had been arrested in South Vietnam for their advocacy of peace and neutrality. "If the opponent was not honorable on this point it would be difficult to achieve national concord," the ambassador said.[3] What would then become of the National Council of National Reconciliation and Concord, the proposed coalition government of the Provisional Revolutionary Government (PRG) and the Saigon regime?[4]

North Vietnam believed that if the United States were truly committed to making peace, a final agreement would be reached before the US presidential election in November. Hanoi suspected that Washington intended to postpone an agreement, however. "The North Vietnamese government intended to act with caution—the Americans could be treacherous," the ambassador said.[5]

Again, the North Vietnamese government requested that the Swedes raise their voices against the bombing: "The pressure of opinion had shown itself to be effective many times."[6]

Wickman's response was decisive: "He could immediately promise continued Swedish support in official forms, and that the government would investigate possibilities to bring diplomatic pressure to bear on the United States for a prompt peaceful settlement."[7] The foreign minister knew Palme's intentions well enough to speak confidently on his behalf.

Nearly a week before the 1972 presidential election in the United States, another official from the North Vietnamese embassy expressed Hanoi's attitude to the Swedish Foreign Ministry. The embassy secretary informed Ekéus that the disputed fine points were not the true reason for Washington's intransigence. "The problem was that the United States wants to prolong already concluded negotiations about an agreement," Ekéus wrote, summarizing the secretary's comments. "The most important thing now is to get the agreement signed. Additionally, a meeting for initialing the agreement in Hanoi was agreed upon. Kissinger now says that he wants to have new discussions in Paris, not for initialing but for continued negotiations."[8]

In retrospect, Kissinger's machinations would not have surprised Ekéus, for the journalist Seymour Hersh would later brief him about the national security advisor's 1968 treachery. "Kissinger was advisor . . . both to Democrats . . . and with Nixon," Ekéus recalled. Learning that a peace agreement was imminent, Kissinger shared the intelligence with Nixon. "But it was clear that Nixon sent a message to the South Vietnamese: 'Don't go make that deal.' . . . They stopped the negotiation"[9]

Without such a settlement even four years later, Stockholm knew that the North Vietnamese were determined to go on fighting, and they did as Kissinger carried out the needlessly protracted negotiations toward the end of 1972.

Stockholm could only witness diplomatic developments from a distance, but what was happening on the ground in Paris? That October, the North Vietnamese had agreed that Thieu could remain in office in Saigon, and the Americans had accepted that North Vietnam and NLF troops would remain in place in South Vietnam. Hanoi would leave the matter of political prisoners held in South Vietnam for the attention of Saigon and the PRG.[10] Hanoi made the concession regarding South Vietnamese President Nguyen Van Thieu under Soviet and Chinese pressure. Le Duc Tho and Kissinger even shook hands with the anticipation that war would end on October 15. Peace could have been achieved then. That November, Kissinger declared that "peace is at hand."[11]

The only problem was that Thieu refused to accept the deal.[12] The US president wrote his South Vietnamese counterpart: "You have my absolute assurance that if Hanoi fails to abide by the terms of this agreement it is my intention to take swift and severe retaliatory action."[13]

OPERATION LINEBACKER II

In support of this assurance, Nixon ordered the bombing of the North Vietnamese cities of Hanoi and Haiphong shortly before Christmas. Officially known as Linebacker II, since the original Linebacker campaign had taken place that May to counter the Spring Offensive, the so-called Christmas Bombings lasted from December 18 to December 29, with a thirty-six-hour truce as a Christmas present. This truce was mainly intended as a signal to the government in Saigon that the US president would maintain his commitment to the regime after the withdrawal of American troops.[14] Kissinger, who had been ready to travel to Hanoi to initial the agreement, had privately observed at the time: "While we have a moral case for bombing North Vietnam when it does not accept our proposals, it seems to be really stretching the point to bomb North Vietnam when it has accepted our proposals and when South Vietnam has not."[15]

The Christmas Bombing had ruined Kissinger's scoop of an imminent peace, but he would claim afterward that they had produced a revised agreement that better protected South Vietnamese self-determination.[16]

Kissinger may have been embarrassed after his premature proclamation of impending peace, but Thomas Pickering, then deputy director of the State Department's Bureau of Political-Military Affairs, would later see no reason to doubt the national security advisor's support for the presidential action: "Well, they were a pretty united team. Otherwise, Kissinger wouldn't have stayed."[17]Thirty-six thousand tons of bombs fell from B-52s flying over North Vietnam. These sorties left more than 1,600 people dead.[18] The air campaign also included the launching of fifty-three Shrike missiles.[19]

Particularly offensive to the Swedes, and to Palme himself, was the fact that Bach Mai hospital in Hanoi had also been hit. Telford Taylor, the veteran counsel for the prosecution at the Nuremberg Trials, afterward visited the ruins of the hospital "with rescue workers carrying patients piggyback, cranes and bulldozers and people using only their hands desperately clearing debris to reach victims said to be buried in the rubble."[20]

The destruction of the hospital was a blow not only for North Vietnam but for the Swedes as well, for they had contributed a great deal of aid to it. Outraged, Palme sent a telegram in French to Pham Van Dong: "In this moment of new difficult tests for your people I express our sympathy with the victims of the bombings and confirm our solidarity with the demand for a speedy settlement that secures the Vietnamese people's right to determine their own future."[21]

THE KITCHEN TABLE SPEECH

Yet Palme felt compelled to do more than reassure the North Vietnamese—he had to confront the Americans. He sought the advice of his Social Democratic counterparts in Austria and West Germany, Bruno Kreisky and Willy Brandt, respectively. According to the minutes of his telephone conversation with Brandt, Palme "said that the bombings now involved systematic destruction of a country," sincerely expressing the same sentiments in private that he would very soon express in public.[22] The West German chancellor mentioned that he had been in touch with Chairman Leonid Brezhnev of the Soviet Union, whose reaction to the Christmas Bombings was "entirely undramatic."[23] Understanding Brezhnev's muted response, the Swedish prime minister observed "that Russians clearly were 'patient' and that they also were economically dependent on the U.S.A."[24] Palme also suspected that Brezhnev believed the American war in Vietnam would somehow exculpate any future Soviet intervention in a Eastern European country.[25]

As for West Germany, the Swedish prime minister proposed that Brandt and French president Georges Pompidou "propose mediation or at least make a public statement."[26] Brandt claimed that his government had already issued a quiet démarche to the Nixon administration and added that he was thinking about making a public statement. The Swedish prime minister promptly reported to Hanoi what the West German chancellor had said.[27]

Palme also consulted with his mentor and predecessor, former Prime Minister Tage Erlander, and with sociologist Alva Myrdal, who was the Swedish minister for disarmament. Another advisor, Anders Ferm, wrote a draft of a speech, which the prime minister revised in his own words at his own kitchen table at home on the night of December 22.[28] As evidence of the prime minister's literary contribution, a draft of the speech in Palme's own handwriting is available at the Labour Movement Archive in Sweden.[29]

"It was not an instant reaction," Palme later recounted. "It was building up inside of me since the bombing resumed. We had many discussions on it over a period of five days or so. And then, that evening, I knew what I had to say about it."[30] The prime minister knew what he had to say, even without the counsel of his own Foreign Ministry.[31] "He didn't ask anybody for permission," Falkman remembered. Nor did he "gather the government, and said: 'Do you think that . . . ?' Then, there would be compromises and he didn't want that."[32]

This self-initiative was a wise move on Palme's part, for Wachtmeister of the Foreign Ministry would disapprove of the speech, as would Sverker Åström, now the state secretary for foreign affairs.[33]

On December 23, Palme recorded a speech that was first broadcast on Swedish radio, and then textually transmitted to international media. He also performed an encore on film for Swedish television. In this speech, Palme dispensed with his customary tact. He had no fear of offending Washington.[34] "We should call things by their proper names," Palme began:

> What is going on in Vietnam today is a form of torture. There cannot be any military justification for the bombing. Military spokesmen in Saigon have denied that there is any evidence of North Vietnamese escalation. Nor can the bombings be a response to North Vietnamese obstinacy at the negotiating table. The resistance to the October agreement comes—as *The New York Times* has pointed out—mainly from President Thieu in Saigon. People are being punished, a nation is being punished in order to humiliate it, to force it to submit to force. That is why the bombings are despicable. Many such atrocities have been perpetrated in recent history. They are often associated with a name: Guernica, Oradour, Babi Yar, Katyn, Lidice, Sharpeville, Treblinka. Violence triumphed. But posterity condemned the perpetrators. Now a new name will be added to the list: Hanoi, Christmas 1972.[35]

The 1940 Soviet execution of Polish officers in Katyn Forest, and the 1960 massacre of South African Blacks in Sharpeville, both count among the foul crimes of modern history. Yet Palme's references to Guernica, Oradour-sur-Glane, Babi Yar, and Treblinka would strike a nerve, for they were all the sites of Nazi crimes. In tandem with the Italian fascists, the Germans had bombed the doomed Spanish town of Guernica in 1937. As acts of reprisal, German forces had also destroyed the Czech village of Lidice in 1942, and the French village of Oradour-sur-Glane two years later. Babi Yar was the site of the massacre of over 30,000 Jews in Nazi-occupied Ukraine in 1941. Treblinka, the death camp that was in German-occupied Poland, killed nearly one million Jews and two thousand Roma from 1942–1943.

Ferm's original draft contained the phrase about calling things by their rightful names, followed by the description of the bombing raids as unjustified torture, but his version was long-winded: "What is now going on Vietnam is therefore nothing more than torture with the aim of forcing North Vietnam to yield at the negotiating table."[36] Palme's version was more economical: "What is going on in Vietnam today is a form of torture." An elegant rearrangement of Ferm's ideas, the prime minister's finished manuscript was also more reflective of his own inner feelings.[37] The final line, a roll call of atrocities: "Guernica, Oradour, Babi Yar, Katyn, Lidice, Sharpeville, and Treblinka," was Palme's own.[38] This was an emotional reaction, not a calculated response. Despite the assistance of others, Palme's refreshingly undiplomatic words truly belonged to him. Now known in Sweden as "the Kitchen Table Speech," the address was the rhetorical triumph of the prime minister's career.[39]

Right-wing critics of Palme have accused him of overlooking Soviet crimes, but that is a distortion. In 1968, he had not hesitated to condemn the Soviet invasion of Czechslovkia.[40] By the time of his Christmas Bombing speech, Katyn was recognized as a Soviet crime. J. K. Zawodny's pathbreaking account of Soviet bloodlust in the forest had already been published in 1962.[41]

One admirer of the address was Ekéus. "I was very proud when he made this . . . this Christmas speech, so to say," Ekéus recalled. "I felt it was very tough, but I felt it was a way to wake up, really."[42]

The text of the speech arrived at the embassy in Washington via telex on Saturday, December 23. Ironically, the Swedish embassy was located at the site of another controversy involving the Nixon administration, the Watergate office complex. As duty officer, Eliasson found his holiday weekend disturbed: "It wasn't a regular working day. I remember I came to the embassy, and it was not open."[43]

Once inside, Eliasson examined the telex: "I read it, and I immediately called Leif Leifland and said to him, 'This is dynamite.'"[44] The Swedish ambassador planned to visit friends in Virginia, but Leifland and Eliasson both realized the situation was urgent. "And I called him and said, 'Ambassador, I have the sense that you should not leave town,'" Eliasson recounted. "I said: 'You will have a reaction during the day from someone, I'm sure.'"[45] De Besche, therefore, awaited the inevitable summons from the State Department.

The "dynamite" could only produce a positive explosion. "I knew Palme," Eliasson said. "I knew his emotions. I'm a diplomat. I wouldn't have used those terms myself, but I mean he did it in his way."[46] Eliasson not only knew Palme's emotions, he understood them. Haiphong, within its city limits, had not been a bombing target before April 1972, and now the bombing had only intensified during Operation Linebacker II.[47] "So, it was an escalation of the warfare," Eliasson explained, "it extended out to the city and its civilian population was affected. He felt that he had reached the limit, and he made this statement."[48]

Eliasson, a former exchange student at an Indiana high school, was long familiar with the United States. As well as he understood the prime minister, he also understood Americans. Eliasson shared his thoughts on strategy with Leifland: "You cannot look like you are regretting things, that you ask for an understanding, apologize, things like that. . . . You don't get respect from that."[49]

Atonement would have won the respect of neither Nixon nor Kissinger. "So," Eliasson went on, "we suggested as an embassy, and Leifland agreed with me, that we should stand firm."[50] Although the reaction from the Nixon administration would come that same day, telegrams from the Swedish embassy in Hanoi gave the prime minister no reason to regret what he had said. Eskil Lundberg, now chargé d'affaires at the embassy, reported that the bombing raids on December 19 and 22 that had struck Bach Mai Hospital had killed one surgeon, fifteen nurses, one pharmacist, and six medical students.[51] With the rest of the local diplomatic corps, Lundberg soon inspected the damage for himself: "One can conclude that the material damage with regard to the buildings is now total."[52]

Visiting the hospital himself two weeks later, the Swedish ambassador concurred with the assessment of his chargé d'affaires. Öberg reported that "the destruction there was total, repeat total. Of the buildings that remain none should be used further."[53] According to the ambassador, the casualty toll was even higher now, with thirty people dead, including five doctors.[54]

Sweden had good reason to be completely horrified. Contradicting the cynical charge that Palme calculatedly engaged in provocative rhetoric to appease and contain the extreme Swedish left, the prime minister realized that the Communists were an electoral nonfactor by this point.[55] The four other major political parties joined C. H. Hermansson of the Left Party Communists in a national condemnation of the Christmas Bombings. A telegram to UN Secretary General Kurt Waldheim bore the signatures of Hermansson, Palme as leader of the Social Democratic Party, Thorbjörn Fälldin of the Centre Party, Gunnar Helén of the Liberal Party, and Gösta Bohman of the Conservative Party. "Against the background of these bombings which have reached an unprecedented level and which severely hit the civilian population, we appeal to you to use once again use your influence in order to put an end to the bombings and to attain peace and independence in Vietnam," Sweden's leading politicians collectively urged Waldheim.[56]

The Liberal Helén, a member of the Opposition, expressed an open antipathy to Nixon's war. "The fact that the bombing has stopped around Hanoi and that talks are about to resume has little bearing," Helén said. "Hundreds have changed their position from a sort of balanced silence to a clear outcry against the bombing. And that includes many of the older people who are now divorcing their memories of postwar America from what's going on now."[57]

Bohman, who had previously attacked the prime minister for his criticism of the war, probably felt pressured to join the protest of his political counterparts. He later argued that Palme had violated Sweden's official position of neutrality.[58]

At any rate, the Swedish public shared their prime minister's disgust. A national petition against the bombings, which had the support of all the political parties, collected 2.7 million signatures. This number exceeded Palme's aspiration for two million names.[59] Quickly putting their money where their mouths were, the Swedish people also contributed 10 million kronor for the reconstruction of Bach Mai Hospital. This collection, which would have been worth 70 million kronor in 2016 currency, took only three months.[60]

The president, who could never handle criticism with good grace, was very angry.[61] "There's no question that Nixon . . . was sort of in a way like Trump, extremely sensitive about being criticized," observed Professor Falk.[62]

True, many Western countries officially criticized the aerial assault on Hanoi and Haiphong. "We found it very difficult to understand the reasons for the bombing," said Mitchell Sharp, the Canadian secretary of state for external affairs, "or the purpose which it intended to serve. We deplore that action."[63]

The chancellor of West Germany privately described the Christmas Bombings as "disgusting and unfathomable," but for all the encouragement that he had given Palme, Brandt did not officially speak out.[64]

According to Bernd Greiner, the prominent German historian and Americanist:

> Brandt never made a public statement—nor did he press the American government behind the scenes, i.e., diplomatically, to speed up the efforts for a cease-fire or peace treaty in Vietnam. He did not even voice any disapproval in private talks with members of the Nixon administration. Whatever misgivings he had, he kept them to himself.[65]

Indeed, I have not found a record of any démarche from Bonn in the United States. West Germany was even more dependent on the good graces of the United States than the Soviet Union was. A spokesman for Brandt merely lamented the lack of a peace agreement in Vietnam, indicating the wish that the peace talks would "soon achieve results."[66] Not that Palme blamed Brandt for his cautious approach, as Ekéus noted:

> Willy Brandt became so important for Sweden, and for Palme, to the end of his life. . . . I think Brandt made clear to Palme that: "We, West Germany, cannot

be, so to say, not be loyal to the United States . . . we have the Soviet Union. We have East Germany. We have these crazy guys." So one can understand . . . it was just like a rational fear. . . . I even participated in conversations with Brandt-Palme . . . one had to be careful. . . . Palme was very, very smart. He understood it absolutely. Absolutely.[67]

Sweden's Nordic neighbors, Finland and Denmark, also had their say. "It is especially difficult to understand on what arguments the vast bombard- ments of the North Vietnam territory have been based," commented Finnish Foreign Minister Ahti Karjalainen.[68] Danish prime minister Anker Jørgensen said that prospects for ending the war and a postwar reconstruction of Vietnam "suffered a tragic setback . . . the parties and particularly the United States assume a heavy responsibility."[69]

Yet the comments of the prime minister of Sweden stood apart in their comparison of the Christmas Bombings to Nazi atrocities.[70] "We were in the Vietnam War," Kissinger said, "and we thought that Swedish policy was insensitive and unfeeling for our problems, and too self-righteous. Now, to be compared to the Nazis, considering that we fought a war of four years against the Nazis, was not acceptable to us."[71]

In World War II, Nixon had served as a naval lieutenant in the Pacific the- ater. Even though the former logistics officer had faced little danger, and only from the Japanese, President Nixon found the comparison to Nazis impos- sible to stomach.[72] Kissinger reported that Palme's reference to the Third Reich was "an aching wisdom tooth" for the president.[73]

The evidence may be circumstantial, I would suggest that the prime minister's words inflicted an even sharper toothache in the mouth of the national security advisor. Nixon had spent much of the Second World War in the South Pacific, but Kissinger, a member of a German-Jewish family, had suffered from direct contact with the Nazi menace. The Nazis had come to power when he was a child. In 1938, he fled with his immediate family from Germany to the United States. No fewer than thirteen relatives who had remained behind died in the Holocaust.[74]

During World War II, the young refugee had then returned to his homeland as an intelligence officer in the US Army. Kissinger even participated in the liberation of a concentration camp, where he beheld the fate of fellow Jews who had not shared his chance to escape.[75] "Consciousness that societies can take a very evil turn," Kissinger said later, "this separates me from many Americans, who have never seen it, can't imagine it."[76]

Kissinger could have applied that statement to the Swedes. As Kissinger probably saw it, Palme knew nothing of evil—only he did. The overly sen- sitive Nixon and Kissinger should have realized that the best way to avoid comparisons to Nazis would have been to refrain from committing atrocities themselves. "But Kissinger resented all the criticism directed at him," no matter the reason, observed historian Robert Dallek.[77]

It is important to remember that Bruno Kreisky himself had lost even more relatives to the Holocaust than Kissinger had, over twenty members of his extended family.[78] Despite his own painful personal history, the Austrian chancellor never criticized the Swedish prime minister's speech for its comparison of the Holocaust to other atrocities. In a collective letter to Palme and Kreisky written three months before the Christmas Bombings, Brandt had pondered that "after Auschwitz and Hiroshima, after Nuremberg and Song My [My Lai], we have just realized the barbarity into which the human being can fall, what strong forces oppose and fight attempts to organize peace and a humane community."[79]

Palme concurred with Brandt, and Kreisky took no offense.[80]

As prone as Kissinger was to pontificate about the Holocaust, he proved remarkably insensitive about one of its few heroes. Swedish diplomat Raoul Wallenberg had rescued tens of thousands of Hungarian Jews in Nazi-occupied Budapest, then mysteriously disappeared into Soviet custody in 1945. In 1973, Wallenberg's elderly mother wrote to Secretary of State Henry A. Kissinger to use his influence with the Soviets to determine the hero's fate. When A. Denis Clift of the National Security Council approached Kissinger for an answer, the new secretary of state responded, "We should not get involved."[81]

Clearly, the Christmas Bombing speech has not escaped scholarly criticism. Swedish historian Gunnar Åselius, in his own excellent study of the Swedish response to the Vietnam War, argued that the comparison was inappropriate because the United States had not deliberately targeted civilians, unlike the Nazis. Yet the Nixon administration knew what it was doing when it bombed heavily populated areas. Åselius also pointed out that the North Vietnamese had advanced weapons at their disposal, in contrast to the helpless Jewish victims of Treblinka. The North Vietnamese may have employed antiaircraft missiles in self-defense but they did not have the means to bomb American cities in retaliation. It could hardly be called a fair fight. Åselius cites Linebacker II's thirty-three American casualties, and the additional thirty-four American pilots taken prisoner, but these losses were minuscule compared to over 1,600 Vietnamese dead.

One must concede that the Nazis intended to every exterminate every Jew on Earth, and that the Nixon administration did not intend do likewise with the Vietnamese people. At the same time, one can also make the case that the Vietnam War, like the Holocaust, qualifies as genocide. After all, Article II of the UN Convention on the Prevention and Punishment of the Crime of Genocide clearly states that "genocide means . . . acts committed with the intent to destroy, in whole or in part, a national, ethnical, racial or religious group." Moreover, Palme was not only addressing the Christmas Bombing; his speech was the product of years of outrage over a war that would ultimately kill two million civilians.[82]

Years later, Falkman contemplated the historical figure of Kissinger. Unlike some international relations theorists who present Kissinger as a tough realist who outsmarted foolish idealists, Falkman argued the opposite:

> Nixon and Kissinger had this illusion to bomb and punish a people that didn't obey their big plans. I mean Kissinger said that the Vietnamese are very egoistic, but you know they're egoistic because they don't want to take part in the big foreign policy game that Kissinger has been leading with China and with the Soviet Union and America. And he thought it was very egoistic to try to become independent. After one hundred years of colonialism, first they had China, then the Americans. They had one goal only: that is, to become independent. This he didn't want to believe because he had idealistic ideas about diplomacy to be led by American dollar policy and American power . . . like it was in Germany, the Westphalia peace . . . So, he was the one who was naïve.[83]

Kissinger, and of course, Nixon had another reason to regard the Swedish stand as a threat. Professor Falk observed that Palme's rhetoric

> was important as a voice of Western conscience in the context, both of the Cold War and the Vietnam War, as suggesting that there were considerations that transcended geopolitics. And that the Cold War justifications for the military intervention by the U.S. in Vietnam should not be allowed to go unchallenged, and of course, it reinforced the Swedish commitment to neutrality in the context in the Cold War . . . and in a way, it encouraged antiwar activism, especially in the European countries, that said: "Why can't our government do what the Swedish government is doing?"[84]

A DIPLOMATIC BREAKDOWN

Immediately after Palme's speech, and on the same day, US Undersecretary of State for Political Affairs U. Alexis Johnson requested the appearance of the Swedish ambassador at the State Department in Washington at noon. Functioning as acting secretary of state, Johnson made a statement to de Besche that was authorized from the highest level:

> I am acting on direct personal instructions of the president. Let me say first, that personally I cannot recall any case of two states with diplomatic and friendly relations, where the chief of government of one state made such outrageous statements with regard to the government of the other state. I cannot recall any statement by the Swedish government about Nazi Germany same as what is now

said in regard to the U.S. The president feels that given the Swedish government's relations with Nazi Germany, and what he feels was the cooperation, that
statement comes with singular ill grace.[85]

Obviously, Palme had borne no responsibility for Sweden's provision of
iron ore to Nazi Germany, or the permitted use of its territory for the transport of German troops to occupied Norway. Nixon, on the other hand, did
directly bear responsibility for his own policy in Southeast Asia. Therefore,
the president's comment about Nazi Germany was the one that came with
singular ill grace. Concluding his attempted history lesson, Undersecretary
Johnson went on:

> The US government, therefore, cannot come to any other conclusion than that
> the Swedish government attaches very little importance or value to its rela-
> tions with the US, or the attitude of the US government towards Sweden. In
> consequence hereof, the charge d'affaires John Guthrie, who is now in the US,
> will not be returning to Sweden. It is further the view of the US government
> that it would not be useful for the successor to Ambassador de Besche, who has
> already got agreement, to come to the US at this time.[86]

So, Yngve Möller, de Besche's newly appointed replacement whom had
received the assent of the Nixon administration in October, would not be
received in Washington, and John Guthrie, who had come home just for
Christmas, would remain in the United States.[87] Furthermore, Holland had
left Stockholm in August, and Washington would not replace him anytime
soon.[88] De Besche was understandably incensed: "I terminated the conversation by concluding that in the U.S.A., one found Palme's statement 'outrageous'—in Sweden, one found the American bombing 'outrageous.'"[89]

Ironically, it was the Swedish American Johnson who had been chosen
to scold de Besche. Reading Johnson's comments in 2018, Pickering said:
"My sense is that those were instructions that were prepared probably with
the support, or at the instigation, of the National Security Council," he said.
Pickering also speculated that the expression "outrageous statements" could
have come from Kissinger himself.[90]

Pickering did not believe that Kissinger could have differed with Nixon on
the handling of US-European relations:

> I think, in general, there was meeting of the meeting of the minds. The question
> of who-influenced-whom-more is an open question even today. But there is no
> question at all that Nixon had a very clear mind of his own, in many issues,
> may well have been the lead. But it's difficult to verify. You'd have to sit and
> talk with Henry, and I'm not sure he'd tell you what he thought or you would

get something that maybe made him look better than Nixon, however he wanted to key it.[91]

Pickering reflected that "in the end, no national security advisor can stay in the job if he or she is directly opposed to the president for any length of time because the president has to count on them to be the supporter of the president's policies, and have somebody in who is going to fight over the policies, not agree with them, is a burden that a president is not going to accept for very long."[92]

As far as the instructions to Johnson were concerned, Pickering said, "They seemed as if, in fact, it may perhaps have come as well heavily from the White House, but that's only a guess. Whatever Undersecretary Johnson may have felt personally, it had not one iota of significance with respect of what he said to the Swedish ambassador."[93]

Johnson, Pickering surmised, feared that the war could spread outside Indochina, affecting countries such as Thailand. At the same time, the undersecretary was also a loyal subordinate of Nixon, and he expressed that loyalty in his confrontation with the Swedish ambassador: "I don't know whether he agreed with the president, but I suspect with these instructions, he probably was reasonably sympathetic with the president on the subject."[94]

As far as de Besche was concerned, the meeting could not have been easy for the Swedish ambassador, either. Palme's style certainly was not his. "He was slightly more critical of the tone of the Swedish government against the United States," Eliasson explained. "He was basically a negotiator on trade . . . he was a professional diplomat. He didn't feel at home with the political temperature of this issue, but he was a loyal civil servant."[95]

Afterward, the ambassador gave an account of his meeting with Johnson to Eliasson. De Besche told the first secretary: "And when I left, I said to him: 'By the way, I think your bombings are outrageous.'"[96] Eliasson laughed in recollection: "And I said to Leif [Leifland], 'He's on our side. The ambassador's on our side.'"[97]

That Christmas Eve, Falkman was on duty at the Foreign Ministry when a coded telegram arrived from the Washington embassy. Well aware of the telegram's sensitive nature, he delivered it personally to Palme's home in the Stockholm suburb of Vällingby. The prime minister read the telegram. Then, "He looked up from the text and said with a pleased smile: 'Imagine, I have broken through!'"[98] Palme realized that his address had more impact on Washington than anything he had ever said before.[99]

Even at that moment of personal triumph, Palme could think of someone else: "Poor Yngve Möller—this is the second time he has gotten caught up in my Vietnam speeches. The last time was in . . . 1965 [in Gävle], when I was his guest. . . . After my speech, journalists rang his phone off the hook.

And now he can't go to Washington! I can hardly call on Christmas Eve and inform him of this."[100]

Two days later in Washington, Acting Secretary Johnson met again with de Besche. Johnson claimed that the US Air Force had been ordered to only bomb military targets. The Swedish ambassador did not contradict him. Likely referring to Öberg, Johnson suggested that certain people in Hanoi were ignorant of official Air Force policy. De Besche explained that Palme had based his speech on Öberg's reports during his home-leave. "He related what he had experienced himself, and it wasn't based on newspaper reports," de Besche said. "In particular, the bombing of the large hospital in Hanoi aroused a strong reaction, especially because that was where a large part of Swedish humanitarian aid had gone."[101] Johnson had no basis to imply Öberg's ignorance. The acting secretary of state probably did not know that Kissinger's own aide, John Negroponte, had complimented Öberg, maintaining that the Swedish ambassador "together with the British consul general would be the best informed in Hanoi."[102]

The second meeting between the acting secretary and the Swedish ambassador failed to resolve the tension. Stockholm and Washington would not reestablish full diplomatic relations for more than a year. No Swede could have been more crushed than Yngve Möller, who had been scheduled to take over the Washington embassy in February.[103] He relinquished his seat in the Riksdag and left his post as editor of the newspaper *Arbetarbladet*. To prepare for his important posting, Möller had read years of dispatches from the Washington embassy.[104] Ironically, Möller opposed the war, but also disapproved of Palme's controversial Nazi reference.[105]

The prime minister hesitated before giving Möller the bad news, even trying to persuade Falkman himself to do the deed. On Christmas Day, Palme finally faced his responsibility as prime minister, and telephoned the expectant ambassador.[106] The prime minister informed Möller that he would wait for the Nixon White House to make the next move. For now, Palme would keep the diplomatic freeze a secret from the party leaders and the rest of the Swedish government. "My spontaneous impression was deep disappointment," Möller wrote, thinking of his wife as well as himself. "Our travel plans were spoiled, my entry into the new office postponed indefinitely. . . . That the disruption would be delayed so long I could not have imagined on this Christmas Day."[107]

The prime minister and Foreign Minister Wickman still anticipated that Möller could soon leave for the United States, when the US embassy leaked the news to the Washington media. Möller later suspected that an American embassy official thought that exposure of the freeze could resolve the situation.[108]

In any case, the secret was out. In his hometown of Gävle, Möller heard locals say: "Here comes the ambassador without an embassy."[109]

With considerable understatement to *The New York Times*, he said, "I'm a little disappointed. I had hoped to go to Washington and improve relations. And I'm still looking forward to it. I hope to go soon."[110]

He never did, becoming ambassador to Oslo instead.[111]

"I would prefer if the United States would recognize the fact that one can have a deep-seated difference of opinion with Washington that calls for arguments rather than diplomatic rebuffs," Palme commented. "They serve no useful purpose."[112] Despite the pressure, Palme held firm. Then, almost paradoxically, the prime minister resorted to the traditionally Swedish instrument of diplomatic tact. At a press conference on December 28, Palme denied likening contemporary American leaders, either political or military, to the Nazis. He said that he had only meant to compare the impact of violence on innocent civilians.[113] In an interview with *The New York Times*, the prime minister insisted that he only used charged historical references as "symbols of meaningless suffering and violence" that did not signify "literal comparisons."[114] Palme was hedging slightly. It is clear from the prime minister's original speech that he viewed the Christmas Bombing as an evil act designed to torture and humiliate the Vietnamese people. If he did not truly intend to compare the bombing to Nazi acts of genocide, among other examples of historical infamy, then there was no reason to specifically list them. Palme's speech was not a simple summary of civilian casualties.

When asked if he thought that Palme had compared American leaders to Nazis, Falkman answered in the affirmative: "Yes, he did that. . . . Yes, he enumerates, for instance, the killing of Jews in Poland by the Nazis, and he compared this killing and also in other parts of the world . . . to the killings in Vietnam because this was the murder of . . . the whole civilian population"[115]

Ekéus, for his part, also believed that Palme had made the historical comparison. The Christmas Bombing speech had to be given in light of the civilian casualties, he later reflected, although "one could say it was unfair to compare with Nazi concentration camps, and so on . . . but the results were terrible," as innocents had also died.[116]

Continuing this more conciliatory approach in collaboration with Åström, the prime minister quickly wrote a letter to Nixon. Palme urged a bombing halt by trying to appeal to the president's patriotism and assumed morality. The Swedish ambassador, during his second meeting with Johnson, had handed over the prime minister's entreaty. Historically, Palme argued, other countries had turned to the United States for ethical guidance. He expressed his own personal appreciation for the United States as an example of popular government. Then, the prime minister turned to express the horror and dismay the Christmas Bombing had created all over the world. "Such reactions are particularly strong among young people and involve the risk that they will lose faith in democracy and democratic values," Palme wrote.[117]

The preceding sentence originally referred to "your people," meaning Americans. Upon the advice of Eliasson, who favored an even more polite tone, "your people" was changed to "young people."[118]

Probably conscious of the damage done by his speech to US-Swedish relations, Palme refrained from personally criticizing the president. Now, he only wanted the violence to stop: "This day, when people are assembled to express their longing for peace, with the deepest seriousness I wish to appeal to the President of the United States to cease with the bombings, which cause so much suffering and destruction, and to renew efforts to find a negotiated solution that will ensure the right of the Vietnamese to shape their own future."[119]

To his credit, though, Palme neither retracted his speech nor apologized for it. "I don't regret it because in this world you have to speak out fairly loud to make anyone listen," Palme said to a journalist. "I can't keep silent on this issue and won't be pressurized into silence."[120] Simultaneous to his polite letter to Nixon, the prime minister issued an open challenge:

"The weapon of democracy is argument, discussion. Bombing is no argument. And you should not prevent civil servants from doing their jobs. I would like to have a public discussion with the President of the United States any time, any place, in any medium, on these principles of democracy."[121]

The president silently declined the challenge. Senator Hugh Scott of Pennsylvania, a fellow Republican, seemed willing to assume Nixon's place in the debate. As the majority leader of the US Senate, Scott took great umbrage at the Palme's Yuletide commentary:

> I am getting a little fed up with the inaffable premier of Sweden, Olof Palme, who can find nothing wrong with the North Vietnamese murderers, assassins and slaughterers, and who pretends, because his majority is so frail that it depends on it, to appease the extreme left by continuous and flaring anti-Americanism. . . . I'm personally glad at the moment that we have no ambassador from Sweden. At the proper time, if the prime minister becomes rational, we will welcome an ambassador.[122]

Unlike Scott, some senators required no apology. According to a *Congressional Quarterly* survey, nineteen senators may have looked upon the Christmas Bombings with favor—nine offered no comment and forty-five openly disapproved.

"We cannot read about the heavy bombing without a deep and despairing sense that peace is not at hand," said Senator Edward M. Kennedy, the Democrat from Massachusetts. "Congress must and will act on the people's mandate for peace."[123]

Democratic senator Hubert Humphrey of Minnesota, the former vice president who had served President Johnson as a public hawk but a privately tormented dove, called the Swedish ambassador in Washington to convey his approval of Palme's speech.[124]

Of greater significance was the reaction of the chairman of the Senate Foreign Relations Committee. Not only did Senator J. William Fulbright publicly censure Nixon for his handling of the affair, but he also composed a sympathetic message for the outgoing Ambassador de Besche:

> I cannot tell you how chagrined I am that my government is so petulant and childish as to react to a legitimate criticism (and one shared by most of the nations of the world) by refusing to receive your successor. . . . I hope that you and your Government will not feel that this is representative of the attitude of the majority of Americans; in fact, I believe that a great majority of people of this country share your Prime Minister's sentiments about the recent bombing of the people of North Vietnam.[125]

Senator Claiborne Pell of Rhode Island appeared on the floor of the Senate to condemn the Nixon administration for its treatment of Sweden: "I believe this action by our government is mistaken, petty, and inappropriate."[126] While acknowledging the frankness and directness of Palme's words, Pell said they only reflected the horror about the Christmas Bombings felt by many of his own congressional colleagues and "many tens of millions" among the American public. The rejection of Sweden's ambassadorial appointment was "perhaps another indication that the administration simply cannot tolerate criticism or opposition to its policies, whether from our friends overseas or from within our own country."[127]

Surely, the senator believed, the leader of a country with as distinguished a humanitarian record as Sweden had the right to condemn terror by air. In the end, Nixon was hurting his own country. "If our government insists on engaging in activities that go against the grain of world opinion," Pell stated, "it cannot improve its standing among the nations of the world by petulantly refusing to receive ambassadors."[128] The senator sent a copy of his speech to his warm friend at the Swedish Foreign Ministry, Wachtmeister.[129]

Soon making his own appearance on the Senate floor, Senator Frank Church of Idaho joined Pell in condemning Nixon's pettiness. Church borrowed a quote from his historic predecessor, Senator William E. Borah, who had represented Idaho from 1907 to 1940: "A good cause is strengthened by opposition, a weak one justly destroyed by it."[130]

Following Fulbright's tenure, Church and Pell would both later serve at different times as chairman of the Senate Foreign Relations Committee. In their defense of Palme, these three important and influential figures represented a powerful constituency within the US foreign policy establishment. Not all Washington policymakers shared the outlook of Nixon and Kissinger. Eliasson, as first secretary, maintained friendly relations with many senatorial aides. Not surprisingly, he was close to staffers of Senator Edward M. Kennedy of Massachusetts as well Senator Church, both liberal Democrats. Kennedy staffer Jerry Tinker was particularly helpful.[131] Democratic Senate staff were frank with Eliasson, and the word "'overreaction' was . . . definitely something I heard all the time from people around Fulbright, Church, and Kennedy."[132]

At the same time, Eliasson kept in touch with the aides of Republican senators Charles Mc. Mathias Jr. of Maryland and Charles Percy of Illinois.[133] In addition to the US Senate, Palme found supporters in the House of Representatives. Representative Benjamin S. Rosenthal, a Democrat from New York, was the chairman of the Subcommittee on Europe of the House Foreign Affairs Committee. He planned to hold hearings on the effect of the Vietnam War on US-European relations. Media hype christened 1973 as "the Year of Europe." For that year, the Nixon administration had anticipated a renewal of the 1941 Atlantic Charter, a renewal that ultimately would never come to pass because the White House prioritized parts of the world beyond Western Europe.[134] Rosenthal was interested in the implications for the forthcoming July 1973 Conference on Security and Cooperation in Europe, cutbacks in troops stationed on the continent, commercial penetration of the Iron Curtain, and American dealings with the growing European Economic Community. "The Administration has announced that 1973 will be a year of concentrated diplomatic efforts in Europe," Rosenthal stated. "I don't see how we can carry out those efforts when Europe is increasingly outraged with the bombing in Vietnam."[135]

Furthermore, the subcommittee chairman requested the testimony of the assistant secretary of state for European affairs, Walter Stoessel. Rosenthal, in making his request to Secretary of State Rogers, was chiefly concerned with the diplomatic freeze with Sweden.[136]

Ultimately, Rosenthal's plan came to naught. Stoessel failed to show up on the requested date, using his vacation as an excuse. His deputy, Russell Fessenden, did not appear, either. Although the assistant secretary did offer to appear on a later date, he was only willing to appear in executive session. "As you know, it is the policy of the subcommittee to proceed in open session except where discussion of security or diplomatic matters is of such overriding importance to make closed hearings mandatory," Rosenthal wrote to the State Department, understandably annoyed. "I do not see the existence of these factors in the areas we asked Secretary Stoessel to cover."[137]

Of course, one must expect opposition to presidential policies within the US Congress, but some opposition existed within the Nixon administration itself, namely the State Department, even though Rogers himself did not object to the president's position. Leifland, the minister at the Swedish embassy, had lunch with unnamed officials from the department's Bureau of European Affairs, one of whom sat at the Scandinavian desk. Whether Stoessel or Fessenden were a party to this gathering is unclear. Those who did attend the meeting, however, expressed the view that Nixon had "overreacted" to Palme's speech.[138]

In a position paper submitted to the White House, these Europeanists in the State Department favored conducting "business as usual but no unusual business."[139] Diplomacy with Sweden could take place at lower levels without ambassadorial contact. They hoped that both countries would quickly resume diplomatic relations at a "normal level."[140] The Europeanists saw a problem, however: "The prime minister's statement to American journalists, the petition, the publicity around the Socialist International's meeting in Paris, statements in the American Congress, and so forth made it difficult for the State Department, meaning those at the White House who favored a quick return to normal relations."[141]

Like Palme, Leifland held firm. "I replied that I also viewed it as my most important task to contribute to the normalization of relations coming about as soon and as painlessly as possible," he reported to Stockholm:

> I also emphasized that I appreciated their concern for Swedish-American relations, but that it is unthinkable that the prime minister or the Swedish government would take back what they have said or keep silent "just to please the president," particularly as it seemed obvious that the internal revolt of opinion must have been one of the factors that contributed to the president's decision to stop the bombing.[142]

When asked about this State Department gathering, Eliasson responded, "I usually went with Leifland to every meeting related to Sweden and Vietnam, so I was probably in on that meeting."[143] Eliasson had no clear memory of this particular meeting, nor could he recall any State Department official describing Nixon's response to the Palme speech as an overreaction, although he did not "know if Leifland heard something that I wasn't present to hear."[144] In fact, Eliasson did not remember anyone from the State Department criticizing Nixon at any formal meeting:

> I must tell you that even if they privately could have been critical of the Christmas Bombing and the Vietnam policy, they were very professional in not disclosing that much officially in any way. Maybe after dinner or a reception, you could hear some hint that they had their doubts about the war, but at meetings at the State Department, they were very correct and loyal to the government as they should.[145]

Nor would Eliasson divulge the identities of the State Department who had even discreetly implied antiwar sentiments in more social settings:

> No, I don't want to name them because they were hinting it so elegantly that you almost had to guess their views, and I don't want to hang them out now much later in my life that they were disloyal to the government. I never respected the diplomats who came out and privately said one thing because I thought you are paid to represent the government. . . . I am there to represent my country's views, and they are there to represent theirs.[146]

One State Department official who was skeptical about the war in Vietnam was Pickering: "I certainly felt massively lukewarm about it, probably should have felt stronger and more negatively about it. I went there two or three times, probably at least once in '72, and found that things like military briefings and visits to military installations were really pretty badly organized and pretty badly presented."[147]

When asked if he regarded the war as wrong, or just badly planned, Pickering responded, "I thought it was wrong and couldn't be won," and then laughed slightly. "But other than that, it was okay," Pickering went on, laughing again.[148]

Did he share his misgivings with Eliasson? "I'm not sure whether we had that conversation or not," Pickering answered. "I wouldn't, at that point, necessarily have gone out of my way to tell him that. But I would not, I think, have run away from the conversation had it come up."[149]

As for Nixon's reaction to the Palme speech, Pickering said, "I thought it was a little extreme, but maybe something that fitted Nixon's style of doing things," concluding with a chuckle.[150]

That did not mean that Pickering agreed with Palme on the Christmas Bombings. He argued that Nixon had employed that tactic to get the peace negotiations moving again, as well as to gain some military advantage. Examining Palme's speech on 2018, Pickering commented:

> Most of us had, of course, gone through the Second World War, when massive bombing was something that we practiced fairly widely against Germany, Italy, and particularly Japan. And the notion that it constituted a war crime of the first order was something that, I think, probably, we would have judged, even if we opposed the war, as maybe an exaggeration beyond what our general sense of it was.[151]

Despite the good intentions of the Bureau of European Affairs, the State Department carried little weight in the Nixon administration. The president and his national security advisor, Kissinger, reserved the key decisions in US foreign policy for themselves. That does not mean the State Department served no purpose. Pickering explained that the National Security Council, which Kissinger ran, "is focused on policy rather than implementation. And the Defense Department, the State Department, and the other agencies are focused on implementation, and generally have the funds to do so."[152]

Pickering confirmed that Nixon and Kissinger often bypassed Secretary of State Rogers and the State Department: "Well, I think for many things they did, things they considered important."[153]

No matter the private feelings of some State Department personnel, Leifland's hope would not come to pass that Möller could assume his post as Swedish ambassador to Washington.[154]

Once the diplomatic freeze from the White House began, Leifland primarily dealt with Helmut Sonnenfeldt of the National Security Council; Joseph Sisco, the assistant secretary of state for Near Eastern affairs; and Arthur Hartman, the assistant secretary of State for European and Eurasian affairs. The White House discouraged State Department contact with the Swedish embassy. "But Hal Sonnenfeldt never declined invitations," Eliasson recalled: "So, Leif and I saw him regularly. . . . Not only we talked about Swedish-American relations, but also he was an expert on Russia, and of course, Russia is very important to Sweden, also. So, we had very important discussions on geopolitical strategic issues, and he was very generous. That was really our most important channel.[155]

Sisco's bailiwick was the Middle East. "He was really a first-rate diplomat," Eliasson said, "with high influence. With him, we mostly spoke Middle East, but he was a good, high-level contact."[156] Eliasson also had lower-level contacts in the White House itself. Nevertheless, these contacts now had limits. "We were in Nixon's doghouse, as we called it," Eliasson said.[157]

Previously, Eliasson had accompanied Leifland to all State Department meetings, but Swedish American relations had now changed: "Actually, I had more contact with the Bureau of European Affairs that he could because he was later in January put on the black list."[158] Therefore, Eliasson met officials of lower and intermediate rank. Among his contacts were two men who successively served at the State Department's Sweden desk: John P. Owens and Bill Bodde. Eliasson also dealt on his own with Pickering, as well as with Hartman himself.

Eliasson was particularly fond of Bodde: "We became friends. We even were invited for Thanksgiving dinner, my wife and I . . . in spite of all this."[159]

Pickering had already formed a fast friendship with Eliasson, remembering:

He invited me to the Swedish embassy. I think we saw one of the films, either *The Emigrants* or *The New Land* [Jan Troell's films about Swedish emigration to the United States]. . . . We were not people who saw each other every day, but we had contact and talked about things back and forth. . . . But it was more of a social contact, although we talked about issues, I'm sure. I had very little to do with Sweden or the Swedish embassy in an official character. So, it was one of those kinds of contacts one develops in diplomacy that are very nice to have because you don't have to do a lot of work. But at the same time, you can talk about issues.[160]

Eliasson also liked Hartman: "He was a very decent person, and I think Leifland met him a few times, but I had frequent contact all the time with the desk."[161]

The regrets of the State Department officials were never fully expressed. Eliasson remembered that "so many people confessed that they were against the war, but we never received an apology. We never expected or asked for one, either. That you have to accept."[162]

It is also likely that the Watergate scandal made working conditions for the Swedish embassy much easier than they would have been. "For every month, Nixon's star was fading," Eliasson pointed out.[163] For Eliasson, the diplomatic freeze proved a rewarding challenge. "It was one of the most exciting periods of my life."[164] Conducting diplomacy in calm circumstances may be pleasant, "but diplomacy when you have a challenge . . . you learn much more uphill."[165]

Among the members of the American Fourth Estate, a few parroted the arguments made by the White House. The *New York Daily News* cheered the diplomatic snub against "Olof Palme, the peacenik premier of Sweden."[166] The newspaper went on to accuse the Swedes of hypocrisy: "We seem to recall they smugly sat out World War II, turned a neat profit doing business with Hitlerite Germany, and even let the Nazis use Sweden as a protected pathway for troops doing occupation duty in suffering Norway."[167]

William F. Buckley Jr., the editor-in-chief of the conservative *National Review*, questioned Palme's ability to think straight: "Perhaps Palme, whose country permitted Nazi troops to march back and forth between Finland and Norway, is psychologically ill at ease with the historical fact that Americans fought to save Europe while the Swedes practiced nude sunbathing, or whatever."[168]

The *New York Daily News* was just a local tabloid, and Buckley represented the right wing, but the mainstream periodicals were not so blithe. America's newspaper of record, *The New York Times*, cautioned the White House for its mistreatment of Palme and another firm opponent of the war, Australian Prime Minister Gough Whitlam, whose Washington embassy had received a nasty phone call from Kissinger in response to his own private letter to Nixon: "The diplomatic rebuffs they received from Washington could not stifle the widespread belief that their comments reflected the unexpressed feelings of many of this country's closest friends and allies abroad."[169]

Rather than accusing Palme of insulting the United States, *The New York Times* blamed the superpower for damaging its own image: "The implications of this worldwide censure extend far beyond Indochina, vitally affecting this country's ability to lead its allies and others toward the generation of peace that President Nixon has repeatedly promised."[170]

The Washington Post, a *Times* competitor that had repeatedly endorsed Johnson's bloody war, published an editorial in support of Palme. The editors may have described the prime minister's speech as "an extravagant statement," but they also made an important point about the diplomatic freeze between the United States and Sweden. When Nixon threw his temper tantrum, "There is no record that he attempted to explain to the Swedes the purpose of the latest bombing, any more than he has to Americans."[171]

The Washington Post detected the inherent contradiction in Nixon's reaction:

> It was not Olof Palme's words that shot almost a score of B-52s out of the skies of North Vietnam during the December raids: it was missiles supplied to Hanoi by the Soviet Union. The two million signatures Mr. Palme is trying to rally for an end-the bombing petition are not killing South Vietnamese: the bullets sent to the Vietcong by the People's Republic of China are. Yet Mr. Nixon keeps his ambassador in Moscow, and Moscow's envoy stays in Washington. As with the Russians, he continues efforts to broaden ties with the Chinese.[172]

Palme was a well-wisher. As the editors observed: "The Swedish attitude—which is, let it be noted, shared in some more or less considerable degree by practically every friend the United States has—expresses essentially, we think, the bafflement with which so many people everywhere view the extended and continuing American involvement in Vietnam."[173]

The reaction from the American public was mixed. In a letter to the Swedish embassy, Gardner Macartney of Methuen, Massachusetts, repeated the arguments already made by conservative forces:

> Your country is very critical of the United States and yet your country, except during the time of the Vikings, has proven to be very cowardly. I site [*sic*] for example your fear and humility before the Nazis. I just thank God that we have a President at last who dares to call a spade a spade . . . and a dog a dog. The best course of action for Sweden would probably be to slink quietly behind the Iron Curtain. You'll probably be dragged there anyway . . . in due time.[174]

Long before, King Charles XII of Sweden had undermined any notions of Swedish cowardice when he took on the Russian army of Tsar Peter the Great in the early eighteenth century's Great Northern War.

From Denver, Colorado, Bertram E. Butland mailed a transcript of the radio commentary of George Putnam, a right-wing media personality. Putnam had rhetorically inquired: "And what did Sweden ever do—what word of opposition was ever spoken against the atrocities of Babi Yar, Katyn Forest, Treblinka, or any of the other instances in which the Nazis practiced atrocities against the whole human race?"[175]

Perhaps Putnam did not know about Swedish diplomat Raoul Wallenberg's historic heroism, or the refuge that Sweden provided to thousands of European Jews during World War II as well. In any case, Putnam's commentary impressed the uninformed Butland, who wrote: "In case you have not seen or heard the above, this should enlighten you Swedes. May be [*sic*] you should send this on to your Olaf [*sic*] Palmer [*sic*]. What the hell has gone wrong with you Swedes?? You use [*sic*] to be a fine bunch of people!"[176]

In the immediate aftermath of the Christmas Bombing speech, a relieved Palme could report that most of the international mail was supportive: "I've never received so much mail from abroad—particularly from the United States—and letters are overwhelmingly positive to the stand we have taken."[177]

Those Americans who did support Palme composed more thoughtful, reflective messages. Arny Reichler of Chicago, Illinois, penned a letter that was entirely free of ethnocentrism, and full of criticism for his own president:

> I have the uncomfortable feeling that America is becoming the greatest menace to humanity since Hitler. There seems no way to stop the constitution dictator. I write to you because you have shown the courage and sense of history and gentleness of a leader of men. I write to you not hoping really that you can do anything more. Frustrating as it is, the pressure must come from my countrymen and even if they did en masse arise to oppose the killing I am not sure it would matter to "our mad bomber."[178]

Albert Epstein of Maywood, New Jersey, empathized with those suffering in Vietnam:

> The merciless bombing of North Vietnam, of Hanoi and Haiphong—hospitals, churches, schools, villages destroyed—men, women, children, babies—the casualties. . . . My countrymen, all of you have seen the child, a little girl running, screaming, her flesh hanging from her body, stripped by napalm. I wonder how those who command and the Generals in the Pentagon, the manufacturers of this hideous form of torture, would welcome napalm poured upon their children.[179]

The most important response probably came from Prime Minister Pham Van Dong of North Vietnam via telegram. "Thank you very sincerely for your concern during the new escalation of the extremely barbaric war of the

United States, and at the same time for your warm support for the Vietnamese people's just fight."[180]

Using Öberg as an intermediary shortly afterward, Dong not only reexpressed his gratitude to Palme but extended another invitation to visit Hanoi. "He added that no head of government enjoyed such confidence and popularity here as the Swedish prime minister," the Swedish ambassador recounted.[181] The North Vietnamese leader also rewarded Palme with a gift, a painting executed by a local defense unit. Palme would never visit Vietnam, the country he had done so much to help.[182]

For all his compliments for Palme, Dong was not quite so complimentary about French president Georges Pompidou, who cared more about cultivating a close relationship with the United States than had his predecessor, Charles de Gaulle. "The prime minister offered scathing criticism of Pompidou's collaborative silence on the Vietnam question," Öberg wrote. "France was more anxious to protect its colonial remnants in South Vietnam than to play an honorable role in Vietnam."[183]

West German chancellor Willy Brant had been just equally silent, but Dong bore him no ill will. "He said he understood the federal chancellor's difficulties in speaking publicly in plain language," the ambassador informed Palme. "Pham Van Dong knows that you were in contact with Brandt during the climax of the bombing right before Christmas."[184] Obviously, the North Vietnamese prime minister was aware that Brandt had advised Palme on his Christmas Bombing speech.

NOTES

1. *"Samtal mellan ambassadör Ngo and utrikesministern,"* Swedish Foreign Ministry, 20 October 1972. *UD-HP Dossierer, Vietnamkriget, Mål: F, Fredsträvanden* 1971–1972, HP 38:20, RA.

2. Ibid.

3. Ibid.

4. Ibid.

5. Ibid.

6. Ibid.

7. Ibid.

8. Memorandum from Rolf Ekéus, *"Samtal med ambassadsekreterare Hung, DRV's ambassad,"* November 1, 1972. *UD HP-Dossierer, Vietnamkriget, Mål:F, Fredsträvanden,* 1972–1973, HP38:21, RA.

9. Ekéus interview.

10. Farrell, *Richard Nixon*, 495–96. Article 8 of the original agreement, in Asselin, *A Bitter Peace*, 195.

11. Luke A. Nichter, *Richard Nixon and Europe: The Reshaping of the Postwar Atlantic World* (Cambridge, UK: Cambridge University Press, 2015), 110; Asselin, *Vietnam's American War*, 197–98, 71; Nguyen, *Hanoi's War*, 258, 272.

12. Schwartz, *Henry Kissinger and American Power*, 193; Asselin, *Vietnam's American War*, 199; Asselin, *A Bitter Peace*, 101; Nguyen, *Hanoi's War*, 258, 279, 294; Prados, *Vietnam*, 506.

13. Prados, *Vietnam*, 508.

14. Young, *The Vietnam Wars*, 278; Schulzinger, "Richard Nixon, Congress, and the War in Vietnam 1969–1974," 292–93; Asselin, *Vietnam's American* War, 202; Nguyen, *Hanoi's War*, 295.

15. Prados, *Vietnam*, 507.

16. Interview with Henry Kissinger by Jan Eliasson.

17. Telephone interview with Thomas Pickering, September 16, 2018.

18. Schwartz, *Henry Kissinger and American* Power, 202; James William Gibson, *The Perfect War: Technowar in Vietnam* (Boston and New York: The Atlantic Monthly Press, 1986), 417; Asselin, *Vietnam's American War*, 203; Nguyen, *Hanoi's War*, 1, 296.

19. Phan Thu, *An Unequal Contest*, 131.

20. Telford Taylor, "Hanoi Is Reported Scarred But Key Services Continued," *New York Times*, December 25, 1972; Åselius, *Vietnamkriget och de svenska diplomaterna*, 466.

21. From *"Palme meddelande med DRV,"* December 20, 1972. From *"Telegram från statsminister Olof Palme till DRV:s regeringschef Pham Van Dong,"* December 20, 1972. *Pressmeddelande, Pressbyrån. Utrikesdepartementet, HP-Dossierer, Vietnamkriget,* 1972–1974, HP38:58, RA.

22. Memorandum by Sverker Åstrom, December 21, 1972. *Utrikesdepartementet, HP-Dossierer, Vietnamkriget,* 1972–1974, HP38:58, RA.

23. Ibid.

24. Ibid.

25. Ibid.

26. Ibid.

27. Ibid.

28. Berggren, *Underbara dagar framför oss*, 463; Alvin Schuster, "Swedish Chilliness Toward U.S. is Limited to Vietnam," *New York Times*, January 8, 1973.

29. Palme's draft of Christmas Bombing speech, *Volym* 2.4.0: 044, *Tal* 1972, OPA, ARAB and www.olofpalme.org.

30. Schuster, "Swedish Chilliness Toward U.S. is Limited to Vietnam."

31. Schuster, "Swedish Chilliness Toward U.S. is Limited to Vietnam"; Agrell, *Fred och Fruktan*, 175; Åselius, *Vietnamkriget och de svenska diplomaterna*, 460.

32. Falkman interview; Wilhelm Agrell, *Fred och Fruktan*, 175.

33. Wachtmeister, *Som Jag Såg Det*, 197; Åström, *Ögonblick*, 164–65.

34. Palme phoned in his speech to the Swedish news agency Tidningarnas Telegrambyrå (The Newspapers' Telegram Bureau); Berggren, *Underbara dagar framför oss*, 463; Göran Hägg, *Retorik i Tiden: 23 historiska recept för framgång* (Stockholm:

Norstedts, 2011), 189–91; Archivist Emeritus Stellan Andersson, ARAB, email, November 7, 2019.

35. http://www.olofpalme.org; the website has only posted the speech in the original Swedish. The English translation is from *Olof Palme Speaking: Articles and speeches*, Gunilla Banks, ed. (Stockholm: Premiss förlag, 2006), 141–42.

36. Anders Ferm, December 12, 1972, *Statsrådsberedningen. Tal, offentliga 1972, Volym* 2.4.:44, OPA, ARAB. In 1988, Anders Ferm furnished copies of his speech draft, along with Palme's handwritten revised version, to ARAB. Anders Ferm, *"Betr. Olof Palmes arkiv,"* 11 February 1988. *Tal, offentliga 1972, Volym* 2.4.0: 044, OPA, ARAB.

37. Göran Hägg made a similar comparison of Ferm's torture statement to Palme's. Hägg, *Retorik I Tiden*, 190.

38. Anders Ferm's rough draft of Christmas Bombing speech, *Volym 2.4.0: 044, Tal 1972*, OPA, ARAB. Palme's draft of Christmas Bombing speech, *Volym 2.4.0: 044, Tal 1972*, OPA, ARAB.

39. Erik Ohlsson, *"Bombflyget tar sikte på sjukhusen,"* *Dagens Nyheter*, August 19, 2016.

40. Berggren, *Underbara dagar framför oss*, 407.

41. See J. K. Zawodny, *Death in the Forest: The Story of the Katyn Forest Massacre*. Notre Dame, IN: University of Notre Dame Press, 1962. Paul Rudny, University of Gothenburg, Sweden.

42. Ekéus interview.

43. Eliasson telephone interview; Eliasson, *Ord och Handling*, 49.

44. Eliasson Stockholm interview.

45. Ibid.

46. Ibid.

47. Adam Land, "Haiphong," in *Encyclopedia of the Vietnam War*, ed. Stanley I. Kutler (New York: Macmillan USA, 1996), 216–17.

48. Eliasson Stockholm interview.

49. Ibid.; Eliasson, *Ord och Handling*, 55–56.

50. Ibid.

51. Telegram 626 from Lundberg to Cabinet Stockholm, *"Re Bombningar Bach Mai-Sjukhuset,"* December 24, 1972. *UD HP-Dossierer, Vietnamkriget, Mål: H. Hanoi's politik, 1972–1975, HP 38:30*, RA. "Largest Hospital in Hanoi Reported Damaged in Raid," *New York Times*, December 23, 1972.

52. Telegram 629 from Lundberg of the Swedish Embassy in Hanoi to Cabinet Stockholm, *"Re Bombningarna Bach Mai-Sjukhuset,"* December 27, 1972. *UD HP-Dossierer, Vietnamkriget, Mål: H. Hanoi's politik, 1972–1975*, HP38:30, RA.

53. Telegram from Jean-Christophe Öberg to Cabinet Stockholm, January 10, 1973. *UD HP-Dossierer, Vietnamkriget, Mål:H, 1972–1975, Hanoi's politik*, HP38:30, RA.

54. Ibid.

55. Scott, *Swedish Social Democracy and the Vietnam War*, 33.

56. Telegram from the leaders of Sweden's five political parties to UN Secretary General Kurt Waldheim, December 28, 1972. *Utrikesdepartementet, HP-Dossierer, Vietnamkriget, 1972–1974, HP 38:58*, RA.

57. Schuster, "Swedish Chilliness Toward U.S. is Limited to Vietnam."

58. Östberg, *I takt med tiden*, 306.

59. Hägg, *Retorik i Tiden*, 192; Erik Ohlsson, *"Bombflyget tar sikte på sjukhusen,"* *Dagens Nyheter*, August 19, 2016; Schuster, "Swedish Chilliness Toward U.S. is Limited to Vietnam."

60. Ohlsson, *"Bombflyget tar sikte på sjukhusen."*

61. See my own book, *Nixon, Kissinger, and Allende: U.S. Involvement in the 1973 Coup in Chile* (Lanham, MD: Lexington Books, 2009). The work of my undergraduate professor, the late Dr. Stanley I. Kutler of the University of Wisconsin, is particularly relevant. See Kutler's *The Wars of Watergate: The Last Crisis of Richard Nixon* (New York: W.W. Norton & Company, 1992) and *Abuse of Power: The New Nixon Tapes* (New York: Touchstone, 1998). For an audio sampling of the true Nixon personality, I would recommend nixontapes.org.

62. Falk interview.

63. Asselin, *A Bitter* Peace, 153.

64. Robert Burns, " . . . As Others See Us," *New York* Times, January 8, 1973; Paul Hofmann, "War Raids Incite Anti-U.S. Feelings in Italy," *New York Times*, January 3, 1973.

65. Bernd Greiner, *Universität Hamburg*, email, January 28, 2021.

66. Ibid.

67. Ekéus interview.

68. Telegram 1651 from Hubert de Besche to Cabinet Stockholm, *"För pol och press,"* December 21, 1972. *UD HP-Dossierer, Vietnamkriget, Mål: C. USA's politik, augusti-december 1972,* 1972–1973, HP 38:15, RA.

69. Ibid.

70. Hägg, *Retorik i Tiden*, 189 and 191.

71. Kristina Lindström and Maud Nycander, *Palme* (2012, Stockholm: B-Reel AB, *Sveriges Television*, and *Film i Väst*), documentary.

72. Stephen E. Ambrose, *Nixon: The Education of a Politician 1913–1962* (New York: Simon & Schuster, 1987), 105–16; Schuster, "Swedish Chilliness Toward U.S. is Limited to Vietnam."

73. Berggren, *Underbara dagar framför oss*, 508.

74. Åström, *Ögonblick*, 165; Walter Isaacson, *Kissinger: A Biography* (New York: Simon & Schuster, 1992), 21–32; Schwartz, *Henry Kissinger and American* Power, 16; Richard H. Immerman, "Confessions of an Eisenhower Revisionist: An Agonizing Reappraisal," *Diplomatic History* 14:3, 337.

75. Isaacson, *Kissinger*, 43–56; Schwartz, *Henry Kissinger and American Power,* 21–22.

76. E. Jarecki, *The Trials of Henry Kissinger* (New York: First Run Features, 2002).

77. Robert Dallek, University of California, Los Angeles, email, October 7, 2020.

78. Kreisky, *The Struggle for a Democratic Austria*, 45; B. Vivekanandan, *Global Visions of Olof Palme, Bruno Kreisky, and Willy Brandt: International Peace and Security, Co-operation, and Development* (Cham, Switzerland: Palgrave Macmillan, 2016), 175; Maria Steiner, *Kreisky Archiv*, Vienna, Austria, email, January 27, 2021.

79. Letter from Willy Brandt to Olof Palme and Bruno Kreisky, September 17, 1972; *Brandt Kreisky Palme* (Kristianstad, Sweden: *Tidens Förlag*, 1976), 48.

80. Letter from Olof Palme to Willy Brandt and Bruno Kreisky, May 10, 1973; *Brandt Kreisky Palme*, 74.

81. Memorandum from A. Denis Clift to Henry A. Kissinger, "Swedish Citizen Requests Your Assistance," September 25, 1973; letter from Maj von Dardel Wallenberg to Henry Kissinger, May 4, 1973. Nixon Presidential Materials Staff, NSC Files, Country Files—Europe, Box 707, RN. *See* Ingrid Carlberg, *Det står ett rum här och väntar på dig. . . .* Stockholm: Norstedts, 2012 and Kati Marton, *Wallenberg: Missing Hero* (New York: Arcade: 1995).

82. Åselius, *Vietnamkriget och de svenska diplomaterna*, 463. Article II, Convention on the Prevention and Punishment of the Crime of Genocide. https://www.un.org/en/genocideprevention/documents/atrocity-crimes/Doc.1_Convention%20on%20the%20Prevention%20and%20Punishment%20of%20the%20Crime%20of%20Genocide.pdf;Prados, *Vietnam*, 531.

83. Falkman interview.

84. Ibid.

85. Telegram 235 from the Swedish Embassy in Washington to Cabinet Stockholm, March 17, 1983. Originally written by Hubert de Besche, December 23, 1972. *Utrikesdepartementet, HP-Dossierer, Vietnamkriget, 1972–1974.* HP 38:38 and HP 38:58, RA.

86. Ibid.

87. Berggren, *Underbara dagar framför oss*, 464; Yngve Möller, *Mina Tre Liv: Publicist, Politiker, Diplomat* (Falköping: Gummessons Tryckeri AB, 1983), 299.

88. Schuster, "Swedish Chilliness Toward U.S. is Limited to Vietnam."

89. Telegram 235, March 17, 1983.

90. Pickering interview.

91. Ibid.

92. Ibid.

93. Ibid.

94. Ibid.

95. Eliasson Stockholm interview; Åselius, *Vietnamkriget och de svenska diplomaterna*, 196–97; Kurt Mälarstedt,*"Frostens År,"* *Dagens Nyheter*, June 5, 1988.

96. Eliasson Stockholm interview.

97. Ibid.

98. Falkman, *Ekot från Vietnam*, 164–65.

99. Ibid., 165.

100. Ibid..

101. Telegram 256 from Hubert de Besche to Cabinet Stockholm, December 26, 1972. *Utrikesdepartementet, HP-Dossierer, Vietnamkriget, 1972–1974*, HP 38:58, RA. U. Alexis Johnson to American Embassy in Stockholm, December 25, 1972. Nixon Presidential Materials Staff, NSC Files, Country Files—Europé, Box 707, RN.

102. Memorandum from Magnus Nordbäck, November 4, 1972, submitted by Hubert de Besche in Washington to the Swedish Foreign Ministry, November 7,

1972. *UD HP-Dossierer, Vietnamkriget, Mål:F, Fredssträvanden,* 1972–1973, HP 38:21, RA.

103. Möller, *Mina Tre Liv,* 295.

104. Ibid., 299.

105. Ibid., 301, 305.

106. Falkman, *Ekot från Vietnam,* 165; Möller, *Mina Tre Liv,* 302.

107. Möller, *Mina Tre Liv,* 304.

108. Ibid., 305.

109. Möller, *Mina Tre Liv,* 312.

110. Schuster, "Swedish Chilliness Toward U.S. is Limited to Vietnam."

111. Möller, *Mina Tre Liv,* 312–13.

112. Schuster, "Swedish Chilliness Toward U.S. is Limited to Vietnam."

113. Telegram from Leif Leifland to Kai Falkman, December 28, 1972. *Utrikesdepartementet, HP-Dossierer, Vietnamkriget* 1972–1974, HP 38:58, RA.

114. Schuster, "Swedish Chilliness Toward U.S. is Limited to Vietnam."

115. Falkman interview.

116. Ekéus interview.

117. "Prime Minister Olof Palme's personal message to President Nixon on Christmas Eve 1972," December 30, 1972. Swedish Foreign Ministry Press Office. *Utrikesdepartementet, HP-Dossierer, Vietnamkriget,* 1972–1974, HP 38:58, RA. *"Herr president,"* Volym 2.4.0: 012, *Tal, OPA, ARAB.* Olof Palme, *Att vilja gå vidare* (Stockholm: Tiden, 1974), 272. Text contained in Letter from Hubert de Besche to the President, December 24, 1972. Forwarded by U. Alexis Johnson to Henry Kissinger, December 24, 1972. Nixon Presidential Materials Staff, NSC Files, Country Files— Europe, Box 707, RN; Eliasson, *Ord och Handling,* 53; Åström, *Ögonblick,* 166–67.

118. Eliasson, *Ord och Handling,* 53–54.

119. Ibid.

120. Schuster, "Swedish Chilliness Toward U.S. is Limited to Vietnam."

121. "Palme Would Debate Nixon," *New York Times,* December 30, 1972.

122. Excerpt from Address of Hugh Scott of Pennsylvania, January 12, 1973. Telegram from Leif Leifland to Cabinet Stockholm, January 12, 1973. *UP HP-Dossierer, Vietnamkriget, Mål:C, USA's politik,* August-December 1972, 1972– 1973, HP38:15, RA.

123. Asselin, *A Bitter Peace,* 152.

124. Leif Leifland to the Swedish Foreign Ministry, *"Den amerikanska reaction på rapporter om svensk kritik av Vietnamkrigföringen m.m.: brev och telefonsamtal,"* January 11, 1973. *UD HP-Dossierer, Vietnamkriget, Mål:C, USA's politik,* 1973– 1974, HP38:16, RA. Prados, *Vietnam,* 114, 260.

125. Telegram 179 from the Swedish embassy in Washington to Cabinet Stockholm, January 3, 1973. Letter from J. William Fulbright of Arkansas to Ambassador and Mrs. de Besche, January 3, 1973, forwarded to Cabinet Secretary Sverker Åstrom by the ambassador, January 8, 1973. *UD-HP Dossierer, Vietnamkriget, Mål:C, USA's politik,* August-December 1973, 1972–1973, HP38:15, RA.

126. "Statement by Senator Claiborne Pell," attached to memorandum by Wilhelm Wachtmeister of the Swedish Foreign Ministry, January 11, 1973. *Utrikesdepartementet, HP-Dossierer, Vietnamkriget,* 1972–1964, HP38:58, RA.

127. Ibid.

128. Ibid.

129. Ibid.

130. Excerpt from Address by Frank Church, January 18, 1973, sent by Leif Leifland to Cabinet Stockholm, January 19, 1973. *UD HP-Dossierer, Vietnamkriget, Mål:C, USA's politik,* 1973–197, HP38:16, RA.

131. Eliasson Stockholm interview.

132. Ibid.

133. Ibid.

134. Nichter, *Richard Nixon and* Europe, 104–05, 108–09, 118.

135. Telegram 180 from the Swedish Embassy in Washington to Cabinet Stockholm, January 3, 1973. *UD HP-Dossierer, Vietnamkriget, Mål:C, USA's politik,* August-December 1972, 1972–1973, HP38:15, RA.

136. Ibid.;"Hearings *om europeiska reaktioner på bombningarna av Vietnam,"* Telegram 26 from Hubert de Besche to Cabinet Stockholm, January 4, 1973. *UD HP-Dossierer, Vietnamkriget, Mål:C, USA's politik,* August-December 1972, 1972–1973, HP38:15, RA.

137. Telegram 26 from Hubert de Besche.

138. Coded telegram from Leif Leifland to the Swedish Foreign Ministry, *"Angående de svensk-amerikanska relationerna,"* January 18, 1973. *Utrikesdepartementet, HP-Dossierer, Vietnamkriget,* 1972–1974, HP38:58, RA. Memorandum from Henry A. Kissinger to the President, "Relations with Sweden," January 13, 1973. Presidential Materials Staff, NSC Files, Country Files—Europe, Box 707, RN.

139. Ibid.

140. Ibid.

141. Ibid.

142. Ibid.

143. Eliasson telephone interview.

144. Ibid.

145. Ibid.

146. Ibid.

147. Pickering interview.

148. Ibid.

149. Ibid.

150. Ibid.

151. Ibid.

152. Ibid.

153. Ibid.

154. *"Angående de svensk-amerikanska relationerna,"* January 18, 1973.

155. Eliasson Stockholm interview.

156. Ibid.

157. Ibid.

158. Ibid.

159. Ibid.

160. Pickering interview.

161. Eliasson Stockholm interview.

162. Ibid.

163. Ibid.

164. Ibid.

165. Ibid.

166. Excerpt from the *New York Daily News*, Telegram from Holm to Cabinet Stockholm, January 4, 1973. *UD HP-Dossierer, Vietnamkriget, Mål:C, USA's politik*, August-December 1972, 1972–1973, HP38:15, RA.

167. Ibid.

168. William F. Buckley Jr., "Not Just a Scandinavian Disease," *The Evening Star* and the *Washington Daily News*, January 11, 1973.

169. Robert Burns, " . . . As Others See Us," *New York Times*, January 8, 1973; Allan Barnes, "From the Archives, 1972: Whitlam's strong protest against US bombing in Vietnam," *The Age*, December 20, 2020; James Curran, "Whitlam V Nixon," The United States Studies Centre, August 1, 2012: https://www.ussc.edu.au/analysis/whitlam-v-nixon.

170. Ibid.

171. "Behind the Rift with Sweden," *Washington Post*, January 12, 1973.

172. Ibid.

173. Ibid.

174. Letter from Gardner Macartney to the Swedish embassy in Washington, postmarked February 20, 1973. Enclosed in package of letters from the Swedish consulate in Chicago to the Swedish embassy, February 27, 1973. *UD HP-Dossierer, Vietnamkriget, Mål:C, USA's politik, 1973–1974, HP38:16, RA.

175. Ibid.

176. Ibid.

177. Excerpts from *The Evening Star* and the *Washington Daily* News, January 14, 1973, in Telegram 102 from the Swedish Embassy in Washington to Cabinet Stockholm, January 15, 1973. *UD HP-Dossierer, Mål:C, 1972–1973, Vietnamkriget, USA's politik*, August-December 1972, HP38:15, RA.

178. Letter from Arny Reichler to Olof Palme, January 26, 1973. Enclosed in package of letters from the Swedish consulate in Chicago to the Swedish embassy, February 27, 1973.

179. Letter from Albert Epstein to the Swedish ambassador, February 6 1973; Ibid.

180. Palme's telegram was in French. Telegram from Pham Van Dong to Olof Palme, December 25, 1972. OPA, *Brevsamling, Volym* 3.2/82, ARAB, Courtesy of Joakim Palme.

181. Coded Telegram 26 from Jean-Christophe Öberg for Olof Palme, January 19, 1973. *UD HP-Dossierer, Vietnamkriget, Mål:H, Hanoi's politik, 1972–1975*, HP38:30, RA.

182. Falkman interview.

183. Coded Telegram 26 from Jean-Christophe Öberg for Olof Palme, January 19, 1973. *UD HP-Dossierer, Vietnamkriget, Mål:H, Hanoi's politik,* 1972–1975, HP38:30, RA. Nichter, *Richard Nixon and* Europe, 99.

184. Coded Telegram 26 from Jean-Christophe Öberg for Olof Palme, January 19, 1973. *UD HP-Dossierer, Vietnamkriget, Mål:H, Hanoi's politik,* 1972–1975, HP38:30, RA.

Chapter 4

Sweden and the American Prisoners of War in North Vietnam

During Palme's December 1970 meeting with the North Vietnamese chargé d'affaires, another important subject came up. The prime minister gave his thanks for the pilot list, which he was confident had "had a very positive impact on opinion in the U.S.A."[1]

SUPPORTING THE ANTIWAR MOVEMENT

Palme was referring to a list of confirmed American prisoners of war (POW) in North Vietnam. In spite of his opposition to the American war in Vietnam, the prime minister felt great compassion for its servicemen who were taken prisoner. After his meeting with the US Senate Foreign Relations Committee in Washington the previous June, Palme had more fully realized that alleviating the suffering of missing American servicemen and their families could help turn the American people more firmly against the war. He had said as much to the Vietnamese ambassador to Moscow during his visit to the Soviet capital shortly afterward. "From the discussions I got a strong impression of the importance to public opinion in your country of the issue of missing American servicemen," Palme wrote Fulbright afterward.[2]

Senator Fulbright concurred with Palme's reasoning:

I am also very pleased that you are pursuing the matter of American prisoners in Vietnam, and I hope that the North Vietnamese will respond. I am sure it is extremely difficult for them to recognize that taking some action for the relief of the prisoners' hardships could be a most powerful influence upon the public opinion of the people of this country. . . . It may be too much to expect that a small country, suffering as it has for so long, could bring itself to show a concern for the humanitarian considerations, but these very difficulties would make it all the more dramatic and effective.[3]

Fulbright had good reason to seek Palme's help. The senator had already written to the late President Ho Chi Minh in June of 1969, and then to Prime Minister Pham Van Dong in June of 1970, in order to request an official list of American prisoners. Ho had rejected Fulbright's request, insisting that only a final settlement of the war would straighten out the POW matter. Pham Van Dong, for his part, had failed to respond at all.[4]

Moreover, POW wives had lobbied the senator. Lieutenant Colonel Bobby Vinson of the US Air Force had been missing in action since April 1968. His wife, Joan, was now the national coordinator for the National League of Families of American Prisoners and Missing in Southeast Asia, and knew in advance of Fulbright's planned meeting with the prime minister. Hoyt Purvis, the senator's press secretary and special assistant, conveyed a message from Mrs. Vinson: "She has made a special plea that when you see Prime Minister Palme Thursday you make brief mention of his possible help in obtaining information on American prisoners in North Vietnam."[5]

Besides helping to turn the American public against the war, what other reasons did Palme have to try to assist the prisoners and their families?

STRENGTHENING SWEDISH-AMERICAN RELATIONS

According to Ekéus, the prime was well-disposed toward the United States: "He was, in a sense, more pro-American than most Swedish politicians . . . he was not an enemy of the United States at all. I think he understood it better than most people, understood and respected . . . its history and so on."[6]

Eliasson, first secretary at the Swedish embassy in Washington, also acknowledged that "this was a way, also, of creating confidence-building vis-à-vis the State Department and the U.S. government."[7]

TRADITIONAL SWEDISH HUMANITARIANISM

Ekéus explains that the prime minister had humanitarian motives, as well: "I think it was far from cynical. On the contrary, I think it was a strongly emotional engagement towards helping.[8]

Indeed, helpfulness was a key component of the Swedish diplomatic tradition. The late UN secretary general Dag Hammarskjöld, as Ekéus noted, had set a powerful example for Palme. Back in 1955, Hammarskjöld had traveled to Beijing to secretly negotiate the release of fifteen American prisoners of war. The Chinese had captured the Americans before the active fighting of the Korean War had concluded in 1953, but their continued imprisonment violated the armistice. Hammarskjöld faced a difficult task, for China did not even respect the authority of the United Nations. After all, Taiwan held the seat in the UN that rightly belonged to Beijing. To make matters worse, the Chinese had already found eleven of the prisoners guilty of espionage. Beijing had no incentive to respect the UN resolution calling for their release.

In a sense, Hammarskjöld approached Chinese Foreign Minister Chou En-lai as a Swedish diplomat rather as head of the United Nations. Beijing had reason to trust Stockholm in any case, for Sweden had voted against the 1951 UN resolution classifying China as an aggressor in the Korean War. Before his departure for China, Hammarskjöld saw the Chinese ambassador in Stockholm to plan his visit. Once in Beijing, the Swedish embassy served as the secretary general's lodgings. After his departure from China, Hammarskjöld carried negotiations via the Swedish embassy in Beijing, and with the additional Swedish diplomats posted elsewhere. Again, the secretary general met with the Chinese ambassador in Stockholm. When China decided to free four of the prisoners, Foreign Minister Chou En-lai informed Hammarskjöld through the Swedish ambassador to Peking. Finally, in August 1955, Chou En-lai notified the Swedish ambassador that the remaining eleven prisoners of war would also be released. Peking had taken this action "in order to maintain friendship with Dag Hammarskjöld and has no connection with the UN resolution."[9]

In the aftermath of the Korean War, Sweden had been in the ideal position to help. The Chinese had seen less incentive in keeping their American prisoners. As long as the war went on in Vietnam, however, the Swedes could now only do the best they could. The Foreign Ministry's Falkman said that "we wanted to play a role there, and that is a role that was accepted by both parties. And as we were the only Western power that had relations with the North Vietnamese, then we thought let's give them some help."[10] Any considerations of realpolitik were not involved: "We had a humanitarian tradition to aid the parties in military conflicts. Our mediation in this case, therefore, was not politically motivated but only a wish to help people in need."[11]

Of course, foreign policy is complex and rarely monocausal. Nevertheless, opposition to the war would emerge as the most significant factor in Swedish POW policy.

No matter the reasons for the Swedish assistance, that assistance was sorely needed. Not only did the North Vietnamese refuse to disclose information about most of the prisoners in their custody, but their publicly expressed attitudes also created concern. Nguyen Tho Chan, the North Vietnamese ambassador to Moscow, and now Stockholm, commented to the Swedish newspaper *Dagens Nyheter*:

> The Geneva Convention's rules for the treatment of prisoners-of-war do not in any way apply to the American pilots who have been shot down. They have

committed countless crimes against Vietnam's people. They have indiscriminately bombed, shelled, and spread poisonous chemicals over churches, pago-
das, schools, hospitals, and market places—areas that they very well knew were
populated by civilians.[12]

Nguyen Tho Chan referred to the prisoners of war as "air pirates."[13]

In 1957, North Vietnam had signed the Geneva Convention (III) relative
to the treatment of prisoners of war, of August 12, 1949. Hanoi's signature
to the Third Geneva Convention, which was one of the four pertaining to
International Humanitarian Law in warfare, came with a reservation, however: "The Democratic Republic of Vietnam declares that prisoners of war
prosecuted and convicted for war crimes or for crimes against humanity, in
accordance with principles laid down by the Nuremberg Court of Justice,
shall not benefit from the present Convention, as specified in Article 85."[14]

As North Vietnam had not even put the American prisoners on trial, its
position was highly questionable.[15] Even if the POWs had gone through
some sort of judicial procedure, the North Vietnamese position would have
remained questionable, and disturbing. Articles 70 and 71 of the Third
Geneva Convention required the detaining power to keep the next of kin
informed about the prisoners, and in epistolary contact with them.[16] As the
North Vietnamese scoffed at this requirement, most families knew absolutely
nothing. Naturally, the families of missing servicemen would have reason
for profound worry, even if these men were still alive. Article 130 of the
Third Geneva Convention, after all, forbids "torture or inhuman treatment."[17]
Article 17, more specifically, states that "no physical or mental torture, nor
any form of coercion, may be inflicted on prisoners of war to secure from
them information of any kind whatsoever."[18]

MRS. SINGLETON

Approximately sixty relatives of servicemen missing in action had reached
out to Palme through the mail, by telephone, or in person by June of 1970.[19]
One wife who traveled to Stockholm to meet Palme was Barbara J. Singleton.
A resident of Dallas, Texas, she was the wife of Air Force Lieutenant Jerry
Allen Singleton. During a rescue mission, his helicopter had been shot down
on November 6, 1965.[20] Raising two children and expecting a third at the time
of her husband's disappearance, Mrs. Singleton would wait five years to learn
her husband's fate.[21]

In July 1966, the US military did revise his status from missing in action
to prisoner of war. Mrs. Singleton received no explanation when she was
informed of the alteration in January 1967, however. She had no evidence

that Lieutenant Singleton was even still alive. Dave L. Garrett, who wrote a well-researched master's thesis on Mrs. Singleton, thought that he had determined the source of information: "Bonnie found out years after the war from a former roommate and classmate of Jerry's, General Mike Butchko, that he had personally seen a satellite photograph of Jerry standing in the doorway of a North Vietnamese prison camp."[22]

Historian Timothy Castle, a retired air force officer, questioned his fellow airman's account. "I don't see that Major General Butchko played any role in POW-MIA work, nor was he involved in intelligence oversight—that I am aware of," stated Castle, also a veteran of the CIA's Center for the Study of Intelligence.[23]

Castle, with his past experience in POW/MIA investigations, could not determine how Butchko could have obtained this information. "On the pure question of technology," Castle continued, "during that period I don't believe satellites provided that degree of resolution."[24]

For purposes of surveillance, the options to satellites were airplanes and drones.[25] "The expert photo interpreters often make judgements using mensuration to determine size, height, etc., of humans and inanimate objects," even today. "But, again, the ability to actually see a face—I think it highly unlikely," concluded Castle about the technical capabilities of the Vietnam War era.[26] If the US military had relied solely on satellite photographs, it could have only guessed that Lieutenant Singleton was a prisoner.

Desperate for answers in September 1969, Mrs. Singleton journeyed to France under the joint sponsorship of the Veterans of Foreign Wars and WFAA, a Dallas television station. WFAA newsman Murphy Martin served as an escort. Along with other wives seeking information, Mrs. Singleton confronted Xuan Thuy, the North Vietnamese negotiator at the Paris Peace Talks.[27] Xuan Thuy and his delegation extended little kindness to the women during their meeting. To the women's faces, the officials depicted the missing airmen as air pirates and war criminals. Her husband was a helicopter rescue pilot, Mrs. Singleton countered. After displaying photographs of bomb damage in North Vietnam, the delegation said they had no information about the airmen, but would look into the matter. If they wished to see their husbands again, the delegation advised, they should join the peace movement.[28]

Hearing nothing from the North Vietnamese, Mrs. Singleton and Mrs. Paula Hartness returned to Paris in December. Air Force Major Greg Hartness had disappeared on November 26, 1968. Again, Martin traveled with them, but this time, the Texas businessman H. Ross Perot underwrote the trip, as he did for fifty-six other wives and ninety-four children. The North Vietnamese delegation gave the women the runaround. Claiming the airmen were war pirates and criminals, the delegation denied that they were entitled to the protections of international law. This second meeting included the implication that the women would have to turn against the war in order to obtain information about their husbands.[29] The women wondered what they could possibly tell their children. They were told: "Your children are in the United States and have it good; there are children in Vietnam who are suffering."[30]

The last resort for these women was the prime minister of Sweden. Telegraphing Palme from Paris, they made the short hop to Stockholm before even receiving an answer. "Sweden, as a neutral state, should have a good chance to influence Hanoi," Mrs. Singleton said at a press conference held at Arlanda Airport. "In the name of humanity, we hope, and with us many at home in the United States, for a Swedish request to at least release the names of the pilots who sit in prison in North Vietnam."[31]

The prime minister duly received Martin and the wives. Although Palme sympathetically described the North Vietnamese as "underdogs fighting against the mightiest nation in the world," he had sympathy for his visitors too.[32] Understanding the friendly relationship between Stockholm and Hanoi, the women requested that the prime minister obtain a list of prisoners. Palme agreed to try.[33] Unlike the North Vietnamese, the Swedish prime minister's offer of assistance came with no strings attached.

In a photograph taken of the meeting, Palme appears stiff and uncomfortable. His discomfort may have been due to worry that he could not help Mrs. Singleton and Mrs. Hartness. Unfortunately, it turned out that no one could help Mrs. Hartness. In 2005, the remains of Colonel Hartness were located in Laos.[34]

Palme's visible discomfort may also have been due to his possible distaste for Murphy Martin, which I shall discuss later.

Obviously, most relatives of prisoners of war could not meet Palme in Stockholm. Therefore, they wrote to him. By the end of 1970, the Swedish government had received approximately five thousand letters from these relatives and other concerned Americans.[35]

MRS. TERRELL

The wife of an air force navigator, Major Irby D. Terrell Jr., had faith in the prime minister's capacity for empathy. Terrell's plane had been lost in January of 1968. That August, the US Defense Department inexplicably altered his status from missing in action to prisoner of war.[36] Still knowing nothing, Greta P. Terrell of Anniston, Alabama, wrote to Palme: "Could you, Mr. Palme, imagine what it would be like to not know if your wife is living or dead? Can you imagine what it would be like to not hear from her, or a beloved child, for years?"[37] Mrs. Terrell beseeched Palme, as the leader of a neutral nation, for his help. "That is why I ask you to search your conscience and decide if, altho [*sic*] you oppose America's role in this war, you also approve of the treatment of these prisoners," the anxious wife continued. "If you are an honest and good man, I am certain that you will decide that their fate and treatment is important."[38]

MRS. HUGHES

Dorothy Hughes of Santa Fe, New Mexico, was ignorant of the fate of her husband, an air force officer. Lieutenant Colonel James Lindberg Hughes had been missing since 1967. Desperate for word by December of 1969, she traveled all the way to Laos to pay a call at the North Vietnamese embassy. Visiting North Vietnam to provide badly needed medication to her husband proved impossible.[39] The following month, Mrs. Hughes forwarded to Palme a copy of a telegram she had sent to Hanoi: "Your officials in Vientiane told me my wounded husband James Lindberg Hughes was a prisoner and well in Hanoi but I still have not heard from him in nearly two years why."[40]

MRS. HALYBURTON

Another anxious wife writing Palme was Marty Halyburton of Decatur, Georgia. On October 17, 1965, Navy Lieutenant (j.g.) Porter Alexander Halyburton had been a radar intercept officer in the backseat of a F-4 fighter. Suddenly, the F-4 was struck. Approximately twelve hours after the shoot-down, Mrs. Halyburton received word. "They said they would make a determination within twenty-four hours of his status," she recalled. "And . . . it was determined within twenty-four hours that he had been killed in action."[41]

She had no reason to believe otherwise. Thirty-five planes had participated in the same strike: "I had telephone calls from his squadron commander and other people who had been on the flight, who witnessed a plane crash into a mountain and explode, and no parachute sighted, or any radio contact."[42]

Of course, Mrs. Halyburton had no way of knowing, but Lieutenant Halyburton had managed to save himself before the plane crashed into the mountain. "The pilot was killed, and I really had no choice but to eject," he explained later. "And so, I did. And we were very low-level; nobody saw my parachute. My radios did not work."[43]

Shortly afterward, Mrs. Halyburton attended a memorial service for her husband.[44]

In February of 1967, Washington upgraded Lieutenant Halyburton's status to POW. Like the wife of Lieutenant Singleton, Mrs. Halyburton received no explanation.

Unbeknownst to her, Lieutenant Halyburton had a cellmate who was permitted to write letters. "When I found out I was dead about the time Marty found out I was alive, we used the next letter that [fellow Navy POW] Dick Ratzlaff wrote home, and this is in 1967," Halyburton remembered. "It contained several references to me that would have identified the fact that I was there. Unfortunately, that letter was never given to the government, and so those messages were not delivered."[45]

One message that had reached the government came from Commander James Bond Stockdale, a navy flier, in January of 1967. Written on carbon paper was a list of more than forty prisoners of war, including Lieutenant Halyburton. Commander Stockdale had performed an invaluable service for his country, but his list was not an absolutely reliable source at the time. Kept in solitary confinement, his primary mode of communication with his fellow prisoners was a system of taps on the walls, in addition to an occasional whisper.[46]

This list was classified and kept secret from the wives, whose only news was the mysterious change in their husbands' status.[47] Therefore, Mrs. Halyburton really had no way of knowing that Lieutenant Halyburton was, in fact, alive. When naval officials showed Mrs. Halyburton photographs of the 1966 forced march of POWs in Hanoi, she repeatedly scanned the photographs but could not find her husband.[48]

Uncertain what to believe, Mrs. Halyburton decided to approach the prime minister of Sweden. She had become involved with the National League of Families of American Prisoners and Missing in Southeast Asia by this time. The organization was aware of "certain countries that had a diplomatic relationship with North Vietnam, and also relations with our countries."[49]

Furthermore, Mrs. Halyburton "saw Sweden as having more of a neutral position, and I felt it was important that there be countries who could be in a position to mediate between those countries who were obviously at war with each other."[50]

In October of 1969, Mrs. Halyburton finally wrote to the prime minister:

Dear Premier Palme: My husband Porter Halyburton has been a prisoner of war in Vietnam for four years. Although the U.S. government believes that he is definitely a prisoner I have had no letters from him or seen his picture in any picture or film release from Hanoi. I am asking for your support on behalf of American prisoners and their families in seeking from Hanoi a list of prisoners and an exchange of mail.[51]

In the fall of 1969, Foreign Minister Nilsson approached the North Vietnamese ambassador to the Soviet Union, Nguyen Tho Chan. Palme's old marching partner from 1968 was a particularly appropriate courier because he was also Hanoi's accredited diplomat in Stockholm as well as Moscow. Nilsson respectfully requested that Hanoi "make a gesture of generosity," namely the identification of the prisoners of war.[52]

Kissinger was skeptical that such a gesture of generosity could help hasten the end of the war, as the Swedish foreign minister believed. The new national security advisor cautioned the president:

> Unfortunately, although we of course might welcome anything which might be done to improve the situation of our POWs, Nilsson missed the mark when he made this particular suggestion. The purpose of our diplomatic efforts is above all to bring pressure to bear to get serious talks underway in Paris, and the effect of Nilsson's intercession may even be to cause Hanoi to respond on the POW issue in order to deflect criticism away from the hard line in the talks. It might be in order, therefore, to go back to the Swedes and point out that the best way to bring peace in Vietnam (and at the same time solve the POW issue) is through movement in the talks, and that they should take the excellent opportunity to make this basic point with the North Vietnamese.[53]

Nixon concurred with Kissinger.[54] For both men, gaining advantage in the war took immediate priority over the alleviation of the suffering of the POW community.

GOOD NEWS

On March 3, 1970, Nguyen Tho Chan handed a list to Swedish ambassador Gunnar Jarring in Moscow. The North Vietnamese diplomat described it as "proof of how much the Vietnamese people appreciate the warm friendship which has been shown by the Swedish people and government."[55]

On March 3, 1970, the Swedish government could now formally confirm that fourteen men were prisoners.[56] This intelligence was remarkable enough for Kissinger to include in the President's Daily Brief.[57]

In November of 1969, David Dellinger and Rennie Davis of the National Mobilization Committee to End the War in Vietnam had confirmed four of the POWs that later appeared on the first Swedish list.[58] Ethel Taylor, Madeline Duckles, and Cora Weiss, who all belonged to the American antinuclear group Women Strike for Peace, had already identified five of them for the first time in December of that year.[59] Five of the names on Sweden's list, however, had never been confirmed by a non-Vietnamese source: Lieutenant

Porter Alexander Halyburton USN; Major Irby Terrell Jr. USAF, Captain Robert Bruce Hinckley USAF, Lieutenant Colonel James Lindberg Hughes USAF, and Lieutenant Jerry Allen Singleton USAF.[60]

Soon afterward, Mrs. Halyburton received a telephone call from her navy contact, who informed her that her husband's name was on the Swedish list.[61] A telegram from Stockholm then arrived on March 6: "I wish to inform you that the Government of the Democratic Republic of Vietnam has confirmed that your husband Porter Halyburton is in prison in North Vietnam . . . .Letter follows from Ministry for Foreign Affairs . . . Olof Palme Prime Minister of Sweden."[62]

Indeed, a letter to Mrs. Halyburton from the Foreign Ministry did follow.[63] As for Mrs. Singleton, her visit to Stockholm had not come in vain, for she also received a telegram from Palme and a letter from the Foreign Ministry.[64] Before the media, Mrs. Singleton posed with a photograph of her husband and Palme's telegram.[65]

In an interview with *Dagens Nyheter*, Mrs. Singleton said, "I am deeply thankful to Prime Minister Palme for his efforts." Referring to her visit with Palme four months before, she continued: "The prime minister expressed his deep and serious sympathy and promised me to see what Sweden could do."[66]

Mrs. Singleton said afterward, "I am so happy. I had hoped the whole time, but this is the first time that I have real certainty."[67]

At about the same time, Mrs. Terrell received direct confirmation from the Swedish Foreign Ministry that "Irby David Terrell, Jr . . . is at present in a prison in the Democratic Republic of North Vietnam."[68]

The women were grateful for the information. "That was a defining moment and so very important, because NVN would now have to account for him," Mrs. Halyburton remembered. "My first letter from Porter came after Olof Palme's announcement and I felt Sweden was responsible for that breakthrough and perhaps many others."[69]

Through her navy contact, the Swedish government had apprised Mrs. Halyburton that a letter from her husband would arrive shortly, and it did it, on May 10.[70]

With Cora Weiss of Women Strike for Peace, the National Mobilization Committee's David Dellinger had established the Committee of Liaison with Families of Servicemen Detained in Vietnam in January of 1970. The Committee of Liaison took over the task of identifying POWs and arranging the exchange of the mail with the families, which Women Strike for Peace had first done in late 1969.[71] Although the Committee of Liaison had been in operation for some time, Mrs. Singleton would not receive any mail from her husband until late April of 1970. His missives, which had been composed in December 1969, made it obvious that he had not seen any of his wife's letters.[72] It is likely that Stockholm's interest in Singleton's case ensured the delivery of his first letter.

Even though Mrs. Hughes had first received confirmation directly from the North Vietnamese one excruciatingly long year before, she acknowledged Palme's confirmation was the first secured by a foreign government. "He must be a wonderful humanitarian to transmit information of this nature directly to the wives," Mrs. Hughes publicly commented.[73]

Just months before the surviving POWs would finally come home, Mrs. Hughes assured Palme that "you have used your good offices to obtain information which has resulted in happiness for many, myself included."[74]

Another relieved wife was Marie Hinckley of Fort Walton Beach, Florida.

"I am writing in appreciation for your efforts in securing information about my husband, Captain Robert Bruce Hinckley," Mrs. Hinckley wrote, "your telegram was the first official confirmation from Hanoi that my husband is held prisoner. My husband is of three-fourths Swedish descent and still has relatives in Sweden. It will be a pleasure to inform my husband, upon his release, that you, specifically, and your country were the first to aid us in the humanitarian effort."[75]

MRS. STOCKDALE

During Palme's visit to the United States in June of 1970, he saw a woman who was making a name for herself. Sybil Stockdale was the wife of Commander Stockdale. After Commander Stockdale had been shot down in September of 1965, Mrs. Stockdale only learned that he was still alive when she received two letters from him the following April. Over time, his generous four-page letters turned into brief messages. Concerned that either poor health or mistreatment prevented her husband from writing longer letters, Mrs. Stockdale looked for help.[76] She wrote to Palme in September of 1969. On March 6, 1970, the prime minister telegraphed the news to Mrs. Stockdale that her husband was still alive: "I am happy to be able to forward this positive message in a matter that must have caused you much anxiety."[77] The Swedish telegram had arrived after antiwar activists David Dellinger and Rennie Davis had first officially confirmed Stockdale's imprisonment in November of 1969.[78] Commander Stockdale would not be freed until the American withdrawal from Vietnam in 1973. Later, in 1992, the retired Vice Admiral Stockdale would run for vice president under independent presidential candidate Ross Perot, a man who had also played a role in the POW matter.[79] For now, freedom and political prominence would have to wait for the naval officer.

His wife was the more prominent Stockdale at the moment. Mrs. Stockdale, cofounder of the National League of Families of American Prisoners and Missing in Southeast Asia, had served as the first national coordinator, and was now chairman of the organization's board. Mrs. Halyburton, who served on the league's board of directors and as coordinator for the southeastern states, thought the world of Mrs. Stockdale. "She was phenomenal," Mrs. Halyburton said. "She had quite a vision. She worked diligently and very hard to include all of the family members, whether it was wives or parents, brothers and sisters. And she worked very hard to be nonpolitical."[80]

Mrs. Stockdale herself would publicly state in 1972: "I 100 percent completely endorse what President Nixon has done and is doing, and he has my vote."[81]

Nevertheless, she insisted that her organization was nonpartisan. In fact, Mrs. Stockdale did express her irritation with the Nixon administration from time to time. The initial slowness of Nixon and Kissinger to meet with her organization annoyed her. In January of 1970, Mrs. Stockdale even scolded the president's armed forces aide, James D. Hughes. She warned him that "just because publicly we, the wives and families, still say that we think our government is doing everything possible to help our men, we do NOT really believe this is the case."[82]

She had a mind of her own. In spite of her personal backing of the president, she was even more hawkish than him. If Hanoi would not free the prisoners and provide information about all those missing in action, Mrs. Stockdale proposed a last resort: "I would land the U.S. Marines in North Vietnam and claim it as U.S. territory."[83]

Nevertheless, Mrs. Stockdale still supported the president and his war. The Swedes doubted the political objectivity of her work. From Washington, the Swedish ambassador recommended that Palme meet her, but warned Stockholm, "Mrs. Stockdale was a likely representative for the hawkish thinkers who dominate POW groups here. One who harbors mistrust for the activity of the peace groups, and clearly, somewhat surprisingly, for the Swedish campaign. Nevertheless, Mrs. Stockdale, who is an intense person, is the foremost spokesman for the pilots' wives."[84]

Palme reached the American capital in June 1970 and received her as part of a delegation from her organization. The minutes indicate that Mrs. Stockdale immediately got down to business, peppering the prime minister with many questions. She wanted more information from the North Vietnamese about the prisoners. As far as her organization was concerned, the available information proved insufficient. A more complete prisoner list was needed. Mrs. Stockdale pressed Palme: "Couldn't one use the Swedish aid to North Vietnam to persuade Hanoi to change its attitude?"[85]

Palme did not favor Mrs. Stockdale's suggestion but chose his words with care: "Any connection between aid to Vietnam and efforts on the prisoner issue only existed in the respect that both aim to help people in need."[86]

The Swedish denial of aid to Vietnam would have punished the suffering Vietnamese masses for the crimes of the North Vietnamese authorities.

Mrs. Stockdale's colleague, Bernard L. Talley, was the secretary treasurer for the National League. Talley, whose son was missing in action, was concerned about the Third Geneva Convention.[87] He asked Palme for both the Swedish and the North Vietnamese interpretations of the Geneva Convention relative to the Treatment of Prisoners of War.

In his answer to Talley, Palme approached the matter of international law with cautious neutrality. "The prime minister described Hanoi's argumentation and pointed out that the cause would be hurt if one entered into a legal dispute with Hanoi over the interpretation of the Geneva Convention," the minutes recorded. "From the Swedish side, one wanted to continue treating the prisoner issue from a purely humanitarian point of view."[88] In other words, shaking one's finger at the North Vietnamese would accomplish nothing.

Within the walls of the Foreign Ministry, a firmer opinion was expressed. Esbjörn Rosenblad of the Ministry's Negotiations Group compared the Korean War to the Vietnam War: "Then as now, the discussion concerns the American pilots' status as prisoners of war. Then as now, the war criminal concept is ventilated. And in both cases, the parties are bound by the 1949 Prisoner of War Convention."[89]

Rosenblad was a specialist in international law, and there is every reason to believe that Palme, legally trained himself, would have privately agreed with him.

Professor Falk, an antiwar activist who had his own expertise in international law, believed that the Swedish prime minister took the correct public position. "I mean whatever approach he took on that question I think is understandable because it is a gray area," Falk said, "and how you interpret the relationship between the Geneva Conventions and the kind of conflict that existed there, of course."[90] He also pointed out that since the terrorist attacks of September 11, 2001, the United States has refused to observe the Geneva Conventions in its treatment of captured insurgents.[91]

Falk agreed that Palme rightly refrained from condemning the North Vietnamese for suspected mistreatment of prisoners. "Yes," the international jurist reflected, "and undoubtedly that was a factor that he would be more effective in helping the prisoners if he didn't try to moralize or legalize their obligation to behave other than what they were behaving."[92]

During Palme's conference with the POW families, Mrs. Stockdale raised another question that would come to irritate Stockholm profoundly: the possible internment of the POWs in Sweden. The prime minister had a ready answer: "On the matter of internment of prisoners of war in a third country, Palme said that such a thing had probably never occurred. Otherwise, he did not want to offer any comments on this. Swedish attention was primarily directed at the possibility of obtaining information about the prisoners in North Vietnam."[93]

As first secretary of the Swedish embassy, Eliasson had accompanied Palme to the meeting, and Mrs. Stockdale made a strong impression on the young diplomat. "A tough lady. Very determined. Very firm," Eliasson observed. "No, I just remember that she was very tough. I think Palme had to remind them that we were meeting to try to help them get the information."[94]

The first secretary suspected the group had fallen under the influence of people ill-disposed toward Palme. When asked if he had liked Mrs. Stockdale, Eliasson replied, "Some people don't understand the importance of the expression, 'You never have a second chance to make a first impression.' If you want people to do something for you, you got to make sure you have a soft start, so that you can make people relax."[95]

Nevertheless, Eliasson regarded Mrs. Stockdale's position with empathy. "I don't complain," he added. "She had her husband sitting in a prison, probably tortured also. So, understandable."[96]

On the whole, Eliasson was pleased with the meeting. Presumably, so was Palme. "It wasn't from the beginning very friendly," Eliasson said, "but in the end, I think it turned out very friendly because they realized that we were going to be the channel to the North Vietnamese."[97]

Indeed, Mrs. Stockdale herself felt better after the meeting, for Palme's obvious intentions gave her "new hope."[98]

The Swedes were determined to identify the Americans who were held prisoner by Hanoi. By the meeting's conclusion, Mrs. Stockdale and her group could recognize that determination. "They were pretty impressed by our desire to get that information," Eliasson said. "We had also got reports about the mistreatment of American prisoners."[99]

In later years, Eliasson could look back with pride on his government's efforts to help the POW families: "We got the information."[100]

Mrs. Stockdale later mailed Palme a list of prisoners of war and missing servicemen, the same list that had been provided by the State Department upon his departure from Washington. "It was very gratifying to meet with you while you were here," Mrs. Stockdale wrote the prime minister, "and we hope that you will soon have something substantive to report to us."[101]

Eventually representing 1,600 families, the National League would develop a friendly relationship with Nixon and his political backers, even gaining access to the Republican National Committee's lists of supporters for fundraising purposes.[102] Courtesy of the White House, the National League also had the benefit of a WATS (Wide-Area Telephone Service) line for long-distance calls.[103]

POLITICAL VIEWS OF THE POW COMMUNITY

Of course, Nixon had admirers among the POW community. Air Force First Lieutenant John L. Borling was captured in 1966 and remained a prisoner for nearly seven years. Decades later, General Borling said that his release came "in accordance with the Peace Accords that were generated over the years, but came to fruition after an operation called Linebacker II that involved heavy bombing of downtown Hanoi and other principal areas."[104] Later, when Nixon resigned, Borling's little girl asked, "Why are they treating him so badly? He brought my daddy home."[105] In retrospect, Borling saw no reason to dispute his daughter's comment:

And I think, overridingly, the personal component of "here was the guy who brought us home," is determinant in my estimation of his value as a president. . . . I think he wished he could have done more and sooner, but at the end of the day, he gave us an opportunity to walk out of there with our heads high, and gave recognition not only to us, but to the whole veteran community, I think, that served in Vietnam, and they number in the millions. So, Richard Nixon has a standing, in my view, and standing I think, not to speak for the group, but would suggest that the vast majority hold him and his memory in high regard.[106]

Commander Halyburton also had high regard for Nixon:

> I think he did everything that he thought he could. I know he was very criticized for sending troops into Cambodia, but Cambodia was being used as a staging unit for the North Vietnamese army, and granting an enemy sanctuary means you can never defeat them. . . . And he was trying to get out with some kind of sense of honor, I guess, rather than just completely withdrawing with no strings attached, like McGovern wanted to do. Anyway, we were all very grateful to President Nixon. . . . You know the bombing of Hanoi in '72 was over the issue of return of POWs and some other issues. By doing that, he forced the Vietnamese to agree to that. And the agreement contained very specific provisions about our release. Had he not done that, who knows what would have been.[107]

When it came to Nixon's Swedish counterpart, however, views of the POW community were mixed. For most of his imprisonment, Borling was denied access to the international media, and even to letters from his wife. He did not even learn of the 1969 moon landing until one year had passed. Borling could remember Olof Palme: "I seem to recall that he was outspoken against it. Help me if I'm incorrect there, that the Swedish government position was basically anti-American at that point, at least my sense was, in a moderated Swedish sense. Reserve, if you will. And I certainly don't harbor any ill-will against the Swedes."[108]

He repeated: "I harbor no ill-will against the Swedes. I harbor no ill-will against anyone, frankly, including the Vietnamese. I've been back to Vietnam."[109] Even in captivity, Borling had had warm feelings for Sweden: "I always had a fantasy that I would somehow escape, jump in the Red River and float down to Haiphong and climb aboard a Swedish freighter. And two months later, I'd be in Stockholm. . . . But that was just a dream."[110]

Looking back, Halyburton could not recall "hearing a great deal about Sweden and Olof Palme. I'm sure that we got every piece of sort-of antiwar propaganda. Anything that was bad for the United States, we got it."[111]

He did not regard critics of the American military effort with any fondness: "And we viewed the antiwar movement as hurting us, prolonging the war, and extending our captivity. And so, things were just sort of black-and-white in that way. If you were antiwar, then you were hurting us. You were hurting our effort to win the war. You were delaying our return, all of that."[112]

Mrs. Halyburton, like her husband, did not remember Palme's antiwar activism, although she warmly recollected the help the late prime minister had provided.[113]

Of course, POW relatives did not blindly support Nixon then, or later. During the war, Mrs. Halyburton shared her husband's regard for the president, believing that McGovern would abandon the POWs in Vietnam. "Well, back then, particularly as the election approached . . . McGovern said he was going to pull out of Vietnam with no strings attached," she recalled, "and so, I felt like Nixon was not going to pull out of Vietnam until the prisoner issue had been solved, and the prisoners came home. So, I was a supporter, a firm supporter of Nixon."[114]

In the years since the war, the revelation that Nixon has sabotaged the 1968 Paris peace talks disturbed Mrs. Halyburton. "And of course, that's disappointing, and I'm disillusioned over hearing that, but a long time has passed," she concluded. "And I'm still grateful to him for bringing my husband home."[115]

Some members of the POW community dissented from White House policy, leaving the National League of Families to form an entirely group. POW/MIA Families for Immediate Release favored a total American pullout from Indochina. An organization of only 350 members, this upstart lobby still managed to raise its voice.[116] Horrified by the intensification of the bombing of North Vietnam in the spring of 1972, POW/MIA Families for Immediate Release issued a press release:

President Nixon uses us and our men as his excuse for continuing the war in Southeast Asia. We are his excuse for breaking off the peace talks. We are his excuse for avoiding meaningful negotiation on ending the war. . . . But he's not really doing these things because of us. He's doing them so that he won't have to admit he sent 20,000 Americans to their deaths for a mistake.[117]

In the spring of 1970, well before the official split of the POW movement, Falkman met with a group of POW wives who paid a call on the Swedish Foreign Ministry. They came under the auspices of a US Air Force colonel who was attached to the Pentagon.[118] "And they were docile women, quite young," Falkman recalled.[119] Wachtmeister, as head of the Foreign Ministry's Political Department, greeted them.

Once Wachtmeister left, Falkman made a bold and courageous move:

From an envelope, I took twelve black-and-white photographs that I laid out on the table. I explained that I had recently returned from a trip to Hanoi and had gotten these pictures at a hospital. They showed children in white beds with horrible injuries from the bombing, faces burned from napalm, wounds over the entire body from fragmentation bombs, some with amputated arms and legs from landmines, others with deformed faces from chemical herbicides. The women stared at the photographs with horror. I said that I had seen these children myself in the white beds, an appalling result of the American bombing campaign.[120]

The American colonel resented Falkman's gesture: "We have not come here to see propaganda pictures from Hanoi!"[121]

The following morning, Falkman received a telephone call from one of the POW wives. She asked to meet with him. Sitting down to coffee and pastry at the elegant Grand Hotel, the young woman confided that the photographs had affected her profoundly: "I was so shocked I couldn't sleep at night. And I don't know. My husband, in Vietnam, he never told me about this."[122] She asked to see Falkman alone:

She told the whole story that she had met this boy. They went to university together. There was no love story between them, but he wanted to get married because he risked his life, etc. in Vietnam. And . . . they got married, but she didn't know him. And now she was hesitating if she would receive him if he came back, etc., etc. I don't know what happened afterwards, but still, I did that because I think this was a moral question.[123]

Palme, for his part, dealt with the issue at the highest diplomatic levels, such as his meeting with British Prime Minister Wilson the following month. Rather than offering to help the American POWs himself, the British prime minister asked his Swedish counterpart for his assistance. Palme had the North Vietnamese connections, after all:

> Mr. Palme said with some difficulty he had obtained 14 names of captured United States pilots from the North Vietnamese, and had informed their next of kin. This had become public knowledge and the claim had been made that some of the names were already known to the Americans. This was true in several cases, but there were others in which pilots next of kin had said that they had had no previous information.[124]

THE SECOND LIST

Palme did not stop there. During his visit to Moscow in late June of 1970, Palme took the time to meet with Ambassador Nguyen Tho Chan. During the ambassador's visit to Hanoi in July, Palme summoned the North Vietnamese chargé d'affaires in Stockholm. The prime minister furnished the chargé d'affaires with a list of 203 missing servicemen, asking him to forward the list to Chan.[125] Four months later, in November, the North Vietnamese confirmed to Stockholm that thirty-six men were in their custody.[126] Another 156 names were not prisoners, the North Vietnamese claimed, and an additional four were dead. Due to a lack of identifying details, Hanoi could not account for ten men.[127] All the names of living prisoners on the latest Swedish list had been originally confirmed by the National Mobilization Committee, Women Strike for Peace, or the Committee of Liaison.[128]

Nevertheless, State Department spokesman Robert J. McCloskey did state at a press conference: "We very much appreciate this act of Sweden to assist the prisoners and their families."[129] An unnamed US State Department official went farther than that, describing the Swedish intelligence as "significant."[130] The Committee of Liaison had obtained its information through the Vietnam Committee for Solidarity with the American People (Viet-My), an organization that acted under the supervision of the North Vietnamese government.[131] At the time, the Viet-My members were varied in their occupations. Phan Hien, who sat on the Viet-My Board, would later serve as deputy minister of foreign affairs and deputy minister of justice after the war and reunification of Vietnam. Viet-My secretary Tran Minh Quoc functioned as an interpreter for visiting peace activists, and three decades later, was Vietnamese ambassador to Italy. Nguyen Thi Hoai Phuong was on the staff of the Vietnamese Communist Party's Commission for External Relations. The poet and musician Do Xuan Oanh had composed the song "19–8" in commemoration of the revolutionary takeover of Hanoi on August 19, 1945, and also served as an interpreter. Although Pham Khac Lam had been secretary to General Vo

Nguyen Giap during the French phase of the war, he was now a journalist.[132] The Viet-My membership all held responsible positions in Vietnamese society, and their own source of information was the North Vietnamese Ministry of Defense.[133] Nevertheless, as a reference for the Committee of Liaison, Viet-My's status was semiformal. In the words of Cora Weiss: "They were official enough . . . but they were unofficial enough so that I could not be accused of negotiating with their government."[134]

Stockholm, by contrast, received its information at the highest diplomatic level. The North Vietnamese Defense Ministry originated the data, as it had done for the antiwar activists, but its mode of transmission to the Swedish embassy was the Ministry of Foreign Affairs in Hanoi. The Swedish statistic of forty-five living prisoners was the highest number officially confirmed by the top ranks of the North Vietnamese government to date. Indeed, unnamed Washington officials confirmed to the Reuters news agency that it was "the longest list of prisoners or suspected prisoners yet received through government channels."[135]

TRAGIC NEWS

Particularly significant was the confirmation of four deaths on the Swedish list of November 1970: Colonel Edward Burke Burdett USAF, Commander Ernest Albert Stamm USN, Lieutenant Commander Terry Arden Dennison USN, and Major Ward Kent Dodge USAF.[136] The Swedes went beyond the usual telegram and letter to try to make personal contact with the four widows.

Ten months before, however, Cora Weiss had reported to the US State Department the following about Commander Stamm and Lieutenant Commander Dennison: "The individuals . . . had either died in their parachutes or had died thereafter from injuries resulting from the incident."[137]

Although Weiss had made the report to the State Department, she declined any contact with officials of the US military. "The information is unverified and its reliability unknown," the US Navy concluded. "For this reason, no status change will be made as a result of the Weiss information."[138]

Apparently, Weiss contacted Mrs. Dennison in Miramar, California. As skeptical as the US Navy was about the information, Mrs. Dennison wrote to Palme: "I have received information from an unreliable dissentent [*sic*] group that my husband Terry Arden Dennison . . . United States Navy died in his air raid over North Vietnam on July 19, 1966. I have evidence that he was alive several months after his accident. Because of your high diplomatic status could you please verify this information?"[139]

Early in November of 1970, Colonel Burdett's death had also been included on the Committee of Liaison's list.[140] Nevertheless, the Swedish government felt obligated to personally confirm the death to Mrs. Burdett.

Stockholm favored a sensitive approach to the wives. Local Swedish consuls would officially inform Mrs. Dennison and Mrs. Stamm of their widowhood.[141] On December 11, 1970, the consul general in San Francisco received orders to contact Mrs. Dennison. Mrs. Ruth Ann Stamm, who lived in Sanford, Florida, would receive a visit from the consul in Jacksonville that same day. Presumably because there were no Swedish consulates close to Macon, Georgia, Ambassador de Besche would personally telephone Mrs. Burdett.[142]

The evidence does not indicate whether the Swedes ever managed to contact Mrs. Dodge. If they did, she probably did not believe them. As late as Christmas Eve of 1970, a local newspaper in Garden City, Kansas, reported the following about Major Dodge: "To this date, neither his parents . . . nor his wife and daughters . . . have received any indication as to whether he is dead or alive and a prisoner of war."[143]

If Mrs. Burdett took Ambassador de Besche's telephone call, it is doubtful that she took his word at face value, either. In 1974, when she learned that her husband's remains would finally come home, she said: "I had hoped he would come back with the prisoners a year ago."[144]

Mrs. Stamm, on the other hand, believed the Swedish government. Her husband, Navy Commander Ernest Albert Stamm, had been shot down on November 25, 1968. "He flew a Vigilante," said his daughter, Katrina Stamm Shoemaker. "I mean it was a reconnaissance mission. They were just taking pictures. The plane is really cool. I mean it was way ahead of its time. It had night vision. It broke the sound barrier."[145]

Ironically, Commander "Tommy" Stamm was at the very end of his tour. As Katrina recalled: "They were days from coming home. . . . They knew it was going to be dangerous, and I also know my dad was not supposed to fly that mission. There was another gentleman who was supposed to fly it. He chickened out. He got drunk, and couldn't fly. And they asked for volunteers. My dad and his navigator . . . said, 'We'll fly it.'"[146]

A second plane accompanied Stamm on the ill-fated mission. "Two planes always went out," his daughter explained, "and one flew Position 1. One flew Position 2. They would check their equipment out. If everything checked out on Plane 1, they would swoop down, and take the pictures, and then if not, Plane 2 would go in."[147]

Commander Stamm piloted Plane 1. "When the plane was initially shot down," his daughter continued, "of course the guy in Plane Position #2 was able to take pictures. . . . They saw one parachute."[148]

It was the report of the parachute that gave Mrs. Stamm some hope, and the US military would eventually conclude that Commander Stamm had been taken prisoner. Still, his wife did not know what to believe. A family friend wrote to the Swedish embassy in Washington on Mrs. Stamm's behalf. Ambassador Besche then replied that he had forwarded the letter to Stockholm: "The Swedish Prime Minister has expressed his great sympathy with the American prisoners of war and their families, and he has stated that he will pay serious attention to the letters he himself and Swedish authorities have received in this matter."[149]

Although it was a polite form letter, the Swedes did far more than extend politeness; they include Commander Stamm's name in the list submitted to the North Vietnamese in July of 1970.[150] That November, the resultant North Vietnamese list classified Stamm as "dead."[151] The more extensive list that would be given to Sweden in December provided a little more detail about the commander's sad fate than had previous reports, "Captured: 25-11-68— Dead: 16-1-69."[152] Mrs. Stamm had been correct to suspect her husband's survival of the shoot-down, but he had apparently died in captivity.

At the time the Swedish government learned about Commander Stamm's death, his family was anticipating a happy holiday season. His son, Ernest August David Stamm, was ten years old, and his daughter, then just Katrina Stamm, was twelve. Mrs. Stamm sternly warned her Navy contact, "If you hear any information, I don't want to know about it. Please do not contact me, I want the kids to have a pleasant holiday. I want to try to make Christmas joyous for them. Please do not contact me unless it's that my husband is walking through my front door."[153]

Of course, the Swedish government was ignorant of Mrs. Stamm's request. On the afternoon of December 11, 1970, the Stamm family returned to their suburban Orlando home from an outing. Then, Mrs. Stamm received a telephone call from a neighbor, who said, "Ruth, I think you need to come over here."[154]

Waiting at the neighbor's house was the Swedish consul, Saga Skafte-Lindblom, who had come there to await Mrs. Stamm's return. "My mom, of course, is in tears," Katrina recalled. "She's crying. Well, Christmas certainly was ruined."[155]

It is unclear if Mrs. Stamm had ever learned of Cora Weiss's report, but it is clear that the news from Sweden came to her as a profound shock. The impact on the widow and her children was such that the Swedish information was possibly entirely new to them.

Mrs. Stamm passed away in 2016, but her surviving daughter can now speak on her behalf. Then only a child, Katrina never saw Mrs. Skafte-Lindblom, and could only identify her afterward as a Swedish lady. To this day, Katrina now refers to her mother's encounter with this messenger as "the Swedish incident."[156] Mrs. Stamm regarded the Swedish attempt to help as an unwarranted interference, and Katrina has the same point of view:

> Well, for whatever reason, and I do not understand, why a Swedish embassy would think it's their job to come to my mom and discuss her husband. If you have information, to me, the proper avenue would have been through our government to tell them, not come to the suburbs and hunt my Mom down, and ringing the bell: "Here, look what I got, this information!" . . . So my mom had made every attempt to try to make tragedy not happen over the holidays . . . and . . . this lady, I don't know why, and I don't know on what basis, and why from Sweden, they would need to send someone to our front door.[157]

When asked about his government's direct contact with the Stamm family, Eliasson was very surprised. The Swedes were quick to notify families that their missing relatives were still alive and in captivity. "We gave the whole list to the State Department and to the families almost at the same time," said Eliasson, who has good reason to know as one of the embassy's first secretaries.[158]

Deaths were another matter entirely. He could not remember "sending out instructions about contacting families directly, but evidently, that was done. I must say I don't recall."[159]

Nor would Eliasson have favored such a practice: "If I were ambassador, I would not have given the green light to such an action. It's not for a foreign embassy to go to individuals and give them information about life and death about other countries' citizens. It should be done through their own official channel."[160]

The problem was that funneling information through the official channel produced little effect. Even though the State Department had acknowledged the reliability of Swedish information as early as November of 1970, the Pentagon apparently did not take it seriously. In spite of that, the US Navy surely knew the Swedish government was in direct communication with POW families. Well before Mrs. Skafte-Lindblom bore her sorrowful message to Mrs. Stamm, Palme had publicly stated that he was sharing whatever news he had with the families, not just the US government.[161] Undoubtedly, the navy also knew that the list provided by Sweden that November had confirmed Commander Stamm's death. It would have been advisable for the navy to convey Mrs. Stamm's Christmas request to the Swedish government.

Mrs. Stamm was understandably bitter. According to Katrina, "My mom then called her Navy contact, and said, 'Why didn't you tell me about this information?'"[162] The official replied, "We are aware of those reports. We do not consider them valid. We have reasons to believe they are incorrect, and we believe Tommy is probably still POW, number one. And number two, you told us not to contact you."[163]

The Stamms withstood a terrible tragedy, and outsiders do not have the right to judge the family for their resentment of the Swedish incident. They are certainly entitled to their feelings. At the same time, Katrina does not recall that her mother held a grudge against Sweden as a whole:

> No, I don't think it was something that she got into having feelings about one way or the other, other than being shocked that this person came to her home. It's just not something that she went around carrying some kind of campaign against the prime minister or something. If you had asked her years later, "What do you think of Sweden?" She would have said, "Oh, that would be a nice country. I'd love to visit there one day."[164]

It is important to remember that the Swedes only acted with the best of intentions. There is every reason to believe they would have held back their information during the Christmas season, had American authorities notified them in time. Yet it would have been impossible for the Swedes to hold back the sad news indefinitely. Stockholm possessed accurate information about Commander Stamm—Washington did not.

In fact, the US government did not formally acknowledge Commander Stamm's death until August 13, 1974.[165]

Nevertheless, Katrina lived with her grief, and some degree of uncertainty. Her family has never learned the cause of Commander Stamm's death: "You know what? I pray that he didn't even make it out of the plane. It's like rather than being tortured in a POW camp, I would like to think he did die then."[166]

She has never accepted his official date of death. She does not even believe that the body shipped back to the United States in 1974 was that of Commander Stamm, who would soon receive a posthumous promotion to the rank of captain.[167] The worst time to lose a father is in childhood. Katrina is a reminder that the actions of both Swedish and American officials had an impact on children.

When it came to the 156 men who remained missing in action according to Sweden's November list, seventeen had already been listed as "never been captured in North Vietnam" by the Committee of Liaison.[168] According to the Reuters report, US government officials noted that the Swedish "listing of three-quarters of the 200 men as never having been captured was in many cases the first indication that they were not prisoners."[169]

Sweden's own information about most of the missing men was reliable; they never returned home. The list also included Eugene DeBruin, a civilian employee of the CIA subsidiary Air America, who had been shot down in Laos in 1963. DeBruin's fate has remained undetermined to this day.[170]

Nevertheless, the Swedish list made some mistakes in classifying some men as missing in action. One name was listed twice. Eight other prisoners, who had been originally confirmed by the National Mobilization Committee or the Committee of Liaison, were now listed as unconfirmed by Sweden.[171] The Swedish government had already confirmed the imprisonment of Robert Bruce Hinckley in March of 1970, but now mistakenly listed him as unconfirmed.[172] Another name, classified as "never captured in Vietnam," was actually that of Jerrie L. Kerr, the wife of Captain Michael Scott Kerr USAF. When Mrs. Kerr received a telegram from Palme incorrectly stating that her husband had never been captured, she must have been very irritated: "I have seven letters from him, the most recent dated Oct. 10."[173]

Sweden would correct most of these mistakes the following month.[174]

Obviously, Stockholm did not bear responsibility for all the errors. Neither the Committee of Liaison nor the Swedish government ever confirmed the imprisonment of Lieutenant Henry James Bediger USN and Army Major Theodore W. Gostas. Both men would return home in 1973. Army Staff Sergeant John Arthur Young would remain unconfirmed by any list when the Committee of Liaison and Vietnam Veterans Against the War distributed a recording of Young's voice from the North Vietnamese in September of 1971.[175] Perhaps Hanoi had refused to confirm their detainment because they had been captured outside of North Vietnam. Bedinger had been shot down in Laos, while Young and Gostas had been seized in South Vietnam.[176] In any case, all three had then been transferred to North Vietnam, although other transferred POWS had been included on at least one Swedish list.[177]

ADDITIONAL REASSURANCE FOR THE BORLING FAMILY

John L. Borling was an additional name on the list. For approximately three years after his 1966 capture, it was assumed that Borling was dead. Then, a fellow prisoner had the chance to send a letter out. This letter included the words: "Tell Aunt Myrna in Chicago that I miss her and love her."[178] Borling hailed from Chicago, and Myrna was the first name of his wife. In six months, Washington figured out who Myrna actually was. "But up to that point, all she said was she thought she could feel me," Borling said.[179]

In March of 1970, the Committee of Liaison informed Mrs. Borling of her husband's captivity. According to the committee, his letter was en route from Hanoi to Chicago.[180]

After a few months, Borling's father wrote to the Swedish prime minister.[181] Either Mr. Edward Borling had done so because the family's exchange of mail with his son had been intermittent, or the worried father had also felt the extra need of reassurance. At least some of Borling's letters had reached home, but his wife would later express her frustration publicly at the very end of the year: "My husband has been a prisoner 4½ years. . . . He received his first letter from me in October of this year—despite all those I wrote. I've always sent pictures and he has received none."[182]

It is impossible to determine precisely why Borling's father had written the prime minister, for his letter does not exist in the Foreign Ministry Collection at Sweden's National Archives, nor among Palme's personal papers. Borling himself, now a retired general, cannot provide me any explanation, either. In any case, his father's letter produced results.

In November of 1970, Borling's name was included in the list given to the Swedish government.[183] The Swedish prime minister informed Borling's father by telegram on December 10. "This is reassuring and vital information," Mr. Edward G. Borling swiftly wired back. "Will appreciate your continued efforts and influence on behalf of U.S. prisoners of war and M.I.A.'s. May God bless you."[184]

Myrna Borling was also relieved at the confirmation her husband's continued survival. "It's great to hear this," Mrs. Borling said. "It's good that he's on the official list because we feel that when the war is over, he'll be accounted for and won't be left behind."[185]

MISSING SERVICEMEN

As for the missing servicemen whom Hanoi had never captured, their families had every reason for despair. In spite of their sorrow, they could still thank Palme for the information. "After a year and a half with no information at all, you sent word to my parents last week about my missing brother, Capt. Laurent J. Gourley, U.S. Air Force," Elzene E. Estes reported to Palme. "Although that news wasn't exactly what we had been praying for, we consider ourselves among the lucky ones because we have some news."[186]

One mother of another missing serviceman, Air Force Captain Thomas J. Beyer, even concurred with Palme about the war. "Thank you . . . for expressing yourself on the 'talk show' while in this country," Mrs. Charles J. Beyer of Fargo, North Dakota, wrote to the prime minister. "We agree with your views completely and especially regarding the corruption of the Southvietnam regime. . . . We are greatful [*sic*] even in America for an honest politician anywhere in the world today—there are so very few it seems."[187]

Moreover, Mrs. Beyer appreciated Palme's attempt to determine her son's fate: "There are simply no words in a case such as this to express ourselves adequately. It is the only answer of any consequence received to the hundreds of letters I have written all over the world imploring aid in the matter."[188]

FINAL LIST

Close to the end of December 1970, the chargé d'affaires of the North Vietnamese embassy provided the Swedish prime minister with a more extensive list of American airmen who had been taken prisoner between August 5, 1964 and November 15, 1970, 368 in all.[189] Nine had been already been released, and nineteen had perished in captivity.[190] The Committee of Liaison had already confirmed the new names on the final list given to Stockholm, but it also included the five living prisoners previously confirmed for the first time by the Swedish government.

Eliasson would later be reluctant to give all the credit to his own government: "It was the combined pressure of us and the American senators who were against the war."[191] North Vietnamese diplomats did provide copies of the same list to representatives of Senators Edward M. Kennedy and J. William Fulbright. The two politicians had dispatched letters to Hanoi in June. These representatives had traveled to Paris for this express purpose. In addition, the Committee of Liaison received its own copy.[192]

Again, the Swedish list was not definitive. As far as I can determine, it should have included three more names.[193]

As far as the Swedish contribution was concerned, Professor Falk appreciated Palme's effort on behalf of the POW community. "I do think his support in a more generic way was helpful in legitimizing the efforts of civil society groups, like the Committee of Liaison, to address these issues," Falk said.[194] He saw another benefit: "It certainly had some value in annoying the U.S. government."[195]

In addition, the professor admired the North Vietnamese in their exercise of statecraft: "They were surprisingly sophisticated about their relations with Sweden and with civil society groups," Falk pointed out. "They, in effect, understood the soft power dimensions of this kind of conflict . . . that helped them sway international public opinion, and they did do a very impressive job in that way, much more so than, for instance, was done during the Korean War than by the North Koreans, let's say."[196]

Falk rightly noted the support given by Stockholm to the Committee of Liaison. Palme may not have originally confirmed all the information on his final list, but his official position gave its transmission a special credibility.

MRS. GRIFFIN

Not all the POW families received happy news from Stockholm. Granted, the deaths confirmed by Sweden for the first time on its final list had been reported elsewhere. Once Stockholm had reconfirmed these deaths in captivity, however, they seemed more final. After the shootdown of Lieutenant Commander James L. Griffin USN on May 19, 1967, his voice was heard on Radio Hanoi. Then, when Griffin's name did not appear on a published POW list in 1970, his wife was deeply upset.[197] She would soon write to Olof Palme, searching for information.[198]

That November, Mrs. Griffin heard a disturbing report from a friendly navy contact. According to this contact, the Committee of Liaison's Cora Weiss had claimed that Lieutenant Griffin had died in captivity. Mrs. Griffin was incredulous. She took the initiative by calling a reporter at *The Atlanta Journal-Constitution.* "They announced on May 19, 1967 that my husband is a prisoner," she told the reporter. "They would not have done that if he were not alive."[199]

The Atlanta Journal-Constitution quoted Mrs. Griffin the following day: "It's a shame that this kind of announcement should come from a dissident group who has no standing whatsoever."[200]

Two days before Christmas of 1970, her telephone rang. The caller, turning out to be Cora Weiss herself, told Mrs. Griffin that her husband was deceased. Mrs. Griffin still could not believe it.[201]

The following month, Stockholm finally responded to her letter. Rune Nyström, head of the division, Royal Ministry of Foreign Affairs, wrote: "It is my sad duty to convey to you the information given to the Swedish Government by the Government of the Democratic Republic of Vietnam, namely, that your husband died in North Vietnam on May 21, 1967."[202]

She regarded this news as plausible: "Now the time for tears has come. But my tears are private. When the children are in bed I pour a glass of Chardonnay, pile sad songs on the record player, and reread the letter over and over. In private, I know."[203]

Officially, she would not accept her husband's death until its confirmation through "proper channels" via "the International Red Cross with endorsement from the U.S. government."[204] As with the Stamm family, Mrs. Griffin would not receive official confirmation from the US government until the war had ended.[205]

All the same, Mrs. Griffin treated Nyström's letter with great seriousness. "I did realize that there was little possibility that I would ever see him again alive," she later commented, "but I was appreciative of the information sent to me by the Swedish Royal Ministry for Foreign Affairs."[206]

The December 1970 list was the last that Stockholm would receive. In June of 1972, the North Vietnamese would bypass the Swedish government, as well as the Committee of Liaison, to give Senator Edward Kennedy letters for the families of twenty-four prisoners of war who had been taken since November of 1970. An official list of these new POWs followed.[207]

REACTIONS OF U.S. GOVERNMENT OFFICIALS

In any case, Palme presented his own list to the American ambassador on the very day that he had received it, December 23, 1970. The prime minister explained that the first two confirmed lists were the direct result of letters from POW families, which he had forwarded to the North Vietnamese. The latest list came from Hanoi without any Swedish prompting. "This is a remarkable achievement," Holland said, undoubtedly realizing that Palme's diplomacy deserved credit for this full compilation of prisoners.[208]

Palme said that he had recently spoken with the chargé d'affaires of the North Vietnamese embassy: "He [the prime minister] had the strong impression that one in Hanoi anticipated the possibility of an escalation of the war from the U.S.A.'s side and that Hanoi regarded this extraordinarily seriously."[209]

Fearing the chance for even greater violence, the Swedish prime minister also regarded this possibility with extraordinary seriousness as well. Through Holland, Palme advised the Nixon administration to treat the prisoner list as an indication that Hanoi wanted to keep lines of communication open with Washington. "Hanoi will not change its policy if the bombing is resumed," said the prime minister, according to the minutes. President Johnson had stopped the bombing of North Vietnam on November 1, 1968, but Nixon had interrupted with the bombing halt with continuous small-scale assaults from the beginning of his presidency. Large-scale aerial operations would come later, but Vietnamese morale would remain strong no matter what.[210]

Holland questioned why Palme foresaw an American military escalation. "The recently conducted bombing raids and President Nixon's language," the prime minister responded. He then went on:

> We cannot understand . . . how one expects that someone could willingly accept overflights by reconnaissance planes. We are ourselves a small country. Last year, we had foreign submarines on our territory. We tried to hit them with bombs. Unfortunately, we did not succeed. We have anxiously asked ourselves if the overflights, etc. are a way to prepare American opinion for an escalation.[211]

There remains the possibility that the submarines came from the Soviet Union. Scandinavia was never a hot spot in the Cold War, but it was a point of increasing warmth produced by the tensions between the Soviet Union and the Western bloc. Sweden, as a nonmember of NATO, felt vulnerable as a small country. The lingering disquiet of the Swedes could only encourage their increasing identification with another small country, Vietnam. Falkman of the Foreign Ministry, confirmed that the Swedes were "fighting for our own ideals, a small country living in the shadow of a big power like Russia, the Soviet Union. We should support small countries which try to liberate themselves from these big powers."[212]

These were precarious days for Sweden, indeed, but the US ambassador tried to convince Palme that recent American activities signified a "bringing-down," not a "build-up." He addressed the prime minister with respect: "You know the American people and know that they all wish for an end to the war." At the end of the meeting, Holland stated that he would share the prime minister's "pertinent observations" with his superiors.[213]

Holland had a polite relationship with the prime minister from the time of his arrival in Sweden. In fact, the ambassador's sympathy for Sweden alarmed the White House. During the first month of his tenure, Holland publicly claimed Sweden's right to provide aid to North Vietnam, and asylum to deserters from the American military. The ambassador even took the time to meet activists from the United NLF Groups, the same activists who had protested against him. After an extended conversation with the American diplomat, the young activists publicly described the meeting as productive.[214]

It is likely that Holland kept his word and transmitted Palme's views to the Nixon administration, and it is just as likely that the Nixon administration disregarded them. Nevertheless, the White House was not the only important building in Washington. Influential people in the US Capitol did appreciate Palme's abilities as an intermediary. Indeed, as Palme mediated with the North Vietnamese, members of Congress wrote to him for assistance. Representatives John Dellenbeck of Oregon and Lawrence J. Hogan of New Jersey asked him to ensure that the North Vietnamese treated the prisoners humanely, according to the relevant Geneva convention.[215] Senators Frank Church of Idaho and Charles Mathias of Maryland asked the Swedish government to forward their own letter to the prime minister of North Vietnam.[216] Interestingly, Dellenbeck, Hogan, and Mathias were Republicans, members of Nixon's own political party.

Stockholm undoubtedly respected Church and Mathias for their antiwar engagement, but it declined to forward their letter for two reasons. The Washington embassy was authorized to inform Church and Mathias that the Swedish government would only approach Hanoi about the POW issue at the request of the prisoners' families. In truth, this was the most important reason. A secondary reason, which Stockholm wished to remain classified, was that "we do not know how the senators could use the fact that Sweden acted as an intermediary. Furthermore, we do not know the contents of the letter, and it would put us in a difficult situation if we would need to enter in a discussion of the letter's contents."[217]

Even Republican congressmen who were politically close to the president approached the Swedish embassy. House Minority Leader Gerald R. Ford of Michigan, who would later serve Nixon as vice president, and then replace him as president, wrote to Ambassador de Besche: "I share the deep concern of our people and would very much appreciate anything you and your government will do to urge the government at Hanoi to provide humane treatment for these men and to inform our government of their condition so that their families may be given a report on their health and welfare."[218]

Senator Howard Baker of Tennessee, who would extend subtle sympathy to Nixon as he investigated the Watergate scandal, also wrote to de Besche: "Please accept this letter as my personal appeal to you and the government of Sweden to assist in assuring that these prisoners of war receive treatment as provided in the Geneva Accords and that they be given at least the minimum medical attention and living conditions required."[219] Baker hoped that Hanoi would permit the prisoners to exchange letters with their loved ones.[220]

Representative Jack Kemp, a Republican from New York, expressed similar views as the other American politicians. Palme responded to the New Yorker in the same way that he responded to the other American politicians. Declining to debate Kemp about the legal status of the POWs, the prime minister merely pointed to the peace negotiations in Paris:

"The question of the captured pilots has been linked with the problems of the presence of foreign troops in South Vietnam and the future composition of the South Vietnamese Government. Consequently, an overall solution by negotiation of the Vietnamese problem seems to be the way to settle also the question of the pilots."[221]

ROSS PEROT

Indeed, Americans of all stripes approached Palme to help the prisoners of war. The prime minister even heard from Ross Perot, the data processing tycoon and future presidential candidate. Forming his own organization, United We Stand, the colorful Texan had singlehandedly tried to negotiate for the release of the prisoners, and his efforts still command the respect of Borling, Halyburton, and other former POWs.[222]

Mrs. Halyburton, for her part, found Perot to be helpful. "He certainly had the means and the determination to make this POW/MIA issue one that all Americans could get behind, no matter what their political leanings were," she said.[223] Not only did Perot make the issue a national one, but "international, too, in that he took a group to Paris. He took a group to Russia."[224]

Stockholm, by contrast, was not impressed with Perot. Eliasson, laboring on the POW issue at the Washington embassy, never met Perot during this period. He only interacted with Perot's organization. "They contacted me, and I received them," Eliasson said. "We talked about our efforts. I didn't work very closely with them."[225]

Unfortunately, Perot's approach had serious limitations. Eliasson himself acknowledged the tycoon's "chances of getting positive treatment by the North Vietnamese were not very high."[226] Perot disregarded the fact that the war was not yet over, but the 1969 Christmas season would quickly disillusion him. Determined to give the POWs some holiday cheer, Perot chartered a plane to carry supplies, medication, and clothing to Hanoi. The planeload also included Christmas gifts and 1,400 canned Christmas dinners. Beyond celebrating a belated Christmas, Perot hoped to negotiate with the North Vietnamese government for the release of the prisoners. Landing in the Laotian capital of Vientiane, Perot requested admittance of himself and his delivery to North Vietnam. After all, Articles 72 and 73 of the Third Geneva Convention do entitle prisoners to relief shipments under certain regulations. Prime Minister Pham Van Dong rebuffed Perot's request, advising him to send his goods through Moscow.[227]

In fairness to Perot, he sincerely intended to deliver the supplies to the POWs. The White House was less sincere. As Alexander Butterfield, the deputy assistant to the president, wrote in a memorandum to Nixon:

> The assumption all along was the North Vietnamese would not allow Ross and his . . . planes into North Vietnam. After widely publicizing their repeated refusals, Ross was to leave the goods with orphaned children in South Vietnam and herd his entourage home by way of India and Europe . . . holding numerous enroute press conferences to continue high-lighting Hanoi's "thoroughly unreasonable" rejection of food, clothes, medicine, etc. and its "inhumane treatment of captured persons." We hate to see him divert from his plan, but have little hope now that won't.[228]

Actually, Perot had announced in Vientiane that he would give the supplies to North Vietnamese orphans in case the POWs could not receive them. The White House tried to discourage Perot's idea, "for it would only be a matter of days before the Communist propaganda machine would turn the gesture into an admission of war crimes guilt on our part."[229] Nixon and his circle preferred *South* Vietnamese orphans as recipients of charity.

Therefore, the White House was displeased by what followed. Perot's plane stopped in Anchorage, Alaska, for the repackaging of the twenty-six tons of supplies into three-kilogram containers that would be acceptable for shipment from Moscow to Hanoi. "There is just no reason why we should make the Soviets look good on this one," Butterfield commented.[230]

Unfortunately for Perot, who had tried to follow Pham Van Dong's demand, the Soviets foiled his scheme by denying his plane landing rights.[231]

Realizing that he could not always buy what he wanted, Perot turned to Palme for help. In a letter addressed to "Prime Minister Olaff [*sic*] Palme,"

Perot wrote: "I seek your help as a humanitarian in convincing the North Vietnamese to release these men, or least operate their camps in accordance with the Geneva Convention.[232]

In 1969, the prime minister had met with Murphy Martin, the Dallas newsman, along with Mrs. Singleton and the other POW wife.[233] Martin was not yet Perot's employee, but the businessman had paid for the trip to Stockholm. At the meeting, Palme made a poor impression on Martin, who later reported to the American embassy that the prime minister "was not very well informed on prisoner question at outset of talk."[234]

Probably, Martin's low estimation was due to the reticence of the prime minister, who "stated that he could not comment on what GOS [Government of Sweden] might be doing with Hanoi Re: prisoners because of 'diplomatic channels involved' although he tried to give impression that he 'would do what he could.'"[235]

It is likely that Martin's personal manner turned Palme off has well. The prime minister avoided Perot and his associates after that. Conflicting values and priorities were the main factor, for the representatives of the Swedish foreign ministry made it clear that they were engaged solely on a humanitarian mission.

The Texas billionaire appointed Martin to serve as president of United We Stand, his advocacy organization, in January 1970.[236] Still persistent, Martin called Leif Leifland of the Foreign Ministry to request another audience with the prime minister. Perot, accompanied by Martin and Mrs. Singleton, would present Palme with a gift as an expression of appreciation for his efforts. Perot's deputy assured Leifland that the ceremony would generate a great deal of attention in the United States, where Palme planned to travel in June. Through Martin, Perot proposed making an offer of economic aid to Hanoi, in exchange for the release of the American prisoners of war. The Swedish prime minister, apparently, would serve as intermediary. Martin, whose background in television reporting failed to inspire trust in Leifland, claimed that he could "make the prime minister's trip to the United States a success. Mr. Palme could be made into a hero."[237]

Leifland concluded, "The proposal of a presentation of a gift to the prime minister as part of a big PR-campaign should be rejected. The Swedish action has not been undertaken for the sake of PR."[238] Furthermore, Leifland opposed Perot's idea of a prisoner exchange for either money or goods. "Mr. Martin, Mr. Perot, and the 'United We Stand' organization should therefore be kept at a distance," he concluded.[239] Palme accepted this advice.[240]

Stockholm's distance from Perot was telling. If the Swedish government had aided POW families with the aim of ingratiating itself with the White House, it would have embraced Perot, a Nixon insider. During the 1968 presidential campaign, Perot had furnished candidate Nixon with personnel from his own company, Electronic Data Systems. These personnel provided advice and performed advance work.[241] Once Nixon became president, Perot founded United We Stand in consultation with the White House. He also arranged for the publication of newspaper advertising, as well as the production of a television special, in support of Nixon's Vietnam policy in the fall of 1969.[242] Perot even contributed $250,000 to a secret White House fund that supported Republican senatorial candidates. Significantly, this illicit fund helped undermine the reelection campaign of antiwar Senator Albert Gore Sr. of Tennessee.[243] The prime minister and his Foreign Ministry could not have known about Perot's secret campaign contribution, but they must have known the tycoon's agenda contradicted their own.

The Perot organization persisted in its campaign to win Stockholm's favor. Martin dropped off a packet at Leifland's office. This packet included a collection of newspaper clips with headlines such as "Response is Huge to Perot's Appeal," "Perot is Not Giving Up," "Perot Puts Hanoi on the Spot," "Perot Shows 'em Up," and "A man with compassion."[244]

The delivery of these promotional materials had been probably Perot's own idea. A quarter-century later, biographer Gerald Posner would have a similar experience with Perot. The billionaire furnished Posner with a biographical packet, which included a list of fifty-nine awards the Texan had received over the years, and a list of charitable contributions, worth a combined $120 million, that he had made.[245]

In the Foreign Ministry files, I came across an old-fashioned magnetic tape of an address Perot had given on March 9, 1970, at the National Press Club in Washington.[246] It had arrived at the Foreign Ministry from the Swedish embassy via air mail. During the question-and-answer session, Perot mispronounced the Swedish prime minister's name as "Pal-mey."[247] The billionaire dismissed the POW list collected by Sweden in March: "They gave Palme fourteen names last week, thirteen of them were old names."[248] Actually, as I have noted, five of the names had been previously unconfirmed by a non-Vietnamese source. Stockholm had produced information—Perot had not.

In the recording of Perot's appearance to the National Press Club, his references to the POWs come across as disrespectful: "I measure Sweden by what they produce, and so far, they've produced thirteen bad names and one good one."[249]

Responding to a question about the importance of Sweden in the POW matter, Perot provoked laughter with a crude remark: "I'd support the devil himself in trying to get these men out," the tycoon said. "And that's not putting Sweden in that category, but I'd deal with whoever I had to deal with to get these men out."[250]

Perot dismissed Sweden's influence. "I've had numerous contacts with Sweden," he said. "Why is Sweden such a key country in these negotiations? I'm not sure it is."[251]

Snubs from Stockholm may have provoked Perot's deprecating comments. Contradicting his own claims of Swedish irrelevance, he still hoped to work with Sweden to identify the POWs and return them to the United States.[252] Perot could not understand that only a peace agreement could produce a wholesale release of the prisoners.

Perot was unceasing with his appeals. The bad chemistry between United We Stand and the Swedish government was due, in part, to a clash of cultures. Swedish culture values modesty and self-effacement. Perot's self-promotional gestures must have come across as vulgar to Stockholm. His public insults would not have helped, either.

Furthermore, Leifland could gather that the work of United We Stand was ineffective from his conversation with its own president. Martin indicated to Leifland

1. That relations between the Department of Defense and "United We Stand" are "strained."
2. The North Vietnamese negotiating team in Paris have refused to receive him—"It seems as if the North Vietnamese want nothing to do with us."[253]

In April of 1970, Leifland received yet another call from United We Stand asking if Perot could meet with the prime minister. United We Stand also offered Palme the chance to "meet eighty or so" journalists who were accompanying Perot. With Palme's backing, Leifland turned the Perot organization down.[254]

While Perot was correct to point out that many of the names of the POWs on Sweden's March 1970 list were not new, their wives did not dismiss the influence of Stockholm. In 1967, for example, *Life* magazine featured a recent photograph of Captain Paul Edward Galanti USN, who had been shot down the previous year.[255] In addition, the North Vietnamese confirmed Captain Galanti's imprisonment to David Dellinger and Rennie Davis in 1969. A year after Perot's National Press Club speech, Mrs. Galanti would meet with Palme in Stockholm to address her concerns. Indicating that she took the prime minister seriously, she came as part of a delegation of ten who brought along 750,000 letters from their fellow Virginians.[256]

Mrs. Galanti probably asked Palme to consider the Swedish internment of her husband and other long-term prisoners, which the prime minister would have politely but promptly rejected. Perhaps hoping that the pressure of Swedish public opinion would do the trick, Mrs. Galanti even took out an advertisement in *Dagens Nyheter* to endorse the idea of Swedish internment: "I have come to Sweden because your nation is known for its neutrality and impartiality . . . my appeal goes over national borders. It comes directly from the heart. All I ask is to be reunited with my husband."[257]

Even though President Nixon never acknowledged Palme's successful humanitarian diplomacy, certain members of his administration seemed as eager for contact with the prime minister as Perot did. Secretary of State William Rogers showed appreciation in August 1970 for Palme's work: "Thanks in part to your efforts, there has been additional mail and information from prisoners since that time."[258] Indeed, it is very likely that Palme's interest in POWs persuaded the North Vietnamese to allow a more regular exchange of mail. A friendly head of a foreign government wielded far more influence in Hanoi than even a friendly foreign peace group.

Palme had other admirers in the US State Department by the end of 1970. Frank Sieverts, the special assistant for prisoner of war issues, informed the Swedish embassy in Washington that Stockholm's assistance had "definitively made an impression on some people (in the White House, State, and Pentagon) who have not been favorable vis-à-vis Sweden."[259]

Understandably resentful, the North Vietnamese did not care to provide the Nixon administration with information about the POWs, but they seemed almost honored to answer Swedish questions. "When you meet Olof Palme, tell him that for my part, I remain personally prepared to help with what he asks me about in this sad matter," North Vietnamese prime minister Phan Van Dong told Öberg in Hanoi. "Unlike the Americans, your prime minister has been wise enough to only act humanely."[260]

Hearing only silence from Hanoi, the US embassy repeatedly pressed the Swedish government for information. Chargé d'affaires John Guthrie visited Wachtmeister shortly after Palme's return from Moscow in June of 1970. Guthrie wanted to know if the prime minister had brought up the POW issue with Ambassador Chan of North Vietnam. "He asked, according to instructions, if this matter had been raised in Palme's discussion with Chan," Wachtmeister would report later to his diplomatic colleagues, as well as the prime minister himself. Wachtmeister informed Guthrie that he did not know the details of the conversation, but could confirm that it had.[261] A few months later, C. Arthur Borg, the embassy's political counselor, approached the Foreign Ministry to inquire about another meeting that Palme had with Ambassador Chan, this time in the Swedish city of Sundsvall.[262] The prime minister did not seem to mind the American inquiries about his diplomatic contacts, writing to Secretary Rogers about his two-hour long conversation with Chan in Moscow:

With him I also discussed the American prisoners. I related my own recent experiences in the United States in order to show how important this issue is to public opinion in your country. As a result of this conversation the Swedish government has now sent to Hanoi a new list of men whose families have appealed to the Swedish government.[263]

Operating under the jurisdiction of the State Department, the USm embassy in Stockholm continued to show an interest in Palme's efforts. In 1972, the US ambassador wrote to Foreign Minister Krister Wickman, who had replaced Nilsson the year before, to thank the prime minister and his government for "actions which resulted obtaining new information about the status of a few individuals."[264] Holland did add that "in other cases the information provided tended to confirm information received through other channels."[265] Nevertheless, the American ambassador concluded by encouraging Stockholm to carry on with its good work.[266]

After the American withdrawal from Vietnam, the National League of Families of American Prisoners and Missing in Southeast Asia acknowledged Palme's record: "We cannot help remembering that in 1970 Sweden accomplished more from a list of names compiled from family requests than our government has ever accomplished with a full and complete list submitted several times."[267]

The Swedes could try to help Americans who were held in North Vietnam because they enjoyed full diplomatic relations with its government. Prisoners in Cambodia and Laos, on the other hand, were out of luck, and Stockholm could only offer their relatives its genuine sympathy. Not only did Sweden lack a full embassy in the Cambodian capital of Phnom Penh and the Laotian capital of Vietniane, it did not have formal relations with either of the respective insurgent forces in either country.[268] At least once, however, Öberg did inform Stockholm that he would approach the local Pathet Lao information office about the disappearance of an Air Force navigator in Laos. Sadly, no information was ever forthcoming.[269]

VIOLATIONS OF THE THIRD GENEVA CONVENTION

As far as the POWs in North Vietnam were concerned, the Swedish government did what they could. It was initial practice for the Swedes to forward letters to POWs through Peking, by way of Moscow. By 1970, Öberg was chargé d'affaires at the new Swedish embassy in Hanoi. When Öberg tried to hand over letters from POW wives to a North Vietnamese official on August 5, however, he was politely but firmly rebuffed. "Every month, the pilots had the right to send and receive letters and presents to and from their relatives," the official said, repeating his government's public position. "Moscow was the right place to arrange these contacts."[270]

As the conversation progressed, the North Vietnamese official grew more candid: "They were not regarded as prisoners of war, but as criminals, since the United States had never declared war."[271]

The North Vietnamese official's interpretation of international law was incorrect, for Article 2 the Third Geneva Convention, states that "the present Convention shall apply to all cases of declared war or of any other armed conflict which may arise between two or more of the High Contracting Parties, even if the state of war is not recognized by one of them."[272]

As Hanoi saw it, the POWs were not entitled to the protections of the Geneva Convention. The official still claimed that the prisoners "however were well-treated and wanted for nothing."[273]

Later on, however, Öberg would sometimes serve as a postal conduit for the POWs and their families, working with the North Vietnamese Red Cross on at least one occasion.[274]

In 1970, Palme may have declined the request of a POW father to give his own interpretation of the Geneva Convention, but his government did speak to the North Vietnamese that year about the general treatment of prisoners in wartime. In Stockholm, the Foreign Ministry's Falkman spoke with Chargé d'Affaires Nguyen Van Than from the North Vietnamese embassy. Falkman said that his government "wished that an international legal system would come into being and be applied for the humane treatment of all people who are taken prisoner during armed conflicts."[275]

Did the Swedes know that the North Vietnamese were, in fact, mistreating the POWs?

I have not come across any evidence that the prime minister, directly and in his own words, ever denied the charges of torture of the POWs. According to Eliasson, "Palme also, like me, had no illusions about how they were treated, but our main focus was to get the list out from the North Vietnamese."[276] That did not indicate Palme's indifference to any prisoner mistreatment: "That, more or less, strengthened him further to get involved."[277]

At the same time, Palme never expressed an opinion to Eliasson on the question of torture: "No, I would say that is action was aiming at getting the list. . . . We thought one thing we could do since Sweden had a humanitarian tradition, that we could try to get at least information about who was in prison, and then, in the end, the release of them."[278]

When an American wrote to Palme to express his concern about Hanoi's treatment of the POWs, Falkman did respond in the prime minister's name, but probably at the behest of the Foreign Ministry, that "we do not think that there is any reason to believe that the pilots are not accorded humane treatment."[279]

In response to a letter from another American, this time the sister of an imprisoned pilot, Falkman wrote: "The former Swedish Minister for Foreign Affairs, Mr Torsten Nilsson, was in Hanoi recently and was then informed by Vietnamese officials that the captured military men in the Democratic Republic of Vietnam are given a lenient and humanitarian treatment."[280]

According to Falkman, the Foreign Ministry had reason to believe the North Vietnamese would not harm the prisoners: "They had orders not to kill the American soldiers when they landed from parachutes, etc., because the Vietnamese understood, of course, they could be used in a big peace exchange."[281]

Öberg possessed considerable expertise on Southeast Asia, and firm opinions on North Vietnamese practices. In one dispatch home, he wrote, "For my part, I believe that one should take the Vietnamese seriously when they assert that they are giving the captured pilots correct treatment."[282]

The Swedish ambassador had reached this conclusion late in the war, however. Perhaps also because he had spent more time in North Vietnam than the other important figures in Swedish diplomacy, he had a more realistic appreciation of torture as a probability *earlier* in the war. When *The New York Times* reporter Seymour Hersh was in Hanoi in March of 1972, he visited Öberg. As the reporter recalled, the Swedish ambassador and his French counterpart "urged me not to be taken in if . . . I was allowed to interview American prisoners of war. They had good reason to believe that some of the prisoners at the infamous Hanoi Hilton had had very bad times."[283]

According to Hersh, the Swedish ambassador had a trusted source:

> He had been repeatedly told . . . by one of his housekeepers who walked past the Hanoi Hilton en route to the Swedish chancery that she often, especially in the earlier years—this was in 1972 . . . could hear the sounds of beating and the cries of those being beaten inside the prison. Öberg told me he did not doubt the woman's account, but did not explain why.[284]

Physical evidence indicated the housekeeper's veracity. She easily could have heard the sounds of torture. "When I visited the prison in 2015 while on a family visit to Hanoi," Hersh pointed out, "I was struck by how close it was to the street in the central part of the city."[285]

In March 1972, Hersh did have the opportunity to interview two POWs in Hanoi. Before *The New York Times* published his article, Hersh shared his impressions with the Swedish ambassador. The first captive was Major Edison W. Miller of the US Marine Corps. He had been shot down October 13, 1967. "He was in good physical condition and excellent mental balance," Öberg reported to Stockholm about Miller.[286]

The second prisoner had only recently been shot down and left badly burned in the process. "He received good medical care," the ambassador noted.[287]

In Hersh's published article, Miller said, "I have never been tortured and I have never been beaten."[288]

Hersh observed that Miller had to watch what he was saying, for a North Vietnamese official was present. The second prisoner, Air Force Captain Edwin A. Hawley, had been just shot down on February 17. Hawley described his treatment obliquely: "When the bombing was still going on heavy, there were hard feelings. If you were antagonistic you were asking for trouble some times [*sic*], but it was not policy and it depended on your personal behavior."[289]

Hersh's article could leave some readers with the impression that treatment of the detainees had improved over time, but that the North Vietnamese did mistreat both disobedient captives, as well as new prisoners who had been captured in the recent bombing raids, such as Hawley. After his return to the United States, Miller would acknowledge losing half of his hearing due to a battering incident, as well as fifty pounds in weight.[290] Immediately after his own release, Hawley declined to talk about the behavior of his former captors, but did admit having dropped twenty pounds.[291] According to the distinguished gastroenterologist Dr. Mohammad H. Bawani, "Mistreatment, depression, inadequate food, and poor living conditions could all contribute" to such weight loss.[292]

In Washington, Eliasson suspected the abuse of American prisoners. Press reports of torture seemed credible to him, even if he did not put his faith in all of them. More importantly, Eliasson was the embassy's contact person for the POW families, whose fears and suspicions convinced him. "When I met with the wives, they were very sad and angry about torture," he said.[293]

When asked about his Foreign Ministry's claim of humane and lenient treatment, Eliasson was surprised: "No, I didn't know that. They shouldn't have done that. . . . If that's the case, they didn't know. . . . We had an embassy in Hanoi. In that case, they should have confirmed it. I don't recall that was done."[294]

Unaware of the attitude of the Foreign Ministry in Stockholm, Eliasson acted on his own initiative in Washington: "I remember telling Palme [during his US visit in 1970], and also writing home, 'You have to be extremely tough with the North Vietnamese because if they are to have legitimacy, they can't use the same methods,' but they did."[295]

Sadly, the North Vietnamese did use the same methods as the Saigon regime and its American patrons. Detainees suffered on both sides of the 17th parallel.

Lieutenant Halyburton was one of the sufferers. On July 6, 1966, the North Vietnamese forced fifty-two POWs to march through the streets of Hanoi.

Remembering the trauma, Lieutenant Halyburton described the scene in a calm voice: "We were handcuffed in pairs. We had guards on either side of us, with rifles with bayonets, fixed bayonets . . . and we were told to bow our heads to show our shame and all of this to the Vietnamese people, and for all the cameras that were there." Still, Halyburton and others were determined to preserve their dignity: "I think most of us tried to walk with our heads up, and we got lots of bangs on the back of the head from these rifles to make us bow our heads."[296]

In addition, he intended to keep his face visible for the cameras from the international media.[297] As the POWs progressed through the North Vietnamese capital, Lieutenant Halyburton could hear the shouting of the English words "war criminals" and "baby killers." He heard screaming in Vietnamese. "People began to crowd in against us," Halyburton said. "And at the time, we were hit with sticks and mud and rocks and fists and everything. And even the guards that were beside us were getting hit."[298]

Halyburton was not seriously hurt, "but I sure had a lot of bruises and knots on my head and cuts and things like that."[299] In spite of the onslaught, Halyburton and his colleagues maintained their courage and presence of mind. "We came to the Hanoi Sports Stadium, and they opened the gates . . . and we all pushed in there," he said. "And I really believe that had we not, if we had stayed in the streets . . . we probably would have been killed."[300]

After the march, Lieutenant Halyburton endured even worse treatment. He was punched. His interrogators tried to terrify him with claims that he would be sentenced to death for war crimes.[301] The torment went beyond that. First, his captors would fasten cuffs, which were designed for the wrists, very tightly on his forearms. The pain did not stop there, however. After connecting his head to his leg irons by means of a rope, his captors gave the rope a tug.[302]

A similar technique was applied to Commander Stockdale after his capture. One particularly excruciating application was the tying of his upper arms and shoulders together with hemp, and then pulling.[303]

Lieutenant Borling also suffered in prison. After his 1966 shootdown, he encountered little leniency or humanity for most of his six-and-a-half years of captivity in North Vietnam. "I would say the first four-and-a-half, five years were very brutal, with some respite," Borling recounted.[304] The fates of Air Force captains John Dramesi and Edwin Atterbury were a grave example. When they were caught trying to escape in 1969, both men were harshly tortured. "Atterbury was killed, tortured to death," Borling said. "The rest of us, this was when the whippings started with coaxial cable or hand belts, and especially amongst the senior guys themselves."[305]

That did not mean that Borling was constantly tortured: "In my own case, it was episodic. You were locked in a very small room, either alone or with one other guy, or maybe two, for years. And you had no windows, and you had limited ventilation. So, it was terribly hot in summer, terribly cold in winter. You had no books. You had no writing materials.[306]

Inadequate dental care aggravated the suffering of the prisoners:

We all broke teeth. I did, and I must tell you, by the grace of God, I didn't have any substantial pain from teeth until the release at Clark [Air Force Base, a US-controlled facility in the Philippines], when three days after I was released, I'm in a dental chair getting a root canal. But it actually has to be needing a root canal for years, for other people. Now, are their faces blown up, well out-of-proportion. . . . Now, they did bring, about five or six years out, as I remember, they did bring a dentist. They just sit you in a lawn chair. They had this foot drill that somebody would pump with a foot. They would drill out your abscesses or your cavities. They wouldn't put anything in them. They just drilled them out with no Novocain.[307]

Conditions became better after Ho Chi Minh died, "when they thrust us into larger groups . . . the food improved."[308] This improvement was only relative. "While torture was not as universal as it was, there was still punishment meted out for such things as a chanced chain-of-command or failure to follow what they would call requests, but which were orders to go see delegations or go do this."[309]

In addition to direct physical torture, which are prohibited by Articles 130 and 17, other aspects of the prisoners' treatment did not comply with several articles of the Third Geneva Convetion. As implied by Borling, the diet was inadequate. In Commander Stockdale's first days at Hoa Lo Prison, he subsisted on two daily servings of pumpkin soup.[310]

Lieutenant Halyburton's early prison diet was downright disgusting, featuring "rice infested with ants and soup with pig fat."[311]

The Third Geneva Convention devotes an entire article, Article 26, to food: "The basic daily food rations shall be sufficient in quantity, quality and variety to keep prisoners of war in good health and to prevent loss of weight or the development of nutritional deficiencies."[312]

Isolation was a breach of the Geneva Convention. Commander Stockdale, for example, spent the first eighteen months of his imprisonment in solitary confinement, and then for some considerable time afterward.[313] Just as the Third Geneva Convention maintains a standard for prisoner nutrition, it also maintains a requirement for prisoner fellowship. Article 22 states: "The Detaining Power shall assemble prisoners of war in camps or camp compounds according to their nationality, language and customs, provided that such prisoners shall not be separated from prisoners of war belonging to the armed forces with which they were serving at the time of their capture, except with their consent."[314]

Verbal threats and insults, such as those directed at Lieutenant Halyburton and his colleagues during the forced march in Hanoi, also fell into the category of acts outlawed by the Third Geneva Convention. "Likewise, prisoners of war must at all times be protected," demands Article 13, "particularly against acts of violence or intimidation and against insults and public curiosity."[315]

Like Borling, Halyburton also noticed that conditions improved upon the September 1969 death of Ho Chi Minh. Hoping to score an international victory on the public relations front, the North Vietnamese Politburo decided to "apply the points of the Geneva Convention that are consistent with our humanitarian policies."[316] Tellingly, the North Vietnamese still did not accept the Geneva Convention in its entirety.

At any rate, Halyburton noted:

> And they found out that torturing people didn't produce what they wanted. And so, they changed their policy . . . they stopped the really abusive treatment, with some exceptions. . . . I think most of us who had been tortured and all of that, they kind of left us alone after that. But when the bombing started again, you know it stopped in 1968, and didn't start again until 1972, some of those people that were shot down then were tortured because . . . we were bombing like crazy, and they were pretty incensed.[317]

Halyburton, of course, was referring to the bombing halt over North Vietnam that was imposed by Lyndon Johnson in 1968, and the intensification of continued bombing at Richard Nixon's orders in 1972.[318]

As far as torture was concerned, the Swedish Foreign Ministry gave assurances based on inadequate information, but it is understandable why they did so. In the first place, no one at the Swedish embassy ever visited the prisoners, although no Swedish official ever tried.

In the fall of 1970, however, Öberg did propose an official Swedish visit to the prisons. In a strictly confidential memorandum to the Foreign Ministry, Öberg wrote, "Perhaps I should recommend a fairly long and detailed personally-formulated letter from the prime minister or foreign minister to the person concerned in Hanoi concluding with a proposal, an offer, to visit the pilots in their camps with the greatest discretion."[319]

Öberg thought that such an offer could remove the main stumbling block in the official Paris peace talks.[320] Swedish assurances of humane treatment would counter American charges of cruel treatment.

Wachtmeister, as head of the Foreign Ministry's Political Division, objected strongly to Öberg's proposal. Regarding American passion for the POWs, Wachtmeister skeptically concluded that "the interest and commitment are only partly spontaneous."[321] He suspected that the Nixon administration was trying to exploit the issue in order to gain concessions at the Paris peace talks, a counterproductive move:

> The pattern has been the following: the administration creates an opinion, this becomes so gradually so strong that it forces the administration to—or gives the administration a reason for—dramatic actions . . . these actions create, in turn, demands and expectations for additional power measures, etc. It has all become a game with echo effects, or like a tennis game where the opponents hit the ball back with increased power each time.[322]

Increased demands, therefore, would only lead to increased violence. Wachtmeister doubted that the Nixon administration cared about the prisoners of war at all, wondering if it "did not lay in Washington's self-interest to keep the prisoners (or in any case, some of them) in North Vietnam? So long as they are there, Nixon has great possibilities to disarm the domestic criticism against an eventual escalation of his warfare in Indochina."[323]

Wachtmeister did not wish to serve Nixon's agenda in Southeast Asia. "We should avoid all spectacular initiatives of the type, for example, that Öberg was in on this fall: the proposal that the prime minister or foreign minister should in 'greatest secrecy and discretion visit the pilots in their camps.'"[324]

Wachtmeister did not believe that the Americans would keep such an initiative secret, for the propaganda value would be too great. Besides, he believed that an official visit to the prisoners should only take place upon the invitation of the North Vietnamese government.[325]

Many years later, Falkman echoed the late Wachtmeister. He doubted that visiting the prisoners would have served any useful purpose: "It would be so propagandistic, in a way."[326] The Swedes did not wish to draw attention to their POW work "because we wanted to play a discreet role. We could do much more by handling the exchange of letters and messages and lists, etc., etc. without talking about it. We didn't talk about it officially."[327]

At least in the beginning of their official relationship with North Vietnam, the Swedes did not even know for certain where the prisoners were kept. When Falkman made his first visit to Hanoi in 1970, he went for a jog around a lake, Le Petit Lac: "And then two days later, I was summoned to the Foreign Ministry, to the protocol: '"Mr. Falkman, we have heard that you are running around in the park. . . . We should advise you not to do that because some of our soldiers or policeman could think that you are a prisoner of war who escaped from the prison.'"[328]

Under a misapprehension, the North Vietnamese official warned, the police could shoot him.[329]

And I said, "All right. I will not do that anymore."[330]

Falkman laughed at the memory, but the strange experience had led him to conclude "that the prison was very close to us, close to the hotel. And then it was, as some people guessed, but we never had any confirmation about it."[331]

In fact, the old Hoa Lo Prison was in that very location. It was just a part of the notorious detention complex renamed "the Hanoi Hilton" by the POWs. Halyburton explained that "the Hanoi Hilton was not just one area. It had several different areas. . . . So, I was in eight different prisons. Some of them were within thirty miles of Hanoi out in the country. At least one was up near the Chinese border. I moved up there during the bombing of Hanoi in 1972."[332] From Loung Lang POW camp, informally known as Dogpatch, China was nine miles away.[333]

As the chargé d'affaires at the Swedish embassy, Falkman also suspected the reason why the United States had avoided bombing the North Vietnamese capital: "The Vietnamese had informed the Americans directly, probably, that your prisoners are in the Central Prison in Hanoi, and perhaps in other prisoners in Hanoi. . . . This is my belief."[334]

In fact, American authorities did not know the precise location of the prisons, although they knew the majority of them were in the Hanoi area. Falkman was still correct to believe the Americans had sought to avoid bombing the prisons.[335]

Those who managed to visit the prisoners did not detect any signs of torture. Professor Falk sympathized with the North Vietnamese, yet his sympathy was not blind. Leaving his critical faculties switched on, he even declined "to endorse a statement that some people in the antiwar movement favored, which denied that North Vietnam was ever responsible for torture."[336] Falk trusted "other sources that there was some torture, particularly when the pilots were captured after parachuting from their planes if they were shot down by the villagers that captured them."[337]

Moreover, Hanoi's reservation against the Geneva Convention troubled Falk considerably, particularly because it enabled the classification of the POWs as war criminals. "If such practice is generalized," Falk wrote in 1971, "it defeats the humanitarian purposes that underlie the Geneva Conventions and probably leads to a general deterioration in treatment accorded POWs."[338]

When Falk met with eight or so prisoners in September of 1972, however, he saw nothing to confirm his suspicions. "I didn't encounter any evidence . . . and they seemed in good health and good spirits," Falk acknowledged. "They were probably being listened to, and therefore it was not too reliable, but to the extent that one could have an impression, it was an impression that they, at least, were not subject to torture."[339]

Neither making denials nor accusations, Falk simply acknowledged the lack of solid information.[340]

In addition, contemporary media reports on prison conditions were contradictory and confusing. *The New York Review of Books* reported that when Hanoi had released three prisoners in 1969, they initially stated that conditions in captivity had been "adequate" and "assured relatives of the Americans left behind in the North Vietnamese camps they had no cause to worry."[341]

Two of the men, Navy Lieutenant Robert F. Frishman and Apprentice Seaman Douglas B. Hegdahl, later "charged that the North Vietnamese had tortured certain prisoners . . . by pulling out fingernails or tying their hands to the ceilings."[342] Frishman said that he had been "forced . . . to sit tied to a stool in an unbearably hot hut," adding "that the North Vietnamese had neglected persons who needed medical treatment and had kept many prisoners in solitary confinement.[343]

In the fall of 1972, the North Vietnamese freed three American pilots: Navy Lieutenant Markham L. Gartley (j.g.), Navy Lieutentant (j.g.) Norris A. Charles, and Major Edward K. Elias of the Air Force. In an interview with Seymour Hersh, one of the pilots described his last view of Navy Lieutenant Commander John S. McCain III: "I saw him very recently, and he's all right."[344] McCain, the future Arizona senator and presidential candidate, had suffered considerable torture.

A second pilot commented to Hersh: "There's been a lot of bad treatment and a lot of good treatment. You have to look at the whole picture."[345] Yet a third said: "Look, there are four essential things in life—food, clothing, shelter, and medical care . . . they've been adequate, to say the least."[346] According to their account, the prisoners could play games of volleyball and basketball. Reading material, including the classics of English literature, was also plentiful. The three pilots had been in captivity for four years or less, and prison conditions had improved by the final stages of the war, which could explain their relatively positive impressions.[347]

Soon after commenting anonymously on his experiences, Gartley went completely on the record at a press conference: "My treatment during capture has been humane. I have not been mistreated . . . when you take into account the standard of living in the country in which we were confined and examine the conditions, you'd have to say we were treated very well."[348]

North Vietnamese manipulation of the prisoners made the situation even more perplexing to the outside world. Borling faintly recollected the visits of international commissions and delegations: "The standard trick was that they would start to torture twenty or thirty guys, and whoever broke first got to go see the delegation, and tell them how well they were being treated."[349] Interpreting the behavior of the prisoners who did speak to the visitors, Borling went on: "I don't know if their spirits were broken, but I think they were bent enough that they went along with it just to be not hurt anymore."[350]

This fact substantiates Falkman's belief that a prison visit by Swedish officials would have amounted to little more than a propaganda exercise.

Most of the POWs faced their ordeal with remarkable courage, however. "I mean you have no idea how much pain was endured trying to resist the propaganda efforts of the North Vietnamese, and trying to be true to ourselves," Borling said. "The chore was to return, but return with honor. And for the most part, there were only a few radical turncoats over the years."[351]

Borling was modest about his own experiences, but he demonstrated considerable ingenuity when handcuffed:

> I never saw a delegation, not that I was particularly brave. I had a nail I kept in my gum, a piece of a nail, that I could use as a kind of a lock pick to open up the friction cuffs, or the "hell" cuffs we called them, but there wasn't a lock per se. There was just a little lever inside, and I could trick it and open up enough to take away the excruciating pain.[352]

As long as the war lasted, Falkman was unaware of the torture. "We had no idea exactly what was happening," he said later. "And we didn't know."[353] When Falkman returned to Vietnam in the summer of 2013, he visited the surviving portion of the old Central Prison in Hanoi: "Horrible, of course. And there were also *guillotines* from the French. And also they would chain the American prisoners."[354] As much as Falkman condemned the inhumanity of the American war in Vietnam, he could now recognize the inhumanity of the wartime prisons: "But still, they made horrible things."[355]

Palme kept his thoughts on torture to himself. As late as June of 1972, Democratic Representative Donald M. Fraser of Minnesota wrote to Palme: "Your efforts to assure adherence to the Convention Relative to the Treatment of Prisoners of War by all participants in the Indochina War are important and appreciated. I know you will continue and augment them."[356]

Palme, in his response to the Democrat from Minnesota, repeated a line from a draft furnished by the Foreign Ministry: "The Swedish Government has been informed by the North Vietnamese Government that the pilots receive humane treatment and that they may exchange letters with their families."[357]

This was a line he repeated to other American politicians.[358] Obviously, the prime minister acted under the guidance of the Foreign Ministry. To his credit, nevertheless, he avoided repeating the mistake of at least two Foreign Ministry letters; he did not claim any belief in the leniency and humaneness of the North Vietnamese captors.

Ultimately, however, only the American withdrawal from Vietnam would liberate the POWs. Palme probably did not criticize the North Vietnamese for their treatment of the American prisoners for two reasons. Any outspokenness on Stockholm's part would have antagonized the North Vietnamese to no good end. After all, the accusations of the Nixon administration had done nothing to alleviate the suffering of the prisoners. "You have to maximize the probability to get what you want out of them," Eliasson explained. "If we had gone out publicly and condemned the North Vietnamese for torturing prisoners, I am not sure that we'd get those lists out. And that was his calculation, and of course, mine."[359]

In a legal sense, the question of torture was probably too complex for the Swedish government to forthrightly answer. International law had not anticipated a conflict like the Vietnam War. "All of International Humanitarian Law, and law generally, was based on territorial conflict between sovereign states," Professor Falk said. "And at the time of the Vietnam War, there was no law that was geared or oriented toward the problems of intervention in an internal conflict."[360]

After clarifying that legal quandary, Falk added that "the Geneva Protocols of 1977 were negotiated in Geneva after the Vietnam War because it was realized there was an important gap in dealing with that gray area."[361]

Amid this juridical controversy, the Swedish Foreign Ministry correctly refrained from joining Nixon and his associates in their accusations against the North Vietnamese. At the same time, the Foreign Ministry should have adopted a uniformly neutral tone toward these accusations. The Foreign Ministry acted with the best of intentions. In retrospect, however, it would have been better to simply assure the families that it had urged Hanoi to treat the POWs with compassion, leaving it at that.

In addition, Stockholm probably found Nixon's moralizing on the issue hypocritical. After all, American servicemen found themselves held captive in Southeast Asia solely because of the aggressive war waged there by their own government. All the United States had to do to liberate their imprisoned servicemen was to militarily disengage from Vietnam. De Besche in Washington probably reflected the attitude of his superiors when he wrote of "the faulty logic in Nixon's statement that American troops would remain so long as American prisoners were detained in North Vietnam."[362]

One figure the Swedish government could not take seriously was the retired astronaut Frank Borman, whom Nixon appointed special representative on prisoners of war. Borman embarked on a world tour in 1970 to draw attention to the POW issue, and one of his stops was Sweden. Palme, who was visiting the city of Karlstad, received Borman in his hotel room for a forty-five-minute conversation.[363] The prime minister and his advisor, Anders Ferm, were not impressed. "Palme/Ferm have informed me that the evaluation of the meeting with Borman was that it was entirely meaningless," Ekéus of the Foreign Ministry reported to Öberg in Hanoi. "Yet because Borman was said to be Nixon's representative, one could not avoid the meeting."[364]

The problem was that the Nixon administration delinked the POW issue and the war itself, preferring to treat them as completely separate matters.[365]

If the former astronaut sensed Palme's skepticism, it did not deter him. When Borman returned to the United States, he gave an address in Washington before a joint session of Congress. The retired Borman could only imagine the suffering of the American prisoners:

> What are the conditions of your imprisonment and your capture? By and large it is a similar story. After your capture you were probably beaten, dragged through villages, in some cases tortured. If you have been a prisoner for any length of time, you have probably lost 45 to 60 pounds. Your food generally consists of two meals, one largely rice and squash soup and an evening meal of pig fat. It is designed barely to keep you alive, it appears, as is the medical care, destined to barely avert death rather than promote health.[366]

Borman insisted that South Vietnam was treating the North Vietnamese and NLF prisoners humanely, as dictated by the relevant Geneva Convention. Among other South Vietnamese detention facilities, Borman had toured Con Son prison, where he claimed the inmates were common criminals, not political prisoners. The infamous tiger cages, the former astronaut said, were empty.[367] Even if the tiger cages had been empty during Borman's visit, one wonders why the tiger cages had not been taken down.

Skeptical of Borman's rhetorical claims, de Besche mailed home a clipping by *Washington Post* columnist Nicholas von Hoffman. The columnist had his own views about South Vietnamese prisons, reporting that the families of political prisoners were not even allowed to give a petition to US vice president Spiro Agnew, who had traveled to Saigon: "If we have dirty hands, then why should our opponents treat our men any better than we and our Saigon payrollers do?"[368]

The suspicions of the Swedish ambassador were confirmed by Tom Harkin, the future US senator for the state of Iowa. Then a young staffer on Capitol Hill, Harkin accompanied a congressional delegation to South Vietnam. Circumventing the official tour, Harkin managed to see the tiger cages for himself. He found that they were, in fact, occupied by hundreds of political prisoners who had dared to disagree with the South Vietnamese regime. In a published article, Harkin reported:

> Each cell is about five feet wide, ten feet long, and ten feet deep. Into each cell are crowded as many as five people, with no fresh air, no sanitary facilities, no water, and no direct sunlight. Many of those in the cages have their ankles shackled to an iron bar about two feet off the floor. They are sometimes kept this way for months and years. None of the men could stand because their legs were paralyzed from being shackled and beaten.[369]

Tinker, an aide to Senator Kennedy, furnished the article to Eliasson at the Swedish embassy. Gravely concerned about the situation in South Vietnam, Eliasson duly dispatched Harkin's article to Stockholm.[370] "It sort of reinforced my view that we need to have contact with all segments of the Vietnamese society," Eliasson explained. "And whatever happened in the end, we should be aware . . . that this regime was carrying out torture, and detaining people under horrible conditions."[371]

Another article in the Foreign Ministry files was written by Professor Falk. He wrote that "the POW issue becomes pernicious when pro-war forces, trading on the genuine sympathies of all Americans for the prisoners, focus public attention on prisoner mistreatment . . . as a way of rallying support for the Administration's program of prolonging and expanding the war."[372] Carefully underlined in Falk's article were the following words: "American POWs in North Vietnam . . . are not legally entitled to release and repatriation until, according to Article 118 of the Geneva Convention on the Treatment of Prisoners of War, after the cessation of hostilities."[373]

THE INTERNMENT SCHEME

Meanwhile, by 1971, Nixon's belligerent approach to Indochina had failed to resolve the POW question. While Palme was happy to be of service to the prisoners of war, he did not agree with the American proposal for their internment in his own country. The year before, Secretary of State Rogers had written to his counterpart, Foreign Minister Nilsson, to propose that Sweden intern selected prisoners of war. Washington could cover all the costs, including transport of sick and wounded prisoners on a Swedish ship. This was the same proposal that Mrs. Stockdale would make to the Swedish prime minister in Washington. The foreign minister, only agreeing to consider the idea, declined to extend it to Hanoi. Nilsson cautioned Rogers that Stockholm's warm relationship with North Vietnam "has to be treated with the utmost care. The matter is very sensitive, and one wrong step can waste whatever usefulness we may have. The little experience we have of the way of reacting in Hanoi supports such a conclusion."[374]

Dissatisfied, Rogers approached the prime minister himself. "In regard to our prisoners, I would like to reiterate our hope that your Government might seek to arrange to intern American prisoners in Sweden, especially any who may be sick or injured and those longest held."[375]

Kennedy, a man who was far more sympathetic to Palme than anyone in the Nixon administration, also favored the idea. The senator appealed directly to President Ton Duc Thang of North Vietnam that he "would hope seriously ill and wounded prisoners could be repatriated through a neutral country, such as Sweden, with the understanding that such prisoners would remain in that country until the end of hostilities in Vietnam."[376]

Senator Claiborne Pell of Rhode Island, who was representing his nation on the United Nations Committee III on Respect for Human Rights in Armed Conflicts, was just as liberal as Kennedy. Just before the Democratic senator made his statement at the UN committee meeting in New York, he had the courtesy to telephone the head of the Foreign Ministry's Political Division to discuss whether he should directly mention Sweden in his statement. Wachtmeister warned the Democratic senator that "so far, we have not considered this idea workable."[377] He indicated his preference that Pell not mention Sweden in this context . . . and that on the whole, I found it wiser not to take up the internment idea in an address before the committee."[378]

While the Rhode Islander still favored the internment idea, he was enough of a gentleman to exclude Sweden from his official statement, only reminding the United Nations that Convention (III) Relative to the Treatment of Prisoners of War "suggests that prisoners who have undergone a long period of captivity be repatriated or interned in a neutral country."[379]

Then, in January of 1971, Deputy Assistant Secretary of State William Sullivan had lunch with Leifland, now minister at the Swedish embassy in Washington. Leifland explained that Article 111 of the Third Geneva Convention required that "the belligerent parties, united, ask the neutral land about this matter. We had no indication North Vietnam would be interested in internment in a third country."[380]

In fact, the Third Geneva Convention did allow the internment in a neutral country of sick, wounded, and long-detained prisoners. Leifland, however, was correct in his reference to Article 111, which explicitly states, "The Detaining Power, the Power on which the prisoners of war depend, and a neutral Power agreed upon by these two Powers, shall endeavor to conclude agreements which will enable prisoners of war to be interned in the territory of the said neutral Power until the close of hostilities."[381]

Undeniably, the North Vietnamese regarded the American POWs as strategic assets of the war. Not only did these unfortunate men serve as bargaining chips, but they also were useful sources of information (e.g., the North Vietnamese learned to counter the Shrike missile by studying missile remnants after the attacks, and by questioning POWs).[382]

They had little incentive go along with the Nixon administration's internment scheme. Did the North Vietnamese have a legal compulsion to do so? Article 109 of the Geneva Convention only makes it optional for prisoners held for a protracted period: "They may . . . conclude agreements with a view to the direct repatriation or internment in a neutral country of able-bodied prisoners of war who have undergone a long period of captivity."[383]

In 2021, legal scholars for the International Committee of the Red Cross published the updated *Commentary on the Third Geneva Convention*. Heleen Hiemstra, whose area of expertise is Article 109, compared the first and second paragraphs. The wording of the first paragraph is quite stringent, stating that "parties to the conflict are bound to send back to their own country . . . seriously wounded and seriously sick prisoners of war, after having cared for them until they are fit to travel."[384]

By contrast, the second paragraph is less stringent: "Throughout the duration of hostilities, Parties to the conflict shall endeavor, with the co-operation of the neutral Parties concerned, to make arrangements for the accommodation in neutral countries of the sick and wounded prisoners of war."[385]

Hiemstra paid close attention to the word *endeavor* in the second paragraph. "The nature of this obligation is different from the compulsory repatriation of seriously wounded and sick prisoners of war provided for in Article 109(1) which is an obligation of result," Hiemstra explained. "Article 109(2) is rather an obligation of means and the exact content of that obligation depends on the circumstances of each case. While a Detaining Power must make their best efforts to come to an agreement with a neutral Power, it is not obliged to accept any offer that is made by a neutral Power."[386]

According to Marco Sassòli, professor of international law at the University of Geneva, the legal obligation only applies to dire cases, who should be sent home directly: "Prisoners of war who are seriously wounded or sick . . . must be repatriated during hostilities, as their internment is no longer needed to prevent them from participating in hostitlies."[387]

Potentially, other prisoners could have qualified for internment in Sweden. "First, the less seriously wounded and sick . . . may be interned in a neutral country if such internment increases their prospects of recovery," Sassòli wrote. "Secondly, for able-bodied POWs who have undergone a long period of captivity, states are entitled to conclude such agreements, although this remains an option rather than an obligation."[388]

Even according to the contemporary interpretation, international law did not automatically compel the North Vietnamese to agree to the internment scheme for those suspected to be seriously ill and wounded. If international law had obligated the North Vietnamese to do so, Article 112 of the Geneva Convention would have required the independent examination of the POWs by Mixed Medical Commissions. These Mixed Medical Commissions would have consisted of two members from a neutral nation, and one selected by the Detaining Power.[389] Given that the death rate for the POWs held in North Vietnam was only 5 percent, it is likely the vast majority of them, in spite of their health issues, still would have been too healthy to qualify for internment in Sweden.[390] Even if the North Vietnamese had violated international law by rejecting the idea of internment in all cases, it would have been pointless for Stockholm to pursue the internment matter without their approval. It is certain that Sweden had no obligation to accept any internees.

In Hanoi, Öberg was no more enthusiastic about the idea than Wachtmeister was in Stockholm. Öberg warned that making an offer to the North Vietnamese to intern their prisoners would make the Swedes seem eager "to please Washington."[391]

Suddenly, from his vacation home in California on May 3, Nixon made a peculiar official statement through White House Press Secretary Ronald L. Ziegler. The press secretary announced that "President Nixon noted with great satisfaction that according to press reports the government of Sweden has offered the use of its vessels and its territory to provide internment of prisoners of war from the conflict in Vietnam."[392] In addition, Ziegler said Nixon "would hope that Hanoi will move promptly to negotiate an agreement on this issue to take advantage of this humanitarian offer on the part of the Swedish government."[393] Oddly enough, Ziegler admitted that Stockholm had not actually made an offer to Washington, but "I'm sure there will be diplomatic discussions with the Swedish government."[394]

Three days later, American diplomat David K. E. Bruce repeated Nixon's statement at a press conference in Paris, where he was an envoy at the official peace talks. Directly addressing the North Vietnamese during the press conference, Bruce said, "I asked today for such agreement on your part so that we can immediately begin discussions with you on detail arrangements."[395]

Things had gone too far for Stockholm. Falkman got in touch with Guthrie. Falkman "pointed out that the Swedish government never indicated any willingness to place vessels at your disposal."[396] Moreover, Falkman said "the condition that the Swedish government will consider, in a positive spirit, which possibilities we have to give our assistance is . . . that the parties reach a concrete agreement on a request and that this is feasible."[397] Without a doubt, the Swedes knew that Hanoi would never make such an agreement with Washington. The North Vietnamese would never alter the status quo for the POWs as long as Nixon failed to establish an actual date for the total withdrawal of American troops from Vietnam.[398]

That does not mean that the Swedes had lost their desire to help the American prisoners of war. As Wachtmeister wrote in an internal memorandum, "In line with our humanitarian traditions, we are always, on principle, prepared to provide assistance in this matter."[399] He was not even averse to the Japanese proposal of assuming responsibility for the prisoners' care in Vietnam itself.[400] At the same time, Wachtmeister understood that Hanoi would never surrender custody of the prisoners, no matter what form. The North Vietnamese would never treat the POWs as an isolated issue. Captivity for the POWs would end when the war itself ended.[401]

Disregarding Falkman's clarification, Guthrie from the US embassy met with Wachtmeister. Even though he personally doubted that Washington would ever reach an agreement with Hanoi for the internment of POWs in a third country, the American chargé d'affaires pointed out that thirty to thirty-five other countries had given their assent to such a scheme. "Here I interjected," Wachtmeister noted afterward, "that I could well understand the motives of those governments for this."[402] Wachtmeister seemed to imply that the other countries agreed to the American request from a position of dependency and subordination. Sweden, however, was different: "For our part, we were not at all entertained by the way in which our willingness to take part in the hypothetical internment case has been exploited before the American public. The internment question is, of course, a very controversial issue, where Sweden does not wish to be used as a pawn in the game."[403]

The North Vietnamese, like Wachtmeister, regarded Nixon's stand on the American prisoners as little more than gamesmanship. As M. Viet, now North Vietnam's chargé d'affaires in Stockholm, had observed to Wachtmeister, "Nixon's maneuvering on the prisoner issue was typical of his endeavor to push this issue in the foreground at the cost of the main problem of American withdrawal from Vietnam."[404] There is no reason to dispute the claim of the North Vietnamese diplomat. Clearly, the Nixon administration used the prisoners of war to justify the continuation of war.

It is interesting to speculate why Nixon tried to make Sweden a pawn in his game. Even as the president officially ignored Sweden's distinguished reputation for humanitarianism, he could hardly overlook it. A public association with Sweden would only have redounded to Nixon's credit, and to the credit of his policy in Indochina. On the other hand, the rejection by the North Vietnamese of an arrangement with Sweden could only have reflected poorly on them. Since Guthrie did not believe the North Vietnamese would agree to the idea, it is likely that Nixon did not believe so, either. Yet the president made the futile proposal. "Nixon has placed us in the middle," an anonymous Swedish official, probably a diplomat in Washington, said to an American reporter. "I'm sure, however, that the North Vietnamese realize what has happened, and that our relations with Hanoi won't be hurt. But we don't like to be used in an American political ploy."[405]

Certainly, the incident was embarrassing for Sweden. In Paris, North Vietnamese delegates said to a Swedish journalist, "Sweden has fallen into Nixon's trap."[406] Any misunderstanding between Hanoi and Stockholm was presumably and quickly cleared up. Even a few lower-level members of the Nixon administration offered their apologies. Sven Kraemer of the White House National Security Council acknowledged to the Swedish embassy's Leifland that the situation "must have been embarrassing for" Stockholm.[407] Kraemer explained that Nixon and Defense Secretary Laird used Sweden's good name for "political purposes" because "your country has such a stand-ing here."[408] Leifland reported back to Stockholm that "none of the Vietnam experts at the White House had been connected to the formulation of Nixon's statement in California."[409] In the end, Nixon's weird public claim betrayed his own awareness of Sweden's importance in world affairs.

THE POW MATTER AND THE PEACE TALKS

The prisoners of war remained a decisive question in attempts to broker a final peace agreement between the United States and North Vietnam. By the spring of 1971, however, the North Vietnamese were showing some signs of flexibility. Mai Van Bo, who had headed the North Vietnamese delegation in Paris and was now posted at the Foreign Ministry in Hanoi, explained his country's position to Öberg. Washington "promised to withdraw its troops by a final, clearly-stated date and honored a cease-fire, Hanoi would guarantee the safety of the American forces, and determine a date to begin talks for the release of the POWs. "This was a clear, logical, and unambiguous negotiat-ing position," Öberg concluded.[410] At this point, the withdrawal of American troops and the liberation of American prisoners would not have to be simul-taneous. The North Vietnamese offered to work out an exchange of prisoners ahead the settlement of all other issues, provided that Washington select a date of withdrawal.[411]

When Mai Van Bo had met Palme in Paris in the spring of 1970, he said to Öberg, "The Swedish prime minister left a strong impression."[412] Palme was refreshing in comparison to aspiring peacemakers such as the late Senator Robert F. Kennedy, the late US Ambassador to the UN Adlai Stevenson, Pope Paul VI, and the Swiss government. They had been "all equally convinced that it was Hanoi that must make concessions and all sacrifices for American propaganda."[413] Unlike them, said Mai Van Bo, Palme actually comprehended the Vietnamese struggle: "He had been surprisingly well-informed on the situation in Vietnam—even in matters of detail—and his judgments had cor-responded to the reality of the war's developments."[414]

While Nixon may have personally disliked Palme, there were members of the US Congress who shared Mai Van Bo's regard for him, taking the prime minister seriously as a potential peacemaker. In the spring of 1971, Senator Vance Hartke of Indiana was one such politician. The midwestern Democrat also received an encouraging signal from Madame Nguyen Thi Binh, who was performing a dual role for the NLF as its foreign minister and its nego-tiator in the official Paris peace talks. Madame Binh let Hartke know that Hanoi would begin talks on freeing the prisoners when Washington set "any reasonable date" for a complete withdrawal of American forces.[415] Actually, the concession had originated in Hanoi in 1970.

The senator seemed even more excited by a letter he had received from Cyrus Eaton, the Canadian American founder of the Pugwash Conferences on Science and World Affairs. In Hanoi, Eaton had recently met with North Vietnamese Prime Minister Pham Van Dong. According to Eaton's letter, the North Vietnamese prime minister had informed the philanthropist that "North Vietnam would release the POWs as soon as the US indicated that it would end the war."[416] Eaton's understanding did not match that of Stockholm at all.

Hartke, who planned to travel to Paris, asked if he could "informally and discreetly have the opportunity to exchange thoughts with any Swede with knowledge of the peace negotiations and 'the Paris scene'" once he arrived in the French capital.[417] The response of the Swedish embassy in Washington was cautious: "We answered Hartke . . . that we could not find Madame Binh's message signaled the softening of attitude on the POW question."[418] The embassy did not even bother to consider the letter from the Pugwash founder.[419]

Like many Americans, nevertheless, the Indiana senator persisted in getting Stockholm's attention. In his capacity as chairman of the Senate Subcommittee on Surface Transportation, the senator intended to visit Stockholm in June. Hartke planned to "study official communications between the suburbs and Stockholm," but he hoped to "meet representatives of the Swedish government to discuss matters concerning Indochina."[420] The senator must also have hoped to meet Palme. Because of Stockholm's interest in antiwar sentiment within the US Congress, de Besche thought it advisable that the foreign minister meet Hartke.[421]

The senator did better than that; he had lunch with the prime minister on June 16, 1971. At Hartke's request, the meal took place with no advance publicity. The senator was optimistic that the proposed McGovern-Hatfield Amendment, which was attached to the Military Procurement Authorization bill, could pass in the US Senate that year, even though it had failed in 1970. Sponsored by Senators George McGovern of South Dakota and Mark Hatfield of Oregon, the second version of the McGovern-Hatfield Amendment would have put a stop to all American military operations in Vietnam, Laos, and Cambodia by December 31, 1971. The exercise of the congressional power of the purse was key to the amendment, which would have denied Nixon the funds to carry on with his war. If the McGovern-Hatfield Amendment had passed, it would have required the North Vietnamese to make "arrangements for the release and repatriation of" the POWs by December 31.[422]

McGovern was a Democrat and Hatfield was a Republican, so this was a remarkably bipartisan effort by the standards of the polarized American present.[423] As for Hartke himself, he hoped that the North Vietnamese would favor the amendment's successful passage as the setting of an acceptable date of withdrawal, and in turn, release the POWs. The senator from Indiana told Palme that three or four votes could make the difference.[424] "You should immediately mention to Mai Van Bo [North Vietnam's negotiator in Paris], for example, that Hartke informed Palme of his judgement," the Foreign Ministry instructed Öberg in Hanoi. "Of course, we cannot assess the correctness of same."[425] It seems that the Foreign Ministry was right to be so cautious, for the McGovern-Hatfield Amendment would ultimately fail to pass.

When Hartke spoke on the floor of the Senate in support of the amendment, he did not mention his talk with Palme nearly a week before. Yet Hartke's speech echoed the prime minister's own rhetoric: "I tell you we are dying of Vietnam. Just as surely as we have given the death stroke to Laos, Cambodia, and Vietnam, we have written our own death sentence as a free and democratic society."[426] The senator urgently insisted that the McGovern-Hatfield Amendment would "commute that sentence while there is still time."[427]

At times, Hartke seemed overeager in his desire to arrange peace in Indochina with Stockholm's help. Then, he gained fresh inspiration from Madame Binh's recent proposal for the concurrent withdrawal of American troops and release of American prisoners. Wickman, the new foreign minister, had spoken approvingly of Madame Binh's seven-point program as well.[428]

In July of 1971, Hartke sought permission to contact Palme by telephone. The senator thought that Madame Binh's recent initiative might have been due to his own conversation with Palme, about which Stockholm had informed Hanoi. Was there a connection?[429] According to the Foreign Ministry, Palme thought that a "'connection' possibly could exist, but that the prime minister himself cannot determine if such is the case."[430] Palme was at his vacation home on the island of Fårö, but in spite of his skepticism, he had made his private telephone number available to the senator. Such was the prime minister's willingness to serve the cause of peace.

American officials may have sought out officials in Stockholm, but the situation was quite often the reverse. Wachtmeister had invited Guthrie, the US chargé d'affaires, to his home for drinks that spring of 1971. In spite of the social lubrication, the conversation was not lighthearted. Wachtmeister reported on Öberg's recent conversation in Hanoi with the North Vietnamese prime minister. Pham Van Dong had assured Öberg that he "was eager as soon as possible to bring about a negotiated peace for all parties under honorable conditions."[431] Obviously, honor to Pham Van Dong did not mean surrender, but he was prepared to offer "generosity in victory."[432]

Significantly, the North Vietnamese prime minister had expressed the desire that his counterpart in Sweden, Palme, receive his words. "Perhaps he had a wish, without any foundation, that his words would go on to

Washington," Wachtmeister said.[433] The Swede believed in Pham Van Dong's sincerity, but the POW question remained the sticking point:

> Nixon had made his statement on continued withdrawals and confirmed that the goal was total withdrawal, yet without indicating a final date of withdrawal. Hanoi has declared itself prepared to discuss the release of the prisoners, after a final date has been indicated. . . . Nixon has said that one must remain so long as Americans were held prisoner. Hanoi has said that the prisoners can be released only after the Americans evacuate. Therefore, a circle of logic exists here. How shall it be broken?[434]

To break this cycle, Wachtmeister suggested "a vehicle for peace" to Guthrie. In essence, this vehicle was the simultaneous, gradual withdrawal of troops and release of prisoners, which the North Vietnamese would, in fact, soon favor themselves. Wachtmeister thought that such a parallel process could instill confidence and trust on both sides, reflecting, "Under these circumstances, could one not imagine that Nixon would be prepared to give a final date of withdrawal—a 'not later than' date?"[435]

Wachtmeister cautioned Guthrie that his proposal was not an official one made by the Swedish government. Nevertheless, the Swede later informed his colleagues that he "had presented these thoughts to the prime minister and foreign minister, who had raised no objection that I had conveyed them to Guthrie in this informal way."[436]

In typical diplomatic fashion, Guthrie thanked Wachtmeister for his report of Öberg's meeting with Pham Van Dong. The American chargé d'affaires added that he would forward Wachtmeister's "interesting" ideas to Washington. Still, Guthrie defended Nixon's policy on Vietnam: "A superpower could not 'withdraw its commitments, anyway.'"[437] The American war in Vietnam would not end for nearly two years. Along with the refusal to finalize a total withdrawal of US forces, and an insistence on a reciprocal withdrawal of the part of the North Vietnamese, the matter of the prisoners of war remained a sticking point because Nixon wished it to remain so.[438]

SENDING THREE POWS HOME

Until dislodged by the Paris Peace Accords in late January 1973, the sticking point remained throughout 1972. That September, the North Vietnamese had decided to release three detained servicemen because of the persuasive powers of former Attorney General Ramsey Clark, who had just made a trip to Hanoi. Therefore, the North Vietnamese issued the invitation to the

Committee of Liaison to escort the three men home.[439] In turn, the Committee of Liaison would turn to Sweden for help.

Committee co-chairmen Cora Weiss and David Dellinger, on this particular mission, also represented the People's Coalition for Peace and Justice. The Reverend William Sloane Coffin and Professor Falk accompanied the cochairmen. The minister was not a member of the Committee of Liaison. Although the professor was listed on the Committee of Liaison letterhead, he later explained that he "was supportive of it more than active in the sense of doing things."[440]

It was on this trip that Falk would meet with the group who would remain in captivity, "To the best of my collection, eight POWs."[441]

Navy Lieutenant Markham L. Gartley (j.g.), Navy Lieutentant (j.g.) Norris A. Charles, and Air Force Major Edward K. Elias, all freed by the North Vietnamese, were all mentioned earlier in this chapter. Both Charles and Elias had been shot down after the Swedish government had obtained its final list of prisoners.[442] The main objective of the escort group, which included Gartley's mother and Charles's wife, was to keep the pilots away from US authorities, as required by the North Vietnamese government. "They were releasing these pilots not to the U.S. government, but to representatives of the international peace movement," the international jurist explained. "And they made a point of saying future releases will depend on whether they are successfully brought back to the United States without governmental interference."[443]

The group took a SAS flight to Copenhagen, Denmark. "The SAS people took us immediately down to the tarmac," Cora Weiss remembered later, "not into the airport where the press were waiting, and took us to a fabulous restaurant in the countryside to wait for the ongoing plane."[444]

Leaving the fabulous restaurant, they "got back on the plane without going through the airport, thanks to SAS and the Swedes, and flew to Bangkok, and that's when we got on the ICC [International Control Commission] plane."[445]

Reaching Hanoi on September 16, the escort group received the three men the following day. They all stayed at the Hoa Binh Hotel.[446]

The pilots themselves had their own reasons to avoid American custody immediately after their release. They anticipated allegations of collaboration with the enemy.

There was also the upcoming presidential election to consider. "So, there was a strong interest on the part of the U.S. government to gain control of these guys so they wouldn't be able to talk to the media," Falk observed, "and there was the assumption that if North Vietnam released them, they would be fervently against the war."[447]

Actually, the three pilots did not hold uniformly antiwar views. In any case, Falk regarded Nixon's motives with skepticism, believing that "he was concerned not for their well-being, these three guys, but for the fact that they could be effective voices against his re-election."[448]

At this point, the Swedish ambassador came to the rescue. Falk rapidly found himself on excellent terms with Öberg, whose energy, opposition to the war, and firm bond with Palme all impressed the professor.[449]

Far more crucially, Öberg allowed the group to use the radio transmitters at the Swedish embassy. "Logistically, we didn't have any good alternative to work out a return set of arrangements that didn't expose us to airports where the U.S. could assert its authority," Falk said.[450] Naturally, the group would have to steer clear of Thailand, Laos, and Cambodia. When North Vietnam had released POWs to antiwar activists in the past, American authorities had pressured the former prisoners to board US military planes in Vientiane, Laos, thereby preventing any independent communication with the media.[451]

The Swedish transmitters were helpful in that regard, but they also served another purpose. In the name of the Committee of Liaison as well as the People's Coalition for Peace and Justice, the escort group telegraphed the following to the president:

> In accordance with the expressed expectations of the North Vietnamese govern-
> ment and in order not to jeopardize the possibility of future releases we believe
> the repatriation of these men should carried out in the following manner STOP
> 1. The men shall proceed home with us and representatives of their families in
> civilian aircraft STOP 2. The men if they wish shall be granted a 10 day furlough
> STOP 3. The men shall receive a complete medical check-up at the hospital of
> their choice civilian or military STOP 4. The men shall do nothing further to
> promote the American war effort in Indochina STOP We believe these terms are
> reasonable and humane and in the best interest of the remaining families and
> their families.[452]

Kissinger mentioned the Committee of Liaison telegram in his Daily Brief to the president.[453] The pilots themselves sent a telegram to Nixon: "In the best interests of all parties concerned we think we should be allowed to return to New York with the escort delegation, and be allowed to spend a few days with our families, if so desired."[454]

Well before the escort group finalized their itinerary, Kissinger was concerned that a possible "stopover in Stockholm may well have been designed to provide maximum propaganda exploitation of the POW's before their return to the US (and to military control)."[455]

As the escort group planned their journey home, the Swedish ambassador performed another key service. "He arranged with the Chinese to take us from Hanoi to Beijing," Weiss said.[456]

The liberated prisoners would fly out of Hanoi on September 25 on CAAC, the Chinese national airline, and on to Moscow. Then, they would take Aeroflot, the Soviet national airline, to Copenhagen rather than Stockholm. Finally, SAS would take them to New York.[457] Although the committee would have preferred to fly from Moscow to Stockholm, it sought to avoid delays, and Copenhagen provided the most direct way home. The prime minister was kept fully informed of this plan.[458] Relying on his own sources, Kissinger informed Nixon of the plan as well.[459]

Through Öberg in Hanoi, Weiss sought Palme's help in arranging a press conference at Kastrup Airport in Copenhagen. She made her case with Öberg with "references to her earlier contacts with the Cabinet Office, the [Washington] embassy, and Olof Palme in New York," presumably during one of his visits to the United States in 1970.[460]

Öberg regarded Weiss's media agenda with some skepticism: "It seems to me fairly far from certain that the release of the pilots will be the public relations coup against the war that from the beginning, Cora Weiss and her group have counted on."[461]

Wishing to conduct the matter as discreetly as possible, Wachtmeister of the Foreign Ministry responded to Öberg: "Concerning Cora Weiss's repeated references to conversations with Palme and the Cabinet Office, I want to state for your information that the Cabinet Office has explained their wish that this matter be handled entirely by the Foreign Ministry."[462]

Weiss also requested the assistance of a SAS representative upon landing in Copenhagen, in order to book the final leg of the journey to New York. In addition, she wished to reserve a facility at Kastrup for the desired press conference. "In strictest confidence, the SAS representative in Moscow is to be informed about the wishes of Cora Weiss above," Cabinet Stockholm instructed the Swedish embassy in Moscow. "At the same time, it should still be made clear that this is not in any way an instruction to the SAS representative from Swedish authorities."[463]

Wachtmeister assured the Danish government that "any action was, of course, an internal Danish matter, and that we only wanted, in the spirit of Nordic consultation, to inform Copenhagen about what was going on."[464]

His counterpart at the Danish Foreign Ministry "commented that a request via Stockholm scarcely seemed to him to be sufficiently strong grounds for the Danish government to act upon Cora Weiss's request. She could have turned directly to Danish authorities."[465]

In spite of the Danes' reluctance, Weiss's approach via Stockholm worked. The Swedish government wanted to assist a good cause, if nothing else. SAS, that symbol of Scandinavian cooperation, received her group with hospitality.

When they landed in Moscow on September 27, they encountered Adolph Dubs, the chargé d'affaires of the US embassy. Accompanied by the embassy's military attaché and doctor, Dubs encouraged the pilots and their relatives to stay at the embassy, and then fly home on a US medevac plane from Copenhagen, "which I assumed would be their next stop."[466] The group did not feel obligated to accept the offer. "Welcome Sweden once more," Weiss said, "the Swedish head of SAS Moscow comes to pick us up in a Swedish SAS van, and takes us to their private apartment in Moscow, where there's a telephone, and says to the three guys. 'Call home.'"[467]

The entire group enjoyed a smorgasbord, and then took SAS out of Moscow. To their displeasure, two officials from the local US embassy joined them on the flight. "So, we fly to Copenhagen," Weiss said, "and we land, and we go to a restaurant again thanks to SAS."[468]

Before their lunch, the group had managed to shake off the chargé d'affaires from the US embassy in Copenhagen, as well as the US counselor and Air Force attaché. The three men had approached them upon landing. The chargé d'affaires, Thomas J. Dunnigan, offered the former POWs the use of an Air Force jet. "Personally, I would prefer to continue on to New York under the circumstances we're in," Gartley said. "I'm in good health, and there are other considerations now."[469]

Elias also preferred to keep the Committee of Liaison as his escort: "I've been told by these people that future releases were contingent on the way it was handled. I don't want to do anything which might affect someone else."[470]

The group did manage to hold their press conference during their layover in Copenhagen. Gartley expressed concern for the pilots who remained in captivity, favoring "whichever policy will bring the men home the fastest is the one I support the most."[471] Elias, whose family had skipped the journey out of respect for the Pentagon's wishes, declined to take a political stand: "As you know I've been sort of shepherded away from the actual issues. I feel there's a lot of reading I have to do."[472]

Charles was outspokenly antiwar. "I would like to say that I am happy," he said, "but I would be much happier when my fellow prisoners-of-war are able to return home. It is my belief, and the belief of the men with whom I lived while in Hanoi, that if the war is terminated, their return home will be certain."[473]

Charles had asked himself who could free the POWs: "It dawned upon me that it was you. It was you, the American people. If you really want to bring these men home, you can do it."[474]

To their surprise, a few American military personnel boarded their plane to New York. The personnel persuaded the former POWs to don uniforms.[475] The liberated prisoners still managed to reach their home country with their original escort group. Upon arrival in the United States on the evening of September 28, however, Swedish assistance had lost its effect. Prompted by US government officials, the three pilots agreed to check into military hospitals. Elias was immediately willing to do so. Gartley and Charles, who had both planned to make extended visits with their families and to communicate with the media outside of military custody, agreed with great reluctance.[476] Yet willingly or reluctantly, the servicemen really had no choice. "My understanding is that these freed POWs were still subject to military discipline," said Falk in retrospect, and that requirement "to submit to the Pentagon for 'medical debriefing' was a legitimate order that could be not be refused by these men without adverse consequences."[477]

Despite the journey's tense conclusion, the Committee of Liaison was indebted to Palme. "You may have some idea of how complicated and difficult the situation was," Cora Weiss wrote afterward to the prime minister, "and you should know how reassuring it was to have your complete confidence and support."[478]

Weiss extended her gratitude to Palme to "the warm and generous help of your Embassy staff in Hanoi and especially Ambassador Ogard [*sic*]."[479]

She also acknowledged that "without the assistance of the staff of SAS we never would have made it."[480]

SAS, with the intervention of the Swedish government as part owner, had made it possible for the three pilots to hold the uncensored press conference in Copenhagen, and then travel freely.

Nixon also expressed his gratitude, only not to Sweden. Crediting the relevant State Department and Foreign Service personnel, the president wrote to Secretary of State Rogers: "Their tact and dignity under difficult and complicated circumstances helped to counter the efforts which were made to exploit the release for propaganda purposes."[481]

Nearly eight hundred American servicemen were held at some point in the course of the Vietnam War.[482] Swedish policymakers attached great importance to their relationship with the United States, but they were willing to risk that relationship in their opposition to the Vietnam War. By supporting the families of American prisoners of war, neutral Sweden also supported the cause of peace.

NOTES

    1. Wachtmeister, Ekéus from Öberg, *"Situationen Vietnam-Indokina,"* December 16, 1970. *UD HP-Dossierer, Vietnamkriget, Mål: H, Hanoi's politik,* 1970–1971, HP38:26, RA.

    2. Courtesy of David Prentice. Letter from Olof Palme to J. William Fulbright of Arkansas, July 3, 1970. Folder 1970, Box 17:4, Subseries 3 Committee Administration, Series 48 Foreign Relations Committee, JWF.

3. Courtesy of David Prentice. Letter from J. William Fulbright to Olof Palme, July 11, 1970. Folder 1970, Box 17:4, Subseries 3 Committee Administration, Series 48 Foreign Relations Committee, JWF.

4. Speech of J. William Fulbright of Arkansas, *The Congressional Record*, December 4, 1970. Box 37, F1, JWF.

5. Ekéus interview. Memorandum from Hoyt Purvis to J. William Fulbright, June 3, 1970. Box 27, Folder 4, J. W. Fulbright Papers. Geoffery Stark, University Libraries Special Collections, University of Arkansas, electronic mail, May 6, 2019. Lieutenant Colonel Bobby Gene Vinson remained missing in action. His remains were returned to the United States in 1998: https://www.pownetwork.org/bios/v/v004.htm.

6. Ekes interview.

7. Eliasson telephone interview.

8. Ekéus interview.

9. Ekéus interview. Esbjörn Rosenblad, Negotiations Group, Swedish Foreign Ministry, *"Dag Hammarskjöld och FN-piloternas frigivning,"* April 21, 1970. *UD HP-Dossierer, Vietnamkriget, Mål:K, Krigsfångefrågan,* January-May 1970, HP38:31, RA; Henrik Berggren, *Dag Hammarskjöld: Att Bära Världen* (Stockholm: Bokförlaget Max Ström, 2016) 128–29, 133–35; Brian Urquhart, *Hammarskjold* (New York: W.W. Norton & Company, 1994), 96–97, 99, 103, 118, 121, and 126; Bjereld, Johansson, and Molin, *Sveriges Säkerhet och Världens Fred,* 126, 129–30.

10. Falkman interview.

11. Falkman, *Ekot från* Vietnam, 11.

12. Bo A. Ericsson, *"Brev till DN om fångar—Hanois man svarar: USA-flygarna pirater men de behandlas väl,"* *Dagens Nyheter,* November 7, 1969.

13. Ibid.

14. Richard Falk, "The American POWs: Pawns in Power Politics," *The Progressive* (March 1971), 16; Stuart I. Rochester and Frederick Kiley, *Honor Bound: American Prisoners of War in Southeast Asia, 1961–1973* (Annapolis, MD: Naval Institute Press, 1998), 189; Richard A. Falk, "International Law Aspects of Repatriation of Prisoners of War During Hostilities," *The American Journal of International Law* 67:3, 468–69; Richard Falk, University of California, Santa Barbara, email, August 11, 2018.

15. Falk, "International Law Aspects of Repatriation of Prisoners of War During Hostilities." Falk email.

16. International Committee of the Red Cross, Articles 70 and 71, *Commentary on the Third Geneva Convention: Convention (III) relative to the Treatment of Prisoners of War, Volume II* (Cambridge, UK: Cambridge University Press, 2021), 1140, 1155.

17. International Committee of the Red Cross, Article 130, *Commentary on the Third Geneva Convention, Volume II,* 1875.

18. International Committee of the Red Cross, Article 17, *Commentary on the Third Geneva Convention: Convention (III) relative to the Treatment of Prisoners of War, Volume I* (Cambridge, UK: Cambridge University Press, 2021), 653.

19. Transcript of *Meet the Press*, National Broadcasting Company, June 7, 1970, Swedish Information Service. *UR talserien Volym* 2.4.0: 021, OPA ARAB.

20. Dave L. Garrett, *The Power of One: Bonnie Singleton and American Prisoners of War in Vietnam*. Master of Science Thesis in History, University of North Texas (August 1999), 20, 24–25.

21. Ibid., 40.

22. Ibid., 42.

23. Timothy Castle, email, May 12, 2019.

24. Castle email. H. Bruce Franklin, email, December 15, 2018.

25. For technical developments in aerial reconnaissance after the U-2, see David Robarge, "Archangel: CIA's Supersonic A-112 Reconnaissance Aircraft," Center for the Study of Intelligence, Central Intelligence Agency, Washington, D.C., 2012: https://www.cia.gov/library/center-for-the-study-of-intelligence/csi-publications/books-and-monographs/a-12/Archangel-2ndEdition-2Feb12.pdf.

26. Ibid.

27. Garrett, *The Power of One*, 46–47, 49–51.

28. Ibid, 52.

29. Garrett, *The Power of One*, 55–56. Speech of Ross Perot at the National Press Club, March 9, 1970. Library of Congress Recorded Sound Research Center, Washington, D.C.

30. Daniel Viklund, *"Flygarhustrur från USA ber Olof Palme om hjälp,"* Dagens Nyheter, November 26, 1969; Hershberger, *Traveling to Vietnam*, 187.

31. Monica Anrep-Nordin, *"Deras män är fångar i Nordvietnam. Barnen frågar varje dag: Har jag också en pappa?,"* Svenska Dagbladet, November 27, 1969.

32. Garrett, *The Power of One*, 57.

33. Ibid., 57.

34. *"Pilotfruarna hos Palme: Sympati och förståelse men inga klara besked,"* Dagens Nyheter, November 28, 1969. Gregg Hartness, Colonel, United States Air Force: http://www.arlingtoncemetery.net/gregg-hartness.htm.

35. Memorandum from Wilhelm Wachtmeister to the Swedish embassy in Washington, December 30, 1970. *UD HP-Dossierer, Vietnamkriget, Krigsfångefrågan, Mål:K,* from December 1970 to January 1971, HP38:33, RA.

36. Anne Plott, "Anniston Woman Joins Vocal Group: Wives of American POWs Are No Longer Silent," *The Anniston Star*, September 28, 1969.

37. Greta P. Terrell's husband Lieutenant Colonel Irby David Terrell Jr. of the United States Air Force. Letter from Greta P. Terrell to Prime Minister Olof Palme, November 1, 1969, *UD HP-Dossierer, Vietnamkriget, Krigsfångefrågan. Korrespondens till Olof Palme* 1968–1974, HP 38:47, RA.

38. Ibid.

39. Associated Press, "Air Force Wife Tries In Vain for Viet Visa, *Fort Walton Beach Playground Daily News,* December 22, 1969.

40. Telegram from Mrs. James Lindberg Hughes to Olof Palme, January 26, 1970. *UD HP-Dossierer, Vietnamkriget, Krisgfångefrågan, Korrespondens till Olof Palme,* 1968–1974, HP38:47, RA.

41. Telephone interview with Porter Halyburton and Marty Halyburton, October 10, 2018; Hirsch, *Two Souls Indivisible*, 62.

42. Interview with Halyburtons. James S; Hirsch, *Two Souls Indivisible: The Friendship That Saved Two POWs in Vietnam* (New York: Houghton Mifflin Company, 2004), 57.

43. Interview with Halyburtons; Hirsch, *Two Souls Indivisible*, 61.

44. Interview with Halyburtons; Hirsch, *Two Souls Indivisible*, 146.

45. Lieutenant Richard Raymond Ratzlaff, USN; Ibid.

46. Jim and Sybil Stockdale, *In Love and War: The Story of a Family's Ordeal and Sacrifice During the Vietnam Years* (New York: Harper and Row, Publishers, 1984), 197; Rochester and Kiley, *Honor Bound*, 205.

47. Jim and Sybil Stockdale, *In Love and War*, 208–09; Mrs. Marty Halyburton, email, November 11, 2018; Gordon I. Peterson and David C. Taylor, "A Shield and a Sword: Intelligence Support to Communications with US POWs in Vietnam," *Studies in Intelligence* 60:1 (March 2016), 5.

48. Hirsch, *Two Souls Indivisible*, 182.

49. Interview with Halyburtons; Hirsh, *Two Souls Indivisible*, 183.

50. Ibid.

51. Letter from Martha Halyburton to Olof Palme, October 18, 1969. *UD HP-Dossierer, Vietnamkriget, Krigsfångefrågan, Korrespondens till Olof Palme, 1968–1974*, HP38:47, RA.

52. Telegram from the American Embassy in Stockholm to the Secretary of State, December 8, 1969. Nixon Presidential Materials Staff, NSC Files, Country Files—Europé, Box 707, RN. Sven Åhman, *"Flygarhustru: Första livstecknet på femtitvå månader,"* *Dagens Nyheter,* March 8, 1970.

53. Memorandum from Henry A. Kissinger to the President, "Swedish Approach to North Vietnamese on Paris Talks," November 8, 1969. Nixon Presidential Materials Staff, NSC Files, Country Files -Europe, Box 707, RN.

54. Ibid.

55. Coded Telegram 74 from Gunnar Jarring to the Foreign Ministry, March 3, 1970. *UD HP-Dossierer, Vietnamkriget, Mål: K, Krigsfångefråan,* January-May 1970, HP38:31, RA. Coded Telegram from Cabinet Stockholm to Hubert de Besche, July 3, 1970. *HP-Dossierer, Vietnamkriget, Mål: K, Krigsfångefråan,* January-May 1970, HP38:32, RA.

56. List of Fourteen American POWs. Given by Nguyen Tho Chan in Moscow for Swedish Torsten Nilsson, March 3, 1970. *UD HP-Dossierer, Vietnamkriget, Krigsfångefrågan, Mål:K,* January-May 1970, HP38:31, RA. *"Brådskande från pressbyrån, re Palmes i dag avsända telegram till amerikanska piloters anhöriga."* Telegram from Foreign Ministry Press Office in Stockholm to the Swedish Embassy in Washington, December 10, 1970. *UD HP-Dossierer, Vietnamkriget, Krigsfångefrågan, Mål:K,* June-December 1970, HP38:32, RA. United Press International, "Sweden Lists 14 U.S. POWs," March 8, 1970.

57. Memorandum from Henry A. Kissinger to the President, March 9, 1970. Nixon Presidential Materials Staff, NSC Files, POW/MIA, President's Daily Briefs, Box 1, RN.

58. The prisoners were Lieutenant Colonel Gordon Albert Larson USAF, Captain Paul Edward Galanti USN, Commander James Bond Stockdale USN, and Lieutenant

Colonel James Alfred Mulligan USN. United Press International, "North Vietnam Releases List of 59 U.S. Prisoners of War," *The San Bernardino County Sun*, November 27, 1969. "'Chicago 7' Releases Names of 59 U.S. PWs," *The Philadelphia Inquirer*, November 27, 1969. Michael J. Allen, *Until the Last Man Comes Home: POWs, MIAs, and the Unending Vietnam War* (Chapel Hill: The University of North Carolina Press, 2009), 37; Hershberger, *Traveling to Vietnam*, 1.

59. The prisoners first confirmed by Women Strike for Peace before appearing on the Swedish list were Lieutenant Everett Alvarez USN, Captain Philip Neal Butler USN, Lieutenant Ralph Thomas Browning USAF, Captain Robert J. Naughton USN, and Lieutenant Darrel Edwin Pyle USAF. For the record, Women Strike for Peace confirmed the imprisonment of 131 American servicemen. Associated Press, "Here Is List of Prisoners and Mail Recipients," *The Miami Herald*, December 24, 1969. Associated Press, "Names of 132 POWs Released," *The Miami Herald*, December 24, 1969. See James W. Clinton, *The Loyal Opposition: Americans in North Vietnam, 1965–1972* (Louisville, CO: University Press of Colorado, 1995).

60. USN=Navy, USAF=Air Force. List of Fourteen American POWs, March 3, 1970. The Committee of Liaison publicized its own confirmation of Lieutenant Halyburton's captivity on March 6, 1970, but given the time difference between Sweden and the United States, the telegrams sent by Olof Palme in the afternoon could have reached the POW wives much earlier that day. In any case, the US Navy had informed Mrs. Halyburton of the Swedish confirmation some time before March 6. Sven Åhman, *"Flygarhustru: Första livstecknet på femtitvå månader,"* Dagens Nyheter, March 8, 1970. "Statement of Mrs. Cora Weiss, Co-Chairman, Committee of Liaison with Families of Servicemen Detained in North Vietnam, New York, N.Y.," March 31, 1971. *American Prisoners of War in Southeast Asia*, 1971, 231. United Press International, "Sweden Gets List of 14 PWs in Hanoi," *The Philadelphia Inquirer*, March 8, 1970.

61. Interview with Halyburtons.

62. Telegram from Olof Palme to Martha Halyburton, March 6, 1970. *UD HP-Dossierer, Vietnamkriget,Mål:K, Krigsfångefrågan*, January-May 1970, HP38:31, RA.

63. Letter from Leif Leifland to Martha Halyburton, March 4, 1970. *UD HP-Dossierer, Vietnamkriget, Mål:K, Krigsfångefrågan*, January-May 1970, HP38:31, RA.

64. Telegram from Olof Palme to Barbara J. Singleton, March 6, 1970. Letter from Leif Leifland, March 4, 1970. *UD HP-Dossierer, Vietnamkriget, Mål:K, Krigsfångefrågan*, January-May 1970, HP38:31, RA.

65. According to the *St. Louis Post-Dispatch*, Irby D. Terrell, Jr.'s name "had not appeared on previous lists of those known captured, although they appear on lists of those missing." Post-Dispatch Wire Services, "Names of 27 American POWs Held by Hanoi Are Made Public," *St. Louis Post-Dispatch*, March 7, 1970.

66. Sven Åhman, *"Flygarhustru: Första livstecknet på femtitva månader,"* Dagens Nyheter, March 8, 1970.

67. Per Forslind, *"27 fångnamn . . . Ingen av 14 namn nya för USA,"* Svenska Dagbladet, March 8, 1970.

68. "Wife of Confirmed POW Still Plans Trip: Seeking Names of Others Missing," *Tucson Daily Citizen*, March 12, 1970. Anne Plott, "POW's Wife Expects Six-Line Letter," *The Anniston* Star, March 12, 1970. Letter to Greta P. Terrell from Leif Leifland of the Swedish Foreign Ministry, March 4, 1970. *UD HP-Dossierer, Vietnam-kriget, Mål: K, Krigsfångefrågan*, January-May 1970, HP38:31, RA.

69. Marty Halyburton, email, October 10, 2018.

70. Telephone interview with Halyburtons; Hirsch, *Two Souls Indivisible*, 213.

71. "Statement of Mrs. Cora Weiss, Co-Chairman, Committee of Liaison with Families of Servicemen Detained in North Vietnam, New York, N.Y.," March 31, 1971. *American Prisoners of War in Southeast Asia, 1971: Hearings before the Sub-committee on National Security Policy and Scientific Developments of the Committee on Foreign Affairs, House of Representatives, Ninety-Second Congress, First Session* (Washington D.C.: U.S. Government Printing Office, 1971), 230; "Cora Weiss" in James W. Clinton, *The Loyal Opposition: Americans in North Vietnam* (Louisville: University Press of Colorado, 1995), 166.

72. Associated Press, "Letters from POW Mates," *Lubbock Avalanche-Journal*, April 28, 1970; United Press International, "Flyers' Wives Relieved, Angry," *The Daily Colonist*, April 28, 1970.

73. United Press International, "Swedish PM Writes to Santa Fe Woman," *Albu-querque Journal*, March 7, 1970.

74. Letter from Martha Lindberg Hughes to Olof Palme, September 17, 1972. *HP UP-Dossierer, Vietnamkriget, Krigsfångefrågan, Korrespondens till Olof Palme*, 1968–1974, HP38:47, RA.

75. Letter from Marie Hinckley to Olof Palme, April 6, 1970. *UD HP-Dossierer, Vietnamkriget, Krigsfångefrågan, Korrespondens med krigsfångars anhöriga*, 1970–1974, HP38:39, RA.

76. "Statement of Mrs. Sybil Stockdale, Coranado, Calif," May 1, 1970. *American Prisoners of War in Southeast Asia, 1970: Hearings before the Subcommittee on National Security Policy and Scientific Developments of the Committee on Foreign Affairs, House of Representatives, Ninety-First Congress, Second Session* (Washington D.C.: U.S. Government Printing Office, 1970), 58–59; Jim and Sybil Stockdale, *In Love and* War, 123–30, 229–30.

77. Bruce Weber, "Sybil Stockdale, Fierce Advocate for P.O.W.s and Their Fami-lies, Dies at 90," *New York Times*, October 15, 2015; Telegram from Olof Palme to Sybil Stockdale, March 6, 1970, and Letter from Leif Leifland to Sybil Stock-dale, March 4, 1970. *UD HP-Dossierer, Vietnamkriget, Mål:K, Krigsfångefrågan*, January-May 1970, HP38:31, RA.

78. List released by David Dellinger and Rennie Davis, November 1969.

79. Steven A. Holmes, "James Stockdale, Perot's Running Mate in '92, Dies at 81," *New York Times*, July 6, 2005.

80. Interview with Halyburtons; Hirsch, *Two Souls Indivisible*, 209.

81. Press Conference of Mrs. Maureen A. Dunn, Mrs. Sybil E. Stockdale, and Mrs. Phyllis E. Galanti, Office of the White House Press Secretary, May 15, 1972. Attach-ment sent by the Swedish embassy in Washington to the Swedish Foreign Ministry, May 16, 1972. *UD HP-Dossierer, Vietnamkriget, Krigsfångefrågan*, HP38:36, RA.

82. Michael J. Allen, *Until the Last Man Comes* Home, 47; Jim and Sybil Stockdale, *In Love and War*, 361–62, 384–85, 390, 407–08, 411–13.

83. Press Conference of Mrs. Maureen A. Dunn, Mrs. Sybil E. Stockdale, and Mrs. Phyllis E. Galanti.

84. Coded Telegram from Hubert de Besche, *"Pow-frågan och statsministerns besök,"* May 28, 1970. *UD HP-Dossierer, Vietnamkriget, Mål:K, Krigsfångefrågan,* January-May 1970, HP38:31, RA.

85. Jan Eliasson, *"Statsministern mottar delegation i krigsfångefrågan,"* June 9, 1970. *UD HP-Dossierer, Vietnamkriget, Mål: K, Krigsfångefrågan,* June-December 1970, HP38:32, RA.

86. Ibid.

87. The imprisonment of Lieutenant Bernard Talley Jr. USAF was later confirmed by the Committee of Liaison. See Committee of Liaison list in *The New York Times*, June 26, 1970. Major Talley would also appear in the lists released by Sweden in November and December.

88. First Lieutenant Bernard L. Talley Jr. was on the list of prisoners given by Hanoi to Palme in December of 1970. See Committee of Liaison list in *The New York Times*, June 26, 1970.

89. Esbjörn Rosenblad, *"Dag Hammarskjöld och FN-piloternas frigivning,"* April 21, 1970. *UD HP-Dossierer, Vietnamkriget, Mål:K, Krigsfångefrågan,* January-May 1970, HP38:31, RA.

90. Falk interview.

91. Ibid.

92. Ibid.

93. Ibid.

94. Eliasson Stockholm interview.

95. Ibid.

96. Ibid.

97. Ibid.

98. Per Forslind, *"Palme lovar nya aktioner om krigsfångar,"* Svenska Dagbladet, June 9, 1970.

99. Ibid.

100. Ibid.

101. Letter from Mrs. James B. Stockdale to Olof Palme of Sweden, August 14, 1970. *UD-HP-Dossierer, Vietnamkriget, Krigsfångefrågan, Korrespondens till Olof Palme,* 1968–1934, HP38:47, RA.

102. Peter Ognibene, "Rift in the Ranks: Politics and POWs," *The New Republic*, June 3, 1972; Michael J. Allen, *Until the Last Man Comes Home*, 40.

103. Allen, *Until the Last Man Comes Home*, 39.

104. John Borling, telephone interview, June 15, 2016.

105. Ibid.

106. Ibid.

107. Interview with Halyburtons.

108. Borling interview.

109. Ibid.

110. Ibid.

111. Interview with Halyburtons.

112. Ibid.

113. Ibid.

114. Interview with Halyburtons; Hirsch, *Two Souls Indivisible*, 215.

115. Interview with Halyburtons. Although Nixon's sabotage was long suspected, the revelations in John A. Farrell's *Richard Nixon: The Life* received extensive media coverage. See Peter Baker, "Nixon Tried to Spoil Johnson's Vietnam Peace Talks in '68, Notes Show, *New York Times*, January 2, 2017, and Aram Goudsouzian, "Deepening the complexity of Richard Nixon from newly released material," *Washington Post*, March 24, 2017.

116. H. Bruce Franklin, *M.I.A. or Mythmaking in America: how and why belief in live POWs has possessed a nation* (New York: Lawrence Hill Books, 1992), 61.

117. Peter Ognibene, "Rift in the Ranks: Politics and POWs." "P.O.W. Politics," *New York Times*, October 3, 1971.

118. Falkman, *Ekot från Vietnam*, 11.

119. Falkman interview; Falkman, *Ekot från Vietnam*, 11.

120. Falkman, *Ekot från Vietnam*, 12.

121. Ibid.

122. Falkman interview.

123. Ibid.

124. Courtesy of David Prentice. Transcript of Harold Wilson's conversation with Olof Palme, April 7, 1970. PREM 13/3552, Public Records Office, Kew, England.

125. Coded Telegram from Cabinet Stockholm to Hubert de Besche at the Washington embassy, July 3, 1970. *HP-Dossierer, Vietnamkriget, Mål: K, Krigsfångefråan,* January-May 1970, HP38:32, RA.

126. *Pressbyrån* Nilsson, *"Pressmeddelande ang amerikanska krigsfångar i Nordvietnam,"* December 23, 1970. *UD HP-Dossierer, Vietnamkriget, Mål: K. Krigsfångefrågan,* December 1970-January 1971, HP 38:33, RA. List of missing American servicemen sent by Olof Palme to M. Nguyen Tho Chan, July 5, 1970. List of confirmed prisoners sent by the North Vietnamese Ministry of Foreign Affairs to the Swedish Embassy in Hanoi, November 25, 1970. *UD HP-Dossierer, Vietnamkriget, Mål: K. Krigsfångefrågan,* June-December 1970, HP 38:32, RA.

127. Robert C. Toth, "Hanoi Gives Sweden Data on POWs," *Newsday*, December 12, 1970.

128. Lists given to Cora Weiss by the Vietnam Committee for Solidarity with the American People, November 6 and 20, 1970. *UD HP-Dossierer, Vietnamkriget, Krigsfångefrågan, Korespondens med krigsfångars anhöriga,* 1970–1974, HP38:39, RA. United Press International, "North Vietnam Releases List of 59 U.S. Prisoners of War." Associated Press, "Here Is List of Prisoners and Mail Recipients." "Names of 334 U.S. Captives Hanoi Admits Holding, *New York Times,* June 26, 1970.

129. Telegram 1359 from Hubert de Besche in Washington to Cabinet Stockholm, December 11, 1970. *UD HP-Dossierer, Vietnamkriget, Mål:K, Krigsfångefrågan,* December 1970 to January 1971, HP38:33, RA.

130. Toth, "Hanoi Gives Sweden Data on POWs," December 12, 1970.

131. Clinton, "Cora Weiss" in *The Loyal Opposition*, 165–66. See lists given to Cora Weiss by the Vietnam Committee for Solidarity with the American People, November 6 and 20, 1970; Bui Nghi, "The Vietnam-USA Society," *Viet-My: A Special Supplement of Vietnam-USA Magazine*, July 2015; Jessica Frazier, email, January 25, 2019.

132. Viet-My General Secretary Bui Van Nghi, email, April 14, 2019.

133. Courtesy of Tran Minh Quoc. Viet-My General Secretary Bui Van Nghi, email, May 7, 2019; Hershberger, *Traveling to Vietnam*, 41.

134. Clinton, "Cora Weiss" in *The Loyal Opposition*, 166.

135. Reuters, "Sweden Gives U.S. a Hanoi P.O.W. List," *New York Times*, December 12, 1970.

136. List of confirmed prisoners sent by the North Vietnamese Ministry of Foreign Affairs to the Swedish Embassy in Hanoi, November 25, 1970.

137. Memorandum from Captain Dean E. Webster USN, Special Assistant for PW Matters, to Executive Assistant to the Chief of Naval Operations, U.S. Navy, January 14, 1970. Library of Congress: https://www.loc.gov/item/powmia/pw160001/.

138. Ibid.

139. Telegram from Cabinet Stockholm to Leif Leifland of the Foreign Ministry, December 9, 1970. *UD HP-Dossierer, Vietnamkriget, Mål:K, Krigsfångefrågan*, June-December 1970-, HP38:32, RA.

140. Lists given to Cora Weiss by the Vietnam Committee for Solidarity with the American People, November 6, 1970.

141. Telegram from Hubert de Besche to the Foreign Ministry, December 7, 1970; Telegram from Cabinet Stockholm to Hubert de Besche, December 8, 1970; Börjesson, *"Tänkbara Frågor och Svar,"* December 9, 1970, Swedish Foreign Ministry; *UD HP-Dossierer, Vietnamkriget, Mål:K, Krigsfångefrågan,* June-December 1970-, HP38:32, RA.

142. Kaj Falkman, Memorandum, December 11, 1970. *UD HP-Dossierer, Vietnamkriget, Mål:K, Krigsfångefrågan,* from December 1970 to January 1971, 1970–1971, HP38:33, RA. Coded telegram from Wilhelm Wachtmeister at the Swedish Foreign Ministry to Swedish Ambassador Hubert de Besche in Washington, December 8, 1970. *UD HP-Dossierer, Vietnamkriget, Mål:K, Krigsfångefrågan,* June-December 1970, HP38:32, RA.

143. Kaj Falkman, Memorandum, December 11, 1970. Wilhelm Wachtmeister to Hubert Besche, December 8, 1970; Nolan Howell, "After Almost 4 Years, Dighton Pilot's Fate Still Unknown," *Garden City Telegram*, December 24, 1970.

144. Associated Press, "Macon Man Is Among MIA Dead," *The Atlanta Constitution*, March 8, 1974.

145. Katrina Stamm Shoemaker, telephone interview, January 17, 2018.

146. Ibid.

147. Ibid.

148. Ibid.

149. Courtesy of Katrina Stamm Shoemaker.

150. List of missing American servicemen sent by Olof Palme to M. Nguyen Tho Chan, July 5, 1970.

151. The North Vietnamese list was in French. List of confirmed prisoners sent by the North Vietnamese Ministry of Foreign Affairs to the Swedish Embassy in Hanoi, November 25, 1970.

152. List of confirmed prisoners sent by the North Vietnamese Ministry of Foreign Affairs to the Swedish Embassy in Hanoi, November 25, 1970.

153. Shoemaker telephone interview. Email message from Katrina Stamm Shoemaker, January 24, 2018.

154. Shoemaker telephone interview; Falkman, Memorandum, December 11, 1970.

155. Shoemaker telephone interview; Falkman, Memorandum, December 11, 1970; *Sveriges Statskalender 1971*, ed. Bengt Sköldenberg (Uppsala: Almqvist & Wiksells Boktryckeri, 1971), 357.

156. Shoemaker interview.

157. Ibid.

158. Eliasson telephone interview.

159. Ibid.

160. Ibid.

161. United Press International, "Sweden Premier Gets Hanoi Reply on POWs," *The Evening Star*, December 11, 1970; United Press International, "Palme Gets Names of 45 U.S. POWs," *Washington Post*, December 12, 1970.

162. Shoemaker telephone interview.

163. Ibid.

164. Ibid.

165. Ibid.

166. Ibid.

167. Ibid.

168. List of confirmed prisoners sent by the North Vietnamese Ministry of Foreign Affairs to the Swedish Embassy in Hanoi, November 25, 1970. Lists given to Cora Weiss by the Vietnam Committee for Solidarity with the American People, November 6 and 20, 1970.

169. Reuters, "Sweden Gives U.S. a Hanoi P.O.W. List."

170. U.S. Department of Defense POW/MIA Accounting Agency, https://dpaa-mil .sites.crmforce.mil/dpaaProfile?id=a0Jt0000000BTNREA4.

171. They were Charles Frederick Baldock Jr., Theodore Arthur Ballard Jr., Charles Graham Boyd, Burton Wayne Campbell, Frederick Austin Crow Jr., Kenneth Adrian Simonet, Loren Harvey Torkelson, and David Robert Wheat. See Committee of Liaison lists published in *The Miami Herald* on December 24, 1969 and in *The New York Times* on June 26, 1970.

172. Lawrence H. Goldberg USAF was listed twice. List of confirmed prisoners sent by the North Vietnamese Ministry of Foreign Affairs to the Swedish Embassy in Hanoi, November 25, 1970. List of Fourteen American POWs. Given by Nguyen Tho Chan to Torsten Nilsson, March 3, 1970.

173. Associated Press, "Wives Say Husbands Held in POW Camps, *The Daily Chronicle* (Centralia, Washington)," December 14, 1970. *"N'a jamais été capture au Nord V.N."* Mrs. Jerrie L. Kerr was the wife of Michael Scott Kerr USAF. List of confirmed prisoners sent by the North Vietnamese Ministry of Foreign Affairs to

the Swedish Embassy in Hanoi, November 25, 1970. See list provided to Sweden by North Vietnam on December 23, 1970.

174. See list provided to Sweden by North Vietnam on December 23, 1970.

175. Don McLeod, "Voices Identified as U.S. POWs Speak Against War," *Daily Times*, September 16, 1971; "Laos and Found," *Las Vegas Sun*, March 26, 1998; United Press International, "Gostas' family going to Denver," *Billings Gazette*, March 19, 1973; "US Prisoners of War who returned home alive from the Vietnam War." Report Prepared: 7/20/2017. U.S. Department of Defense POW/MIA Accounting Agency: http://www.dpaa.mil/portals/85/Documents/VietnamAccounting/pmsea _returnee.pdf.

176. Bedinger, Henry James, POW Network: https://www.pownetwork.org/bios/b /b133.htm Gostas, Theodore W., POW Network: https://www.pownetwork.org/bios /g/g054.htm John Arthur Young, POW Network: https://www.pownetwork.org/bios /y/y003.htm.

177. For example, Lieutenant Lance Sijan USMC had been shot down in Laos, but his death was confirmed by Sweden in December 1970. See Swedish list from December of 1970, as well as Cora Weiss's list from November 20, 1970. Stuart I. Rochester and Frederick Kiley, *Honor Bound*, 289.

178. John Borling was released on February 12, 1973; Borling interview.

179. Borling interview.

180. "PW's wife awaits 1st letter," *Chicago Sun-Times*, March 12, 1970.

181. "Area PW's wife, family assured by Swedish he's alive," *Chicago Sun-Times*, December 12, 1970.

182. David Sutton, "2 POW Wives Call N. Viet Film Phony," *Chicago Tribune*, December 29, 1970.

183. List of confirmed prisoners sent by the North Vietnamese Ministry of Foreign Affairs to the Swedish Embassy in Hanoi, November 25, 1970. "U.S. Pilots Captured in the Democratic Republic of Vietnam (from August 5, 1964, to November 15, 1970)," December 23, 1970, from the North Vietnamese embassy in Stockholm to Prime Minister Olof Palme.

184. Telegram from Edward G. Borling of Chicago, Illinois, to Olof Palme, December 12, 1970. *UD HP-Dossierer, Vietnamkriget, Krigsfångefrågan, Korrespondens with Krigsfångars anhöriga, 1970–1974*, HP38:39, RA.

185. "Area PW's wife, family assured by Swedish he's alive."

186. In 2002, Gourley's remains were returned to the United States. Gourley, Laurent Lee, POW Network: https://www.pownetwork.org/bios/g/g067.htm.

Letter from Elzene E. Estes to Swedish Prime Minister Olof Palme, December 14, 1970. OPA, *Brevsamling, Volym* 3.2/51, ARAB, Courtesy of Joakim Palme.

187. In 2010, Beyer's remains were returned to the United States. Beyer, Thomas John, POW Network: https://www.pownetwork.org/bios/b/b021.htm.

Letter from Mrs. Charles J. Beyer to Swedish Prime Minister Olof Palme, December 14, 1970. OPA, *Brevsamling, Volym* 3.2/51, ARAB, Courtesy of Joakim Palme.

188 Ibid.

189. "U.S. Pilots Captured in the Democratic Republic of Vietnam (from August 5, 1964 to November 15, 1970)," Ministry of National Defense, Democratic Republic of

Vietnam. Presented by the Embassy of the Democratic Republic of Vietnam, Stockholm, to Swedish Prime Minister Olof Palme, December 23, 1970. *UD HP-Dossierer, Vietnamkriget, Mål: K. Krigsfångefrågan,* from December 1970 to January 1971, HP 38: 33, RA.

190. Ibid.

191. Eliasson telephone interview.

192. J. W. Fulbright, *Congressional Record*, December 22, 1970; Associated Press, "Kennedy gets list of 368 PWs," *Chicago Sun-Times*, December 23, 1970. J. William Fulbright and Edward Kennedy, along with the Committee of Liaison, received the same information in December of 1970. United Press International, "Prisoners of War Held by North Vietnam Are Listed," *Brownsville Herald*, December 23, 1970; Associated Press, "Kennedy gets list of 368 PWs," *Chicago Sun-Times*, December 23, 1970; Terence Smith, "Senators Receive Hanoi P.O.W. List," *New York Times*, December 23, 1970.

193. Ronald Wayne Dodge USN was captured in 1967 and died in captivity. Jerry Donald Driscoll USAF and Louis Frank Makowski USAF were both captured in 1966 and released in 1973. Associated Press, "Many Missing in Southeast Asia," *Abilene Reporter-News*, February 27, 1973; "Midlander Due Release as POW," *The Odessa American*, January 24, 1973; "U.S. Accounted-for from the Vietnam War: Prisoners of War, Escapees, Returnees, and Remains Recovered," U.S. Department of Defense POW/MIA Accounting Agency, November 9, 2017: https://www.dpaa.mil/Our-Missing/Vietnam-War/Vietnam-War-POW-MIA-List/. Driscoll, Jerry Donald. POW Network: https://www.pownetwork.org/bios/d/d060.htm.

194. Falk telephone interview.

195. Ibid.

196. Ibid.

197. Dora Griffin Bell, *The Heroes' Wife* (Bloomington, IN: AuthorHouse, 2006), 35–53.

198. Email message from Dora Griffin Bell, October 15, 2018.

199. Bell, *The Heroes' Wife*, 352–53.

200. Frank Wells, "Wife Questions Report of PW's Death," *Atlanta Constitution*, November 13, 1970; Bell, *The Heroes' Wife*, 353.

201. Bell, *The Heroes' Wife*, 352–54, 358–59. The death of James L. Bell was included in Cora Weiss's list of November 6, 1970.

202. Bell, *The Heroes' Wife*, 352–54, 358–59. His death was included in the Swedish list of December 23, 1970.

203. Ibid.

204. Ibid. Email message from Dora Griffin Bell.

205. The telegram from Vice Admiral David H. Bagley, Chief of Naval Personnel, arrived on January 28, 1973, one day after the signing of the Paris Peace Accords. Bell, *The Heroes' Wife*, 370–71.

206. Email message from Dora Griffin Bell.

207. Neil Sheehan, "Kennedy and Hanoi Letters Discuss P.O.W's," *New York Times*, July 26, 1972. United Press International, "Hanoi Lists Arkansan Among 24

Prisoners," *Arkansas Gazette*, June 25, 1972. Roger Munck, *Riksarkivet*, email, June 10, 2019.

208. The meeting was conducted in English, but the minutes were taken in Swedish. *"Ambassador Holland hos Statsministern,"* Anders Ferm, December 23, 1970. Memorandum attached to R. Nyström, *"Promemoria,"* January 8, 1971. *UD HP-Dossierer, Vietnamkriget, Mål: K, Krigsfångefrågan,* December 1970 to January 1971, RA.

209. Ibid.

210. Ibid.; Asselin, *Vietnam's American War*, 170, 29.

211. Ibid.

212. Falkman interview.

213. *"Ambassador Holland hos Statsministern."*

214. Thorsell, *Sverige i Vita Huset*, 166.

215. Letter from John Dellenback to Olof Palme, June 8, 1972. Letter from Lawrence J. Hogan to Olof Palme, July 11, 1972. *UD HP-Dossierer, Vietnamkriget, Krigsfångefrågan, Korrespondens till Olof Palme 1968–1974*, HP 38:47, RA.

216. Coded telegram from Hubert de Besche to *Polchefen* at the Swedish Foreign Ministry, 26 June 1970. *UD HP-Dossierer, Vietnamkriget, Mål:K, Krigsfångefrågan,* June-December 1970-, HP38:32, RA.

217. Cabinet Stockholm to the Washington Embassy, *"krigsfångefrågan,"* Coded Telegram 155, July 1, 1970. *UD HP-Dossierer, Vietnamkriget, Mål: K, Krigsfångefrågan,* June-December, 1970-, HP38:32, RA.

218. Letter from Gerald R. Ford to Hubert de Besche, July 27, 1970. *UD HP-Dossierer, Vietnamkriget, Mål:K, Krigsfångefrågan,* June-December 1970, HP38:32, RA.

219. Letter from Howard H. Baker Jr. to Hubert de Besche, July 8, 1970. *UD HP-Dossierer, Vietnamkriget, Mål:K, Krigsfångefrågan,* June-December 1970, HP38:32, RA.

220. Ibid.

221. Letter from Olof Palme to Jack Kemp, October 31, 1972. Letter from Jack Kemp to Olof Palme, August 28, 1972. OPA, *Brevsamling, Volym* 3.2/80, ARAB, Courtesy of Joakim Palme.

222. Borling interview. Interview with Halyburtons

223. Interview with Halyburtons.

224. Ibid.

225. Eliasson telephone interview.

226. Ibid.

227. In the 1990s, *United We Stand America* would also be the name of Perot's political organization. Letters from Ross Perot to Olof Palme, January 9 and January 17, 1970, UD *HP-Dossierer, Vietnamkriget, Krigsfångefrågan, Korrespondens till Olof Palme 1968–1974*, HP 38:47, RA. Gerald Posner, *Citizen Perot: His Life & Times* (New York: Random House, 1996), 61–62. Speech of Ross Perot at the National Press Club, March 9, 1970. International Committee of the Red Cross, Articles 72 and 73, *Commentary on the Third Geneva Convention, Volume II*, 1173, 1183.

228. Posner, *Citizen Perot*, 62.

229. Ibid.

230. Ibid.

231. Poster, *Citizen Perot*, 63. Speech of Ross Perot at the National Press Club, March 9, 1970.

232. Ibid.

233. Leif Leifland, *"Tillägg,"* 2 April 1970. *UD HP-Dossierer, Vietnamkriget, Mål:K, Krigsfångefrågan,* January-May 1970, HP38:31, RA.

234. Telegram from the American Embassy in Stockholm to the Secretary of State, November 28, 1969. Nixon Presidential Materials Staff, NSC Files, Country Files— Europe, Box 707, RN.

235. Ibid.

236. United We Stand Press Release, January 11, 1970. *UD HP-Dossierer, Vietnamkriget, Krigsfångefrågan, Korrespondens till Olof Palme,* 1968–1974, HP38:47, RA.

237. Memorandum by Leif Leifland, *"Telefonsamtal med Mr. Murphy Martin,"* March 7, 1970. *UD HP-Dossierer, Vietnamkriget, Mål: K. Krigsfångefrågan,* January-May 1970, HP 38:31, RA.

238. Ibid.

239. Ibid.

240. Ibid.

241. Ehrlichman, *Witness to* Power, 42–43; Posner, *Citizen Perot,* 52–53.

242. Posner, *Citizen Perot,* 58–59.

243. Kyle Longley, "The Reluctant 'Volunteer': The Origins of Senator Albert A. Gore's Opposition to the Vietnam War," *Vietnam and the American Political Tradition,* ed. Randall B. Woods (New York: Cambridge University Press, 2003), 235.

244. Leif Leifland, *"Amerikanska krigsfångar i Vietnam,"* March 12, 1970. *UD HP-Dossierer, Mål:K, Krigsfångefrågan,* January-May 1970, HP38:31, RA.

245. Posner, *Citizen Perot,* x.

246. *"Bandinspelning Mr. Perot's anförande, 9.3.1970,"* *UD HP-Dossierer, Vietnamkriget, Mål:K, Krigsfångefrågan,* January-May 1970, HP38:31 RA.

247. Speech of Ross Perot at the National Press Club, March 9, 1970. Memorandum 264 from Ambassador Hubert de Besche in Washington to Cabinet Stockholm, March 12, 1970. *UD HP-Dossierer, Vietnamkriget, Mål:K, Krigsfångefrågan,* January-May 1970, HP38:31, RA.

248. Speech of Ross Perot at the National Press Club, March 9, 1970.

249. Ibid.

250. Speech of Ross Perot at National Press Club, March 9, 1970.

251. Ibid.

252. Ibid.

253. Leif Leifland, *"Amerikanska krigsfångar i Vietnam,"* March 12, 1970.

254. Leif Leifland, *"Amerikanska krigsfångarna i Vietnam,"* April 9, 1970. *UD HP-Dossierer, Vietnamkriget, Krigsfångefrågan,* January-May 1970, HP38:31, RA.

255. Cover of *Life*, October 20, 1967. Rochester and Kiley, *Honor Bound,* 354.

256. Telegram from Mrs. Paul Edward Galanti to Swedish Prime Minister Olof Palme, received February 8, 1971. OPA, *Brevsamling, Volym* 3.2/61, ARAB,

Courtesy of Joakim Palme. A captioned photo of Phyllis Galanti, *Dagens Nyheter*, March 10, 1971.

257. Phyllis Galanti's advertisement in *Dagens Nyheter*, March 12, 1971.

258. Email from Rachel Johnston of the Richard M. Nixon Presidential Library, Yorba Linda, California, March 16, 2017. Letter from William P. Rogers to Olof Palme, August 10, 1970. *UD HP-Dossierer, Vietnamkriget, Mål:K, Krigsfångefrågan*, June-December 1970, HP38:32, RA.

259. "(i *Vita Huset, State och Pentagon*)" *UD HP-Dossierer, Vietnamkriget, Mål:K, Krigsfångefrågan*, December 1970-January 1971, 1970–1971, HP38:33, RA.

260. Jean-Christophe Öberg to Torsten Nilsson, March 29, 1971. *UD HP-Dossierer, Vietnamkriget, Mål:H, Hanoi's politik*, 1970–1971, HP38:26.

261. Memorandum from Wilhelm Wachtmeister to the Swedish Foreign Ministry, June 29, 1970. *UD HP-Dossierer, Vietnamkriget, Mål: K, Krigsfångefrågan*, June-December 1970, 1970-, HP38:32, RA.

262. Memorandum from Marc Giron to the Swedish Foreign Ministry, "*Mötet mellan statsminister Palme och nordvietnamesiske ambassadören Chen in Sundsvall,*" September 11, 1970. *UD HP-Dossierer, Vietnamkriget, Mål: K, Krigsfångefrågan*, June-December 1970-, HP38:32, RA.

263. Copy of Letter from Olof Palme of Sweden to William P. Rogers, July 14, 1970. *UD HP-Dossierer, Vietnamkriget, Mål:K, Krigsfångefrågan*, June-December 1970, HP38:32, RA.

264. Letter to Krister Wickman from Jerome Holland, March 22, 1972. *HP-Dossierer, Vietnamkriget, Krigsfångefrågan*, 1972–1974, HP38:36, RA.

265. Ibid.

266. Ibid.

267. Letter from National League of Families of American Prisoners and Missing in Southeast Asia to Prime Minister Olof Palme, March 8, 1974, UD *HP-Dossierer, Vietnamkriget, Krigsfångefrågan, Korrespondens till Olof Palme 1968–1974, UD HP* 38:47, RA.

268. Palme also explained Sweden's lack of diplomatic contact with the NLF and Pathet Lao to Mrs. Sybil Stockdale. Jan Eliasson, "*Statsminister mottar delegation i krigsfångefrågan,*" June 9, 1970. Letter from Hubert de Besche to Mr. and Mrs. Ross O'Laughlin, September 1, 1970. Letter from Kai Falkman to Mr. Jerome E. DeBruin, September 9, 1970. *UD HP-Dossierer, Krigsfångefrågan, Vietnamkriget, Mål: K,* June-December 1970-, HP38:32, RA. Åselius, *Vietnamkriget och de svenska diplomaterna*, 361–62.

269. Captain Donald E. Shay Jr. USAF remains missing to this day. Letter from Donald E. Shay to Kaj Falkman at the Swedish Foreign Ministry, January 27, 1972. Letter from Jean-Christophe Öberg in Hanoi to Kaj Falkman at the Swedish Foreign Ministry, February 22, 1972. *UD HP-Dossierer, Vietnamkriget, Krigsfångefrågan*, HP38:36, RA. Donald Emerson Shay Jr., pownetwork.org.

270. The letters were from POW wives who had visited the Swedish Foreign Ministry in Stockholm: Mrs. Alan F. Ashall, Mrs. R. Duncan, Mrs. Paul E. Galanti, and Mrs. Richard C. Nelson. Jean-Christophe Öberg in Hanoi to the Foreign Ministry,

"Amerikanska pilothustrurs brev till sina män," August 5, 1970. *UD HP-Dossierer, Vietnamkriget, Mål:K, Krigsfångefrågan,* June-December 1970, HP38:32, RA.

271. Ibid.

272. International Committee of the Red Cross, Article 2, *Commentary on the Third Geneva Convention, Volume I*, 81.

273. Ibid.

274. *"Pilotfrågan,"* Memorandum from Jean-Christophe Öberg at the Hanoi embassy to Swedish Foreign Ministry, November 12, 1970. Confidential memorandum from Jean-Christophe Öberg to Leif Leifland, 24 August 1970. *UD HP-Dossierer, Vietnamkriget, Krigsfångefrågan, Mål:K,* HP38:32, RA.

275. Memorandum of Kai Falkman, December 3, 1970. *UD HP-Dossierer, Vietnamkriget, Mål:K, Krigsfångefrågan,* June-December 1970, HP38:32, RA.

276. Jan Eliasson, telephone interview, June 17, 2018.

277. Ibid.

278. Ibid.

279. Letter from Kai Falkman to Mr. G.T. Aronson, November 11, 1970. *UD HP-Dossierer, Vietnamkriget, Krigsfångefrågan,* 1972–1974, HP38:32, RA.

280. Letter from Kai Falkman to Mrs. Robert D. Watson, sister of Lt. James W. Bailey, November 24, 1971. *UD HP-Dossierer, Vietnamkriget, Krigsfångefrågan,* 1972–1974, HP38:36, RA.

281. Falkman interview.

282. *"Pilotfrågan,"* Memorandum from Jean-Christophe Öberg in Hanoi to Wilhelm Wachtmeister, January 14, 1972. *UD HP-Dossierer, Vietnamkriget, Krigsfångefrågan,* HP38:36, RA.

283. Seymour M. Hersh, *Reporter: A Memoir* (New York: Alfred A. Knopf, 2018), 152; Seymour M. Hersh, email, October 18, 2018.

284. Hersh email.

285. Ibid.

286. *"Falkman. Re pilotfrågan,"* [Censored] Telegram from Jean-Christophe Öberg to the Swedish Foreign Ministry, March 1972.

287. Ibid.

288. Seymour M. Hersh, "P.O.W.'s Secondary, Hanoi Says," *New York Times,* March 24, 1972.

289. Hersh, "P.O.W.'s Secondary, Hanoi Says." Hawley, Edwin Alexander Jr., pownetwork.org.

290. John Kendall, "Brown's Controversial Appointee: Edison Miller: From Marine Pilot to Censured POW to Supervisor," *Los Angeles Times*, August 6, 1979.

291. Associated Press, "Bombs drop near camp says POW," *Anniston Star*, February 28, 1972.

292. Mohammad H. Bawani, M.D., email, May 30, 2019.

293. Eliasson telephone interview.

294. Eliasson Stockholm interview.

295. Ibid.

296. Interview with Halyburtons.

297. Hirsch, *Two Souls Indivisible*, 136–37.

298. Interview with Halyburtons; Hirsch, *Two Souls Indivisible*, 138.

299. Interview with Halyburtons.

300. Ibid.

301. Hirsch, *Two Souls Indivisible*, 141.

302 Ibid., 165.

303. Jim and Sybil Stockdale, *In Love and War*, 170–71.

304. Borling interview.

305. Ibid.

306. Ibid.

307. Ibid.

308. Ibid.

309. Borling interview; Rochester and Kiley, *Honor Bound*, 490–91.

310. Jim and Sybil Stockdale, *In Love and War*, 157; International Committee of the Red Cross, Article 130, *Commentary on the Third Geneva Convention, Volume II*, 1875;

International Committee of the Red Cross, Article 17, *Commentary on the Third Geneva Convention, Volume I*, 653.

311. Hirsch, *Two Souls Indivisible*, 72.

312. International Committee of the Red Cross, Article 26, *Commentary on the Third Geneva Convention, Volume I*, 765.

313. Jim and Sybil Stockdale, *In Love and War*, 245, 249, 326, 340, 360.

314. International Committee of the Red Cross, Article 22, *Commentary on the Third Geneva Convention, Volume I*, 716.

315. International Committee of the Red Cross, Article 13, *Commentary on the Third Geneva Convention, Volume I*, 572.

316. Jessica M. Frazier, *Women's Antiwar Diplomacy During the Vietnam War* (Chapel Hill: The University of North Carolina Press, 2017), 48.

317. Interview with Halyburtons.

318. Michael J. Allen, *Until the Last Man Comes* Home, 18.

319. Memorandum from Jean-Christophe Öberg to Marc Giron, October 16, 1970. *UD HP-Dossierer, Vietnamkriget, Krigsfångefrågan, Mål:K*, June-December 1970, HP38:32, RA.

320. Ibid.

321. *"Pilotfrågan,"* Memorandum from Wilhelm Wachtmeister to the Swedish embassy in Washington, December 30, 1970. *UD HP-Dossierer, Vietnamkriget, Krigsfångefrågan, Mål:K*, from December 1970 to January 1971, HP38:33, RA.

322. Ibid.

323. Ibid.

324. Ibid.

325. Ibid.

326. Falkman interview. *"Brådskande från pressbyrån, re Palmes i dag avsända telegram till amerikanska piloters anhöriga."* Telegram from Foreign Ministry Press Office in Stockholm to the Swedish Embassy in Washington, December 10, 1970. *UD HP-Dossierer, Vietnamkriget, Krigsfångefrågan, Mål:K*, June-December 1970, HP38:32. RA.

327. Ibid.

328. Falkman interview; Falkman, *Ekot från Vietnam*, 194.

329. Falkman, *Ekot från Vietnam*, 194.

330. Falkman interview.

331. Ibid.

332. Interview with Halyburtons.

333. Hirsch, *Two Souls Indivisible*, 221. Rochester and Kiley, *Honor Bound*, 598.

334. Ibid.

335. Franklin, *M.I.A. or Mythmaking in America*, 65.

336. Falk interview.

337. Ibid.; Falk, "The American POWs: Pawns in Power Politics," 17.

338. Falk, "The American POWs: Pawns in Power Politics," 16.

339. Ibid.

340. Falk interview.

341. Jon M. Van Dyke, "Nixon and the Prisoners of War," *New York Review of Books*, January 7, 1971.

342. Ibid.

343. Ibid.

344. Seymour M. Hersh, "P.O.W.'s Organize Camps to Keep the Morale High," *New York Times*, October 1, 1972; Ralph Blumenthal, "Ex-P.O.W. Calls Camps Humane," *New York Times*, October 2, 1972.

345. Hersh, P.O.W.'s Organize Camps to Keep the Morale High."

346. Ibid.

347. Ibid.

348. Ralph Blumenthal, "Ex-P.O.W. Calls Camps Humane," *New York Times*, October 2, 1972.

349. Borling interview.

350. Ibid.

351. Ibid.

352. Ibid.

353. Falkman interview.

354. Falkman interview; Falkman, *Ekot från* Vietnam, 194.

355. Ibid.

356. Letter from Donald M. Fraser to Olof Palme, June 29, 1972. OPA, *Brevsamling, Volym* 3.2/77, ARAB, courtesy of Joakim Palme.

357. Letter from Olof Palme to Donald M. Fraser, August 24, 1972. Draft of Letter from Palme to Fraser, sent by Karl Rune Nyström to Jan Karlsson, 11 August 19 1972. OPA, *Brevsamling, Volym* 3.2/77, ARAB, Courtesy of Joakim Palme.

358. See Letter from Olof Palme to Jack Kemp, October 31, 1972. OPA, *Brevsamling, Volym* 3.2/80, ARAB, Courtesy of Joakim Palme.

359. Ibid.

360. Falk telephone interview.

361. Ibid.

362. Coded Telegram 66 from Hubert de Besche to the Foreign Ministry, March 20, 1971. *UD HP-Dossierer, Vietnamkriget, Mål:K, Krigsfångefrågan,* February-May 1971, HP38:34, RA.

363. Telegram from Leif Leifland to Jean-Christophe Öberg, *"krigsfångeutväxling i Vietnam,"* August 17, 1970.

364. Coded Telegram from Rolf Ekéus to Jean-Christophe Öberg, August 21, 1970. *UD HP-Dossierer, Vietnamkriget, Mål:K, Krigsfångefrågan,* June-December 1970, HP38:32, RA.

365. Ibid.

366. News Bulletin from the United States Information Service, "Excerpts from Colonel Frank Borman's Address before Congress on War Prisoners," September 22, 1970. *UD HP-Dossierer, Vietnamkriget, Mål:K, Krigsfångefrågan,* June-December 1970, HP38:32, RA.

367. Ibid.

368. Nicholas von Hoffman, "'Peace Heroes' and POWs," *Washington Post,* September 25, 1970; Hubert de Besche to the Foreign Ministry, *"Krigsfångefrågan,"* October 1, 1970. *UD HP-Dossierer, Vietnamkriget, Mål:K, Krigsfångefrågan,* June-December 1970, HP38:32, RA.

369. Thomas Harkin, "Vietnam Whitewash: The Congressional Jury that Convicted Itself," *The Progressive* (October 1970), 19.

370. Jan Eliasson, *"Fångar i Vietnam,"* April 6, 1971. *UD HP-Dossierer, Vietnamkriget, Mål:K, Krigsfångefrågan,* February-May 1971, HP38:34, RA.

371. Eliasson Stockholm interview.

372. Falk, "The American POWs: Pawns in Power Politics," 14. *UD HP-Dossierer, Vietnamkriget, Mål:K, Krigsfångefrågan,* February-May 1971, HP38:34, RA.

373. Ibid. International Committee of the Red Cross, Article 118, *Commentary on the Third Geneva Convention, Volume II,* 1624.

374. Text of Letter from Torsten Nilsson to William Rogers, November 17, 1969, in Telegram from Secretary of State in Washington, D.C. to American Embassy in Stockholm, November 22, 1969. Text of Letter from William Rogers to Torsten Nilsson, November 7, 1969, in Telegram from Secretary of State to the American Embassy in Stockholm, November 10, 1969. Nixon Presidential Materials Staff, NSC Files, Country Files—Europe, Box 707, RN. Letter from William P. Rogers to Olof Palme, August 10, 1970. *UD HP-Dossierer, VK, Mål: K, KF,* June-December 1970, HP38:32, RA.

375. Letter from William P. Rogers to Olof Palme, August 10, 1970. *UD HP-Dossierer, Vietnamkriget, Mål: K, Krigsfångefrågan,* June-December 1970, HP38:32, RA.

376. Letter from Edward M. Kennedy to Ton Duc Thang, June 23, 1970. Leif Leifland of the Washington Embassy to the Foreign Ministry, *"Senator Kennedys skrivelse om de amerikanska piloterna i Nordvietnam,"* January 7, 1971. *HP UD-Dossierer, Vietnamkriget, Mål:K, Krigsfångefrågan,* December 1970-January 1971, 1970–1971, HP38:33, RA.

377. Memorandum from Wilhelm Wachtmeister, November 6, 1970. *UD HP-Dossierer, Vietnamkriget, Mål: K, Krigsfångefrågan,* June-December 1970, HP38:32, RA.

378. Ibid.

379. Statement by Claiborne Pell on Respect for Human Rights in Armed Conflicts, United States Mission to the United Nations, November 6, 1970. *UD HP-Dossierer, Vietnamkriget, Mål: K, Krigsfångefrågan,* June-December 1970, HP38:32, RA.

380. Hubert de Besche to the Foreign Ministry, Coded Telegram 248, January 2, 1971. *UD HP-Dossierer, Vietnamkriget, Mål:K, Krigsfångefrågan,* December 1970-January 1971, 1970–1971, HP38:33, RA.

381. International Committee of the Red Cross, Article 111, *Commentary on the Third Geneva Convention, Volume II,* 1579.

382. Phan Thu, *An Unequal Contest,* 121.

383. International Committee of the Red Cross, Article 109, *Commentary on the Third Geneva Convention, Volume* II, 1547.

384. Ibid.

385. Ibid.

386. Heleen Hiemstra, International Committee of the Red Cross. Email exchange with Jean-Marie Henckaerts, Head, Commentaries Update Unit, International Committee of the Red Cross, May 24, 2019. Notes 4292 and 4293, International Committee of the Red Cross, *Commentary on the Third Geneva Convention, Volume II,* 1564.

387. Marco Sassòli, "Release, Accommodation in Neutral Countries, and Repatriation of Prisoners of War," in *The 1949 Geneva Conventions: A Commentary,* eds, Andrew Clapham, Paola Gaeta, and Marco Sassòli (Oxford: Oxford University Press, 2015), 1041.

388. Sassòli, "Release, Accommodation in Neutral Countries, and Repatriation of Prisoners of War," 1044.

389. Article 112, *Commentary on the Third Geneva Convention, Volume II,* 1585. Note 4353, *Commentary on the Third Geneva Convention, Volume II,* 1589.

390. Michael J. Allen, *Until the Last Man Comes Home,* 18.

391. Memorandum from Jean-Christophe Öberg to the Swedish Foreign Ministry, January 22, 1971. *UD HP-Dossierer, Vietnamkriget, Mål:K, Krigsfångefrågan,* December 1970-January 1971, 1970–1971, HP38:33, RA.

392. "Nixon Hails Swedish Bid to Intern War Prisoners," *Washington Post,* May 4, 1971.

393. Ibid.

394. Associated Press Telegram from San Clemente, California, May 4, 1971. *UD-HP Dossierer, Vietnamkriget, Mål: K, Krigsfångefrågan,* February-May 1971, HP38:34, RA.

395. *"Samtal med ambassadrådet Guthrie angående internering i Sverige av fångar från Indokina,"* Memorandum from the Swedish Foreign Ministry, May 17, 1971. *UD-HP Dossierer, Vietnamkriget, Mål:K, Krigsfångefrågan,* February-May 1971, HP38:34, RA.

396. Ibid.

397. Ibid.

398. United Press International, "Hanoi Rejects POW Internment in Sweden," *Los Angeles Times*, May 5, 1971.

399. Wilhelm Wachtmeister, *"Amerikanska krigsfångarna i Vietnam,"* May 4, 1971, Foreign Ministry Memorandum. *UD HP-Dossierer, Vietnamkriget, Krigsfånge-frågan,* February-May 1971, 1971-, HP38:34, RA.

400. Ibid.

401. Jean-Christophe Öberg, *"Pilotfrågan,"* January 22, 1971. Wachtmeister, *"Amerikanska fångar i Vietnam,"* May 5, 1971.

402. Wilhelm Wachtmeister, *"Samtal med ambassadrådet Guthrie,"* May 11, 1971. *UD HP-Dossierer, Vietnamkriget, Krigsfångefrågan,* February-May 1971, HP38:34, RA.

403. Ibid.

404. Wilhelm Wachtmeister, *"Amerikanska fångar i Vietnam,"* May 5, 1971, Foreign Ministry Memorandum. *UD HP-Dossierer, Vietnamkriget, Krigsfångefrågan,* February-May 1971, 1971-, HP38:34, RA.

405. Robert Skole, "Sweden Feels in Middle of POW Propaganda," *The Evening Star*, May 18, 1971.

406. Ibid.

407. Coded Telegram from Ambassador Hubert de Besche at the Washington embassy to the Foreign Ministry, May 25, 1971. *UD HP-Dossierer, Vietnamkriget, Mål:K, Krigsfångefrågan,* June-December 1971, HP38:35, RA.

408. Ibid.

409. Ibid.

410. Jean-Christophe Öberg to Wilhelm Wachtmeister, May 14, 1971. *ED HP-Dossierer, Vietnamkriget, Mål:H, Hanoi's politik,* 1970–1971, HP38:26, RA.

411. Franklin, *M.I.A. or Mythmaking in America*, 61–62.

412. Ibid.

413. Ibid.

414. Ibid.

415. Coded Telegram 76 from Hubert de Besche to the Foreign Ministry, March 31, 1971. *UD HP-Dossierer, Vietnamkriget, Mål:C, USA's politik,* January-May 1971, HP38:10, RA.

416. Ibid.; Asselin, *A Bitter Peace*, 27; Nguyen, *Hanoi's War*, 212.

417. Ibid.

418. Ibid.

419. Ibid.

420. Coded Telegram 109 from Hubert de Besche to the Foreign Ministry, May 12, 1971. *HP UD-Dossierer, Vietnamkriget, Mål:C, USA's politik*, April-June 1971, HP38:11, RA.

421. Ibid.

422. McGovern-Hatfield Amendment, attached to press release from Senator George McGovern of South Dakota, June 4, 1971. Sent from the Washington embassy to the Swedish Foreign Ministry, June 4, 1971. *UD HP-Dossierer, Vietnamkriget, Mål: USA's politik,* April-June 1970, HP38:11, RA; Knock, "The Story of George McGovern," 112.

423. There was considerable antiwar sentiment among liberal Republicans. See Fredrik Logevall, "A Delicate Balance: John Sherman Cooper and the Republican Opposition to the Vietnam War," *Vietnam and the American Political Tradition: The Politics of Dissent,* Randal Bennett Woods, ed. (New York: Cambridge University Press, 2003).

424. Coded Telegram 109 from Hubert de Besche, May 12, 1971, HP38:11. Coded Telegram from the Political Division of the Foreign Ministry to Jean-Christophe Öberg. *UD HP-Dossierer, Vietnamkriget, Mål:K,*

425. Telegram from Political Division to Öberg, June 14, 1971.

426. Vance Hartke, *Congressional Record,* June 16, 1971. Sent by Jan Eliasson, *"Anförande av Vance Hartke i senatens Indokina-debatt den 16 juni,"* June 22, 1971. *UD HP-Dossierer, Vietnamkriget, Mål:K, USA's politik,* July-August 1971, HP38:12, RA.

427. Ibid.

428. "7-Point Statement Made by Mrs. Nguyen Thi Binh, Chief of the PRC Delegation to the Paris Connerence on Vietnam, 1/7/1971," presented by PRC's Information Bureau in Stockholm to Krister Wickman, 7 July 1971. *"Uttalande av utrikesminister Krister Wickman om madame Binhs 7-punktsförslag,"* "Press Office, Swedish Foreign Minister, July 6, 1971." *UD HP-Dossierer, Vietnamkriget, Mål:F, Fredssträvanden,* 1971–1972, HP38:20, RA.

429. Coded Talegram 143 from Hubert de Besche to the Foreign Ménistry, 1 July 1971. $*UD HP-Dïssierer, Vietnamkriget, Mål:C, USA's politik,* July-August 1971, HP38:12. *"Pilotfrågan—bortdragande av amerikanska trupper,"* Memorandum for Jean-Christophe Öberg to the Foreign Ministry, July 2, 1971. *UD HP-Dossierer, Vietnamkriget, Mål:H, Hanoi's politik,* 1970–1971, HP38:26, RA.

430. *UD HP-Dossierer, Vietnamkriget, Mål:C, USA's politik,* July-August 1971, HP38:12, RA.

431. Memorandum from Wilhelm Wachtmeister, April 25, 1971. *UD HP-Dossierer, Vietnamkriget, Mål:F, Fredsträvanden,* 1970–1971, HP38:19, RA.

432. Ibid.

433. Ibid.

434. Ibid.

435. Ibid.

436. Ibid.

437. Ibid.

438. Asselin, *A Bitter Peace,* 26.

439. Per Forslind, *"Spänd väntan i USA: När friges fångarna?,"* *Svenska Dagbladet,* September 3, 1972; Hershberger, *Traveling to Vietnam,* 215.

440. Falk interview. Letter from Cora Weiss to Olof Palme, October 16, 1972. OPA, *Brevsamling, Volym* 3.2/86, ARAB, courtesy of Joakim Palme. Warren Goldstein, University of Hartford, email, January 7, 2019; Warren Goldstein, *William Sloane Coffin Jr.: A Holy Impatience* (New Haven: Yale University Press, 2004), 261–65; Clinton, *The Loyal Opposition: Americans in North Vietnam, 1965–1972,* 289.

441. Falk interview. Richard Falk, email, August 11, 2018.

442. According to pownetwork.org, Norris A. Charles was shot down on December 30, 1971, and Edward K. Elias on April 20, 1972. According to the Hall of Valor Database at valor.militarytimes.com, Markham L. Gartley was shot down on August 17, 1968.

443. Falk interview; Falk, "International Law Aspects of Repatriation of Prisoners of War During Hostilities," 465.

444. Cora Weiss Oral History Project, Session 4, 68. *The Reminiscences of Cora Weiss.* Columbia Center for Oral History, Columbia University, 2014. Clinton, "Cora Weiss" in *The Loyal Opposition*, 168.

445. Ibid.

446. Falk, "International Law Aspects of Repatriation of Prisoners of War During Hostilities," 466.

447. Falk interview.

448. Ibid.

449. Ibid.

450. Ibid.

451. Hershberger, *Traveling to Vietnam*, 149–50.

452. Telegram from Jean-Christophe Öberg to Cabinet Stockholm, September 24, 1972. *UD HP-Dossierer, Vietnamkriget, Krigsfångefrågan,* HP38:36, RA.

453. Memorandum from Henry A. Kissinger to President Nixon, September 23, 1972. Nixon Presidential Materials Staff, NSC Files, POW/MIA, President's Daily Briefs, Box 1, RN.

454. Telegram from Edward Elias, Mark Gartley, and Norris Charles to Richard M. Nixon, September 24, 1972. Nixon Presidential Materials Staff, NSC Files, POW/MIA, President's Daily Briefs, Box 1, RN. Telegram 477 from Jean-Christophe Öberg to Cabinet Stockholm, September 25, 1972. *UD HP-Dossierer, Vietnamkriget, Krigsfångefrågan,* HP38:36, RA.

455. Memorandum from Henry A. Kissinger to the President, September 15, 1972. Nixon Presidential Materials Staff, NSC Files, POW/MIA, President's Daily Briefs, Box 1, RN.

456. Cora Weiss Oral History Project, Session 4, 74.

457. Memorandum from Rune Nyström, September 26, 1972. *HP UD-Dossierer, Vietnamkriget, Krigsfångefrågan,* HP38:36, RA. Cora Weiss Oral History Project, Session 4, 74. Falk, "International Law Aspects of Repatriation of Prisoners of War During Hostilities," 466–68.

458. Memorandum from Rune Nyström, September 26, 1972. Letter from Cora Weiss to Olof Palme, October 16, 1972. OPA, *Brevsamling, Volym* 3.2/86, ARAB, courtesy of Joakim Palme.

459. Memorandum from Henry A. Kissinger to the President, September 27, 1972. Nixon Presidential Materials Staff, NSC Files, POW/MIA, President's Daily Briefs, Box 1, RN.

460. Cora Weiss recalled meeting Palme in New York in 1969, but he did not visit the United States that year. In 1970, he visited the United States twice. *"åberopande sina tidigare kontakter med statsrådsberedningen, ambassaden och Olof Palme i New York."* Memorandum from Jean-Christophe Öberg to the Swedish Foreign Ministry,

September 24, 1972. Reported by Rune Nyström within the Foreign Minstry, September 25, 1972. *UD HP-Dossierer, Vietnamkriget, Krigsfångefrågan,* HP38:36, RA. Archivist Emeritus Stellan Andersson of ARAB, email, March 31, 2019.

461. Ibid.

462. [Censored] Telegram from Wilhelm Wachtmeister to Jean-Christophe Öberg in Stockholm, September 1972. *UD HP-Dossierer, Vietnamkriget, Krigsfångefrågan,* HP38:36, RA.

463. [Censored] *"de frigivna amerikanska Vietnam-piloterna."* Urgent message from Cabinet Stockholm to the Swedish embassy in Moscow, September 1972. *UD HP-Dossierer, Vietnamkriget, Krigsfångefrågan,* HP38:36, RA.

464. [Censored] Telegram from Wilhelm Wachtmeister to Jean-Christophe Öberg in Stockholm, September 1972.

465. Memorandum by Wilhelm Wachtmeister, Political Division, Swedish Foreign Ministry, September 25, 1972. *UD HP-Dossierer, Vietnamkriget, Krigsfångefrågan,* HP38:36, RA.

466. Telegram from Adolph Dubs to the Secretary of State, September 27, 1972. Nixon Presidential Materials Staff, NSC Files, POW/MIA, Vietnam Subject Files, Box 2, RN; Falk, "International Law Aspects of Repatriation of Prisoners of War During Hostilities," 467–68; Associated Press, *"Bråk i Moskva om piloterna," Svenska Dagbladet,* September 28, 1972.

467. Cora Weiss Oral History Project, Session 4, 76.

468. Cora Weiss Oral History Project, Session 4, 77. Attached Notice to Memorandum from Danish Foreign Ministry to Wilhelm Wachtmeister, September 28, 1972. *UD HP-Dossierer, Vietnamkriget, Krigsfångefrågan,* HP38:36, RA.

469. Memorandum from Danish Foreign Ministry, September 28, 1972; Seymour M. Hersh, "3 Freed P.O.W.'s Return; Dispute Flares over Leave," *New York Times,* September 29, 1972.

470. Seymour M. Hersh, "3 Freed P.O.W.'s Return."

471. Goldstein, *William Sloane Coffin Jr.: A Holy Impatience,* 264.

472. Ibid.; Hershberger, *Traveling to Vietnam,* 216.

473. Press Conference in Copenhagen with Three American Pilots; Edward Elias, Markham Gartley, and Norris Charles, Released by North Vietnam, 28 September 1972. Associated Press Archive: https://www.youtube.com/watch?v=1nR3pfevy8M.

474. Cora Weiss Oral History Project, Session 4, 76.

475. Ibid., 77.

476. Ibid., 468.

477. Falk email.

478. Letter from Cora Weiss to Olof Palme, October 16, 1972. OPA, *Brevsamling, Volym* 3.2/86, ARAB, Courtesy of Joakim Palme.

479. Ibid.

480. Ibid.

481. Letter from Richard Nixon to William Rogers, October 31, 1972. White House Central Files (WHCF), Alphabetical Name Files, William P. Rogers, Box 115, RN.

482. Rochester and Kiley, *Honor Bound,* 589.

Chapter 5

Reconciliation with Washington

While the diplomatic freeze between Washington and Stockholm remained solid as ice, the chilly winds did not blow in just one direction. Kissinger planned to attend the annual meeting of the Bilderberg Group in the spring of 1973. That year, the Bilderberg Group would gather in Saltsjöbaden, an elegant Swedish town on the Baltic Sea. The US national security advisor had no reason to miss this assembly of the elite of Western Europe and North America. Distinguished figures from the fields of politics, business, and academia all celebrated the principle of Atlanticism, a close relationship between the United States and Western Europe. In conversation with the chargé d'affaires of the US embassy, Foreign Minister Wickman encouraged Kissinger to skip the Bilderberg meeting, which the national security advisor proceeded to do. "As I recall," Ekéus recounted, "Wickman's action was motivated to avoid violent and angry demonstrations against Kissinger and the USA, thus protect the US/Sweden security cooperation."[1]

Furthermore, Wickman feared that that if Kissinger encountered Palme, accompanied by his ministers of Finance and Industry, it would aggravate already existing tensions.[2]

Kissinger, for his part, could not appreciate Stockholm's point of view. Secretary of State Rogers instructed the Stockholm embassy, "You should also use occasion to point out to Wickman that Swedish attitude on this question does not contribute to creating atmosphere conducive to improving US-Swedish relations."[3]

Kissinger claimed to Nixon, "I really screwed this fellow Palme, Mr. President," although it is unclear how the national security adviser had actually screwed the prime minister.[4]

"Pal-may?" the president questioned.[5]

"The Swede," Kissinger replied, "and I had agreed to come six months ago" to the Bilderberg meeting. "So, the Swedish foreign minister called in our chargé and said it would be very unfortunate if I came, under these conditions, and with the feelings, even though it's a private conference."[6]

Therefore, Kissinger told Nixon: "I said, under these conditions, I can't come."[7]

The national security advisor thought that he had an ally in Prince Bernhard, the chairman of the conference, and the husband of Queen Juliana of the Netherlands. Kissinger claimed to the president that "Bernhard is now canceling the conference, and taking it out of Sweden."[8]

Nixon was pleased: "Ha! Good. It's a small thing, but it helps."[9]

Prince Bernhard had done no such thing, for the conference would take place as scheduled in Sweden. Perhaps the royal personage had just told Kissinger what he had wanted to hear.

THE PARIS PEACE ACCORDS

The Paris Peace Accords had already been signed, officially ending the American war in Vietnam. Falkman represented the Swedish government as an observer. At the reception following the ceremony, diplomats lined up for a handshake with Kissinger. Falkman was the exception: "After the Christmas Bombings, I felt no desire to join the line."[10]

There were no significant alternations to the original peace agreement that had been reached in October of 1972. Pierre Asselin, a leading historical expert on the Vietnam War, agrees with Jonathan Aitken, the former minister of state for defense procurement under British Prime Minister John Major, who described the Christmas bombing as "a 'cruel necessity.'"[11]

Nevertheless, Asselin includes the texts of the original agreement, and the final agreement that was signed. I have read both and can detect no substantial difference between the two.[12]

The most notable change was that the final agreement dropped the expression "administrative structure," meaning that the National Council on Reconciliation and Concord would not be classified as a coalition government in South Vietnam.[13] In effect, South Vietnam would have two governments: the Provisional Revolutionary Government and the Saigon regime.

Palme issued a public statement in response to the Peace Accords:

> The announcement that an agreement on ending the war and restoring peace in Vietnam has now been reached is greeted by the entire Swedish nation with great relief and satisfaction. Killing and destruction will now cease. The feeling of despair and hopelessness in the face of the madness and cruelty of war has lifted at last. We hope that this agreement will lay the foundation for peace, national self-determination and reconciliation.[14]

The American prisoners of war, whose families were beneficiaries of Palme, could now return home, and the United States would withdraw from South Vietnam. "The principles of the Geneva Agreements on the independence, unity and territorial integrity of Vietnam are recognized," the Swedish prime minister asserted. "A National Council of National Reconciliation and Concord of three segments will be set up in South Vietnam. General elections are to be held and democratic rights respected."[15]

A warning accompanied Palme's optimism: "A laborious and difficult road towards reconciliation has now been embarked upon. It is extremely important that the parties abide by the agreement."[16]

North Vietnam made an initial effort to respect to the Paris Accords, but the evidence indicates that the United States violated the Peace Accords from the very beginning. Even though the treaty recognized two official governing bodies in South Vietnam, Nixon immediately declared that the Thieu dictatorship was "the sole legitimate government of South Vietnam."[17] Thieu, for his part, announced his intention to "arrest or shoot on the spot" people who were associated with the PRG.[18]

In early 1974, 2,800 military officers and technicians remained in Vietnam, advising the Saigon regime in an officially civilian capacity. The South Vietnamese government also consulted with officials from the Central Intelligence Agency on intelligence and police issues. For fiscal year 1974, Washington provided South Vietnam $813 million in military aid, and the Nixon administration requested an additional $1.45 billion from Congress for the following year.[19]

Rather than respecting his official partner, the Provisional Revolutionary Government, President Thieu tried to seize as much of its territory as he could. Of course, a new infusion of war materiel from Washington made Thieu's campaign possible. The North Vietnamese had no choice but to respond in kind.[20]

From Hanoi, Öberg understood the reasons for Thieu's aggressive strategy. "In fact, Thieu committed political suicide when he accepted signing the Paris Accords," Öberg concluded in a dispatch to Palme.[21] Since the treaty had weakened his authority even in the areas under his own control, Thieu became even more repressive:

> Terror, torture, violence, and other methods belonging to the police state meet no understanding in the Vietnamese Buddhist folk tradition. Western, often Americanized, political methods constitute an incomprehensible element in the Vietnamese community, where the president has increasingly come to be regarded as a foreign war machine that can only promise continued war.[22]

Even as the Vietnamese witnessed the gradual American withdrawal from their land, the Cambodians still felt American pressure from the air. Stockholm did not have diplomatic relations with Phnom Penh, but that did not mean that Sweden was indifferent to Cambodia's fate. As early as 1971, Öberg composed a deeply reflective memorandum about Cambodia for Foreign Minister Wickman.

"The invasion of Cambodia in the spring of 1970 was the first sign of Washington's double-dealing, and Nixon's so-called peace initiative in October of last year a confirmation that the president was using the war for domestic political aims," Öberg wrote.[23]

Before his overthrow, Prince Norodom Sihanouk had managed to keep Cambodia out of the war in Southeast Asia. Now, Öberg noted, "Cambodia was now a land on fire."[24] Who had ignited that fire? South Vietnamese forces, supported by heavy US bombing raids, "who are burning, plundering, and raping in Cambodia."[25] The US-sponsored coup had destroyed any semblance of order and justice: "A corrupt military junta in Phnom Penh battles more internally over American dollars than against an enemy, who often consists of the country's intellectual elite, with unassailable patriotic fervor."[26]

Prince Sihanouk had tried to keep Cambodia free of the influence of Communist North Vietnam. As Öberg saw it, the American intervention in Southeast Asia had paradoxically destroyed any political alternatives to communism: "It cannot be ruled out that communism's foremost ally in Indochina is Richard Milhous Nixon's Vietnamization policy, a form of military tourism across borders, which shocks the entire world, but strengthens Indochinese solidarity."[27] Tragically, Öberg's prediction would come true with the rise of the genocidal Khmer Rouge in Cambodia.

Wickman, who would give public expression to Öberg's thoughts on Cambodia, proved more compatible with Palme than Nilsson had been. "Wickman and Palme were the same generation . . . not a labor family, what we call a bourgeois family, so they got on very well," Ekéus explained. "Some felt that Wickman should be the prime minister instead, but he was more an economist. He was not a politically smart mind like Palme."[28] According to Ekéus, Palme was privately pleased to accept Nilsson's resignation: "Of course, he was very happy to get his friend, Krister Wickman, as the new foreign minister."[29]

Eliasson held Wickman in high regard, as well. "He really was a success. . . . He was a very intellectual person, and a good foreign minister."[30]

In any case, Palme's new chief diplomat treated the American intervention in Cambodia as part of Nixon's Vietnamization policy, a policy that "aimed for a military and not for a political solution of the conflict."[31] Wickman respected Öberg's thoughts enough to borrow some of them verbatim for a public debate. The foreign minister described Cambodia as a "now a land on fire."[32] Like Öberg, Wickman saw the Cambodian junta squabbling over dollars. He also regarded the bombing of North Vietnam, as well as the ground invasions of Laos and Cambodia, "as a form of military tourism."[33]

The continued war throughout Indochina gave Palme ample opportunity to speak his mind. Even though the 1973 Paris Peace Accords had officially terminated the American war in Vietnam in January, they had inadequately addressed the matter of Laos and Cambodia. In the case of Cambodia, the American bombing continued until halted by Congress on August 15. Just little more than a week before the air campaign came to an end, the United States accidentally bombed the village of Neak Luong, creating an estimated four hundred casualties.[34]

On August 7, Palme once again spoke out. "All who are assembled here feel sympathy in the face of this human suffering, which brutally and without any forewarning affected private individuals," the prime minister addressed his audience in Sundsvall. "But we do not only feel sympathy. We feel indignation."[35]

Indeed, Palme's indignation was readily apparent:

The American president wanted to continue the bombings, but promised to stop on August 15. For one more week, therefore, the bombs will fall. For one more week, people will experience terror and fear. For one more week, people will die by bombs. It is difficult to imagine anything more senseless than a continued war by bombs in Cambodia.[36]

Once again, a statement from Palme provoked a reaction from the Nixon administration. Owens, as desk officer for Sweden at the State Department, warned the Swedish embassy that the Cambodia speech would probably not "go over particularly well" at the White House.[37] He felt that Palme's use of the words "brutally" and "indignation" would probably not be appreciated in the West Wing.[38] Speaking in a measured manner that was entirely free of hostility, Owens doubted that the US government would make an official response.[39] By this point, of course, Nixon was deeply mired in the Watergate scandal.

The Swedish prime minister still appreciated the potential of the Paris Peace Accords, but undeterred in early 1974, observed that "Vietnam's people have not yet gotten peace. The fighting continues in South Vietnam."[40] While North Vietnam was no longer a target for American bombs, Palme pointed out that "in Saigon a brutal, oppressive regime still seeks to consolidate its power. . . . A great number of political prisoners are detained under inhuman conditions."[41]

THE THAW

In November of 1973, the deep diplomatic freeze between the United States and Sweden began to thaw. Attending the UN General Assembly in New York, as was his practice every year, Wachtmeister received an invitation to Washington. The influential Senator Pell had pressured Kissinger into receiving his friend. The new secretary of state only granted Wachtmeister a curt ten minutes of his time. According to Wachtmeister's account, "Kissinger began by turning to [Assistant Secretary Walter] Stoessel with a question about what level Swedes were received at the State Department, a downright tactless gesture in my presence. 'On Director's level,' answered Stoessel."[42]

According to the State Department minutes, Wachtmeister said that "he hoped relations would soon be back on former good basis."[43]

The minutes went on:

> Secretary commented that cooling of relations between US and Sweden has been due in large part to rhetoric: Also, we had noted existence of what appeared to be one-sided policy in Sweden. He thought it should not be beyond wit of man to develop means of normalizing relations between Sweden and US. There were no basic conflicts of interest: On contrary, there existed a community of values between the two countries.[44]

Regardless of Kissinger's initial rudeness, the meeting ended on a positive note. "I think with some human ingenuity, ways can be found for Sweden and America to co-exist," Kissinger said, "and furthermore, I want to get those Minnesota senators off my back."[45] Senators Hubert Humphrey and Walter Mondale of Minnesota would naturally consider the views of their Swedish American constituents. Mondale had written to Kissinger to urge the exchange of new ambassadors. Moreover, Kissinger had felt pressure from the Senate Foreign Relations Committee during his confirmation hearings for his appointment as secretary of state. He had promised to reevaluate the American relationship with Sweden.

On October 4, 1973, the Senate had approved Resolution 149 under the sponsorship of Humphrey. Resolution 149 advised "that the United States Government and Sweden should restore their normal friendly relations, and confirm this return to normalcy by appointing and dispatching ambassadors to their respective capitals on an immediate basis."[46]

Now, Kissinger had to work on Nixon. The secretary of state had his own reasons to favor an exchange of ambassadors. Swedish Defense Minister Sven Andersson had become foreign minister in November of 1973, and the secretary of state viewed him as friendlier to Washington than Wickman had been. Moreover, Kissinger appreciated Palme's lobbying of the Icelandic prime minister at the October 1973 meeting of the Nordic Council. The Swedish prime minister, Kissinger noted to Nixon, had placed great emphasis on "the importance to Western security of the retention of the Icelandic Defense Force. This intercession was particularly timely in view of our current negotiations with Iceland on the future of the IDF.[47]

If Palme was conciliatory to the White House, he was not excessively so. The Swedish ambassador to Chile, Harald Edelstam, rescued 1,300 Chileans from the bloody dictatorship of General Augusto Pinochet during this period. Edelstam acted with the full support of the Swedish prime minister. At the time, intelligent people reasonably suspected American sponsorship of the 1973 coup that had brought Pinochet to power, but until the declassification of the relevant US documents almost thirty years later, that sponsorship could not be confirmed. Nonetheless, the suspicion remained. Not only did the Swedish rescue operation reflect poorly on Pinochet, it also reflected poorly on his sponsor, the Nixon administration. Leifland, as minister at the Washington embassy, blamed Edelstam for the extended length of the diplomatic freeze. During this period, Leifland even informed the State Department that "his own relations with USG [U.S. Government] were better than with Edelstam."[48]

On March 14, 1974, the diplomatic freeze officially melted. Nixon approved the reestablishment of full diplomatic relations with Sweden, and the appointment of a new ambassador to Stockholm, Robert Strausz-Hupé.[49] When Palme attended the funeral of French President Georges Pompidou on April 4, he saw Nixon for the second and last time. The prime minister approached the president as soon as he spotted him. This time, Nixon was cordial. Palme expressed his pleasure that Stockholm and Washington would soon exchange ambassadors. The president concurred, adding that his new appointee, the Austrian-born Strausz-Hupé, was a remarkable European with whom one could speak freely, in spite of his age. Palme observed that wisdom came with age, and then they both laughed. Praising the splendid qualities of his own newly appointed ambassador, Count Wilhelm Wachtmeister, who had served as head of the Foreign Ministry's Political Division, the prime minister observed that Swedes tended to have a good time in Washington. The president said that Swedes were popular in Washington. At that, they laughed again.[50] Had Nixon forgiven Palme? Certainly, the Watergate scandal had fatally weakened the president, draining him of some of the energy that can fuel hatred. At the same time, however, Nixon was prone to lifelong grudges. It is often easier to be polite face-to-face with one's adversaries. More likely than not, Nixon resented Palme for the rest of his life.

Regardless of the president's inner feelings, he accepted the credentials presented by Wachtmeister in the Blue Room of the White House on June 5, 1974. The Swedish diplomat had already been in Washington for a month, and

Nixon gave him as much time as Kissinger had done in November. The president went through the appropriate motions, but he seemed distracted by his own looming political destruction. "We had a rocky road for a while," Nixon acknowledged, yet also expressed the desire for a productive relationship.[51]

"This was the first and only time I met Richard Nixon," the Swedish ambassador remembered.[52] Two months later, the president resigned and left Washington for good.

By then Strausz-Hupé was ensconced at the US embassy in Stockholm. As professor of political science at the University of Pennsylvania, he had founded the Foreign Policy Research Institute, and he carried great weight within foreign policy circles. Fulbright, unimpressed on Capitol Hill, regarded Strausz-Hupé as "the very epitome of a hard-line, no compromise" hawk.[53] Strausz-Hupé accepted the post without enthusiasm. Within months of his appointment, the ambassador submitted his resignation to President Gerald R. Ford, also writing to White House Chief of Staff Alexander Haig: "I wish to return to useful employment in the NATO area, my interests and experience being far more relevant to the care of the Western alliance than the guardianship of our relations with neutral, though meddlesome Sweden."[54]

Strausz-Hupé would eventually become the US ambassador to NATO in March of 1976, but until then, he would remain in Stockholm. Despite his belief that US-Swedish relations had fully recovered, he still had a considerable amount work to do.[55] Shortly after Nixon's resignation, the new ambassador advised the State Department to raise no objections to the Swedish government's decision to promote the status of the information office of the Provisional Revolutionary Government in Stockholm. Strausz-Hupé feared that any objections "could diminish our effectiveness at a later date in dissuading the GOS from actually recognizing the PRG."[56]

The ambassador wanted to avoid

> giving the radical left an opportunity to stoke once again the fires of anti-Americanism which have been burning low in recent months. I think it important that we have to keep in mind that our leverage here is quite limited in this area, unlike fellow Scandinavians Norway and Denmark, Sweden is not our ally, and the GOS is extremely sensitive to its right to set the lines of its neutral foreign policy. Too heavy handed pressure on the GOS could only lead to the lessening of our prestige and influence here.[57]

Ultimately, the ambassador's concerns would prove pointless, for Sweden would not formally recognize the PRG until Saigon's fall.[58]

In the fall of 1974, the United States suspected that the North Vietnamese and the PRG were preparing for a military offensive. As the war approached its end, Washington had to deal with Foreign Minister Andersson.

Kissinger assumed Palme had selected "the more conservative and pro-US Sven Andersson" in a bid to appease Washington.[59] As far as Eliasson knew, however, Wickman had not been replaced for ideological reasons, "but it was also a matter of personality."[60] Eliasson thought that the appointment of the "solid, quiet" Andersson had its advantages: "Wickman was a very intellectual foreign minister. He had around him a number of advisors who were very intellectual, while Sven Andersson was sort of a middle-of-the-road, working-class background, party secretary."[61]

Carl-Magnus Hyltenius, the new foreign minister's private secretary, observed that Andersson brought considerable experience and political advantages to his position. Previous to his last assignment as defense minister, Andersson had served as minister without portfolio and then as minister of communications. Long before he had even joined the cabinet, he had also been secretary-general of the Social Democratic Party. Unusually for such a political heavyweight, his appointment did not inspire domestic opposition. "He was very respected also among the opposition parties," Hyltenius recalled. "There were political differences, of course . . . when it came to social policy issues and things like that . . . but on foreign policy, I don't think it was very controversial."[62] Unity on matters of foreign policy was key. "Maybe Palme chose him to have some stability, so to speak," Hyltenius concluded.[63]

Andersson was always accompanied by his private secretary on his travels abroad, where the subordinate could observe the foreign minister fulfilling the essential role of his position, that of diplomacy. Hyltenius moonlighted as an interpreter. The foreign minister understood English, but his working-class youth had not trained him for communication in foreign languages. "And what he wanted to say, I translated everything to English or German or French or whatever," his personal secretary added.[64]

In the early fall of 1974, Andersson delivered a speech at the Waldorf-Astoria hotel in New York. The foreign minister shared the stage with his American counterpart, Secretary of State Kissinger, who had retained his position as national security advisor upon his new appointment the year before. Andersson also met privately with the secretary of state in Kissinger's suite, their first and only meeting. "It was sort of a getting-back to the relations at the top level," as Hyltenius put it.[65]

Andersson asked Kissinger, "May I ask you how we can prevent a new war in Vietnam?"[66]

The secretary of state replied,

I am not very optimistic. We do not have much leverage. If North Vietnam were to abide by its treaty obligations we would have a better chance. If the Soviets and Chinese were prepared to respect the Paris Accords . . . new arms supply would be strictly limited to replacement. For our part, we would be prepared to be very diligent about respecting this commitment. Do you have much influence with them?[67]

The foreign minister conceded that his own country did not. Then, Kissinger referred to Öberg, another indication of the close attention that Washington had paid to the legendary Swedish diplomat: "Do you still have that active Ambassador there?"[68]

To Kissinger's probable relief, Andersson answered, "We have a new Ambassador in Hanoi. He knows the political situation quite well. We understand North Vietnam is receiving more and more weapons from China."[69]

The secretary of state insisted:

> We support continuing negotiations. I think in the next few months the South will make a new proposal. Of course, flexibility in negotiations is not a distinguishing trait of the North. I listened to Le Duc Tho make the same speech for four years, but don't misunderstand me. They are skilled and tough negotiators. The representative of a tenth-rate industrial power was negotiating with the representative of the most powerful country in the world and was very disciplined and able and I respect him.[70]

Notwithstanding his personal respect for his negotiating counterpart, Le Duc Tho, Kissinger could not help but condescend to the North Vietnamese.

Back in Stockholm, the foreign minister obviously met with foreign emissaries as well, and he relied heavily on his personal secretary. "I was dealing with his schedule," Hyltenius said. "Everyone who wanted to see the minister had to go through me. And I participated in all meetings. When there were visitors coming to see the minister, often one by one, I was present. I took notes."[71]

Naturally, Hyltenius attended two meetings between the foreign minister and the new American ambassador in November of 1974. "I can see him before me," Hyltenius said more than forty years later. "Strausz-Hupé. He was an elderly gentleman."[72]

Both meetings took place within a week of each other at the Foreign Ministry. The first was relatively insignificant. "I think it was a more general discussion, probably about the situation in Vietnam," Hyltenius remembered.[73]

What has become controversial is the second meeting, the conversation of November 11, 1974. Now that the diplomatic freeze had finally ended, the American ambassador appealed to the foreign minister. Strausz-Hupé asked if Sweden "could use its influence" with the North Vietnamese to persuade them to hold back on its planned offensive, and resume negotiations.[74]

Andersson denied that his country had any political influence with Hanoi. All Stockholm had provided was economic aid. Moreover, the foreign minister was skeptical that Hanoi and the PRG would even consider new talks. According to the minutes taken by Hyltenius, Andersson "referred to a case about a year ago when representatives for the PRG who had arrived for negotiations were shot. . . . Another factor that would prevent a resumption was that the exchange of prisoners of war has not taken place in the way that was anticipated in the Paris Accords."[75]

In his memoir of his time as minister of the Washington embassy, Leifland would cite an American document claiming that Andersson had leaked information about the planned North Vietnamese offensive.[76]

Leifland's account of the meeting is implausible. As the minutes indicated, it had been the other way around. The American ambassador had leaked information to the Swedish foreign minister. The foreign minister had not disclosed any intelligence to the American ambassador. As a witness to the exchange, Hyltenius had reason to know what he was talking about:

> To me, it sounds very unlikely. Sven Andersson certainly . . . had a positive attitude toward the United States, but he had also, of course, a critical view on the Vietnam War, as Palme had. I don't see there were differences of opinion there. So, I can't believe it because Strausz-Hupé refers to the build-up as a fact, and asks Sven Andersson to try to somehow to influence the Vietnamese to hold, so to speak, and go back to the negotiating table.[77]

Andersson could be as blunt in public as he was in private because a speech he gave in January 1975 irritated Kissinger. Speaking before the Swedish Committee on Vietnam, Andersson criticized the Saigon regime for its failure to respect the Paris Accords. Rejecting the concept of coexistence with the Provisional Revolutionary Government, President Thieu, via military means, tried to seize areas controlled by the PRG in South Vietnam. The foreign minister noted that since the signing of Paris Accords, one hundred thousand Vietnamese had died: "Responsibility for this development rests heavily on the Saigon regime and those who support its policy."[78]

The Paris Accords prohibited any foreign military presence in Vietnam, or any foreign influence on public policy, but the Ford administration disregarded these prohibitions: "The latest military setbacks for Saigon have led the American president to announce that he intends to request still more money for the Saigon regime, whose warfare is almost entirely funded by the USA."[79]

The United States had tried to justify its own violations of the Paris Accords by pointing the violations allegedly committed by the other side, but Andersson could see no justifications. Such an attitude was an "extraordinarily worrying perspective. The government in Saigon has been able to cling to power exclusively as a consequence of American support. . . . An increased American involvement will therefore only further prolong the conflict."[80]

Simultaneously, as the ambassador called on the foreign minister of Stockholm, the State Department in Washington summoned Curt Lidgard of the Swedish embassy for a meeting. James Lowenstein, the deputy assistant secretary of state for European affairs, said that "Secretary of State Kissinger had personally instructed him" to issue an aide-mémoire because Andersson had employed "insulting language."[81] Furthermore, Lowenstein charged the Swedish foreign minister with "putting all the blame on one side."[82] Because it was an aide-mémoire, the communication would remain unofficial.[83]

On the same day as the aide-mémoire, Strausze-Hupé assured Kissinger, "I will call on Foreign Minister Andersson tomorrow afternoon to express our surprise and concern that he has chosen to publicly criticize the United States on such a forum, and to make a one-sided, extremely biased presentation of the true situation in Vietnam."[84]

A foreign minister eager to please the Americans with classified data would not have challenged them with outspoken rhetoric. Andersson, by contrast, openly opposed the American engagement with Southeast Asia. "So, it was . . . rather heated," Hyltenius said in reference to rhetoric of the day, "but altogether, I don't think that Sven Andersson used any insulting language. That would not be like him."[85]

As displeased with Andersson as he was with Palme, Kissinger opposed the possibility of further Swedish participation in peace negotiations. He warned Strausz-Hupé,

> At this time, we do not think it desirable to interject Palme into a delicate situa-
> tion in which a number of other efforts are at work. Therefore, you should take
> no further initiatives with Swedes whom we doubt could produce anything of
> real value toward a solution. If Palme or his foreign minister raise the matter
> with you, you should listen to what they have to say, but you are to avoid even
> appearing to give them a talking brief on our behalf.[86]

Just before the ultimate Communist victory in South Vietnam, Öberg was now the Swedish minister in Paris. To a PRG representative, Öberg promoted the negotiations with Saigon as a means to prevent further killing. The Foreign Ministry in Stockholm promoted the same idea to the PRG representative stationed there. Informed of these Swedish overtures, Strausz-Hupé reported to Kisinger, "I made no comment but said I would inform my government."[87]

It seems that Kissinger had overestimated the pro-American conservatism of Andersson. The Swedish foreign minister wished to maintain a construc-tive relationship with the United States, but that wish did not prevent him from challenging the capitalist superpower on matters of principle. Over time, the Palme government grew increasingly and directly critical of US involvement in the 1973 coup d'état in Chile. In public commemoration of the coup's third anniversary in 1976, Andersson himself blamed the Nixon administration and the CIA in 1976 for sponsoring the Chilean military's ouster of Allende.[88] Kissinger caught wind of Andersson's criticisms. While flying on an airplane, the secretary of state was agitated enough to demand that Hartman, the assistant secretary of state for European and Eurasian Affairs, confront Ambassador Wachtmeister. Kissinger wanted Hartman to tell Wachtmeister that "A. Claim that USG instrumental in overthrow of Allende is totally false. B. Andersson's comments are totally unacceptable to the USG. C. In any event, the entire subject is none of Sweden's business."[89]

The Ford administration, like its predecessor, welcomed neither critical rhetoric nor offers of mediation from the Swedish Foreign Ministry. The only difference was that Ford, unlike Nixon, possessed the psychological maturity to tolerate differences of opinion without freezing diplomatic relations. After all, political commentator Mark Shields once described Ford as "the most emotionally healthy president" in American history.[90]

NOTES

1. Rolf Ekéus, email, July 24, 2017. Telegram from Secretary of State to American Embassy in Stockholm, "Kissinger Visit to Sweden," April 28, 1973. Nixon Presidential Materials Staff, NSC Files, Country Files—Europe, Box 707, RN.

2. Telegram from American Embassy in Stockholm to Secretary of State, "Foreign Minister Wickman Comments on Possible Kissinger Visit to Sweden," April 27, 1973. Nixon Presidential Materials Staff, White House Central Files, Subject Files, CO, Box 67, RN.

3. "Kissinger visit to Sweden," April 28, 1973.

4. Richard M. Nixon and Henry A. Kissinger. Oval Office Conversation 909–006, May 2, 1973. The Nixon Tapes, RN: https://www.nixonlibrary.gov/white-house-tapes /909.

Luke A. Nichter, Chapman University, email, June 27, 2022.

5. Ibid.

6. Ibid.

7. Ibid.

8. Ibid.

9. Ibid.

10. Falkman, *Ekot från Vietnam*, 239.

11. Asselin, *A Bitter Peace*, 165.

12 Ibid., 191–216.

13. Schwartz, *Henry Kissinger and American Power*, 207; Prados, *Vietnam*, 513. Article 9 of the original agreement, in Asselin, *A Bitter Peace*, 194, and Article 12 of the signed agreement in Asselin, *A Bitter Peace*, 206.

14. Unofficial translation of Olof Palme's statement, *Pressbyrån*, Swedish Ministry of Foreign Affairs, January 24, 1973. *Utrikesdepartementet, HP-Dossierer, Vietnamkriget,* 1972–1974, HP38:58, RA.

15. Ibid.

16. Ibid.

17. Fred Branfman, "Indochina: The Illusion of Withdrawal," *Harper's Magazine*, May 1973; Asselin, *Vietnam's American War*, 213–14, 220–21; Prados, *Vietnam*, 518.

18. Ibid.

19. David K. Shipler, "Vast Aid from U.S. Backs Saigon in Continuing War," *New York Times*, February 25, 1974.

20. Gareth Porter, "Report from North Vietnam: Pressing Ford to Drop Thieu," *New Republic*, February 8, 1975.

21. Jean-Christophe Öberg to Krister Wickman, *"Vietnam: Syd sett från Nord,"* May 15, 1973. *UD HP-Dossierer, Vietnamkriget, Mål:H, Hanoi's politik,* 1972–1975, HP38:30, RA.

22. Ibid.

23. *"Indokina,"* Jean-Christophe Öberg to Krister Wickman, March 10, 1971. *UD HP-Dossierer, Vietnamkriget, Mål:H, Hanoi's politik,* 1970–1971, HP38:26, RA.

24. Ibid.

25. Ibid.

26. Ibid.

27. Ibid.

28. Ekéus interview.

29. Ibid.

30. Eliasson Stockholm interview.

31. Excerpt of Krister Wickman in foreign policy debate, Cabinet Stockholm to the Washington embassy, April 2, 1971. *Utrikesdepartementet, HP-Dossierer, Vietnamkriget,* 1970–1972, *Svenska ställningstäganden,* HP38:57, RA.

32. Ibid.

33. Ibid.

34. Sydney Schanberg, "Cambodia," *Crimes of War*: http://www.crimesofwar.org /a-z-guide/cambodia/. Associated Press, "A U.S. Plane Hits Cambodia Village in 2nd Bomb Error," *New York Times*, August 8, 1973; Robert Schulzinger, "Nixon, Congress, and the War in Vietnam, 1969–1974," 297; Prados, *Vietnam*, 520–21.

35. *"Fran Pressbyråns Vakthavande Re Palmes Tal i Sundsvall,"* August 8, 1973. *Utrikesdepartementet, HP-Dossierer, Vietnamkriget,* 1972–1974, HP38:58, RA.

36. Ibid.

37. Memorandum, *"Amerikanska kommentarer till statsminister Palmes Kambodja-uttalande,"* August 10, 1973. *Utrikesdepartementet, HP-Dossierer, Vietnamkriget,* 1972–1974, HP38:58, RA.

38. Ibid.

39. Ibid.

40. Telegram from the Swedish Foreign Ministry, January 30, 1974. *Utrikesdepartementet, HP-Dossierer, Vietnamkriget,* 1972–1974, HP38:58, RA.

41. Ibid.

42. Wachtmeister, *Som Jag Såg Det,* 203. Kurt Mälarstedt, *"Frostens År: Nixon tog emot i Vita Huset,"* Dagens Nyheter, June 7, 1988.

43. Telegram from Secretary of State to American Embassy in Stockholm, "Wachtmeister's Call on Secretary," November 24, 1973. Nixon Presidential Materials Staff, NSC Files, Country Files—Europe, Box 707, RN.

44. Ibid.

45. Wachtmeister, *Som Jag Såg Det,* 203; Eliasson, *Ord och Handling,* 56–57.

46. Henry Kissinger, "Memorandum for the President. Subject: Our Relations with Sweden," November 26, 1973. Nixon Presidential Materials Staff, NSC Files, Country Files—Europe, Box 707. Senate Resolution 149, "On the Senate of the United States," October 4, 1973, enclosed with letter from Francis R. Valeo to Henry A. Kissinger, October 9, 1973. Letter from Henry A. Kissinger to Walter F. Mondale, September 15, 1973. Nixon Presidential Materials Staff, White House Central Files, Subject Files, CO, Box 67, RN.

47. Henry Kissinger, "Memorandum for the President. Subject: Our Relations with Sweden," November 26, 1973. Wachtmeister, *Som Jag Såg Det,* 203. Kurt Mälarstedt, *"Frostens År: Nixon tog emot i Vita Huset,"* Dagens Nyheter, June 7, 1988.

48. Telegram from Secretary of State to the American Embassy in Stockholm, "U.S.-Swedish Relations," March 11, 1974, Nixon Presidential Materials Staff, NSC Files, Country Files—Europe, Box 707, RN Leif Leifland, *Frostens år,* 192. Kurt Mälarstedt, *"Frostens År: Nixon tog emot i Vita Huset,"* Dagens Nyheter, June 7, 1988. Berggren, *Underbara dagar framför oss,* 506. Again, see my own book, *Nixon, Kissinger, and Allende: U.S. Involvement in the 1973 Coup in Chile.*

49. Memorandum from Henry A. Kissinger to the President, "Restoration of Relations with Sweden," March 14, 1974. Nixon Presidential Materials Staff, NSC Files, Country Files—Europe, Box 707, RN.

50. Thorsell, *Sverige i Vita Huset,* 202–03.

51. Wachtmeister, *Som Jag Såg Det,* 207–08. Mälarstedt, *"Frostens År: Nixon tog emot i Vita Huset."*

52. Ibid., 208.

53. Paul Lewis, "Robert Strausz-Hupé, Envoy And Cold-War Stalwart, 98, *New York Times,* February 26, 2002.

54. Letter from Robert Strausz-Hupé to Alexander M. Haig, Jr., August 12, 1974. National Security Advisor Presidential Country Files for Europe and Canada. Country Files: Romania—State Department Telegrams, Box 12, Gerald R. Ford Presidential Library, Ann Arbor, Michigan (GRF).

55. Ibid.

56. Telegram from Robert Strausz-Hupé to the Secretary of State, "Sweden and the PRG," August 16, 1974. National Security Adviser, Presidential Country Files for Europe and Canada. Country File: Romania—State Department Telegrams, Box 12, GRF.

57. Ibid.

58. Flora Lewis, "Saigon Reds Look to Nonalignment," *New York Times*, May 1, 1975.

59. Memorandum from Henry A. Kissinger to the President, "US-Swedish Relations," December 14, 1973. Nixon Presidential Materials Staff, NSC Files, Country Files—Europe, Box 707, RN.

60. Eliasson Stockholm interview. Åselius, *Vietnamkriget och de svenska diplomaterna*, 489.

61. Ibid.

62. Carl-Magnus Hyltenius, Interview in Stockholm, Sweden, December 20, 2017.

63. Ibid.

64. Ibid.

65. Ibid.

66. "Meeting of Secretary with Minister of Foreign Affairs of Sweden Sven Andersson," Department of State Memorandum of Conversation, October 2, 1974. Mem Con 10-2-1976, NSC Europe, Canada, Ocean Affairs Staff Files, Box 23, GRF, courtesy of Stacy Davis. Carl-Magnus Hyltenius, email, June 13, 2022.

67. Ibid.

68. Ibid.

69. Ibid.

70. Ibid.

71. Hyltenius interview.

72. Ibid.

73. Ibid.

74. Memorandum by Carl-Magnus Hyltenius, *"Samtal mellan utrikesministern och amerikanske ambassadören,"* Swedish Foreign Ministry, November 11, 1974. *HP-Dossierer, Vietnamkriget, Mål:C,* 1974, HP38:17, RA.

75. Ibid.

76. Leifland, *Frostens år*, 188–89.

77. Hyltenius interview.

78. *"Anförande av utrikesminister Andersson den 27 januari vid Svenska Vietnamkommitténs möte i Stockholm,"* Utrikesfrågor: Offentliga dokument m.m. rörande viktigare svenska utrikesfrågor 1975* (Stockholm: Norstedts Tryckeri, 1976), 161.

79. Ibid.

80. Ibid.

81. Coded Telegram from Curt Lidgard to Cabinet Stockholm, January 29, 1975. *UD HP-Dossierer, Vietnamkriget, Mål:C, USA's politik,* 1975, HP38:18, RA.

82. Ibid.

83. Ibid.

84. Telegram from Robert Strausz-Hupé to Henry Kissinger, "Swedish Foreign Minister's Vietnam Speech," GRF.

85. Hyltenius interview.

86. Telegram from Henry Kissinger to Robert Strausz-Hupé, "Swedish Views on Vietnam Negotiations," April 23, 1975. National Security Advisor, Presidential Country Files for Europé and Canada. Country File: Romania—State Department Telegrams, Box 12, GRF.

87. Telegram from Robert Strausz-Hupé to Henry Kissinger, "Swedish Views on Vietnam Negotiations," April 24, 1975. National Security Advisor Presidential Country Files for Europe and Canada. Country File: Romania—State Department Telelgrams, Box 12, GRF.

88. *"Utrikesminister Anderssons anförande vid Chile-kommissionens möte den 11 september," Utrikesfrågor: Offentliga dokument m.m. rörande viktigare svenska utrikesfragor 1976* (Stockholm: Norstedts Tryckeri, 1977), 170–71.

89. Telegram from U.S. Delegation Secretary Aircraft to the State Department in Washington, "Swedish FM's Comments on the U.S. and Allende," September 14, 1976. National Security Adviser, Trip Briefing Books and Cables for Henry Kissinger, 1974–1976. Kissinger Trip File, September 13–24, 1976, South Africa, London—SECTO, Box 43, GRF.

90. Clyde Haberman, "Mark Shields, TV Pundit Known for His Sharp Wit, Dies at 85," *New York Times*, June 18, 2022.

Chapter 6

The Postwar Reconstruction of Vietnam and Swedish-American Relations

Development Assistance

As always, Swedish support for Vietnam ended neither in rhetoric, nor in mediation. The Palme government did not lose interest once in Vietnam once the war ended. In June of 1973, Foreign Minister Wickman, Andersson's predecessor, traveled to Hanoi to arrange reconstruction aid. "I flew with him there," Ekéus said, "and then Palme was very nervous."[1] Wickman and Ekéus were two radicals in the Foreign Ministry. Palme's close aide, Ferm, would serve as his eyes and ears. "So, he flew with us to check that Wickman didn't go overboard with me, to be too enthusiastic," Ekéus said.[2] That did not mean Palme had such great differences with the radicals. "Now," Ekéus pointed out, "I was strongly supporting Palme."[3]

Wickman assured the North Vietnamese: "The Democratic Republic of Vietnam will thus be on the top of the list of countries with whom my government will collaborate in this respect."[4] In order to facilitate the planned reconstruction, the Swedish foreign minister encouraged Hanoi to join the United Nations. Foreign Minister Nguyen Duy Trinh, representing the Vietnamese government, reacted to the proposal with reluctance, effectively dismissing the UN as a Washington-dominated organization.[5] The Vietnamese foreign minister favored bilateral aid programs with countries such as Sweden. Of key interest for him was Swedish support for the development of Vietnam's forest industry and medical care system. Trinh may have been cynical about the United Nations, but he regarded the Swedes without a trace of cynicism:

One had been moved to learn how Prime Minister Palme himself had collected signatures on the street for the benefit of Vietnam; how the five Swedish party leaders, through their appeal for a bombing halt, had supported the peace movement; and how a committee with former Prime Minister Erlander at the head, and the crown prince as honorary chairman, collected funds for Bach Mai's reconstruction.[6]

Wickman believed that the productive relationship between Sweden and Vietnam, which had begun during the war, would continue in peacetime: "Both were small or medium-sized countries that were resolutely waging an independent policy. Swedish support for the Democratic Republic of Vietnam lay in line with Swedish policy to assert the interests of small and medium-sized states."[7]

The North Vietnamese had no reason to doubt Wickman's word about Swedish aid. As a British consul-general said after encountering Wickman in Hanoi: "Say what you will about Sweden or Swedish actions in Vietnam, but they live up to what they say. How many others do that?"[8]

Palme and his associates believed the Vietnamese people deserved reconstruction aid in compensation for their suffering. Wickman had expressed himself with great frankness on the subject, insisting upon the obligation of Americans to provide for reconstruction of Vietnam after all the damage they had inflicted there. "The prestige of the superpower forbids the United States from owning up to a real debt to Vietnam's people," Wickman scathingly observed in a public address.[9]

The absence of a moral debt on Sweden's part had not prevented its government from providing nonmilitary aid to the North Vietnamese as early as 1965. In response to repeated American bombing operations, Sweden had provided medication and medical equipment to meet the needs of the injured, along with textiles and food to meet the needs of the consumers of damaged industries. North Vietnamese children received condensed milk. Stockholm even furnished the paper required for the publication of academic textbooks. The North Vietnamese Red Cross received these vitally needed goods through its counterpart organization in Sweden.[10]

The aid did not stop there, however. "After the mass bombing of North Vietnam, an extensive aid within the health care sector began," Falkman wrote later. "Two of North Vietnam's leading hospitals were built with Swedish aid."[11]

Wickman's own predecessor, Nilsson, had served as foreign minister under Prime Minister Erlander, and had maintained his appointment when Palme assumed office in 1969. Nilsson had expanded this assistance in 1969 by allocating 225 million kronor in aid to cover a three-year period. This was in keeping with Nilsson's controversial promise at the 1969 party congress. Out of this allocation, 75 million kronor had been earmarked for humanitarian assistance, and this amount would be increased later to more than 95 million kronor.[12]

By 1972, the Swedish government had resolved to provide North Vietnam with reconstruction aid.[13] The escalating bombing campaigns against North Vietnam that spring, however, compelled the Swedish government to spend 150 million kronor, which had been originally set aside for the eventual reconstruction of Vietnam, on emergency humanitarian assistance.[14] The next year, Stockholm decided to divert an additional 190 million kronor from reconstruction programs to humanitarian aid for North Vietnam. The reconstruction of Bach Mai Hospital, which had been destroyed during the Christmas Bombings, would cost Sweden another 10 million kronor. Beyond that, Sweden planned to provide Hanoi 100 million kronor in development aid for fiscal year 1973/74, and 130 million kronor for fiscal year 1974/75.[15] In the latter fiscal year, Sweden would become the first country to ever answer the United Nations call for member nations to provide of .7 percent of its GNP in international aid. The Palme government would reserve 1 percent of its GNP for international aid the following fiscal year.[16]

A substantial aid portion of Swedish reconstruction aid went to forest cultivation and paper production. Seeking to establish a forestry industry in North Vietnam, a visiting delegation from that country's State Planning Commission had first requested help from the Swedish government in September of 1969. Apart from industrial development, alleviating the severe paper shortage in North Vietnam could help remedy the program of illiteracy, a sad legacy of French colonialism.[17]

In his address before the 1969 Party Congress, Foreign Minister Nilsson had promoted reconstruction aid in general for the Democratic Republic of Vietnam, but he first promoted plans for the forestry program after his visit to North Vietnam in 1971.[18] The East Germans had begun to assist North Vietnam in tree planting in the Quang Tri Province, and expressed interest in experimenting with Swedish planting methods.[19] Swedish support for the North Vietnamese paper industry would prove controversial back in Stockholm. Ekéus recalled that "this famous or infamous development of Vietnamese forests and [the] paper production facility . . . was very criticized by the opposition parties at that time. And it was . . . very difficult."[20]

Öberg brought forestry experts to Vietnam, and then requested a plane from the legendary General Vo Nguyen Giap. The 1954 victor of Dienbienphu was now Minister of Defense. The Swedish diplomat wanted to give the industrial team a bird's-eye view of the North Vietnamese forest, which happened to be the location of key air defense installations and other military assets. The general laughingly rejected the solicitation: "You want to fly over Vietnam.. . . . We are hiding in the forest, and you want to take photographs of the air. You are crazy!"[21]

In August of 1974, the Swedish government made a formal agreement with North Vietnam to support the construction of the Bai Bang paper mill in Viet Tri, in addition to the establishment of a children's hospital in Hanoi, and a clinic for outpatients in Mon Bai.[22]

The development of the forestry industry came in stages. As Falkman explained,

> To build and operationalize the factory required the efforts of 600 Swedish technicians and a prefabricated village of housing, a restaurant, a swimming pool, a school, and hospital. Between 1974 and 1990, Sweden invested more than two billion kronor in a pulp-and-paper factory, and a forestry company for planting and timbering. The project was completed with a harbor installation, barges for the transport of timber, and a technical school.[23]

The Moderate Party opposed the project because of cost overruns. The original 770 million-kronor budget eventually expanded to 2.8 billion kronor over approximately twenty-five years. The production of paper at Bai Bang, scheduled to begin in 1979, did not start until 1983. "Not until 1996 was the paper mill operating at full capacity," noted Pierre Schori, the former deputy foreign minister responsible for issues of foreign aid and migration.[24]

Despite the right-wing opposition to the project, the investment in the Bai Bang project eventually proved worth the effort. "Now, that project turned out to be a tremendous success," Ekéus pointed out in 2016. "As late as five years ago, the Australian government made a study of major development assistance, and listed this as one of the greatest success stories, the way we had in Vietnam."[25]

Beyond the forestry industry, Swedish support for North Vietnam's family planning program was also important. It was a collaborative effort between the two countries rather a top-down charitable operation. "The Swedish expert who visited Hanoi had been impressed by what had been seen of the infrastructural side of family planning activities," Öberg told North Vietnamese prime minister Pham Van Dong in 1971.[26] Sweden did not condescend to the North Vietnamese, but gave them the greater opportunity to help themselves.

At the end of 1972, Wickman again received Madame Binh in Stockholm. The Swedish foreign minister suggested to his fellow diplomat that the United Nations administer an international reconstruction fund for Vietnam. Donor countries could contribute to this fund. Madame Binh distrusted such a scheme, fearing that the United States would manipulate the fund, directing much of it to the Saigon regime. The American intervention in her country had left her deeply embittered and puzzled. Many years later, Madame Binh would say to Falkman, "We Vietnamese ask ourselves why over two and a half million Americans crossed the Pacific Ocean to fight us Vietnamese. We have never done them harm"[27]

Indeed, Prime Minister Phan Van Dong would prove reluctant to apply for UN membership, so distrusted was the international organization by North Vietnam. "The UN . . . offered the possibility of reducing the superpowers' influence," Wickman assured her.[28] Madame Binh thought it preferable for Vietnam to receive aid either bilaterally from friendly countries, or from a consortium of such countries. Nevertheless, she agreed to discuss the proposal with rest of the PRG.[29]

While the Swedish government did not have diplomatic relations with the Saigon regime, it extended its assistance to the people of South Vietnam. Approximately 7 million kronor worth of aid, primarily medication and medical equipment, reached PRG-controlled areas by the fall of 1972. Stockholm then appropriated an additional 10 million kronor worth of aid to be channeled through the government-run SIDA, an acronym for the Swedish International Development Cooperation Agency, as well as the nongovernmental organizations Save the Children and the Red Cross.[30]

Although the Swedes had yet not formally recognized the Provisional Revolution Government as a governing body, they did provide the PRG with 3 million kronor in direct humanitarian aid in fiscal year 1971/72, raising that amount to 13.5 million for fiscal year 1973/74.[31]

As the war drew to a final close in 1974, Swedish officials began to explore the NLF-controlled areas of South Vietnam. The Swedish ambassador finally crossed the fabled the 17th parallel in early January. "Welcome to our land," a customs official said in French, "we know Olof Palme's statements on the Vietnam question, and you Swedes have always given your support to Vietnam's cause."[32]

Öberg found that the areas controlled by Thieu were surrounded by new strongholds and barbed wire. Anyone who tried to enter these areas either faced arrest or risked getting shot. The areas controlled by the PRG, by contrast, were free and open. The ambassador traveled independently, accompanied only by his own interpreter from Hanoi. The Swedish ambassador sought out ordinary people for conversation: "Simple, often illiterate people honestly answered my questions, often laughing that one could ask such stupid questions. Naturally, everything had become better. The end to the Saigon army's brutal exploitation, where theft, violence, and harassment clearly were a part of the routine."[33]

In order to determine aid requirements, the first secretary of the Swedish embassy, accompanied by the aid attaché, traveled down from Hanoi to South Vietnam at the end of the year, where the "visit consisted of hospitals, schools, farms, land reclaiming schemes, and sawmills, among other things."[34] Despite the lack of formal diplomatic relationship with the PRG, the Swedes were making plans for the future.[35]

A few months before the war came to an end, Lennart Klackenberg, in his role as a Swedish delegate, did petition the United Nations to provide $2.9 million to the Provisional Revolutionary Government rather than the Saigon regime, for which the multilateral aid had been originally intended.[36]

Between 1967 and 2013, Sweden provided Vietnam with over $1.8 billion in official development assistance, commonly known as ODA. The annual disbursements increased dramatically after Palme took office.[37]

Swedish development aid to Vietnam ended in 2013. "We don't think it's necessary," Falkman said, "and we regard them as independent and no need for Swedish aid, except commercial relations with them. And we regard us as equal countries."[38]

Once the war ended, the Swedes could turn some focus on what they did best: business. The state-owned Petroswede, for example, engaged in talks with Vietnam to collaborate on oil-exploration projects. SAS asked for the right to fly over South Vietnam, as former President Thieu had permitted the carrier to do.[39] It has been charged that the Swedes sided with North Vietnam during the war in a cynical pursuit of their own business interests. While Stockholm undeniably appreciated Vietnam's commercial potential, it is important to remember two things. First, Swedish commercial investment in a truly independent Vietnam would aid the country's development. Second, Swedish trade with the United States had been far more important, and Palme's activism had come at the risk of that trade.

Even though Washington bore the primary responsibility for Vietnam's destruction, it failed to honor its own pledge in the 1973 Paris Peace Accords to provide its former enemy with reconstruction aid.[40] Certainly, Americans bore considerable bitterness toward North Vietnam at war's end, but postwar assistance would not have been politically impossible. The US Congress in the early 1970s was strongly antiwar and liberal in philosophy—liberal enough for the senior senator of Massachusetts to feel comfortable advocating postwar assistance for Vietnam.

The Swedes closely followed Kennedy's work as chairman of the Subcommittee to Investigate Problems Connected with Refugees and Escapees, which was part of the Senate Judiciary Committee. In November of 1970, Kennedy's subcommittee had released a report on refugees in Indochina. For de Besche in Washington, the report brought to mind the proposal made by Palme when the prime minister had come to the United States several months before: "It seems to me the difference lies in the report's proposal that humanitarian aid should be provided during the ongoing conflict while the Swedish proposal primarily aims for a program of international reconstruction after the war."[41] One of the authors of the Senate report then informed the Swedish ambassador that Kennedy would request that Secretary of State Rogers introduce the idea of a UN conference on postwar humanitarian aid.[42]

That December, Kennedy more fully described his plan to Ola Ullsten, a member of the Swedish delegation at the UN. With a bipartisan group of senatorial colleagues, Kennedy intended to write to Rogers to propose the international program for humanitarian assistance. The senator offered specific and informed suggestions: "Kennedy considered that the UN, or maybe better, a specialized agency within the UN, provided the best framework for such a program."[43] He also favored carrying out the program in stages. The priority would be to help the wounded and injured "casualties of war," as well as refugee children. Then, aid for all Indochinese refugees would follow.[44]

That does not mean that the senator had any illusions, however: "Kennedy was not particularly optimistic concerning the administration's reaction to the proposal."[45] Since he could not insist that the Americans themselves make the actual proposal, he preferred a sponsor with "credibility as well in the North as in the South," referring to the two states of Vietnam.[46] Kennedy then praised Sweden's "great traditions" of international philanthropy.[47]

The meeting ended in a manner that indicated Kennedy's recognition of Sweden's importance in international affairs. It was likely that Palme's own initiative on aid to Indochina influenced the senator: "Senator Kennedy seemed eager to maintain contact with the embassy on this matter. He was also informed of the prime minister's proposal concerning postwar aid to Vietnam. He would allow the embassy to get part of the letter to Secretary Rogers as soon as it was delivered to the State Department."[48]

The prime minister, for his part, seemed just as eager to maintain contact with the liberal lion from Massachusetts, even hosting a dinner in Stockholm in his honor.[49]

On June 18, 1972, the Democratic stalwart introduced two amendments to the Foreign Assistance Act. One amendment stated, "The Congress affirms the willingness of the United States to share the burden for the immediate and post-war relief and rehabilitation of the people of Indochina, including South Vietnam, North Vietnam, Laos, and Cambodia."[50] Kennedy's amendment called for the US government to provide humanitarian assistance through a special United Nations fund. "Such a fund has many precedents in the history of the United Nations and has proven to be an effective way to internationalize funding for special projects," Kennedy said on the floor of the Senate. "Because the United States bears a special responsibility to the people of Indochina, we bear a special burden in supporting such a fund."[51]

The amendment would advise the president to ask the UN Secretary General to hold an international conference on humanitarian assistance for

Indochina. In its own copy of the *Congressional Record*, the Swedish embassy in Washington drew a line by a particular passage in Kennedy's speech:

> It is my impression, having talked with a number of the representatives at the United Nations, that a number of countries throughout the world would like to participate in humanitarian relief efforts in Vietnam. There is very little opportunity for them to do so now. They would welcome leadership by the United States in this field at the present time, not later.[52]

Kennedy had obviously been referring to Sweden, among other nations. After the formal reunification of the newly named Socialist Republic of Vietnam in 1976, the recovering country would join the United Nations the following year.[53] The UN, therefore, could have served as the ideal venue for humanitarian aid.

As the Senate considered Kennedy's first amendment, which was the proposal for international reconstruction aid, it easily passed his second by a vote of 75 to 7. The second amendment would appropriate $70 million for the medical relief of refugees in South Vietnam, and to meet the compensation claims of bombing victims in that area.[54] At a time of general congressional hostility to military appropriations for Vietnam, legislators still willingly approved *humanitarian* appropriations for the people of South Vietnam.

Fourteen months after the American war in Vietnam came to its official termination, Kennedy remained deeply concerned about the violence that continued with Washington's sponsorship. He also remained committed to the idea of aid. The senator wrote to Henry Kissinger to inquire about "the current status of negotiations between Washington and Hanoi on American reconstruction assistance to North Vietnam," among other matters.[55]

Kissinger soon offered a reply:

> These talks have been suspended since last July. The Administration's position, which we believe is shared by the great majority of members of Congress, is that the U.S. cannot at this time move forward with an assistance program for North Viet-Nam. To date, North Viet-Nam has failed substantially to live up to a number of the essential terms of the Agreement, including those relating to the introduction of troops and war materiel into South Viet-Nam, the cessation of military activities in Cambodia and Laos, and the accounting of our missing-in-action.[56]

In his letter, Kissinger overlooked his own country's violations. In the end, did North Vietnamese violations of the Paris Peace Accords really matter? Washington and Hanoi were not equally to blame. US military aggression had nearly destroyed Vietnam, and Washington owed a debt.

The stinginess of the Nixon administration carried over to the Ford administration, where the secretary of state initially maintained his personalized grip on US foreign policy.

Unfortunately for Vietnam, the World Bank also tightened its wallet. Much to Palme's dismay, the multinational lending institution simultaneously kept its wallet open for the Pinochet dictatorship in Chile. Perhaps not so coincidentally, the president of the World Bank was former Secretary of Defense Robert McNamara, one of the original architects of the Vietnam War. McNamara defended this double standard to the Swedish prime minister:

> My first objective in making any Bank loan is to help the people, and ultimately the poorest people, of the country. I believe that this loan does help some 130,000 of the most disadvantaged of Chile's population, and our supervision of the project will ensure that the help goes where it is intended and needed. It is not an endorsement or a support of the present Government of Chile.[57]

Under a consistent policy of political neutrality, the World Bank could have assisted Hanoi, carefully managing the funds for the benefit of the most vulnerable sectors of Vietnamese society. One could not make the case that either Pham Van Dong or Le Duan was more loathsome than Augusto Pinochet. Yet the World Bank president was adamant: "I will only recommend a loan to the Board if I am satisfied that it can and will help the people of the land, irrespective of political circumstances. Such a condition has not been met to date and we have therefore made no loan to Vietnam."[58]

McNamara presented no evidence to Palme, the prime minister of a World Bank member nation, that a loan would not benefit the Vietnamese people.

One could argue that with time and effort, Kennedy could have persuaded Congress to also help the people of North Vietnam, provided he had had the active support of the Nixon administration. Unfortunately, that active support never came. It came from elsewhere. Sweden would assume the leadership role that Senator Kennedy had envisioned for the United States.

A VIETNAMESE VISITOR

The Vietnamese were undoubtedly grateful to the Swedish government. While Palme never accepted Pham Van Dong's repeated invitations to visit Hanoi, the Vietnamese prime minister did finally travel to Sweden in April of 1974. Sweden was the first Western country to officially receive a Vietnamese head of government. Because he was such a distinguished foreign visitor, Haga Palace served as his guesthouse. Here, in the outskirts of Stockholm, Palme hosted a dinner for Pham Van Dong. Former Prime Minister Erlander was a guest that evening, along with former Foreign Ministers Nilsson and Wickman. Öberg took notes while Pham Van Dong reflected on the events of late 1972/early 1973:

> The chief U.S. negotiator had said to American journalists that he personally was against the Christmas Bombings. It was not true. It was Kissinger's refusal to honor the agreement that had been reached with Le Duc in October in Paris that led to the bombings. Pham Van Dong related how Kissinger, when he visited Hanoi after the signing of the agreement, had tried to strike a joking, smiling tone when they met. Pham Van Dong had reacted with physical discomfort to Kissinger's behavior. How could he be a friend, even be able to appreciate a person who caused the deaths of tens of thousands of his countrymen? There are limits here in the world, Pham Van Dong observed, bitter and emotional.[59]

Pham Van Dong formed happier impressions in the northern province of Ångermanland. At the home of Öberg's parents-in-law, the Vietnamese prime minister found himself lunching not only with Palme, but with Mr. and Mrs. Thorbjörn Fälldin. The leader of the Centre Party, Fälldin was a key political opponent of the Swedish prime minister, and would defeat him in 1976. Pham Van Dong assumed such friendliness and civility characterized Swedish society as a whole.[60] It should not have come as a surprise. After all, Fälldin had joined Palme in his condemnation of the Christmas Bombing in 1972.

FULL RECONCILIATION

Ironically, Kissinger cultivated a friendship with Palme once the war ended. They first saw each other face-to-face at the 1975 Helsinki Conference on Security and Cooperation in Europe. Even though Palme and Andersson politely discussed Portugal, Angola, Israel, and the world economy with the secretary of state, it was an awkward meeting. When Kissinger brought up Portugal, Palme contended that the Portuguese Communists had minimal influence, and the Soviet Union would not want to assume the financial burden of aiding them. Palme stressed the importance of cultivating the Socialists in Portugal. When it came to Angola, a former Portuguese colony, Palme mentioned that Sweden had provided the African nation with approximately $5 million in humanitarian assistance. The prime minister argued that liberation movements were nationalistic in nature and would prefer to maintain their independence from the Communist bloc.[61] Tellingly, Palme had made the same argument about another Third World country, Vietnam.

According to Falkman, Kissinger had given the prime minister a call and said, "Let's forget about our enmities during the Vietnam War. We should have discussions about foreign policies of today but between the Soviet and America, etc., etc., the global view."[62] Not all Swedish officials were pleased with Palme's "flattered" response, as Falkman recalled:

> Some of us were astonished that he immediately sort of said yes to Kissinger about this . . . and then they had some quite good relations, I think, in a way. Because also, you understand that we are a small country amidst the Americans and Russians, etc. And the Americans, the executive of the democratic world, liberal world. And then, of course, we are impressed like our prime minister last month or something [Prime Minister Stefan Löfven in May 2016], he was received by President Obama in the White House together with other Nordic countries' heads of government.[63]

Kissinger is not a man known for demonstrations of remorse. He may never have regretted his past mistreatment of Palme. As national security advisor and secretary of state, Kissinger effectively transcended the role of presidential subordinate. He had been partners with Nixon in the execution of American foreign policy. The president's decision to punish Sweden had Kissinger's full support.

Despite all that past wartime vindictiveness, Kissinger accepted Palme's invitation to visit Stockholm in 1976. The secretary of state still sought assurances from the foreign minister about prospective demonstrations in Sweden's capital. The State Department informed Strausz-Hupé that while Kissinger

> has no doubt about the Swedish government's ability to give physical protection, his concern is for the impact on Swedish-American relations and for the political effect in the United States of such visible demonstrations, in the highly charged political climate of the United States on the day immediately preceding several primaries, it would certainly not be helpful to the president.[64]

Indeed, just as Kissinger had worried over the impact of warfare in Vietnam on Nixon's electoral prospects, now he worried over the impact of peaceful protest in Sweden on those for Ford.[65] The Republican incumbent faced a challenge from his party's right wing in the person of former Governor Ronald Reagan of California. Kissinger was prepared to cancel the visit, if necessary.[66] Eliasson, who had returned to Stockholm to take up a post at the Foreign Ministry in 1974, assured the American embassy that "Secretary Kissinger and his party are very welcome in Sweden."[67]

Eliasson said that foreign minister would release a statement to that effect that very day.[68]

In the end, Kissinger could report to Ford: "My visit to Stockholm went surprisingly well. Student demonstrations were hardly anywhere to been seen (having finished their major activity before we arrived), and for every bearded youth who shouted something when we went by, there were ten people applauding us."[69]

Nevertheless, the protest that took place before his arrival was not insignificant. Thirteen thousand demonstrators shouted out, "Kissinger murderer!"[70]

Like most American officials, Kissinger assumed that domestic politics in Sweden were the primary motivator for Palme's moves in foreign policy, including this meeting. The prime minister "needs this respectability that he gained from this for his own tight election fight this fall, was in better humor and much less stiff than when we saw him at Helsinki this summer"[71]

Palme believed that Sweden's strong defense helped preserve Finland, as well as his own country, free from Soviet domination. The Swedish prime minister had no love for Moscow, but he would not mouth the standard Cold War shibboleths favored by Kissinger: "He believes that détente among the superpowers—I was unable to get him to use 'peace through strength'—is absolutely essential to Sweden's security."[72]

As Kissinger saw it, Palme could not comprehend the realities of power politics. "I told Palme that we had to concern ourselves with international implications of local situations, such as Angola," the secretary of state informed the president. "While Sweden's principles made them more concerned with the internal social aspects of these situations."[73]

To Kissinger, Angola was a battlefield of the Cold War rather than a sovereign nation.

Kissinger apparently liked Palme on a personal level, however, for he could appreciate the prime minister's intelligence and wit in their discussion of the international scene. "We had an extended dialogue . . . out of which grew, I think, mutual respect for the alternative points of view, but also increasing recognitions that the post-Vietnam world required some bridging of the gaps that had developed," Kissinger said in 2017. "So, I consider, and consider today, Palme a significant statesman, who illustrates that we can differ, and still share common objectives."[74]

Eliasson attended this meeting. "And Kissinger and Palme really hit it off," Eliasson recalled. "I took the notes. . . . And I remember it was horribly difficult. It was like a tennis game with only volleys. There were so quick between themselves."[75]

Kissinger respected Palme's analytical mind, up to a point. His praise for the late prime minister after his death also contained a note of subtle condescension. As far as the debate over the Vietnam War was concerned, "Palme was the prime minister of a European country. We had to think of our global responsibilities."[76]

In other words, a Swedish leader could never appreciate the responsibilities faced by a superpower, such as the United States, in countries as diverse as Vietnam and Angola. At the same time, "Palme was extremely clever. So, he often found formulations for his views that were particularly grating, and President Nixon reacted with great sensitivity to this."[77]

The term "clever" has a negative connotation, implying insincerity and manipulativeness. For all his praise for Palme, Kissinger has never claimed to have learned anything from the late prime minister's antiwar critique. "I think the challenge of Vietnam was that it turned into a debate of absolute good against absolute wrong, and it wasn't that," he insisted in 2017. "It was more complex, and someday it will be studied in its complexity, but certainly there were major divisions."[78]

By that point, historians had studied the Vietnam War in all its complexity. A scholarly consensus is a rare phenomenon, but most diplomatic historians now make the same arguments about the war that Palme had once made. Perhaps Kissinger, who had abandoned the labor of serious scholarship decades before, did not understand that. Then again, the former secretary of state simply preferred to ignore any scholars bold enough to challenge him.

The crimes against Indochina would never be forgotten.

All the same, Eliasson saw no reason to regret the meeting:

I'm a great believer in dialogue. It is exactly when you have tough times . . . when you need diplomacy. I don't like embargoes, isolation. I think they are counterproductive in many cases. In some cases, they are legitimate, like in South Africa. . . . But, in general, like in relationship to Iran, in relationship to Cuba, it really doesn't lead to results that you expect. I believe much more in open doors, open windows, open dialogue, seeing people. I even negotiated with Saddam Hussein during the Iran-Iraq War.[79]

Palme and Kissinger had a productive exchange in 1976. Two years before, leftist military officers had overthrown their authoritarian government in Portugal. Palme, along with his Social Democratic counterparts such West German Chancellor Brandt, favored the inclusion of the new Portuguese regime in the Western European family. Both Palme and Brandt were concerned that Portuguese communists might unduly influence the demo-cratic process in their country. In 1975, Kissinger had directly reported to President Ford:

Prime Minister Olaf [*sic*] Palme instructed the Swedish Ambassador in Moscow to express this Swedish concern to Soviet officials and Palme himself sum-moned the Soviet ambassador to Stockholm for a discussion of Portuguese events. He warned the ambassador the entire Soviet policy of détente in Europe as well as the outcome of CSCE [Conference on Security and Cooperation in Europe] would be jeopardized if the Portuguese communists violated basic democratic rights.[80]

At the same time, the Swedes, along with the West Germans, pushed hard for the acceptance of the newly Socialist Portugal. "While Kissinger and Americans at the time were very pessimistic about the direction this military would go, because they were openly Communist," Eliasson said, "we claimed very much that through dialogue, we would be sure that in the end, Portugal would come in the Western democracies' side."[81]

The newly independent African nations of Angola and Mozambique, both former Portuguese colonies, naturally came up for discussion as well.[82]

Sonnenfeldt, formerly of the US National Security Council, attended the Stockholm meeting as counselor to the US State Department. According to Sonnenfeldt, Palme impressed the visiting Americans as a "tough cookie" on the Soviet Union. Just the same, Palme and his visitors disagreed on most issues.[83]

As the Vietnam War receded into history, guilt remained an unfamiliar emotion for Kissinger. Other US officials, however, did regret what the Nixon administration had done. In 1979, Vice President Walter Mondale made an official visit to Sweden. When still a US senator from Minnesota, Mondale had resented the references to Nazis in Palme's Christmas Bombing speech, in spite of his support for friendly Swedish-American relations. "At the dinner, which took place in the Foreign Ministry's wonderful dining room," Eliasson remembered, "Mondale said about the Vietnam War: 'You were right and we were wrong.'"[84]

Perhaps this contrite attitude explained Washington's support the following year for the appointment of Palme as the UN special representative to mediate the Iran-Iraq War. When Eliasson learned that the five permanent members of the UN Security Council had unanimously approved the appointment, he said to Palme, "Maybe the change was actually earlier when Mondale said this at this dinner."[85]

Yet the contrition remained partially unexpressed. "It was never an apology," Eliasson reflected, "but it was a recognition that our opposition to the war was understandable."[86]

While Kissinger may have liked Palme to some extent, it remains questionable whether Palme should have liked Kissinger. Dialogue is a diplomatic necessity; personal friendship is not. Kissinger had never objected when Nixon had discussed Palme in an insulting manner, and had even encouraged this presidential tendency by disparaging the Swede himself.[87] As far as I know, Kissinger never apologized to Palme for the diplomatic freeze. Yet Kissinger had a history of charming principled people who should not have been charmed. Asked if Kissinger had genuinely liked Palme, Thomas Pickering answered, "There's no reason why you couldn't ask him that question. What he would tell you, I think, would be how he currently thinks he should respond to it."[88]

For the record, Kissinger, has never responded to my two letters.

NOTES

1. Ekéus interview.

2. Ibid.

3. Ibid.

4. *"Utrikesminister Krister Wickmans tal vid utrikesminister Nguyen Duy Trinhs mottagning i Hanoi den 7 juni 1973,"* UD *HP-Dossierer, Politiska avdelningens ärenden, Politik allmänt. Mål: G/Vietnam, regeringsledamoternas resor 1972-*, HP1: 61, RA.

5. "Extracts from a memorandum on the Swedish Foreign Minister's talks in Hanoi in June 1973," July 3, 1973. *Politiska avdelningens ärenden, Politik allmänt, Mål:G/ Vietnam, regeringsledamöternas resor, 1972*, HP1:G1, *UD HP-Dossierer*, RA.

6. *"Överläggningar mellan utrikesminister Krister Wickman och DRV:s utrikes-minister Nguyen Duy Trinh i Hanoi den 8 och 11 June 1973,"* June 26, 1973. *UD HP-Dossierer, Vietnamkriget, Mål:F, Fredsträvanden*, June-December 1973, 1973–1975, HP38:24, RA.

7. Ibid.

8. *"Promemoria, Utrikesministerns Hanoi-besök"* from Jean-Christophe Öberg to the Swedish Foreign Ministry, June 20, 1973, *UD HP-Dossierer. Politiska avdelningens ärenden, Politik allmänt. Mål: G/Vietnam, regeringsledamoternas resor 1972-*, HP1: 61, RA.

9. *"Stormaktsprestigen förbjuder Förenta staternas regering att vidgå en verklig skuld till Vietnams folk."* Swedish Foreign Ministry Press Office, *"Utrikesministerns anförande i Stockholms FCO,"* November 1, 1972. Delivered by Krister Wickman, October 31, 1972. *Utrikesdepartementet, HP-Dossierer, Vietnamkriget, Svenska ställ-ningstaganden,* 1970–1972, HP 38:57, RA. *Utrikesminsterns anförande i Stockholms FCO,* 31 October 1972.

10. Falkman, *Ekot från Vietnam*, 168; Wickman,*"Stormaktsprestigen förbjuder Förenta staternas regering att vidgå en verklig skuld till Vietnams folk."*

11. Falkman, *Ekot från Vietnam*, 168.

12. Wickman, *"Stormaktsprestigen förbjuder Förenta staternas regering att vidgå en verklig skuld till Vietnams folk."*

13. Falkman, *Ekot från Vietnam*, 169.

14. Wickman, *"Stormaktsprestigen förbjuder Förenta staternas regering att vidgå en verklig skuld till Vietnams folk."*

15. *"Svar på interpellationer av herr Hermansson ang. åtgärder för att uttrycka solidaritet med det vietnamesiska folket, av fru Dahl ang. händelseutvecklingen i Indokina mm. och av herr Antonsson om en internationell återuppbyggnadsplan för Vietnam,"* prepared by the Swedish Foreign Ministry for Krister Wickman, March 1973. *Utrikesdepartementet, HP-Dossierer, Vietnamkriget,* 1972–1974, HP38:58, RA.

16. Bjereld, Johansson, and Molin, *Sveriges Säkerhet och Världens Fred,* 244; Ekengren, *Olof Palme och utrikespolitiken,* 167; Östberg, *När vinden vände,* 142.

17. Falkman, *Ekot från Vietnam*, 169.

18. Ibid. *"Intervju med Torsten Nilsson efter besök I Nordvietnam,"* Inslag i Kväll-söppet, TV 2, 8 November 1971, Press Office, Swedish Foreign Ministry. *UD-HP Dossierer, Vietnamkriget, Mål:H, Hanoi's politik,* 1971–1972, HP38:27, RA.

19. Coded Telegram from Jean-Christophe Öberg, December 29, 1971. *UD-HP Dossierer, Vietnamkriget, Mål:H, Hanoi's politik,* 1971–1972, HP38:27, RA.

20. Ekéus interview.

21. Falkman interview; Falkman, *Ekot från Vietnam*, 169–70.

22. Intelligence Information for the Central Intelligence Agency Directorate of Operations, "Status of Foreign Aid Projects in North Vietnam and PRG-Controlled Areas of South Vietnam," November 22, 1974. Gerald R. Ford Papers, National Security Advisor NSC Vietnam Information Group, Intelligence and Other Reports, 1967–1975. Subject File: National Liberation Front, Box 8, GRF.

23. Falkman, *Ekot från Vietnam*, 170.

24. Schori, "The Legacy of Olof Palme and Sweden."

25. Ekéus interview. Åselius, *Vietnamkriget och de svenska diplomaterna*, 472–73; Östberg, *När vinden vände*, 142; Love Jordell, *Bai Bang-projektet: Från idé till första spadtag, 1969–1974.* Master's Thesis in History, Stockholm University, (2015). 5, 60. Courtesy of Elisabeth Elgán, Department of History, Stockholm University.

26. Jean-Christophe Öberg to Torsten Nilsson, March 29, 1971. *UD HP-Dossierer, Vietnamkriget, Mål:H, Hanoi's politik,* 1970–1971, HP38:26, RA.

27. Falkman, *Ekot från Vietnam*, 234.

28. Peter Landelius, *"Samtal med Madame Binh,"* Swedish Foreign Ministry, December 21, 1972. *UD HP-Dossierer, Vietnamkriget, Mål:F, Fredssträvanden,* 1972–1973, HP 38:21. "Extracts from a memorandum on the Swedish Foreign Minister's talks in Hanoi in June 1973," Swedish Foreign Ministry, July 3, 1973. *UD HP-Dossierer, Politiska avdelningens ärenden, Politik allmänt, Mål:G/Vietnam, regeringsledamöternas resor,* 1972, HP1:G1, RA.

29. Ibid.

30. *"Svar på interpellationer av herr Hermansson ang. Åtgärder för att uttrycka solidaritet med det vietnamesiska folket, av fru Dahl ang. Händelseutvecklingen i Indokina mm. Och av herr Antonsson om en internationell återuppbyggnadsplan för Vietnam,"* prepared by the Swedish Foreign Ministry for Foreign Minister Krister Wickman, March 1973.

31. Ibid.

32. In his memorandum, Öberg translated the customs officer 's words into Swed-ish. Memorandum from Jean-Christophe Öberg to Sven Andersson, January 7, 1974. *UD HP-Dossierer, Vietnamkriget, Mål:H, Hanoi's politik,* 1972–1975, HP38:30, RA.

33. Ibid.

34. Coded Telegram 392 from Bo Kjéllen in Hanoi to the Swedish Foreign Min-istry, December 20, 1974. *UD HP-Dossierer, Vietnamkriget, Mål:G, FNL's politik,* 1970–1974, HP38:25, RA.

35. Ibid.

36. Telegram from the Swedish embassy in Hanoi to Cabinet Stockholm, January 27, 1975. *UD HP-Dossierer, Vietnamkriget, Mål:H, Hanoi's politik,* 1972–1975, HP38:30, RA.

37. The yearly disbursements were less than $1 million and the end of the Erlander period and then leaped to $4.66 million in 1971. Dataset: Aid (ODA) disbursements to countries and regions, Vietnam. Electrronic mail from Sara Järvi, Swedish Ministry for Foreign Affairs, December 7, 2022.

38. Falkman interview. Jordell, *Bai Bang-projektet: Från idé till första spadtag, 1969–1974,* 67. Schori, "The Legacy of Olof Palme and Sweden." Email correspondence with Hedda Eriksson, Press Officer, Swedish Ministry for Foreign Affairs, December 13, 2022.

39. Memorandum by Jan Lundvik, *"Samtal mellan Arne Geijer och Pham Van Dong,"* Swedish Foreign Ministry, September 9, 1975. *UD HP-Dossierer, Politiska avdelningens ärenden, Politik allmänt, Mål:G/Vietnam, regerings ledamöternas resor,* 1972-, HP1:61, RA.

40. Young, *The Vietnam Wars,* 279, 301, and 303.

41. Hubert de Besche in Washington to Wilhelm Wachtmeister, *"Kongressrapport med förslag rörande bistånd till Indokina,"* November 24, 1970. *UD HP-Dossierer, Vietnamkriget, Mål: C, USA's politik,* 1971–1972, HP38:13, RA.

42. Ibid.

43. Leif Leifland, *"Bistånd till Indokina,"* December 15, 1970. *UD HP-Dossierer, Vietnamkriget, Mål: C, USA's politik,* HP38:13, RA.

44. Ibid.

45. Ibid.

46. Ibid.

47. Ibid.

48. Ibid.

49. Letter from Jerome H. Holland to Olof Palme, September 27, 1971. OPA, *Brevsamling, Volym* 3.2/61, ARAB, Courtesy of Joakim Palme.

50. Edward M. Kennedy, "Foreign Assistance Act of 1972," *Congressional Record,* Vol. 118, No. 111, 18 July 1972. Forwarded by the Swedish Embassy in Washington to the Swedish Foreign Ministry, *"Senatebeslut om bistånd till Indokina,"* July 24, 1972. *UD HP-Dossierer, Mål: C, USA's politik,* Vietnamkriget, April–June 1972, HP38: 14, RA.

51. Ibid.

52. Ibid.

53. Bühler, *State Succession and Membership in International Organizations,* 80–82.

54. Kennedy, "Foreign Assistance Act of 1972," *Congressional Quarterly.*

55. Letter from Edward M. Kennedy to Henry Kissinger, March 13, 1974, enclosed with *"Skriftväxling Kennedy-Kissinger om Indokina,"* Washington embassy to the Swedish Foreign Ministry, April 2, 1974. *UD HP-Dossierer, Vietnamkriget, Mål:C, USA's politik,* 1974-, HP38:17, RA.

56. Letter from Henry Kissinger to Edward Kennedy, March 25, 1974, enclosed with *"Skriftväxling Kennedy-Kissinger om Indokina."*

57. Letter from Robert S. McNamara to Olof Palme, March 5, 1975. OPA, *Brevsamling, Volym* 3.2/130, ARAB, Courtesy of Joakim Palme.

58. Ibid.

59. Falkman, *Ekot från Vietnam*, 161; Schori, "The Legacy of Olof Palme and Sweden."

60. Ibid.

61. Telegram from the U.S. Delegation in Helsinki to the Secretary of State, "Secretary's Meeting with Swedish Primin Palme, Helsinki, July 30, 1975," August 1, 1975, National Security Adviser, Trip Briefing Books and Cables, Box 15, Folder: July 26–August 4, 1975, SECTO 2, EXDIS and NODIS, GRF. *"'Försoningsmöte' Kissinger-Palme,"* Svenska Dagbladet, July 31, 1975. Kurt Mälarstedt, *"Frostens År: Ogillande vändes i vänskap,"* Dagens Nyheter, June 10, 1988.

62. Falkman interview.

63. Falkman interview. Mälarstedt, *"Frostens År: Ogillande vändes i vänskap."*

64. Telegram from U.S. Delegation Secretary in Oslo to American Embassy in Oslo to the American Embassy in Stockholm, "Secvisit Sweden," May 21, 1976. Selected page from Trip BB + Cables for HAK: May 19–27, 1976, SECTO, Box 36, GRF, Courtesy of Stacy Davis.

65. Schwartz, *Henry Kissinger and American Power*, 70, 72.

66. Ibid.

67. Telegram from American embassy in Stockholm to American embassy in Oslo, "Secvisit—Sweden," May 21, 1976. Trip BB + Cables for HAK: May 19–27, 1976, Box 35, GRF, Courtesy of Stacy Davis; Eliasson, *Ord och Handling*, 60.

68. Ibid.

69. Memorandum for the President from Brent Scowcroft, May 27, 1976. Trip BB + Cables for HAK: May 19–27, 1976, HAK message to Pres., Box 35, GRF, Courtesy of Stacy Davis.

70. Craig R. Whitney, "Kissinger in Sweden: Vietnam Echoes," *New York Times*, May 25, 1976.

71. Ibid.

72. Ibid.

73. Ibid.

74. Interview of Henry Kissinger by Jan Eliasson.

75. Eliasson Stockholm interview.

76. Interview of Henry Kissinger by Jan Eliasson.

77. Ibid.

78. Ibid.

79. Eliasson Stockholm interview.

80. Memorandum from Henry A. Kissinger for the President, April 26 1975. National Security Adviser, White House Situation Room, NSC Vietnam Information Group: Intelligence and Other Reports, 1967–1975. Subject File: National Liberation Front, Box 8, GRF.

81. Eliasson Stockholm interview.

82. Ibid.

83. Mälarstedt, *"Frostens år: Ogillande vändes i vänskap."*

84. Eliasson Stockholm interview; Wachtmeister, *Som Jag Såg Det*, 197.
85. Ibid.
86. Ibid.
87. Nixon Tapes 783–004 and 909–006.
88. Pickering interview.

Afterword

Kissinger, a man notorious for the cultivation and exploitation of his friends, regarded the former prime minister as useful. Palme's Social Democrats may have lost the 1976 elections, but he remained leader of his own party, and Kissinger undoubtedly expected the Swede to return to power. In 1982, the former secretary of state would establish an international consulting firm, Kissinger Associates, Inc. Therefore, he required an international network. "Kissinger was always eager to have good contacts in all camps," an unnamed Swedish diplomat observed, "and Palme was a good representative for the European left."[1]

While promoting his business interests, Kissinger long harbored hopes of returning to public office.[2] Palme could have been even more useful to an official diplomat.

Indeed, their rapport extended beyond their terms of public office. "Olof Palme became a friend whose thinking I appreciated, and whose human qualities I greatly respected," Kissinger said, noting that he "never visited Europe for that period without seeing Olof Palme."[3] After Kissinger had triple bypass surgery in early 1982, Palme took a break from his mediation of the Iran-Iraq War to telephone the former secretary of state as he recovered at the hospital.[4]

Later that year, Palme assumed power for the second time. On February 28, 1986, the prime minister was assassinated. The murder remained a mystery until 2018, when journalist Thomas Pettersson fingered the late Stig Engström as the assassin.[5] In 2020, Swedish prosecutor Krister Petersson officially identified Engström as the assassin.[6] Both investigations are credible.

Failure and personal insecurity likely drove Engström to resort to violence as a means of psychological compensation. This is certainly the case for most assassins, no matter their ideology.[7] At the same time, Engström also moved in right-wing circles in Sweden.[8] Only those on the extreme right could have wished Palme any harm, but Swedish conservatives, as a rule, favored an unconditional adherence to Washington's agenda, an agenda that had been Kissinger's own.

Palme's 1986 murder left Kissinger genuinely saddened. He spoke at Palme's Washington memorial service at the National Presbyterian Church: "So for all whose lives Olof Palme touched, the world has become a far lonelier place. It has been a privilege to be Olof Palme's contemporary. It has been an honor to know Olof Palme as a man."[9]

Edward Kennedy's tribute to Palme at this memorial service had more depth and meaning. Upon a death, many of us struggle to find polite words for the deceased, but not the senior senator from Massachusetts: "Sometimes, it seems that hate and violence cannot abide those who stand for reason and peace. Olof Palme died, walking among his people, with his wife's hand in his. He was a prophet so honored in his own country that he refused to be afraid. But in a truest sense, he belonged to all of us."[10]

The senator, the youngest sibling of martyrs, placed Palme in their company: "Today I regard him as a brother."[11] Maintaining his composure with effort, Kennedy honored the late prime minister in 1986 with the same words he had spoken in farewell to his own brother, Robert, in 1968: "Olof Palme saw war—and tried to stop it. Let us pray that he was for us—and what he wished for others—will someday come to pass for all the world."[12]

In the years since Palme's death, Swedish-American relations have become friendlier and less complicated. In 2002, President George W. Bush hosted a reception at the White House for American Nobel Laureates, including former President Jimmy Carter, who had just won the Nobel Peace Prize that year. Eliasson, who had served as first secretary at the Washington embassy during the Vietnam War, was now the Swedish ambassador himself. At the request of Bush and his gracious wife, Laura, Ambassador and Mrs. Eliasson joined the First Couple in the receiving line. Kissinger, who had inexplicably won the Nobel Peace Prize in 1973, was one of the guests.

Eliasson knew that former secretary of state "long had a shadow cast over him from the Vietnam War and Allende's fall in Chile," but the Swede also respected Kissinger's diplomatic contributions to détente.[13]

"Mr. Ambassador," said the former secretary of state, "I would never have expected to be greeted by the Swedish ambassador in the White House."[14] The Swedish ambassador correctly interpreted Kissinger's remark as a joke.[15] Yet even the most hilarious wisecrack can convey a serious note. The insecure Kissinger, the commissioner of many crimes, cannot handle any criticism. Shortly after the publication of *The Trial of Henry Kissinger* by the British journalist Christopher Hitchens, the former secretary of state spoke at the National Press Club. As a condition for his appearance at the National Press Club, Kissinger would take no questions about the highly critical Hitchens.[16]

This rule even applied to a friendly interview on Swedish television with Eliasson, who had recently stepped down as deputy secretary general of the United Nations. Kissinger blocked any discussion of past American support of Latin American dictatorships.[17] Obviously, this meant that Kissinger did not wish to discuss his own personal support of Latin American coups, including the 1973 overthrow of Chilean president Salvador Allende.

Therefore, it is doubtful that Kissinger has ever forgiven the late prime minister for his Christmas Bombing speech. Palme's words must gnaw at the old man to this day, with his resentment seeping out even in his lighter moments.

That said, Kissinger was only one man among many who have engaged in service to the American empire. US foreign policy has changed little since the American War in Vietnam, an unjustified intervention that not only sacrificed the lives of over fifty-eight thousand American servicemen, but also approximately three million Vietnamese, of whom two million were civilians.[18] The lessons of Vietnam remain relevant today, and Washington has still not fully comprehended the warnings of Olof Palme.

NOTES

1. Mälarstedt, *"Frostens År: Ogillande vändes i vänskap."*

2. Schwartz, *Henry Kissinger and American Power*, 362–64, 374–75, 382.

3. Interview of Henry Kissinger by Jan Eliasson.

4. Henry Kissinger, "Olof Palme and I Were Friends," *Washington Post*, March 9, 1986; United Press International, "Kissinger 'Excellent' After Triple Bypass in Coronary Surgery," *New York* Times, February 11, 1982; Mälarstedt, *"Frostens År: Ogillande vändes i vänskap"*; Eliasson, *Ord och Handling*, 57.

5. See Thomas Pettersson, *Den Osannolika Mördaren: Skandiamannen och mordet på Olof Palme* (Gothenburg: Offside Press, 2018).

6. Thomas Erdbrink and Christina Andersson, "After 34 Years, Sweden Says It Knows the Killer of Olof Palme," *New York Times*, June 10, 2020, A11.

7. Pettersson, *Den Osannolika Mördaren*, 185, 228–32.

8. Ibid., 39, 64, 175, 181–84, 203–06.

9. Henry Kissinger, "Olof Palme and I Were Friends." Memorial Service for Olof Palme, National Presbyterian Church, Washington, D.C., March 7, 1986. Henry A. Kissinger Papers, Part II, Series III, Post-Government Career, Box 704, Folder 3, Yale University Library Digital Repository (YDR).

10. Remarks of Senator Edward M. Kennedy, Memorial Service for Olof Palme, National Presbyterian Church, Washington, D.C., March 7, 1986. Henry A. Kissinger Papers, Box 704, Folder 3, YDR.

11. Ibid.

12. Ibid.; Marjorie Hyer, "Olof Palme Eulogized as 'Prophet,'" *Washington Post*, March 8, 1986.

13. Eliasson, *Ord och Handling*, 51.

14. Ibid.; Eliasson telephone interview; Eliasson, *Ord och Handling,* 179–80.

15. Eliasson Stockholm interview.

16. Christopher Hitchens, *The Trial of Henry* Kissinger (New York: Verso, 2002); Russell Mokhiber and Robert Weissman, "Did Henry Kissinger Slander Christopher Hitchens?" *History News Network,* July 5, 2002, https://historynewsnetwork.org/article/123.

17. Interview of Henry Kissinger by Jan Eliasson.

18. Prados, *Vietnam*, 531.

Bibliography

"A Bureaucratic Insider." In Merrill, Dennis and Thomas G. Paterson, eds. *Major Problems in American Foreign Relations, Volume II: Since 1914, Sixth Edition*, edited by Dennis Merrill and Thomas G. Paterson, 422–23. Boston and New York: Houghton Mifflin Company, 2005.

"A Career Diplomat." *The New York Times*, October 21, 1972. *New York Times* Article Archive.

Agrell, Wilhelm. *Fred och fruktan: Sveriges säkerhetspolitiska historia 1918–2000*. Lund: Historiska Media, 2000.

Åhman, Sven. *"Även Åsea får kritik i Amerika."* *Dagens Nyheter*, October 10, 1969. *Svenska Dagtidningar*, Royal Library, Stockholm, Sweden.

———. *"Flygarhustru: Första livstecknet på femtitvå månader."* *Dagens Nyheter*, March 8, 1970. *Svenska Dagstidningar*, Royal Library, Stockholm, Sweden.

Albons, Bengt. *"USA hemlig vän i kalla kriget."* *Dagens Nyheter*, December 21, 2002. *Svenska Dagtidningar*, Royal Library, Stockholm, Sweden.

Allen, Michael J. *Until the Last Man Comes Home: POWs, MIAs, and the Unending Vietnam War*. Chapel Hill: The University of North Carolina Press, 2009.

American Prisoners of War in Southeast Asia, 1970: Hearings before the Subcommittee on National Security Policy and Scientific Developments of the Committee on Foreign Affairs. House of Representatives, Ninety-First Congress, Second Session. Washington D.C.: U.S. Government Printing Office, 1970.

Ambrose, Stephen E. *Nixon: The Education of a Politician 1913–1962*. New York: Simon & Schuster, 1987.

Anrep-Nordin, Monica. *"Deras män är fångar i Nordvietnam. Barnen frågar varje dag: Har jag också en pappa?"* *Svenska Dagbladet*, November 27, 1969. *Svenska Dagtidningar*, Royal Library, Stockholm, Sweden.

"Area PW's wife, family assured by Swedish he's alive." December 12, 1970. Northwestern University Main Library, Evanston, Illinois.

Arlington National Cemetery Unofficial Site. http://www.arlington.cemetery.net.

Åselius, Gunnar. *Vietnamkriget och de svenska diplomaterna*. Stockholm: Dialogos, 2019.

Åström, Sverker. *Ögonblick: Från ett halvsekel i UD-tjänst*. Stockholm, 2003.

Ashby, LeRoy and Rod Gramer. *Fighting the Odds: The Life of Senator Frank Church.* Pullman: Washington State University Press, 1994.

Asselin, Pierre. *A Bitter Peace: Washington, Hanoi, and the Making of the Paris Agreement* Chapel Hill: The University of North Carolina Press, 2002.

———. *Vietnam's American War: A History.* Cambridge, U.K.: Cambridge University Press, 2018.

Associated Press. "Air Force Wife Tries In Vain for Viet Visa." *Fort Walton Beach Playground Daily News,* December 22, 1969. Newspapers.com.

———. "Bombs drop near camp says POW." *The Anniston Star*, February 28, 1972. Newspapers.com.

———. *"Bråk i Moskva om piloterna."* *Svenska Dagbladet,* September 28, 1972. *Svenska Dagstidningar*, Royal Library, Stockholm, Sweden.

———. "A U.S. Plane Hits Cambodia Village in 2nd Bomb Error." *The New York Times*, August 8, 1973. *New York Times* Article Archive.

———. "Here Is List of Prisoners and Mail Recipients." *The Miami Herald,* December 24, 1969. Newspapers.com.

———. "Kennedy gets list of 368 PWs." *Chicago Sun-Times*, December 23, 1970. Northwestern University Main Library, Evanston, Illinois.

———. "Letters from POW Mates." *Lubbock Avalanche-Journal*, April 28, 1970. Newspapers.com.

———. "Macon Man Is Among MIA Dead." *The Atlanta Constitution*, March 8, 1974. Newspapers.com.

———. "Many Missing in Southeast Asia." Abilene Reporter-News, February 27, 1973. Newspapers.com.

———. "Names of 132 POWs Released." *The Miami Herald*, December 24, 1969. Newspapers.com.

———. "Soviet Arms Aid to Hanoi is Down." *The New York Times*, April 13, 1972. *New York Times* Article Archive.

———. "Wives Say Husbands Held in POW Camps." *The Daily Chronicle* (Centralia, Washington), December 14, 1970. Newspapers.com.

Baker, Don H. Jr. and Gertrude N. Greenspoon. "Arsenic." In *Minerals yearbook: Metals and minerals (except fuels) 1961,* Bureau of Mines, 275–79. Washington, D.C.: U.S. Government Printing Office, 1962.

Baker, Peter. "Nixon Tried to Spoil Johnson's Vietnam Peace Talks in '68, Notes Show." *The New York Times,* January 2, 2017. https://www.nytimes.com/2017 /01/02/us/politics/nixon-tried-to-spoil-johnsons-vietnam-peace-talks-in-68-notes -show.html.

Bell, Dora Griffin. *The Heroes' Wife.* Bloomington, IN: AuthorHouse, 2006.

Bencko, Vladimir and Florence Yan Li Foong. "The history of arsenical pesticides and health risks related to Agent Blue." *Annals of Agricultural and Environmental Medicine* 24, no. 2 (2017): 312–16.

Berggren, Henrik. *Dag Hammarskjöld: Att Bära Världen.* Stockholm: Bokförlaget Max Ström, 2016.

———. *Underbara dagar framför oss: en biografi över Olof Palme.* Stockholm: Norstedts, 2010.

Berman, William C. *William Fulbright and the Vietnam* War. Kent, OH: The Kent State University Press, 1988.

Bjelf, Lars. *"'Irriterat Läge' Sverige-USA,"* Aftonbladet, June 14, 1972. *Svenska Dagstidningar*, Royal Library, Stockholm, Sweden.

Bjereld, Ulf. *Kritiker eller medlare: Sveriges utrikespolitiska roller 1945–1990.* Stockholm: Nerenius & Santérus Förlag, 1992.

Bjereld, Ulf, Alf W. Johansson, and Karl Molin. *Sveriges säkerhet och världens fred.* Stockholm: Santérus Förlag, 2008.

Bjurström, Sture, trans. *Senatsförhören om Vietnam.* Stockholm: Beckmans, 1967.

Blumenthal, Ralph. "Ex-P.O.W. Calls Camps Humane." *The New York Times,* October 2, 1972. *New York Times* Article Archive.

Branfman, Fred. "Indochina: The Illusion of Withdrawal." *Harper's Magazine,* May 1973.

Brandt Kreisky Palme. Kristianstad, Sweden: *Tidens Förlag,* 1976.

Bring, Ove. *Neutralitetens uppgång och fall—Eller Den Gemensamma Säkerhetens Historia* Stockholm: Atlantis, 2008.

Buckley, William F. Jr. "Not Just a Scandinavian Disease." *The Evening Star and the Washington Daily News,* January 11, 1973. *Riksarkivet,* Arninge, Sweden.

Burns, Robert. "As Others See Us." *The New York Times,* January 8, 1973. *New York Times* Article Archive.

"Bättre besked hade hindrat missförstånd." Dagens Nyheter, October 10, 1969. *Svenska Dagstidningar*, Royal Library, Stockholm, Sweden.

Bühler, Konrad G. *State Succession and Membership in International Organizations: Legal Theories* versus *Political Pragmatism.* The Hague: Kluwer Law International, 2001.

"Campaign Pressed in U.N." *The New York Times,* November 25, 1969. *New York Times* Article Archive.

Carlberg, Ingrid. *Det står ett rum här och väntar på dig. . . .* Stockholm: Norstedts, 2012.

"'Chicago 7' Releases Names of 59 U.S. PWs." *The Philadelphia Inquirer,* November 27, 1969. Newspapers.com.

CIA Center for the Study of Intelligence. https://www.cia.gov/resources/csi/.

Columbia Center for Oral History Research. https://www.ccohr.incite.columbia.edu.

"Cora Weiss." In *The Loyal Opposition: Americans in North Vietnam, 1965–1972,* edited by James W. Clinton. Louisville: University Press of Colorado, 1995.

Cottey, Andrew, "European Neutrality in Historical Perspective." In *The European Neutrals and NATO: Non-alignment, Partnership, Membership*, edited by Andrew Cottey, 21–44. London: Palgrave Macmillan 2018.

Cowie, Jefferson. "The 'Hard Hat Riot' Was a Preview of Today's Political Divisions." *The New York Times,* May 11, 2020. https://www.nytimes.com/2020/05/11/nyregion/hard-hat-riot.html.

Davidson, Thore. *"Har Nixon nobbat Palme? Nej—Palme har aldrig bett att få träffa Nixon,"* Aftonbladet, March 30, 1970. *Svenska Dagstidningar,* Royal Library, Stockholm, Sweden.

Defense POW/MIA Accounting Agency. https://www.dpaa.mil.

Derfler, Leslie. *The Fall and Rise of Political Leaders: Olof Palme, Olusegun Obasanjo, and Indira Gandhi.* London: Palgrave Macmillan, 2011.

"Dockers in Newark Refuse to Unload Swedish Cars." *The New York Times,* June 14, 1970. *New York Times* Article Archive.

Editorial. "Correction: The Lavelle Case." *The New York Times,* August 7, 2010. https://www.nytimes.com/2010/08/08/opinion/08sun3.html.

Ehrlichman, John. *Witness to Power: The Nixon Years.* New York: Simon and Schuster, 1982.

Ekengren, Ann-Marie. *Olof Palme och utrikespolitken.* Umeå, Sweden: Boréa, 2005.

Ekéus, Rolf. *"Kissinger och svensk säkerhetspolitik under det kalla kriget."* In *En diplomatins hantverkare: vänbok till Jan Eliasson,* edited by Dag Klackenberg, Maud Kronberg, and Monica Lundqvist, 277–86. Stockholm: Bokförlaget Atlantis, 2010.

Ekéus, Rolf. *"Mytbildning om Neutralitetspolitiken."* In *Internationella Studier,* no. 1 (2015): 25–33.

Eliasson, Jan. *Ord och Handling: Ett liv i diplomatins tjänst.* Stockholm: Albert Bonniers Förlag, 2022.

Elmbrant, Björn. *Palme.* Stockholm: Atlas Vintage, 2011.

Erdbrink, Thomas and Christina Andersson. "After 34 Years, Sweden Says It Knows the Killer of Olof Palme." *The New York Times,* June 10, 2020. https://www.nytimes.com/2020/06/10/world/europe/sweden-olof-palme-murder.html.

Ericsson, Bo A. *"Brev till DN om fångar—Hanois man svarar: USA-flygarna pirater men de behandlas väl."* *Dagens Nyheter,* November 7, 1969. *Svenska Dagtidningar,* Royal Library, Stockholm, Sweden.

"Erlander vill ej ha ny Stockholmssession." *Dagens Nyheter,* May 9, 1967. *Svenska Dagstidningar,* Royal Library, Stockholm, Sweden.

Falk, Richard. "International Law Aspects of Repatriation of Prisoners of War During Hostilities." *The American Journal of International Law* 67, no. 3 (July 1973): 465–78.

———. "The American POWs: Pawns in Power Politics." *The Progressive,* March 1971.

Falkman, Kaj. *Ekot från Vietnam: En diplomats minnen från kriget och återbesök fyrtio år senare.* Stockholm: Carlssons, 2014.

Farrell, John A. *Richard Nixon: The Life.* New York: Doubleday, 2017.

Franklin, H. Bruce. *M.I.A. or Mythmaking in America: how and why belief in live POWs has possessed a nation.* New York: Lawrence Hill Books, 1992.

Frazier, Jessica M. *Women's Antiwar Diplomacy During the Vietnam War.* Chapel Hill: The University of North Carolina Press, 2017.

Fredriksson, Gunnar. *"En Diplomat Måste Också Reagera som en Människa,"* *Aftonbladet,* June 28, 1972. *Svenska Dagstidningar,* Royal Library, Stockholm, Sweden.

"Från kritik mot Nordstaterna." *Dagens Nyheter,* December 5, 1966. *Svenska Dagstidningar,* Royal Library, Stockholm, Sweden.

Forslind, Per. *"27 fångnamn . . . Ingen av 14 namn nya för USA."* *Svenska Dagbladet*, March 8, 1970. *Svenska Dagstidningar,* Royal Library, Stockholm, Sweden.

———. *"Palme lovar nya aktioner om krigsfångar."* *Svenska Dagbladet,* June 9, 1970. *Svenska Dagstidningar*, Royal Library, Stockholm, Sweden.

———. *"Spänd väntan i USA: När friges fångarna?"* *Svenska Dagbladet,* September 3, 1972. *Svenska Dagstidningar,* Royal Library, Stockholm, Sweden.

Frohlin, Jonas and Eva Tillberg. *Året var 1970.* Sveriges Television, 2019.

Garrett, Dave L. "The Power of One: Bonnie Singleton and American Prisoners of War in Vietnam." Master of Science Thesis, University of North Texas, 1999.

Gibson, James William. *The Perfect War: Technowar in Vietnam.* Boston and New York: The Atlantic Monthly Press, 1986.

Goldstein, Warren. *William Sloane Coffin Jr.: A Holy Impatience.* New Haven, CT: Yale University Press, 2004.

Goscha, Christopher. *Vietnam: A New History.* New York: Basic Books, 2016.

Goudsouzian, Aram. "Deepening the complexity of Richard Nixon from newly released material." *The Washington Post*, March 24, 2017.

Haberman, Clyde. "Mark Shields, TV Pundit Known for His Sharp Wit, Dies at 85." *The New York Times*, June 18, 2022. https://www.nytimes.com/2022/06/18/us/politics/mark-shields-dead.html.

Hall of Valor Database. https://valor.militarytimes.com.

Harkin, Thomas. "Vietnam Whitewash: The Congressional Jury that Convicted Itself." *The Progressive*, October 1970.

Henry A. Kissinger Papers, Yale University Library Digital Repository. https://web.library.yale.edu/news/2016/05/henry-kissinger-papers.

Hersh, Seymour M. "Aide Says Lavelle Ordered Bombings." *The New York Times*, September 20, 1972. *New York Times* Article Archive.

———. "P.O.W.'s Organize Camps to Keep the Morale High." *The New York Times*, October 2, 1972. *New York Times* Article Archive,

———. "P.O.W.'s Secondary, Hanoi Says." *The New York Times*, March 24, 1972. *New York Times* Article Archive.

———. *The Price of Power: Kissinger in the Nixon White House.* New York: Summit Books, 1983.

———. "3 Freed P.O.W.'s Return; Dispute Flares over Leave." *The New York Times*, September 29, 1972. *New York Times* Article Archive.

———. *Reporter: A Memoir.* New York: Alfred A. Knopf, 2018.

Hershberg, James. *Marigold: The Lost Chance for Peace in Vietnam.* Stanford, CA: Stanford University Press, 2012.

Hershberg, Mary. *Traveling to Vietnam: American Peace Activists and the War.* Syracuse, NY: Syracuse University Press, 1998.

"Hijackers Hold Plane in Sweden, Forcing the Release of Croatians." *The New York Times*, September 16, 1972. *New York Times* Article Archive.

Hirsch, James S. *Two Souls Indivisible: The Friendship That Saved Two POWs in Vietnam.* Boston and New York: Houghton Mifflin Company, 2004.

Hitchens, Christopher. *The Trial of Henry Kissinger.* New York: Verso, 2002.

Hofmann, Paul. "War Raids Incite Anti-U.S. Feelings in Italy." *The New York Times* Article Archive.

Holland, Joseph. *From Harlem With Love: An Ivy Leaguer's Inner City Odyssey*. New York: Lantern Books, 2012.

Holmes, Steven A. "James Stockdale, Perot's Running Mate in '92, Dies at 81." *The New York Times*, July 6, 2005. https://www.nytimes.com/2005/07/06/politics/james -stockdale-perots-running-mate-in-92-dies-at-81.html.

Howell, Nolan. "After Almost 4 Years, Dighton Pilot's Fate Still Unknown." *Garden City Telegram*, December 24, 1970. Newspapers.com.

Hägg, Göran. *Retorik i Tiden: 23 historiska recept för framgång.* Stockholm: Norstedts, 2011.

Immerman, Richard H. "Confessions of an Eisenhower Revisionist: An Agonizing Reappraisal." In *Diplomatic History* 14, no. 3 (Summer 1990): 319–42.

International Committee of the Red Cross. *Commentary on the Third Geneva Convention: Convention (III) relative to the Treatment of Prisoners of War, Volume I.* Cambridge, UK: Cambridge University Press, 2021.

———. *Commentary on the Third Geneva Convention: Convention (III) relative to the Treatment of Prisoners of War, Volume II.* Cambridge, UK: Cambridge University Press, 2021.

Isaacson, Walter. *Kissinger: A Biography*. New York: Simon & Schuster, 2005.

Jarecki, E. *The Trials of Henry Kissinger*. New York: First Run Features, 2002.

Jordell, Love. *"Bai Bang-projektet: Från idé till första spadtag, 1969–1974."* Master's Thesis in History, Stockholm University, 2015.

Julin, Gösta. *"Ambassadören i Vietnammarsch: Sverige 'Informeras.'"* *Dagens Nyheter*, February 21, 1968. *Svenska Dagstidningar*, Royal Library, Stockholm, Sweden.

Karlsson, Birgit. *Svensk försvarsindustri 1945–1992.* Karlskrona: Printfabriken, 2015.

Kendall, John. "Brown's Controversial Appointee: Edison Miller: From Marine Pilot to Censured POW to Supervisor." *The Los Angeles Times*, August 6, 1979. Newspapers.com.

Kiernan, Ben and Taylor Owen. "Iraq, Another Vietnam?" In *The United States, Southeast Asia, and Historical Memory*, edited by Mark Pavlick with Caroline Luft, 75–84. Chicago: Haymarket Books, 2019.

Kimball, Jeffrey. *Nixon's Vietnam Wars*. Lawrence: University Press of Kansas, 1998.

Kissinger, Henry. *Toppmötet 2, Avsnitt 4.* Interview by Jan Eliasson. FLX, Sveriges Television, November 30, 2017.

Knock, Thomas J. "'Come Home, America': The Story of George McGovern." In *Vietnam and the American Political Tradition: The Politics of Dissent*, edited by Randall B. Woods, 82–120. New York: Cambridge University Press, 2003.

"Krigets offer klädde av sig på tribunalen." *Aftonbladet*, May 6, 1967. *Svenska Dagstidningar*, Royal Library, Stockholm, Sweden.

Kutler, Stanley I. *Abuse of Power: The New Nixon Tapes.* New York: Touchstone, 1998.

———. *The Wars of Watergate: The Last Crisis of Richard Nixon.* New York: W.W. Norton & Company, 1992.

Lansche, Arnold M. "Arsenic." In *Minerals yearbook: Metals and minerals (except fuels) 1963,* Bureau of Mines, 245–49. Washington, D.C.: U.S. Government Printing Office, 1964.

"Laos and Found." *Las Vegas Sun,* March 26, 1998. Newspapers.com.

"Largest Hospital in Hanoi Reported Damaged in Raid." *The New York Times,* December 23, 1972. *New York Times* Article Archive.

Leifland, Leif. *Frostens år—om USA:s diplomatiska utfrysning av Sverige.* Stockholm: Nerenius & Santérus Förlag, 1997.

Lewis, Anthony. "Abroad at Home." *The New York Times,* October 14, 1972. *New York Times* Article Archive.

Lewis, Flora. "Saigon Reds Look to Nonalignment." *The New York Times,* May 1, 1975. *New York Times* Article Archive.

Lewis, Paul. "Robert Strausz-Hupé, Envoy And Cold War Stalwart, 98." *The New York Times,* February 26, 2002. https://www.nytimes.com/2002/02/26/world/robert-strausz-hupe-envoy-and-cold-war-stalwart-98.html.

Library of Congress. https://www.loc.gov.

Lindström, Kristina and Maud Nycander. *Palme.* Stockholm: B-Reel AB, *Sveriges Television,* and *Film i Väst,* 2012.

Logevall, Fredrik. "A Delicate Balance: John Sherman Cooper and the Republican Opposition to the Vietnam War." In *Vietnam and the American Political Tradition: The Politics of Dissent,* edited by Randall B. Woods, 237–58. New York: Cambridge University Press, 2003.

———. *Choosing War: The Lost Chance for Peace and the Escalation of War in Vietnam.* Berkeley: University of California Press, 1999.

Longley, Kyle. "The 'Reluctant' Volunteer: The Origins of Senator Albert Gore's Opposition to the Vietnam War." In Woods, Randall B. *Vietnam and the American Political Tradition: The Politics of Dissent,* edited by Randall B. Woods, 204–36. New York: Cambridge University Press, 2003.

Marton, Kati. *Wallenberg: Missing Hero.* New York: Arcade, 1995.

McLeod, Don. "Voices Identified as U.S. POWs Speak Against War." *The Daily Times,* September 16, 1971. Newspapers.com.

McNamara, Robert S. with Brian VanDeMark. *In Retrospect: The Tragedy and Lessons of Vietnam.* New York: Vintage, 1996.

"Midlander Due Release as POW." *The Odessa American,* January 24, 1973. Newspapers.com.

Mitchell, Alison. "Opening to Vietnam: The Overview; U.S. Grants Vietnam Full Ties; Time for Healing, Clinton Says." *The New York Times,* July 12, 1995. https://www.nytimes.com/1995/07/12/world/opening-vietnam-overview-us-grants-vietnam-full-ties-time-for-healing-clinton.html.

"Mitt under Miljökonferensen i Stockholm: USA-fartyg 14 000 ton gift till Vietnam—Sverige." *Aftonbladet,* 8 June 1972. *Svenska Dagstidningar,* Royal Library, Stockholm, Sweden.

Mokhiber, Russell and Robert Weissman. "Did Henry Kissinger Slander Christopher Hitchens?" *History News Network,* July 5, 2002. https://historynewsnetwork.org/article/123.

Morris, Roger. *Uncertain Greatness: Henry Kissinger and American Foreign Policy.* New York; Harper & Row, Publishers, 1977.

Mälarstedt, Kurt. *"Frostens År."* *Dagens Nyheter*, June 5, 1988. *Svenska Dagstidningar*, Royal Library, Stockholm, Sweden.

———. *"Frostens År: Nixon tog emot i Vita Huset,"* *Dagens Nyheter,* June 7, 1988. *Svenska Dagstidningar*, Royal Library, Stockholm, Sweden.

———. *"Frostens År: Ogillande vändes i vänskap."* *Dagens Nyheter*, June 10, 1988. *Svenska Dagstidningar*, Royal Library, Stockholm, Sweden.

Möller, Yngve. *Mina Tre Liv: Publicist, Politiker, Diplomat.* Falköping: Gummessons Tryckeri AB, 1983.

"Names of 334 U.S. Captives Hanoi Admits Holding." *The New York Times*, June 26, 1970. *New York Times* Article Archive.

Nichter, Luke A. *Richard Nixon and Europe: The Reshaping of the Postwar Atlantic World.* Cambridge, U.K.: Cambridge University Press, 2015.

Nixon Tapes, Richard M. Nixon Presidential Library. https:/www.nixonlibrary.gov/ white-house-tapes/.

Nguyen, Lien-Hang T. *Hanoi's War: An International History of the War for Peace in Vietnam.* Chapel Hill: The University of North Carolina Press, 2012.

Nordell, Erik. *"'Kolonialkriget hemma': Bilden av Amerika inom den svenska marxist-leninistiskaa vänstern 1963–1977."* Master's Thesis in History, Uppsala University, 2012.

Öberg, Jean-Christophe. *Varför Vietnam?* Stockholm: Rabén & Sjögren, 1985.

Office of the Historian, U.S. Department of State. https://history.state.gov.

Ognibene, Peter. "Rift in the Ranks: Politics and POWs." *The New Republic*, June 3, 1972.

Ohlsson, Erik. *"Bombflyget tar sikte på sjukhusen."* *Dagens Nyheter,* August 19, 2016. *Svenska Dagstidningar*, Royal Library, Stockholm, Sweden.

Olofpalme.org.

Olson, Kenneth and Larry Cihacek. "The Fate of Agent Blue, the Arsenic Based Herbicide, Used in South Vietnam during the Vietnam War." *Open Journal of Soil Science* 10 (2020): 518–77.

Östberg, Kjell. *I takt med tiden: Olof Palme 1927–1969.* Stockholm: Leopard Förlag, 2012.

———. *När vinden vände: Olof Palme 1969–1986.* Stockholm: Leopard Förlag, 2009.

Paglia, Eric. "The Swedish initiative and the 1972 Conference: the decisive role of science diplomacy in the emergence of global environmental governance." *Humanities & Social Sciences Communications* 8, no. 2 (2021): 1–10.

"Palme i attack mot USA:s krig: Ett Hot Mot Demokratin." *Dagens Nyheter,* February 22, 1968. *Svenska Dagstidningar*, Royal Library, Stockholm, Sweden.

"Palme Would Debate Nixon." *The New York Times,* December 30, 1972. *New York Times* Article Archive.

The Pentagon Papers, Gravel Edition, Vol. 1. Boston: Beacon Press, 1971.

Phan Thu. *An Unequal Contest.* Ho Chi Minh City, Vietnam: Tre Publishing House, 2014.

"Pilotfruarna hos Palme: Sympati och förståelse men inga klara besked." Dagens *Nyheter,* November 28, 1969. *Svenska Dagstidningar,* Royal Library, Stockholm, Sweden.

Plott, Anne. "Anniston Woman Joins Vocal Group: Wives of American POWs Are No Longer Silent." *The Anniston Star,* September 28, 1969. Newspapers.com.

———. "POW's Wife Expects Six-Line Letter." *The Anniston* Star, March 12, 1970.

Porter, D. Gareth. "Nixon's Next Options: Bombing the Dikes." *The New Republic,* June 3, 1972.

———. "Report from North Vietnam: Pressing Ford to Drop Thieu." *The New Republic,* February 8, 1975.

Posner, Gerald. *Citizen Perot: His Life & Times.* New York: Random House, 1996.

Post-Dispatch Wire Services. "Names of 27 American POWs Held by Hanoi Are Made Public." *St. Louis Post-Dispatch,* March 7, 1970.

POW Network. https://www.pownetwork.org.

"P.O.W. Politics." *The New York Times,* October 3, 1971. *New York Times* Article Archive.

Peterson, Gordon I. and David C. Taylor. "A Shield and a Sword: Intelligence Support to Communications with US POWs in Vietnam." *Studies in Intelligence* 60, no. 1 (March 2016): 1–15.

Prados, John. *Vietnam: The History of an Unwinnable War, 1945–1975.* Lawrence: University Press of Kansas, 2009.

Protokoll, Sveriges Socialdemokratiska Arbetarepartis 24:e Kongress 28 september-4 oktober 1969. Stockholm: Tiden-Barnängen, 1970.

"PW's wife awaits 1st letter." *Chicago Sun-Times,* March 12, 1970. Northwestern University Main Library, Evanston, Illinois.

Qureshi, Lubna Z. *Nixon, Kissinger, and Allende: U.S. Involvement in the 1973 Coup in Chile.* Lanham, MD: Lexington Books, 2009.

Reuters. "Demonstrators Greet U.S. Envoy in Sweden." *The New York Times,* April 10, 1970. *New York Times* Article Archive.

———. "Sweden Gives U.S. a Hanoi P.O.W. List." *The New York Times,* December 12, 1970. *New York Times* Article Archive.

———. "Yugoslav Envoy to Sweden Dies of Wounds by Croats." *The New York Times,* April 15, 1971. *New York Times* Article Archive.

Rochester, Stuart I. and Frederick Kiley. *Honor Bound: American Prisoners of War in Southeast Asia, 1961–1973.* Annapolis, MD: Naval Institute Press, 1998.

Sassòli, Marco. "Release, Accommodation in Neutral Countries, and Repatriation of Prisoners of War." In *The 1949 Geneva Conventions: A Commentary,* edited by Andrew Clapham, Paola Gaeta, and Marco Sassòli, 1039–66. Oxford: Oxford University Press, 2015.

Schanberg, Sydney. "Cambodia." In *Crimes of War:* http://crimesofwar.org.

Schori, Pierre. "The Legacy of Olof Palme and Sweden." Address by the Swedish Prime Minister's Special Representative at the Ho Chi Minh Political Academy, Hanoi, 2 June 2016.

Schulzinger, Robert D. "Nixon, Congress, and the Vietnam War, 1969–1974." In *Vietnam and the American Political Tradition: The Politics of Dissent*, edited by Randall B. Woods, 282–300. New York: Cambridge University Press, 2003.

Schuster, Alvin D. "Swedish Chilliness Toward U.S. is Limited to Vietnam." *The New York Times,* January 8, 1973. *New York Times* Article Archive.

Schwartz, Thomas A. *Henry Kissinger and American Power: A Political Biography.* New York: Hill and Wang, 2020.

Schwartz, Thomas Alan. *Lyndon Johnson and Europe: In the Shadow of Vietnam.* Cambridge, MA: Harvard University Press, 2003.

Scott, Carl-Gustaf. *"A good offense is the best defense": Swedish Social Democracy, Europe, and the Vietnam War."* PhD diss., University of Wisconsin-Madison, 2005.

———. *Swedish Social Democracy and the Vietnam War.* Huddinge, Sweden: Södertörn University, 2017.

Secor, Laura. "Henry Kissinger is Worried About 'Disequilibrium.'" *The Wall Street Journal*, August 12, 2022. https://www.wsj.com/articles/henry-kissinger-is -worried-about-disequilibrium-11660325251.

Senats förhören om Vietnam, translated by Sture Biurström. Stockholm: Beckmans, 1967.

Sheehan, Neil. "Kennedy and Hanoi Letters Discuss P.O.W's." *The New York Times*, July 26, 1972. *New York Times* Article Archive.

Shipler, David K. "Vast Aid from U.S. Backs Saigon in Continuing War." *The New York Times*, February 25, 1974. *New York Times* Article Archive.

Skole, Robert. "Sweden Feels in Middle of POW Propaganda." *The Evening Star*, May 18, 1971. *Riksarkivet*, Arninge, Sweden.

Smith, Robert M. "Swedish Leader, in U.S., Avows Amity." *The New York Times*, June 5, 1970. *New York Times* Article Archive.

Smith, Terence. "Senators Receive Hanoi P.O.W. List." *The New York Times*, December 23, 1970. *New York Times* Article Archive.

Sterba, James P. "Last U.S. Troops Leave Cambodia." *The New York Times*, July 1, 1970. *New York Times* Article Archive.

Stockdale, Jim and Sybil Stockdale. *In Love and War: The Story of a Family's Ordeal and Sacrifice During the Vietnam Years.* New York: Harper and Row, 1984.

Stellman, Jeanne Mager, Steven D. Stellman, Richard Christian, Tracy Weber, and Carrie Tomasallo. "The extent and patterns of usage of Agent Orange and other herbicides in Vietnam." *Nature* 422 (2003): 681–87.

"Stoppa arsenik-exporten till USA," *Proletären*, No. 30 (1972). Special Collections. Royal Library, Stockholm, Sweden.

Sutton, David. "2 POW Wives Call N. Viet Film Phony." *Chicago Tribune*, December 29, 1970. Newspapers.com.

Svedgård, Lars. *"Palme Tar Kallt på Nya USA-Attacken."* *Aftonbladet,* 8 June 1972. *Svsnska Dagstidningar*, Royal Library, Stockholm, Sweden.

"Svenskt besked till USA':Vi vill stoppa miljömord." *Dagens Nyheter,* June 15, 1972. *Svenska Dagtidningar*, Royal Library, Stockholm, Sweden.

Säkerhets utredningen, Fred och säkerhet: Svensk säkerhetspolitik 1969–1989, SOU 2002:108. Stockholm: *Statens Offentliga Utredningar*, 2002.

Takman, John, ed. *Napalm*. Stockholm: Raben & Sjögren, 1968.

Taylor, Telford. "Hanoi is Reported Scarred But Key Services Continue," *The New York Times*, December 25, 1972. *New York Times* Article Archive.

Thorsell, Staffan. *Sverige i Vita Huset.* Stockholm: Bonnier Fakta, 2004.

Toth, Robert C. "Hanoi Gives Sweden Data on POWs." *Newsday*, December 12, 1970. *Riksarkivet*, Arninge, Sweden.

———. "U.S. May Recall Envoy to Sweden Over Insults." *The Los Angeles Times*, May 28, 1970. *Riksarkivet*, Arninge, Sweden.

Tucson Daily Citizen.

United Nations Office on Genocide Prevention and the Responsibility to Protect. https://www.un.org/en/genocideprevention/genocide.shtml.

United Press International. "Flyers' Wives Relieved, Angry." *The Daily Colonist* (Victoria, British Columbia), April 28, 1970. Newspapers.com.

———. "Gostas' family going to Denver." *The Billings Gazette*, March 19, 1973. Newspapers.com.

———. "Hanoi Lists Arkansan Among 24 Prisoners." *Arkansas Gazette*, June 25, 1972. Newspapers.com.

———. "Hanoi Rejects POW Internment in Sweden." *The Los Angeles Times*, May 5, 1971. *Riksarkivet*, Arninge, Sweden.

———. "Kissinger 'Excellent' After Triple Bypass in Coronary Surgery." *The New York Times*, February 11, 1982. *New York Times* Article Archive.

———. "North Vietnam Releases List of 59 U.S. Prisoners of War." *The San Bernardino County Sun*, 27 November 1969. Newspapers.com.

———. "Prisoners of War Held by North Vietnam Are Listed." *The Brownsville Herald*, December 23, 1970. Newspapers.com.

———. "Sweden Gets List of 14 PWs in Hanoi." *The Philadelphia Inquirer*, March 8, 1970. Newspapers.com.

———. "Sweden Plans to Establish Permanent Hanoi Mission." *The New York Times*, June 30, 1970. *New York Times* Article Archive.

———. "Swedish PM Writes to Santa Fe Woman." *Albuquerque Journal*, March 7, 1970. Newspapers.com.

———. "Sweden Premier Gets Hanoi Reply on POWs." *The Evening Star*, December 11,1970. *Riksarkivet*, Arninge, Sweden.

Urquhart, Brian. *Hammarskjöld.* New York: W.W. Norton & Company, 1994.

"USA till motattack: Skarp protest mot Palmes tal." *Dagens Nyheter,* June 8, 1972. *Svenska Dagstidningar*, Royal Library, Stockholm, Sweden.

U.S. Embassy and Consulate of Hanoi. https://vn.usembassy.gov.

Utrikesfrågor: Offentliga dokument M.M. Rörande Viktigare Svenska Utrikespolitiska Frågor 1965. Stockholm: Norstedts Tryckeri, 1966.

Utrikesfrågor: Offentliga dokument M.M. Rörande Viktigare Svenska Utrikespolitiska Frågor 1975. Stockholm: Norstedts Tryckeri, 1976.

Utrikesfrågor: Offentliga dokument M.M. Rörande Viktigare Svenska Utrikespolitiska Frågor 1976. Stockholm: Norstedts Tryckeri, 1977.

Van Dyke, Jon M. "Nixon and the Prisoners of War." *The New York Review of Books*, January 7, 1971.

Viet-My: A Special Supplement of Vietnam-USA Magazine.

"Vietnam: Impact of War on its Environment." *Congressional Quarterly Weekly Report*, June 29, 1972.

The Vietnam Hearings, with an introduction by J. William Fulbright. New York: Vintage Books, 1966.

Van Atta, Dale. *With Honor: Melvin Laird in War, Peace, and Politics.* Madison: The University of Wisconsin Press, 2008.

Viklund, Daniel. *"Flygarhustrur från USA ber Olof Palme om hjälp."Dagens Nyheter*, November 26, 1969. *Svenska Dagstidningar*, Royal Library, Stockholm, Sweden.

Vivekanandan, B. *Global Visions of Olof Palme, Bruno Kreisky and Willy Brandt: International Peace and Security, Co-operation, and Development.* Cham, Switzerland: Palgrave Macmillan, 2016.

"Vår man i Hanoi m m," Dagens Nyheter, June 9, 1972. *Svenska Dagstidningar*, Royal Library, Stockholm, Sweden.

Wachtmeister, Wilhelm. *Som Jag Såg Det: Händelser och människor på världsscenen.* Stockholm: Norstedts, 1996.

The Washington Post.

Weber, Bruce. "Sybil Stockdale, Fierce Advocate for P.O.W.s and their Families, Dies at 90." *The New York Times*, October 15, 2015. https://www.nytimes.com/2015/10 /16/us/sybil-stockdale-fierce-advocate-for-pows-dies-at-90.html.

Wells, Frank. "Wife Questions Report of PW's Death." *The Atlanta Constitution*, November 13, 1970. Newspapers.com.

Westing, Arthur H. *Ecological Consequences of the Second Indochina War.* Stockholm: Almqvist & Wiksell, 1976.

Whitney, Craig R. "Kissinger in Sweden: Vietnam Echoes." *The New York Times*, May 25, 1976. *New York Times* Article Archive.

Wideman, F. I. and Gertrude N. Greenspoon. "Arsenic," in Bureau of Mines, *Minerals yearbook: Metals and minerals (except fuels) 1962,* Bureau of Mines, 253–58. Washington, D.C.: U.S. Government Printing Office, 1963.

"Wife of Confirmed POW Still Plans Trip: Seeking Names of Others Missing." *Tucson Daily Citizen*, March 12, 1970. Newspapers.com.

"Yngsta tribunalvittnet: 'När jag vaktade boskapen kom tre plan över fältet.'" Dagens Nyheter, May 7, 1967. *Svenska Dagstidningar*, Royal Library, Stockholm, Sweden.

Young, Marilyn B. *The Vietnam Wars: 1945–1990.* New York: HarperPerennial, 1991.

YouTube.

Zawodny, J. K. *Death in the Forest: The Story of the Katyn Forest Massacre.* Notre Dame, IN: University of Notre Dame Press, 1962.

Index

Agent Blue, 65–66
Agent Orange, 63
Agnew, Spiro, 170
Aitken, Jonathan, 210
Allende, Salvador, 221
American Friends Service
   Committee, 54–55
American Revolution, 38
Andersson, Sven, 214, 216–
   221, 227, 236
Angola, 236, 238–240
Ansul Company, 65
ASEA, 27
Åselius, Gunnar, 98
Asselin, Pierre, 210
Åström, Sverker, 60, 92, 103
Atterbury, Edwin, 162
Australia, 23, 110

Bai Bang paper mill, 230
Babi Yar, 93–94, 111
Baker, Howard, 151
Bach Mai Hospital, 91–92, 94, 102, 229
Ball, George, 6, 9
Bediger, Henry James, 146
Beijing, *see also* China, 49–53,
   124–125, 161
Belgium, 23

De Besche, Hubert, 31, 45, 62, 94, 101–
   102, 104–105, 133, 169–170, 232
Beyer, Mrs. Charles J., 147
Beyer, Thomas J., 147
Bilderberg Group, 209–210
Binh, Madame Nguyen Thi, 70, 176–
   178, 230–231
Björnberg, Arne, 49
Blix, Hans, 46
Bodde, William, Jr. (Bill), 109
Bofors, 39–40
Bohman, Gösta, 15, 95–96
Boliden, 65–66
Borah, William E., 105
Borling, Edward, 146–147
Borling, John L., 137, 146–147, 162–
   164, 167–168
Borling, Myrna, 146–147
Borg, C. Arthur, 157
Borman, Frank, 169–170
Brandt, Willy, 92, 96, 98, 113, 239
Brezhnev, Leonid, 92
Bruce, David, K.E., 174
Brzezinski, Zbigniew, 43
Buckley, William F., Jr., 110.
Bui Diem, 17
Bundy, William, 6
Burdett, Edward Burke, 141
Burdett, Mrs., 141–142

Bush, George H.W., 67
Bush, George W., 248
Bush, Laura, 248
Butland, Bertram E., 111
Butterfield, Alexander, 153

CAAC (Chinese national airline), 182
Carlsson, Ingvar, 12
Cambodia, 23, 27–28, 32–34, 49, 60,
    158, 181, 212–213, 233
Canada, 23, 96
Carter, Jimmy, 248
Castle, Timothy, 127
Castro, Fidel, 32
Center party, 95, 236
Central Intelligence Agency, 58, 211,
    221; Air America, 145
Charles, King XIII, 111
Charles, Norris A., 167, 180, 183–184
Chennault, Anna, 17
Chile, 215, 221, 235
China, *see also* Beijing, 5–6, 12, 15,
    38, 47–49, 51–53, 60, 99, 111, 124–
    125, 166, 218
Christmas Bombings, 91–92, 95– 98,
    104–105, 107–108, 112–113,
    210, 229, 236,
Church, Frank, 105, 151
Clark, Mark, 57–59
Clark, Ramsey, 179
Clift, A. Denis, 98
Coffin, William Sloane, 180
Committee of Liaison with Familes of
    Servicemen Detained in Vietnam,
    132, 140, 145–146, 148–149,
    180–181, 184
Communist Party of Sweden
    (*Kommunistiska Förbundet Marxist–
    Leninisterna*), 12
Conference on Security and Cooperation
    In Europé, 106, 236, 239
Conservative party
    (*Högerpartiet*), 16, 95

Davis, Rennie, 131, 133, 156

DeBruin, Eugene, 145
Dellenback, John, 151
Dellinger, David, 131–133, 156, 180
Defense Intelligence Agency, 58
Denmark, 23, 26, 97, 182–183, 216
Dennison, Mrs., 141–142
Dennison, Terry Arden, 341
Dodge, Ward Kent, 141–142
Do Van Ngoc, 61
Dramesi, John, 162
Dubs, Adolph, 182–183
Duckles, Madeline, 131
Dulles, John Foster, 6
Dunnigan, Thomas J., 183

East Germany, *see* German
    Democratic Republic
Eaton, Cyrus, 177
Edelstam, Harald, 215
Ekengren, Ann–Marie, viii
Eisenhower, Dwight D., 6, 15, 32
Ekéus, Rolf, 24–26, 40–41, 43–44,
    48–49, 53–54, 56, 70, 90, 94,
    96, 103, 123–124, 169, 209,
    212, 227, 229
Electronic Data Systems, 154
Elias, Edward K., 167, 180, 183–184
Eliasson, Jan, 13–14, 36, 40–41, 47,
    56–57, 62, 66, 94–95, 101, 105,
    107–110, 124, 136, 144, 148, 152,
    159, 161, 169, 171, 212, 237–
    240, 248–249
Ellsberg, Daniel, 45
Engström, Stig, 247–248
Ehrlichman, John, 61–62
Epstein, Albert, 112
Erlander, Tage, 3, 4, 7, 11–13, 16,
    24–25, 31, 41, 92, 228
Estes, Elzene E., 147.
European Economic Community, 106
Export-Import Bank (Exim Bank), 26

Falk, Richard, 55, 96, 99, 135, 148, 166,
    169, 171, 180–181, 184
Falkenäs, Björn, 30

Falkman, Kai, 1, 3, 39–41,49–52, 56, 69–71, 92, 98–99, 101, 102, 125, 139, 150, 159–160, 165–166–168, 174–175, 210, 227, 230, 236
Ferm, Anders, 92–94, 169, 227
Fessenden, Russell, 106
Finland, 42, 44, 97, 238
Forced March in Hanoi, 130, 161–162
Ford, Gerald R., 151–152, 216, 221, 237–239
Foreign Policy Research Institute, 216
France, 2–4, 14, 23, 38, 113; French diplomatic mission in Hanoi, 67–69
Fraser, Donald, 168
Frishman, Robert F., 167
Fulbright, J. William, 9–11, 16–17, 36, 104–105, 123–124, 148, 216
Fälldin, Thorbjörn, 95, 236

Galanti, Mrs., 156
Galanti, Paul Edward, 156
Garrett, Dave L., 127
Gartley, Markham L., 167, 180, 183–184
Gaulle, Charles de, 113
Gavin, James M., 9
Geneva Accords of 1954, 6–7, 14, 49
Geneva Convention (III) relative to the Treatment of Prisoners of War, 125, 168–169; Article 2, 159; Article 13, 163–164; Article 17, 126, 163; Article 22, 163; Article 26, 163; Article 70, 126; Article 71, 126; Article 72, 153; Article 73, 153; Article 109, 172–173; Article 111, 172; Article 112, 173; Article 130, 126, 163
Geijer, Lennart, 13
Geijer, S., 55
Georgia, 44
German Democratic Republic, 23, 42, 53, 229
Giap, Vo Nguyen, 229
Giron, Marc, 39
Gore, Albert, Sr., 155

Gostas, Theodore W., 146
Gourley, Laurent J., 147
Great Britain, *see* United Kingdom
Great Northern War, 111
Greiner, Berndt, 96
Griffin, Dora (now Dora Griffin Bell), 148–149
Griffin, james L., 148–149
Gruening, Ernest, 9
Guernica, 92, 94
Gulf of Tonkin, 9, 71
Gustaf VI Adolf, King, 29
Guthrie, John, 100, 157, 174, 178–179
Gyllenhammar, Pehr, 49

Hagen, Tord
Haig, Alexander, 216
Halyburton, Marty, 129–130, 132–133, 138, 152
Halyburton, Porter, 129–131, 137, 161–164, 166
Hammarskjöld, Dag, 10, 124–125
Hanoi, *see also* North Vietnam, 7–9, 23, 26, 28, 38, 46, 48–57, 59, 63, 67–69, 71, 90–93, 95–96, 101–102, 111–113, 126, 128–131, 133–137, 139–141, 146–148, 150–155, 157–166, 168–169, 171, 174–184, 211, 218–219, 227–231, 234–236
Hard Hats, *see* International Longshoreman's Union
Harkin, Tom 170
Hartke, Vance, 176–178
Hartman, Arthur, 109–110, 221
Hartness, Greg, 127–128
Hartness, Paula, 127–128
Hatfield, Mark, 177
Hawley, Edwin A., 161
Heath, Edward, 47
Heath, William, 12, 16
Herbicides, 60–66; Operation Ranch Hand, 64
Hegdahl, Douglas B., 167
Helén, Gunnar, 66, 95
Hermansson, C.H., 12, 95

Hersh, Seymour, 90, 160–161, 164, 167
Hickel, Walter J., 34
Hiemstra, Heleen, 173
Hillenbrand, Martin J., 45, 154
Hinckley, Marie, 133
Hinckley, Robert Bruce, 132–133, 145
Hirdman, Sven, 43
Hitchens, Christopher, 248
Ho Chi Minh, 4, 6–7, 124, 163–164
Ho Chi Minh Trail, 23
Hogan, Lawrence J., 151
Holland, Jerome, 29–31, 34, 42, 62,
    149–151, 158
Holland, Joseph, 29–30
Holmberg, Yngve, 16
Holocaust, comparisons to, 98
Hughes, Dorothy, 129, 133
Hughes, James Lindberg, 129, 132
Humphrey, Hubert, 7–8, 17,
    31, 104, 214
Hyltenius, Carl–Magnus, 217–220

Iceland, 214–215
Indonesia, 48
International Committee of the Red
    Cross, 173
International Control Commission, 180
International Longshoreman's
    Association (ILA), 35–36, 38
International War Crimes
    Tribunal, 11, 61
Israel, 236
Italy, 23

Japan, 15
Johnson, Lyndon Baines, 6–7, 9, 11, 164
Joint Chiefs of Staff, 55
Johnson, U. Alexis, 99–101
Jørgensen, Anker, 97

Kahn, Herman, 42
Karjalainen, Ahti, 97
Katyn Massacre, 93, 111
Kemp, Jack, 152
Kennan, George, 9

Kennedy, David M., 34
Kennedy, Edward M., 104–105, 148,
    171–172, 232, 233–235, 248
Kennedy, John F., 43
Kennedy, Robert F., 16, 176, 248
Kenyon College, 1, 16, 35–36
Kerr, Jerrie L, 145–146
Kerr, Michael Scott, 146
Kissinger, Henry A., 35, 43, 45, 53,
    67, 98–99, 110, 181, 217–218, 236;
    attitude about Christmas Bombing,
    91; attitude about Holocaust, 97–98;
    attitude about troop withdrawal,
    24; diplomatic thaw, 214–216;
    disinvited to meeting of Bilderberg
    Group, 209–210; indifference about
    Raoul Wallenberg, 98; justification
    of bombing of Cambodia and Laos,
    23–24; political motives, 24; POW
    views of, 137; President's Daily
    Brief, 131; reaction to Christmas
    Bombing speech, 97, 100, 108, 239;
    reconciliation with Palme, 236–249;
    rejection of postwar aid program for
    Vietnam, 234–235; sabotage of 1968
    Paris Peace talks, 17, 90; skepticism
    of Swedish help to POWs, 131;
    snubbing Palme during 1970 visit,
    31–32; speech at Palme memorial
    service in Washington, 248; and
    Sven Andersson, 217–218, 220–221;
    on Ukraine, 44–45; unofficial talks
    in Paris, 27, 90–91; undermining of
    State Department, 34, 108–109
Klackenberg, Lennart, 24, 232
Korean War, 57–58, 124–125
Kraemer, Sven, 175
Kreisky, Bruno, 92, 97–98

Laird, Melvin, 55, 68, 175
Laos, 23, 27, 145–146, 158,
    181, 213, 233
Laraki, Ahmad 33
Lavelle, John D., 57
Le Duc Tho, 27, 53, 91

Left Party Communists (*Vänsterpartiet Kommunisterna*), vii–viii, 61, 66, 95
Le Duan, 7, 38, 235
Leifland, Leif, 62, 94, 106–107, 109, 154–156, 172, 175–176, 215
Lundberg, Eskil, 95
Liberal People's party (*Folkpartiet liberalerna*), 5, 16, 66, 95
Lidgard, Curt, 220
Lidice, 93
Lodge, Henry Cabot, 4
Lon Nol, 33
Lowenstein, James, 220
Löfven, Stefan, 237

Macartney, Gardner, 111
Mai Van Bo, 50, 59, 176
Martin, Murphy, 127–128, 154–156
Mathias, Charles Mc., Jr., 106, 151
McCain, John III, 167
McCarthy, Eugene, 16
McCloskey, Robert J., 140
McGovern, George, 6, 71, 138
McGovern-Hatfield Amendment, 71, 177
McNamara, Robert S., 6, 235
McNaughton, John, 6
Miller, Edison, 160–161
Moderate party (*Moderaterna*), 15, 230
Mondale, Walter, 214, 240
Moorer, Thomas, 42
Morse, Wayne, 9
Morocco, 33
Moscow, *see also* Soviet Union, 7, 12, 35, 48, 50–53, 57, 111, 123, 125, 131, 140, 153, 157–158, 182–183, 238–239
Mozambique, 240
M. Viet, 175
Myrdal, Alva, 92
Myrdal, Gunnar, 46
Möller, Yngve, 100–102

National Council on Reconciliation and Concord, 210–211

National League of Familes of American Prisoners and Missing in Southeast Asia, 124, 130, 133–134, 136, 158
National Liberation Front (NLF), 6, 14, 38, 65
National Mobilization Committee to End the War in Vietnam, 131–132, 140, 145
National Review, 110
National Security Council, 24, 32–33, 55, 98, 175
NATO (North Atlantic Treaty Organization), 23, 43–45, 150, 216
Neak Luong, 213
Negroponte, John, 102
The Netherlands, 23
New York Daily News, 110
New York Times, 110
Nguyen Co Thach, 52
Nguyen Dinh Thanh, 27–28, 46
Nguyen Duy Trinh, 8, 53, 227
Nguyen Huu Ngo, 89
Nguyen Tho Chan, 12–16, 125–126, 130, 140, 157
Nilsson, Torsten, 4–8, 11–12, 24–27, 69, 130, 158–160, 171, 212, 228–229, 236
Nixon, Richard M., 17, 23–24, 26, 31–32, 3–35, 45, 47, 51, 55, 67, 71, 96, 99–100, 103–105, 108, 110–111, 131, 137–138, 154, 157, 164, 171, 174–176, 179, 181, 184, 209–213, 215–216, 221
Nordic Council, 12, 215
North Vietnam (Democratic Republic of Vietnam), *see also* Hanoi, 6–9, 11–17, 23, 25–28, 34–42, 46, 48–60, 63, 66–71, 89–93, 97–98, 104–105, 111–113, 123–141, 143, 145–153, 156–162, 164–181, 211–213, 216–219, 227–235, 233–234; Ministry of Defense, 140–141
Norway, 23, 26, 40, 102, 216
Nuremberg Tribunal, 58, 91, 126

Nyström, Rune, 149

Obama, Barack, 237
Öberg, Jean–Christophe, 7, 24, 28,
    69, 101, 218, 220, 229, 236; as
    ambassador to Hanoi, 53–54, 59,
    67–68, 94, 113, 157–158, 160,
    181–182, 184, 211, 231; background,
    3–4, 49–50; on bombing of French
    diplomatic mission, 68; on bombing
    of Red River dikes, 54–55; as chargé
    d'affaires in Hanoi, 48–50, 59, 158–
    159, 164, 169, 174, 176, 178–179,
    212, 230; opinion of Dean Rusk,
    8–9; service in Bangkok and Saigon,
    3, 49; surveillance by Pentagon,
    55–57; views of French war in
    Vietnam of, 4
Ohlin, Bertil, 5
Operation Aspen. *See* Sweden,
    mediation efforts of
Operation Linebacker, 50, 59, 67, 94
Operation Linebacker II, *see* also
    Christmas Bombings), 91, 98
Operation Marigold, 9
Operation Rolling Thunder, 7
Oradour–sur–Glane, 93–94
Owens, John P., 213

Palme, Olof: accession, 24;
    assassination, 247–248; attitude
    about North Vietnamese treatment
    of POWs, 135, 152, 159, 168;
    appreciation of positive mail, 112;
    on aid to Democratic Republic of
    Vietnam and Socialist Republic
    of Vietnam, 25–26, 28, 134–135,
    227–228, 232–233; appearance on
    Issues and Answers, 46; appearance
    on *Meet the Press*, 37; appearance
    on *Today*, 37; assistance in bringing
    three POWs home, 184; attitude
    about arms trade, 41; attitude about
    military collaboration with the
    United States, 42–43; on Cambodia,

213; childhood of, 1; Christmas
    Bombing speech, 93–94, 98–99,
    103, 240; criticism of, vii–viii, 5,
    15, 94, 98–99, 108; dealings with
    Joseph Holland, 30–31; on détente,
    47–48; early travels in America, 1–2;
    education of, 1–2, 10; on embassy
    in Hanoi, 28, 48; family background
    of, 1; gratitude from Pham Van
    Dong, 60, 112–113, 157; as host of
    Pham Van Dong, 235–236; initial
    reaction to Christmas Bombings,
    91–92; and Jean–Christophe Öberg,
    4, 53, 101–102, 211; knowledge of
    Kissinger's secret talks in Paris, 27;
    letter from Cora Weiss, 184; letter
    to Nixon, 103–104, 134; lobbying
    of Iceland, 214–215; meeting with
    Frank Borman, 169; meeting with
    Nguyen Tho Chan in 1968, 13, 15;
    meeting with POW relatives, 128,
    136; meeting the Senate Foreign
    Relations Committee, 36; military
    service of, 2–3; motives for helping
    POWs, 123, 150; petition and
    letter to Kurt Waldheim, 95–96;
    opinion of internment proposal,
    135–136, 171; on Pentagon Papers,
    45; political convictions 13–14;
    political evolution of, 2–3; political
    strategy, 13; possible dislike of
    Murphy Martin, 128, 154; reaction
    to diplomatic freeze, 101–104, 209;
    reasons for helping POW families,
    123–125; reconciliation with
    Kissinger, 236–247; relationship
    with Swedish business community,
    49; respect of North Vietnamese,
    176; response to signing of Paris
    Peace Accords, 210–211; second
    meeting with Nixon, 215; service to
    Tage Erlander, 3; speech on ecocide,
    61–63; speech at Gävle, 5; speech at
    Kenyon College, 34–36; speech at
    the National Press Club, 36; speech

at Sergels Torg, 14–15; speech at Social Democratic Youth League, 64; support of Harald Edelstam, 215; student activism of, 2–3; travels in America, 1–2; understanding of Brandt's silence, 96; views on American war in Southeast Asia of, 5–6, 11, 14, 28, 32–34, 37–38, 46, 48; views on communism of, 2–3; views on American war in Southeast Asia of, 5–6, 11, 14, 28, 32–34, 37–38, 45; views on French war in Vietnam of, 2, 14; visit to the United States in June of 1970, 28–29, 31–34, 36, 38; and White House dinner, 47

Palmstierna, Hans, 60, 64

Paris Peace Accords, 179, 210–211, 213, 218–219, 232, 234

Pathet Lao, 158

Paul, Pope VI, 176

Pell, Claiborne, 105, 172, 214

Pentagon Papers, 45

People's Coalition for Peace and Justice, 180–181

Percy, Charles, 106

Perot, H. Ross, 127, 133, 152–156

Petersson, Krister, 247

Petroswede, 232

Pettersson, Thomas, 247

Pfeiffer, Egbert W., 60–61, 63

Pham Van Dong, 60, 112–113, 124, 152, 157, 178–179, 230–231, 235–236

Phan Thi Kim Phuc, 64

Pickering, Thomas, 91, 100–101, 108–109, 241

Pinochet, Augusto, 215, 235

Poland, 9, 44

Pompidou, Georges, 113, 215

Portugal, 236, 239–240

Posner, Gerald, 155

POW/MIA Families for Immediate Release, 138

Prisoners of War (POWs), 34, 36, 71, 89, 123–184, 211

Provisional Revolutionary Government (PRG), 70, 210–211, 216, 219–220, 231–232

Pugwash Conferences on Science and World Affairs, 177

Purvis, Hoyt, 124

Putnam, George, 111–112

Reagan, Ronald, 237

Redeyes, 41–41

Reichler, Andy, 112

Richardson, Ellliot, 32–33

Riksdag (Swedish Parliament), 12, 27, 47, 61

Ringborg, Ethel, 24

Rogers, William, 31–34, 45, 6–68, 157, 171, 184, 209, 233

Rolovic, Vladimir, 67

Rosenblad, Esbjörn, 135

Rosenthal, Benjamin S., 106.

Rostow, Walt, 11

Rusk, Dean, 7–9

Russell, Bertrand, *see* International War Crimes Tribunal

Russia, *see also* the Soviet Union, 42, 44–45, 48

Saab, 40

Saigon, *see also* South Vietnam, 3–4, 9, 12, 14, 17, 48–49, 54, 71, 89–91, 93, 161, 170, 210–211, 213, 216, 219–220, 230–232

Save the Children, 231

Sassòli, Marco, 173

Scandinavian Airlines System (SAS), 26, 66, 180, 182–184, 232

Schori, Pierre, 230

Schumann, Maurice, 69

Schwartz, Thomas A., 17

Scientists' Institute for Public Information (SIPI), 60

Scott, Hugh, 104

Seyss–Inquart, Arthur, 58

Sharp, Mitchell, 96

Sharpeville, 93

Shields, Mark, 221
Sieverts, Frank, 157
Shoemaker, Katrina Stamm, 142–145
Shrike the, 67, 172
Sihanouk, Norodom, 33, 212
Singapore, 40, 48
Singleton, Barbara J., 126–
    128, 132, 154
Singleton, Jerry Allen, 126–127, 132
Sisco, Joseph, 109
Sjölin, Åke, 3
Skafte-Lindblom, Saga, 143–144
Social Democratic party, vii, xi, xix–xx,
    xxi, 24, 29, 95, 217
Sonnenfeldt, Helmut (Hal), 32, 43, 109
South Africa, 93
South Vietnam (Republic of Vietnam),
    see also Saigon 3, 6, 8, 14, 17,
    24–25, 28, 38, 49, 51–52, 59–60,
    63–65, 69–71, 85, 89–91, 111, 113,
    146, 152–153, 170–171, 210–211,
    213, 219, 230, 233–234
Soviet Union, *see also* Moscow, 5–6,
    12, 23, 35, 44, 47, 50–53, 60, 92, 96,
    99, 111, 150, 236, 240
Spring Offensive of 1974, 218–219
Stamm, Ernest Albert
    "Tommy," 141–145
Stamm, Ruth, 141–144
Stans, Maurice, 26
Stevenson, Adlai, 176
Stockdale, James 130, 133, 163
Stockdale, Sybil, 133–136, 171
Stockholm International Peace Research
    Institute (SIPRI), 46
Stoessel, Walter, 214
Strausz–Hupé, Robert, 43, 215–216,
    218, 220, 237
Stoessel, Walter, 106
Stora Kopparberg, 27
Sträng, Gunnar, 25–26
Susini, Pierre, 68
Sullivan, William, 172
Svensson, Ulf, 24

Sweden: aid to Democratic Republic of
    Vietnam and the Socialist Republic
    of Vietnam, 24–28, 227–230, 232;
    aid to PRG, 231; arms trade, 39–4;
    campaign to ban herbicidal warfare,
    60; collaboration with Nazis of, 99,
    110–112; diplomatic freeze with the
    United States, 100–113; diplomatic
    thaw with the United States,
    214–216; embassy in Hanoi, 28; on
    herbicides, 46, 65; mediation efforts
    of (Operation Aspen), 7–9, 11–13,
    48; military collaboration with the
    United States, 41–42; neutrality,
    33–34, 37, 40, 42–45, 96, 150, 216,
    238; Nordic Balance, 44–45; official
    stand against war, 11–12, 45; on
    possible use of Swedish arsenic in
    manufacture of Agent blue, 65–66;
    POW list of March 1970, 131, 140,
    155; POW list of November 1970,
    141, 147; POW list of December
    1970, 147–149; POW views of, 134;
    protests, 11–12, 30; and racism,
    29–30; recognition of North Vietnam
    (Democratic Republic of Vietnam),
    23, 71n1; recognition of Provisional
    Revolutionary Government, 70–71,
    216; status of South Vietnam
    (Republic of Vietnam), 3, 12, 49;
    trade relations with the United States,
    38; on secret U.S. contingency plan
    to defend Sweden, 42–43
Swedish Committee for Vietnam, 12
Swedish Defence Materiel
    Adminisitration, 55
Swedish Environmental Protection
    Agency, 60
Swedish International Devlopment
    Cooperation Agency (SIDA), 231
Swedish Red Cross, 26, 28, 231
Swedish Social Democratic Youth
    League, 54, 64
Switzerland, 176
Synnergren, Stig, 42

Takman, Johan (John), 61, 66
Talley, Bernard L., 135
Taylor, Ethel, 131
Taylor, Telford, 91
Terrell, Greta, 128–129, 132
Terrell, Irby D., 128, 131
Thailand, 48, 101, 181
Thieu, Nguyen Van, 90–91,
   211, 219, 232
Tinker, Jerry, 105, 171
Thomson, James, 6
Ton Duc Thang, 171
Train, Russell, 61–62
Treblinka, 93, 98, 112
Tunney, James, 55

Ukraine, 44–45
Ullsten, Ola, 233
Unger, Leonard S., 5
United Kingdom (Great Britain), 23
United Nations (UN), 14, 46–47, 60, 66,
   95, 124, 172, 214, 227, 231, 233
United Nations Conference on the
   Human Environment, 60–61
United Nations Convention on the
   Prevention and Punishment of the
   Crime of Genocide, 98
United Nations Security Council, 240
United NLF Groups (*De förenade FNL-
   grupperna*), 12–13, 151
United We Stand, 152, 154, 156
U.S. Bombings of Dikes, 54–55, 57–58
U.S. Defense Department (Pentagon),
   55–57, 108, 144
U.S. House Committee on Foreign
   Affairs; Subcommittee on
   Europe, 106
U.S. Reluctance to Reach a
   Settlement, 89–90, 93
U.S. Senate, 104, 234;
   Resolution 149, 214

U.S. Senate Foreign Relations
   Committee, xvii, xxiv, 36, 76, 104–
   105, 123, 214
U.S. Senate Judiciary Committee,
   232; Subcommittee to Investigate
   Problems Connected with Refugees
   and Escapees, 212
U.S. State Department, 30–34, 36–37,
   39, 43, 47, 54, 57, 62, 65, 91, 94, 99,
   106–109, 136, 140, 144, 184

Viet-My, 140–141
Vietnamization, 24, 27, 48, 212
Vinson, Bobby, 124
Vinson, 124
Volvo, 49
von Hoffman, Nicholas, 170

Wachtmeister, Wilhelm, 12–13, 42, 92,
   129, 157, 164–165, 172, 174–175,
   178–179, 182, 214–215, 221
Waldheim, Kurt, 95
Wallenberg, Raoul, 98,112
Washington Post, 111
Weinberger, Caspar, 43
Weiss, Cora, 131–132, 141, 143, 149,
   180–182, 184
West Germany (Federal Republic of
   Germany), 92, 96, 113, 240
Westing, Arthur H., 60–61, 63
Weyland, Otto P., 58
Wedén, Sven, 16
Whitlam, Gough, 110
Wickman, Krister, 69–70, 89–90, 102,
   158, 209, 212–214, 216–217, 227–
   228, 230–231, 236
Widén, Jerker, 43
Wilson, Harold, 27, 48, 139
World Bank, 235
Women Strike for Peace, 131–132, 140
Wåhlin, Sten, 55

Xuan Thuy, 127

Yarborough, Ralph, 36
Young, John Arthur, 146

Yugoslavia, 42, 67

Ziegler, Ronald L., 174

About the Author

Lubna Z. Qureshi earned her doctorate in US history at the University of California, Berkeley in 2006. She also holds a master's degree in military and diplomatic history from Temple University, and a bachelor's degree in history from the University of Wisconsin-Madison.

Her first book, *Nixon, Kissinger, and Allende: U.S. Involvement in the 1973 Coup in Chile*, was published in 2008, also by Lexington Books.

In support of the research for this book, Qureshi received support from the Swedish Institute, the Olof Palme Memorial Fund, the Åke Wiberg Foundation, and the Gerald R. Ford Presidential Foundation.

www.ingramcontent.com/pod-product-compliance
Lightning Source LLC
Chambersburg PA
CBHW071846270326
41929CB00013B/2122